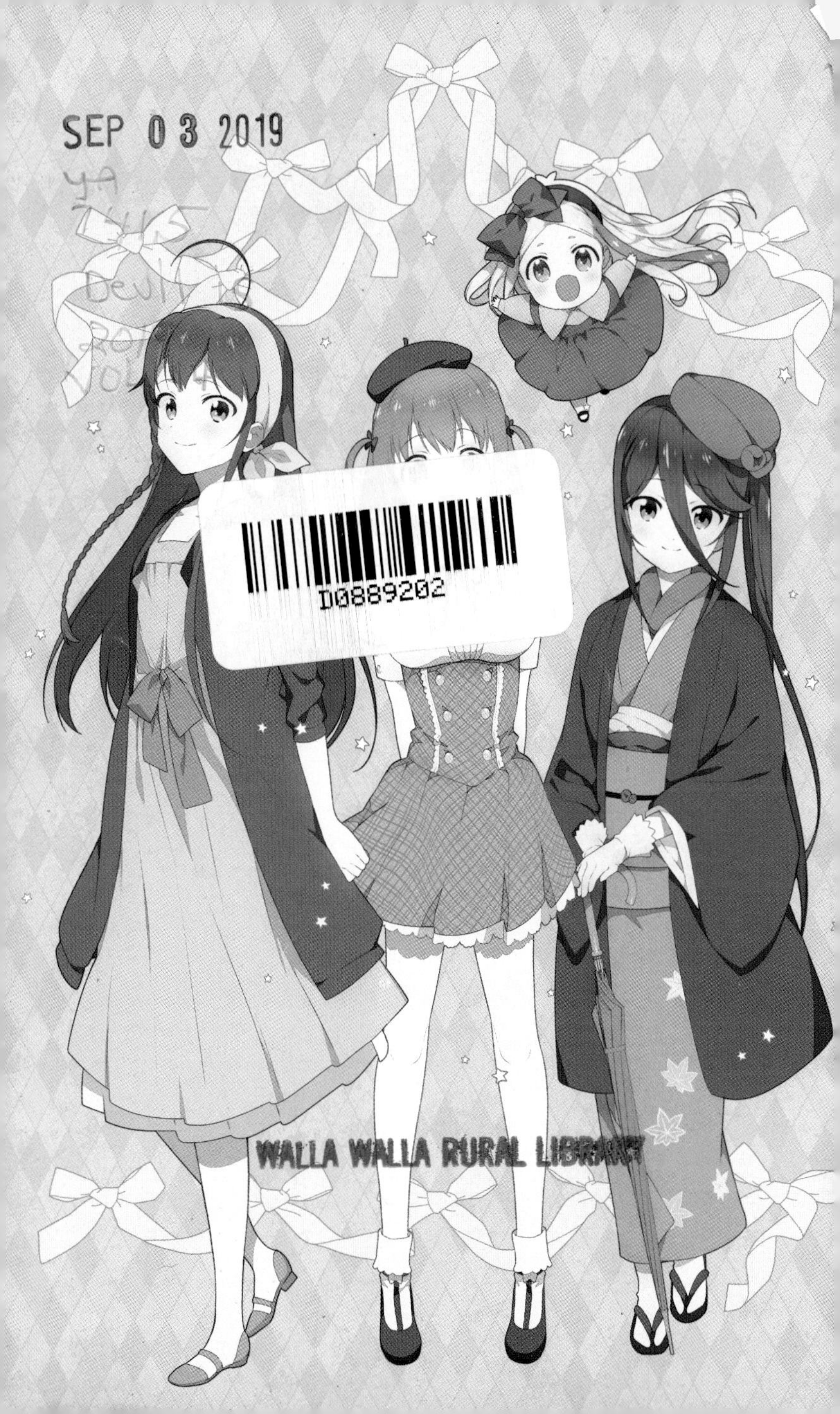

THE DEVIL IS A PART-TIMER! 14

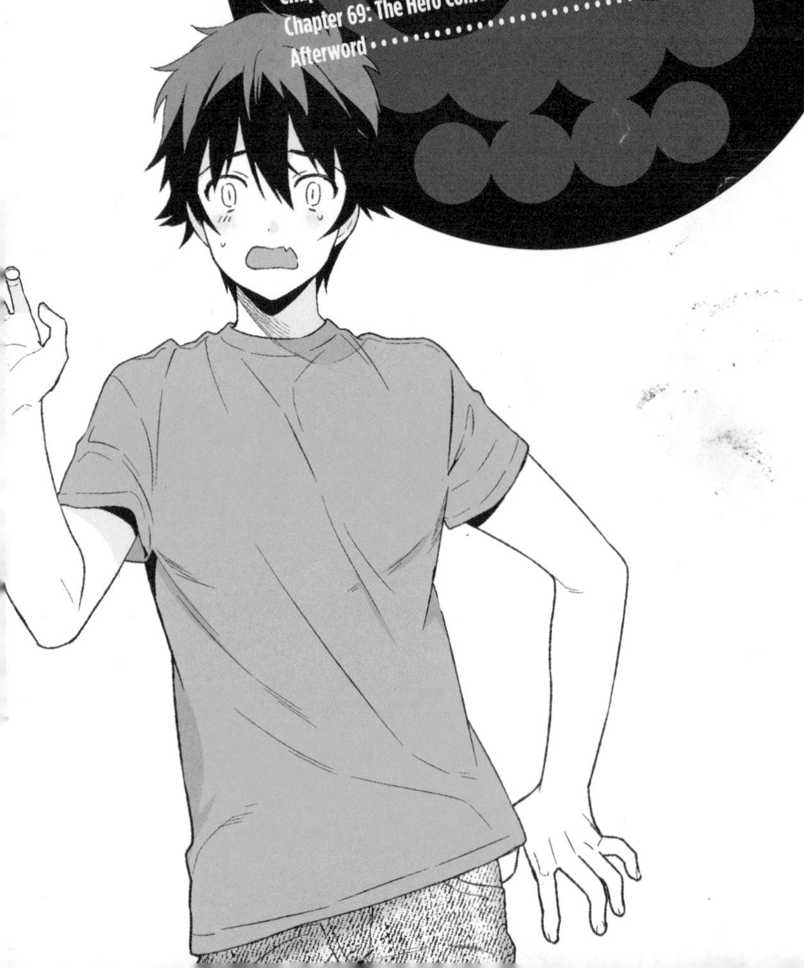

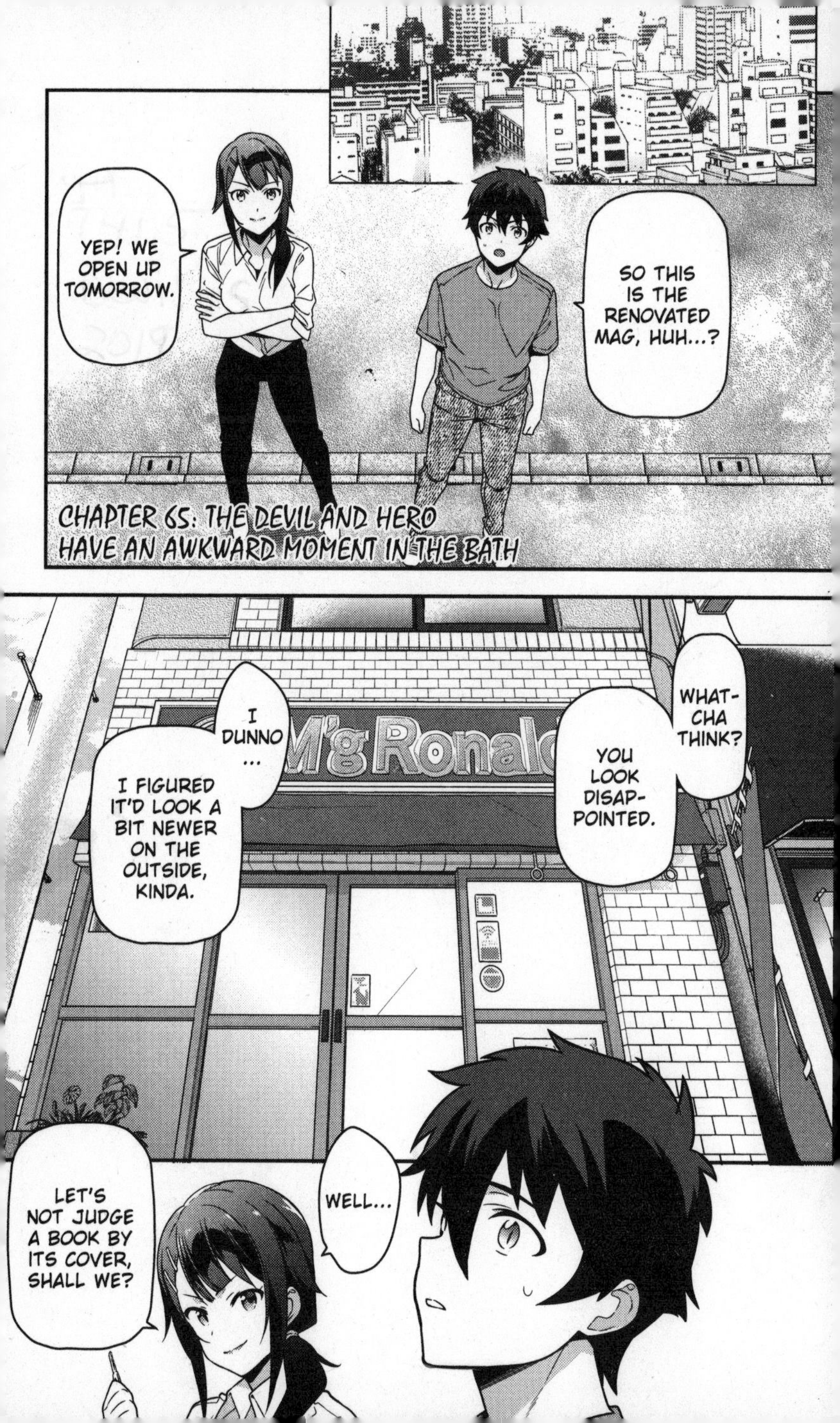
SO THIS IS THE RENOVATED MAG, HUH...?
YEP! WE OPEN UP TOMORROW.
CHAPTER 65: THE DEVIL AND HERO HAVE AN AWKWARD MOMENT IN THE BATH
WHAT-CHA THINK?
YOU LOOK DISAP-POINTED.
I DUNNO...
I FIGURED IT'D LOOK A BIT NEWER ON THE OUTSIDE, KINDA.
WELL...
LET'S NOT JUDGE A BOOK BY ITS COVER, SHALL WE?

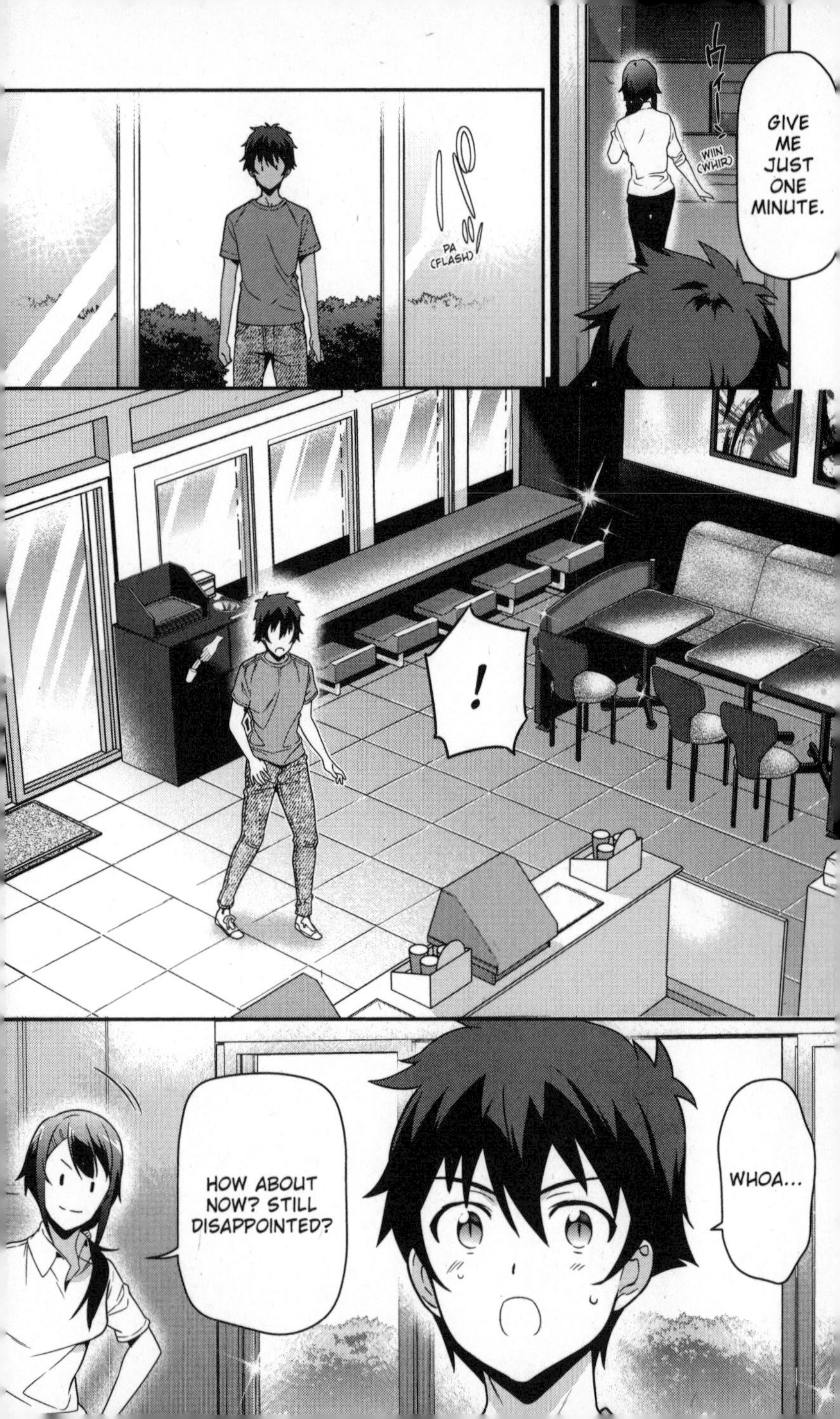
GIVE ME JUST ONE MINUTE.
WIIN (WHIR)
PA (FLASH)
!
WHOA...
HOW ABOUT NOW? STILL DISAPPOINTED?

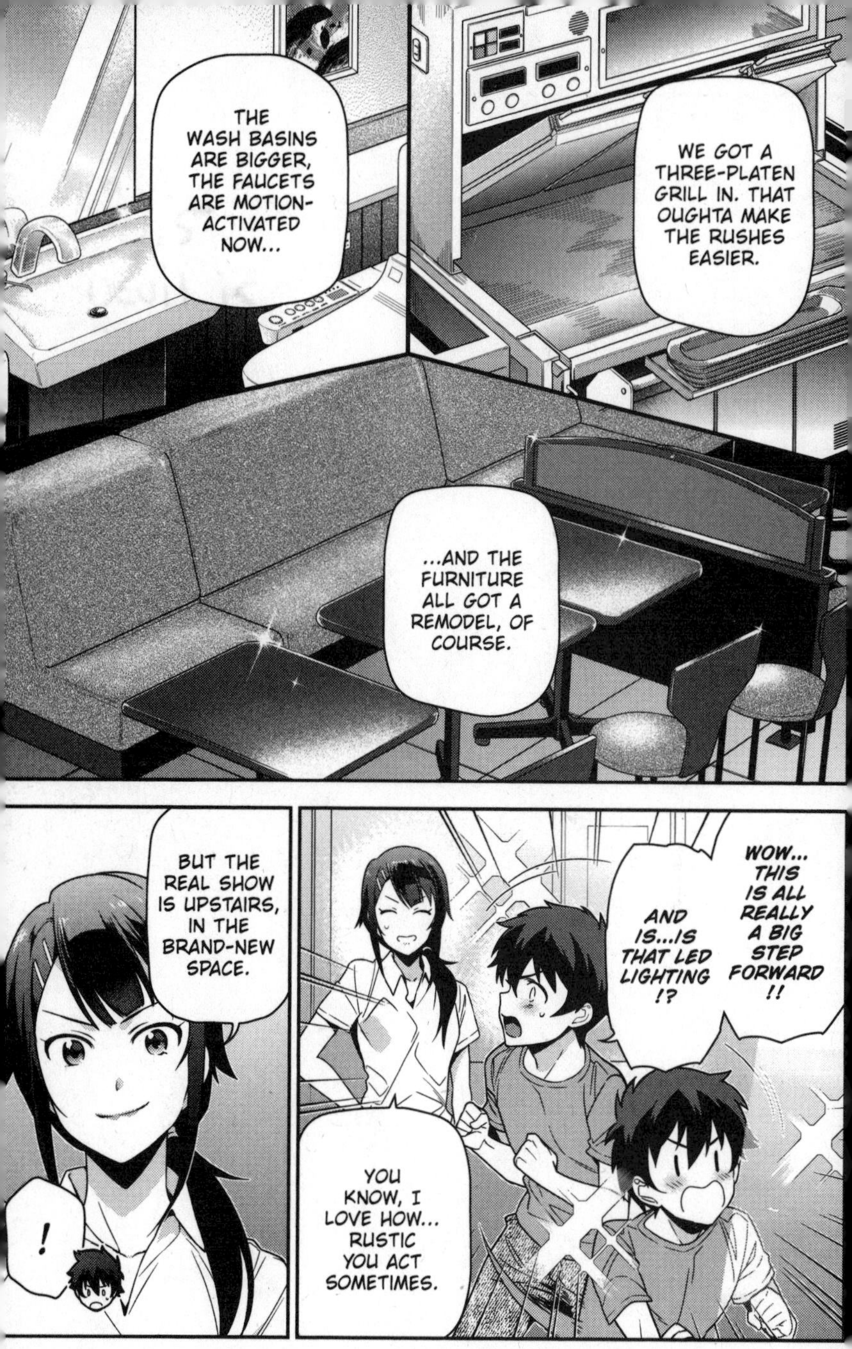
WE GOT A THREE-PLATEN GRILL IN. THAT OUGHTA MAKE THE RUSHES EASIER.
THE WASH BASINS ARE BIGGER, THE FAUCETS ARE MOTION-ACTIVATED NOW...
...AND THE FURNITURE ALL GOT A REMODEL, OF COURSE.
WOW... THIS IS ALL REALLY A BIG STEP FORWARD!!
AND IS...IS THAT LED LIGHTING!?
YOU KNOW, I LOVE HOW... RUSTIC YOU ACT SOMETIMES.
BUT THE REAL SHOW IS UPSTAIRS, IN THE BRAND-NEW SPACE.
!

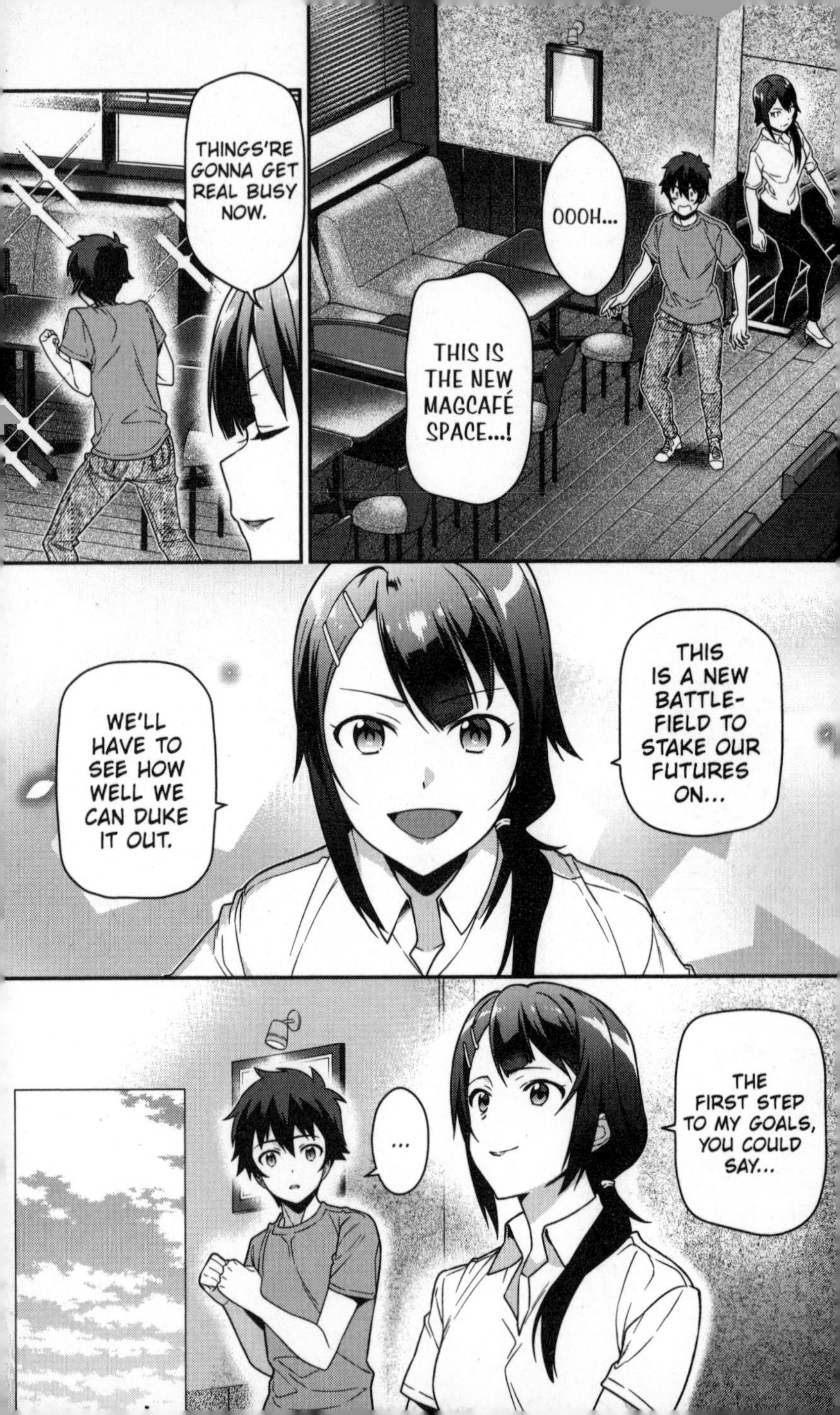

OOOH...
THIS IS THE NEW MAGCAFÉ SPACE...!
THINGS'RE GONNA GET REAL BUSY NOW.
THIS IS A NEW BATTLE-FIELD TO STAKE OUR FUTURES ON...
WE'LL HAVE TO SEE HOW WELL WE CAN DUKE IT OUT.
THE FIRST STEP TO MY GOALS, YOU COULD SAY...
...

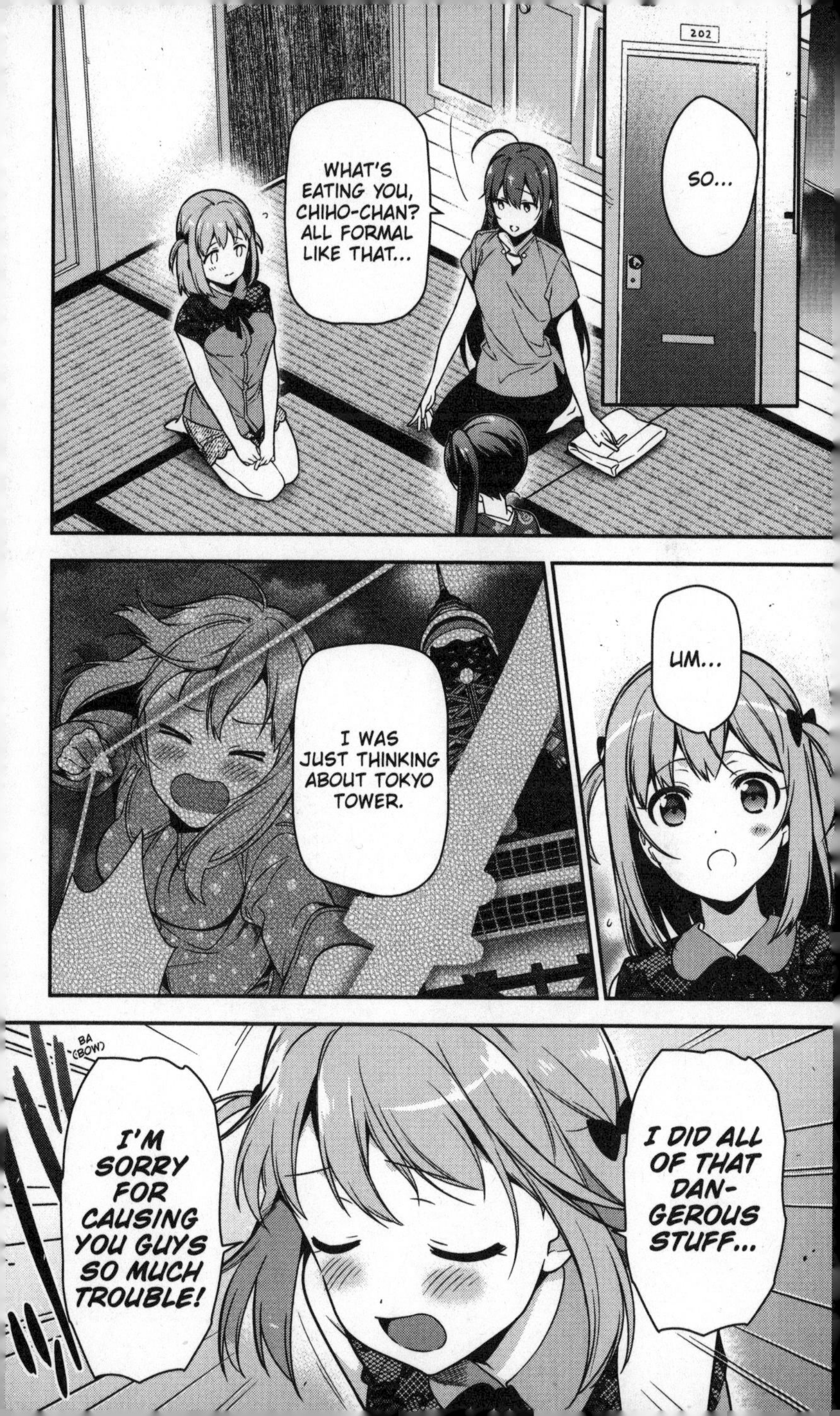
SO...
WHAT'S EATING YOU, CHIHO-CHAN? ALL FORMAL LIKE THAT...
UM...
I WAS JUST THINKING ABOUT TOKYO TOWER.
I DID ALL OF THAT DAN-GEROUS STUFF...
BA (BOW)
I'M SORRY FOR CAUSING YOU GUYS SO MUCH TROUBLE!

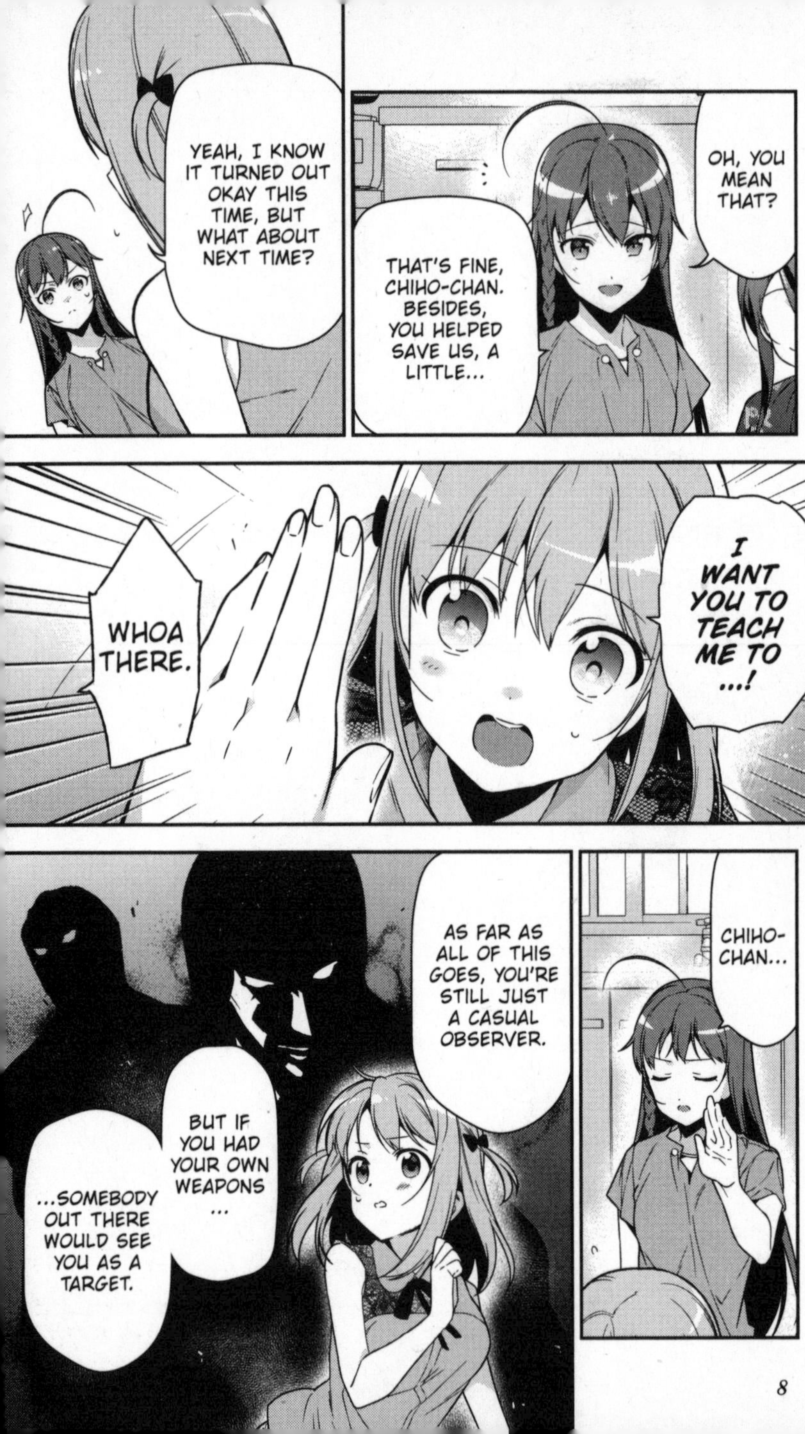
OH, YOU MEAN THAT?
THAT'S FINE, CHIHO-CHAN. BESIDES, YOU HELPED SAVE US, A LITTLE...
YEAH, I KNOW IT TURNED OUT OKAY THIS TIME, BUT WHAT ABOUT NEXT TIME?
I WANT YOU TO TEACH ME TO ...!
WHOA THERE.
CHIHO-CHAN...
AS FAR AS ALL OF THIS GOES, YOU'RE STILL JUST A CASUAL OBSERVER.
BUT IF YOU HAD YOUR OWN WEAPONS ...
...SOMEBODY OUT THERE WOULD SEE YOU AS A TARGET.

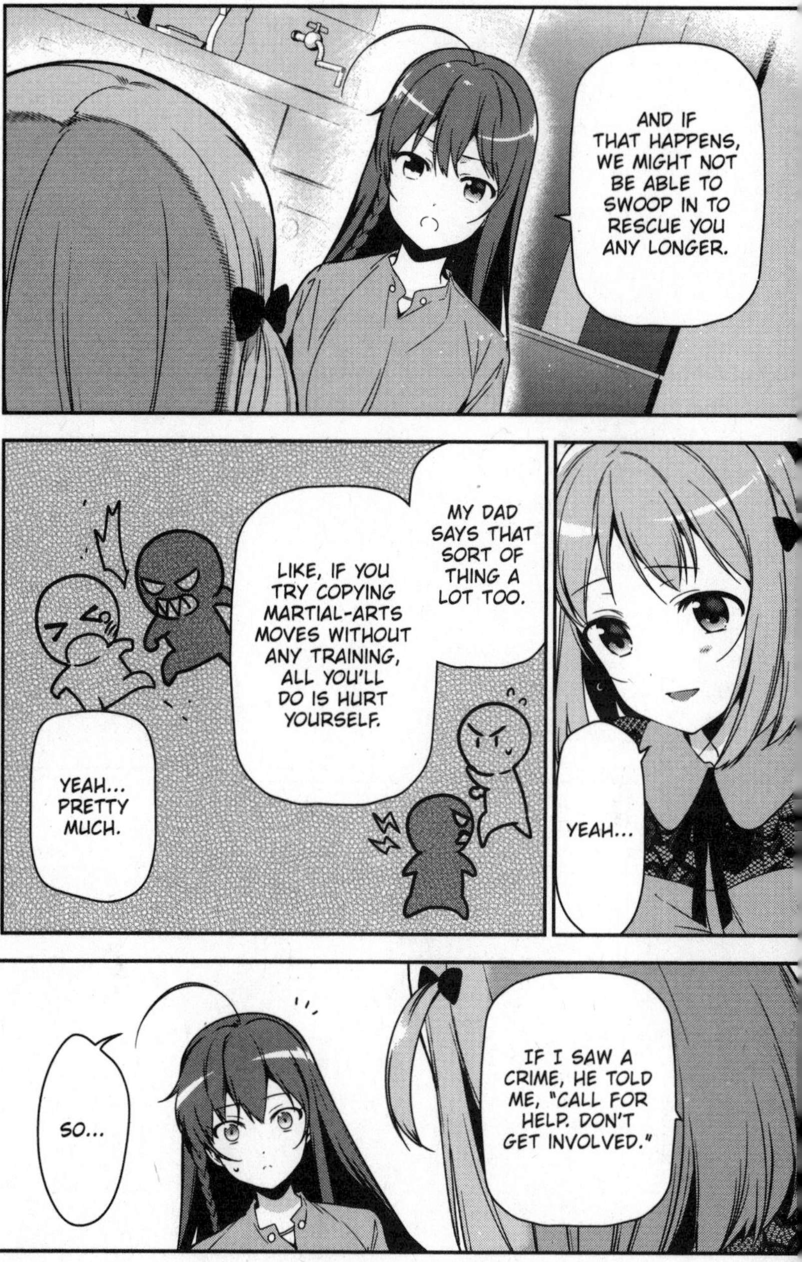
AND IF THAT HAPPENS, WE MIGHT NOT BE ABLE TO SWOOP IN TO RESCUE YOU ANY LONGER.
YEAH...
MY DAD SAYS THAT SORT OF THING A LOT TOO.
LIKE, IF YOU TRY COPYING MARTIAL-ARTS MOVES WITHOUT ANY TRAINING, ALL YOU'LL DO IS HURT YOURSELF.
YEAH... PRETTY MUCH.
IF I SAW A CRIME, HE TOLD ME, "CALL FOR HELP. DON'T GET INVOLVED."
SO...

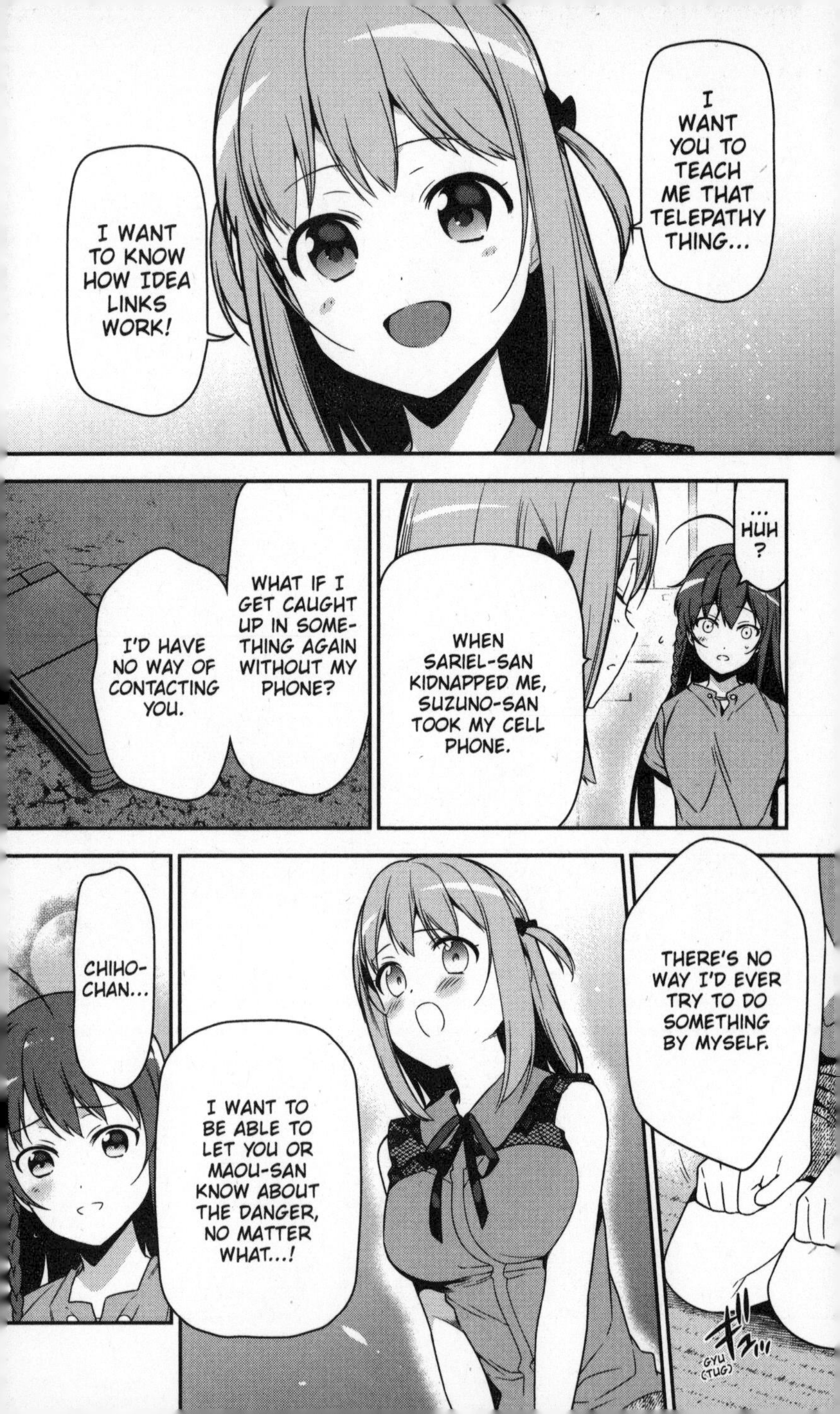
I WANT YOU TO TEACH ME THAT TELEPATHY THING...
I WANT TO KNOW HOW IDEA LINKS WORK!
...HUH?
WHEN SARIEL-SAN KIDNAPPED ME, SUZUNO-SAN TOOK MY CELL PHONE.
WHAT IF I GET CAUGHT UP IN SOME-THING AGAIN WITHOUT MY PHONE?
I'D HAVE NO WAY OF CONTACTING YOU.
THERE'S NO WAY I'D EVER TRY TO DO SOMETHING BY MYSELF.
GYU (TUG)
I WANT TO BE ABLE TO LET YOU OR MAOU-SAN KNOW ABOUT THE DANGER, NO MATTER WHAT...!
CHIHO-CHAN...

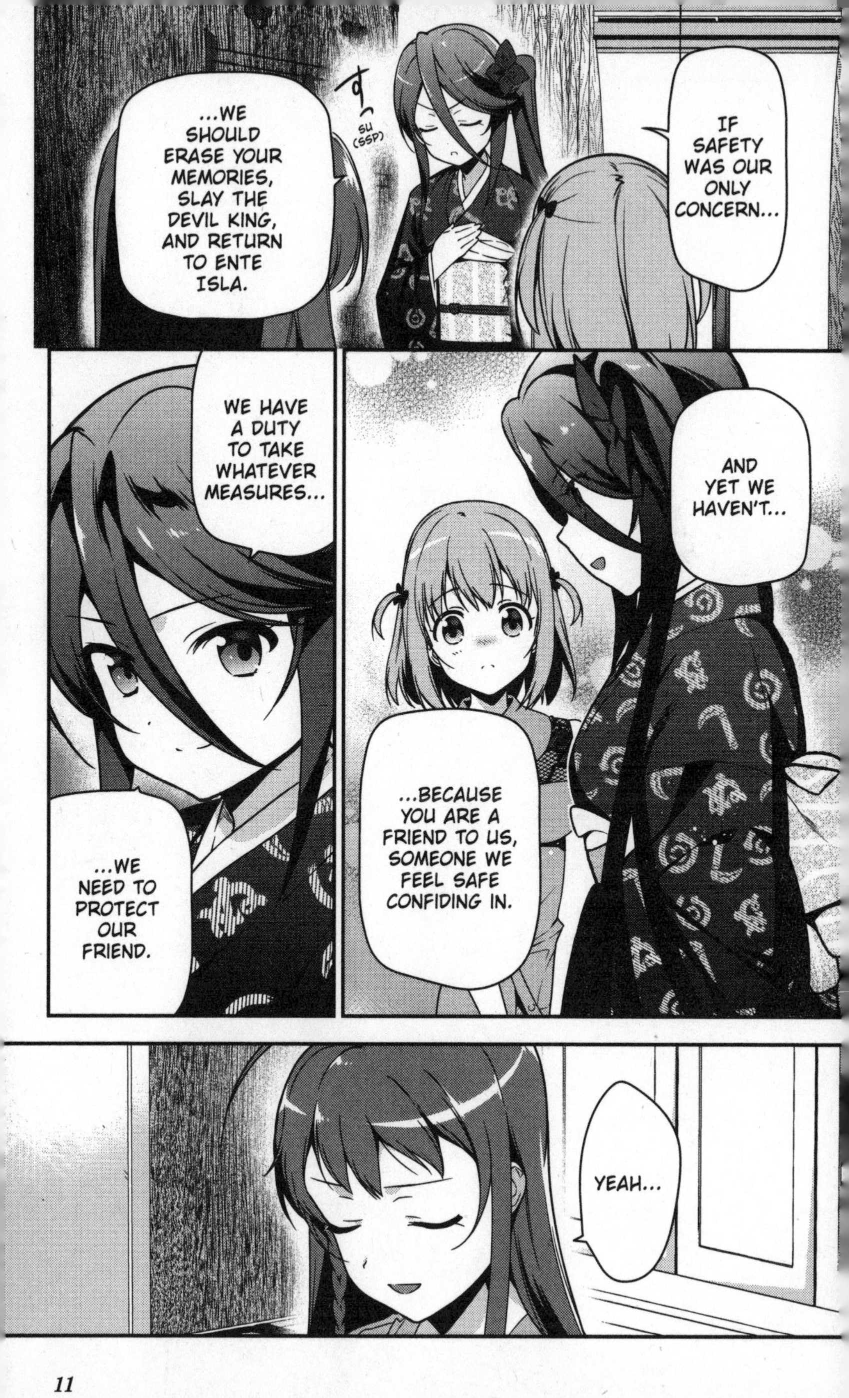
IF SAFETY WAS OUR ONLY CONCERN...
す
SU (SSP)
...WE SHOULD ERASE YOUR MEMORIES, SLAY THE DEVIL KING, AND RETURN TO ENTE ISLA.
AND YET WE HAVEN'T...
...BECAUSE YOU ARE A FRIEND TO US, SOMEONE WE FEEL SAFE CONFIDING IN.
WE HAVE A DUTY TO TAKE WHATEVER MEASURES...
...WE NEED TO PROTECT OUR FRIEND.
YEAH...

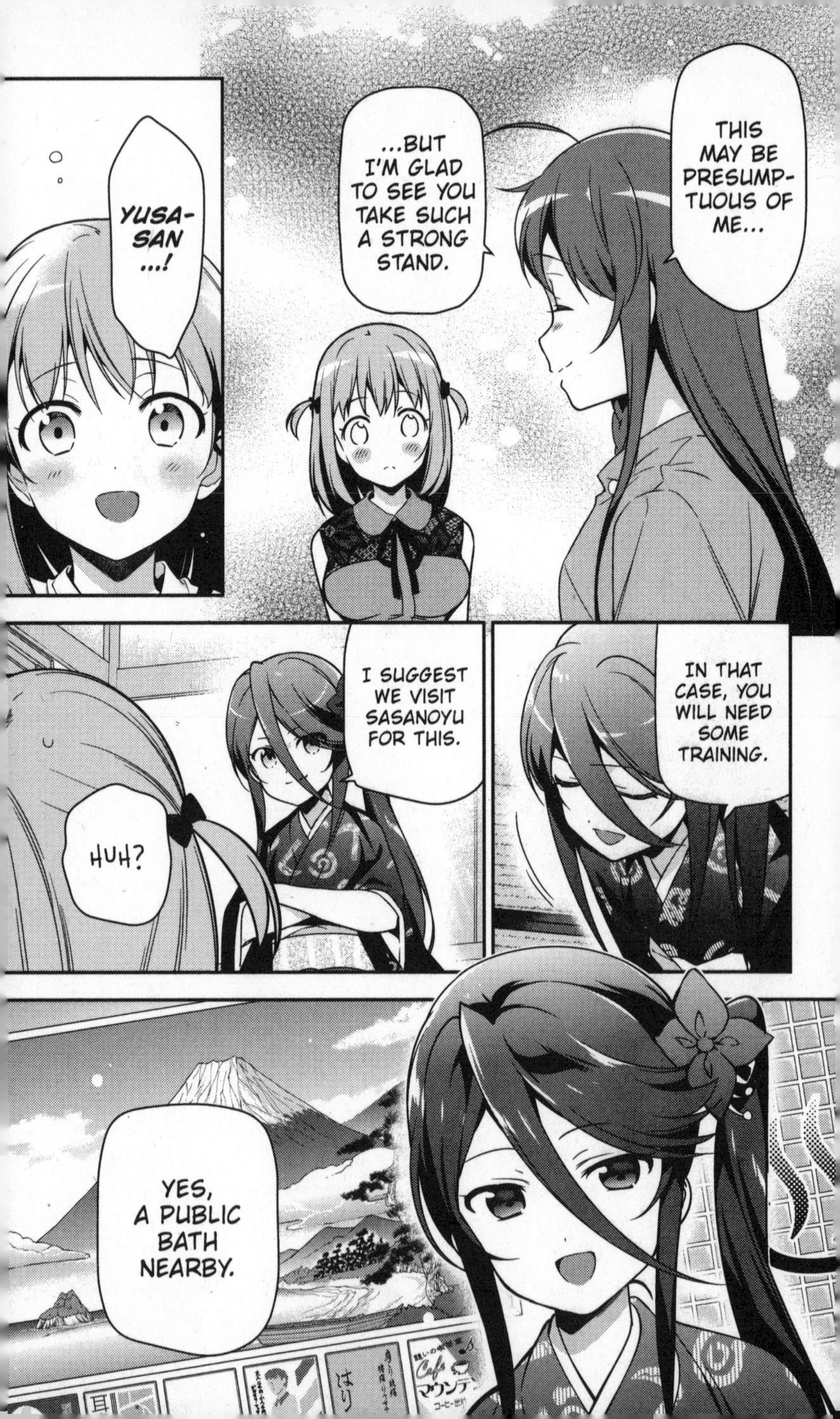
THIS MAY BE PRESUMPTUOUS OF ME...
...BUT I'M GLAD TO SEE YOU TAKE SUCH A STRONG STAND.
YUSA-SAN ...!
IN THAT CASE, YOU WILL NEED SOME TRAINING.
I SUGGEST WE VISIT SASANOYU FOR THIS.
HUH?
YES, A PUBLIC BATH NEARBY.

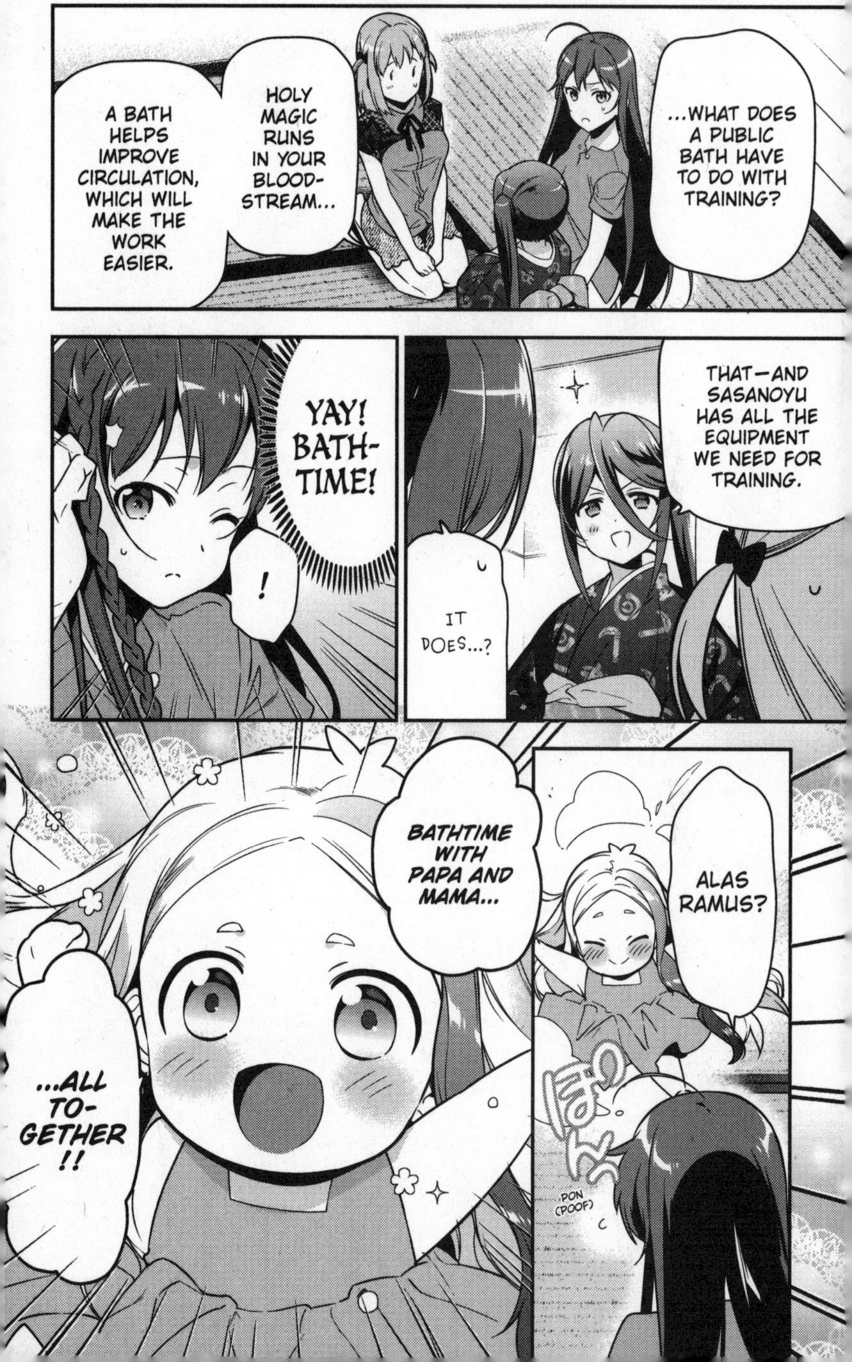
...WHAT DOES A PUBLIC BATH HAVE TO DO WITH TRAINING?
HOLY MAGIC RUNS IN YOUR BLOOD-STREAM...
A BATH HELPS IMPROVE CIRCULATION, WHICH WILL MAKE THE WORK EASIER.
THAT—AND SASANOYU HAS ALL THE EQUIPMENT WE NEED FOR TRAINING.
IT DOES...?
YAY! BATH-TIME!
!
ALAS RAMUS?
PON (POOF)
BATHTIME WITH PAPA AND MAMA...
...ALL TO-GETHER!!

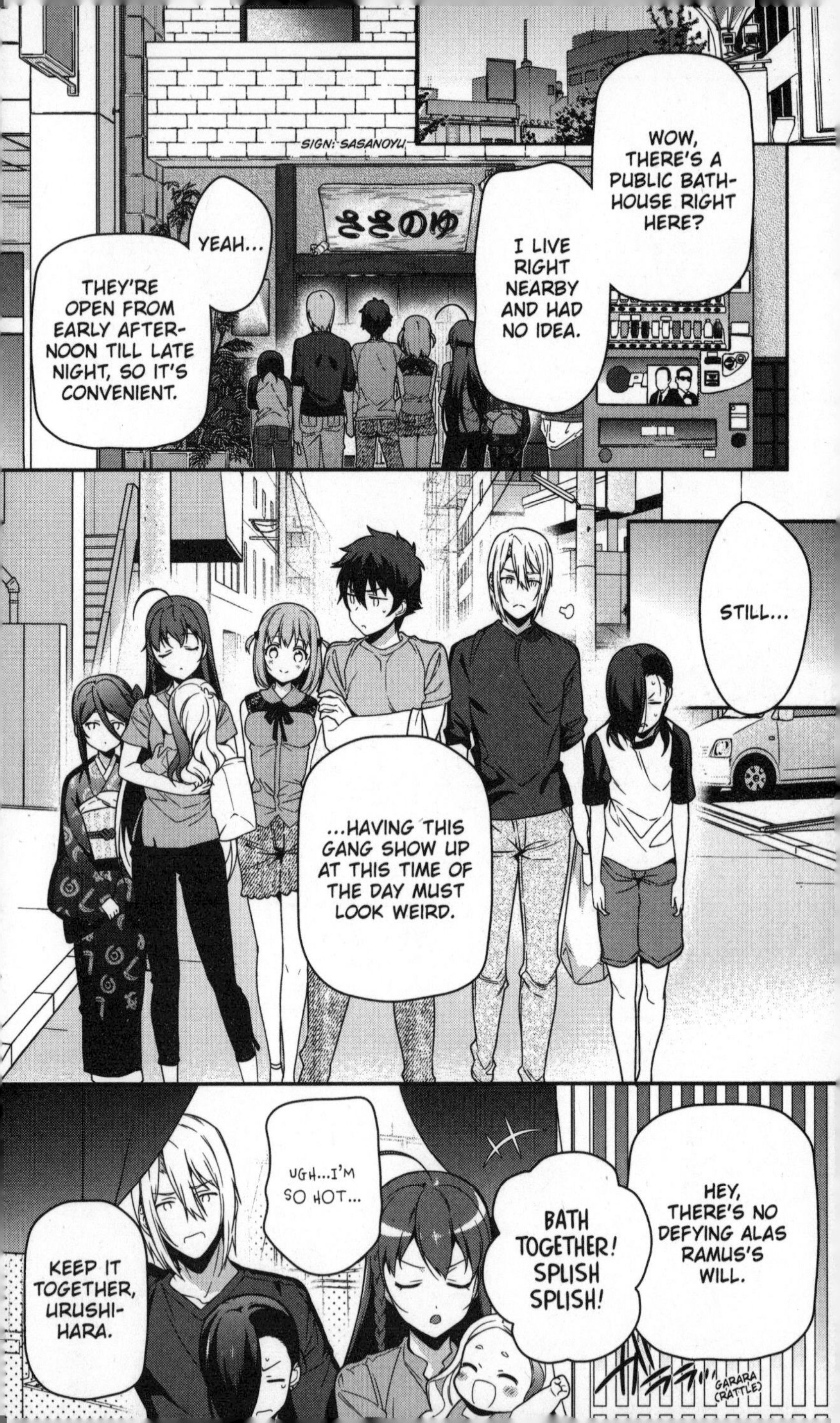
WOW, THERE'S A PUBLIC BATHHOUSE RIGHT HERE?
I LIVE RIGHT NEARBY AND HAD NO IDEA.
SIGN: SASANOYU
ささのゆ
YEAH...
THEY'RE OPEN FROM EARLY AFTERNOON TILL LATE NIGHT, SO IT'S CONVENIENT.
STILL...
...HAVING THIS GANG SHOW UP AT THIS TIME OF THE DAY MUST LOOK WEIRD.
HEY, THERE'S NO DEFYING ALAS RAMUS'S WILL.
BATH TOGETHER! SPLISH SPLISH!
GARARA (RATTLE)
UGH...I'M SO HOT...
KEEP IT TOGETHER, URUSHIHARA.

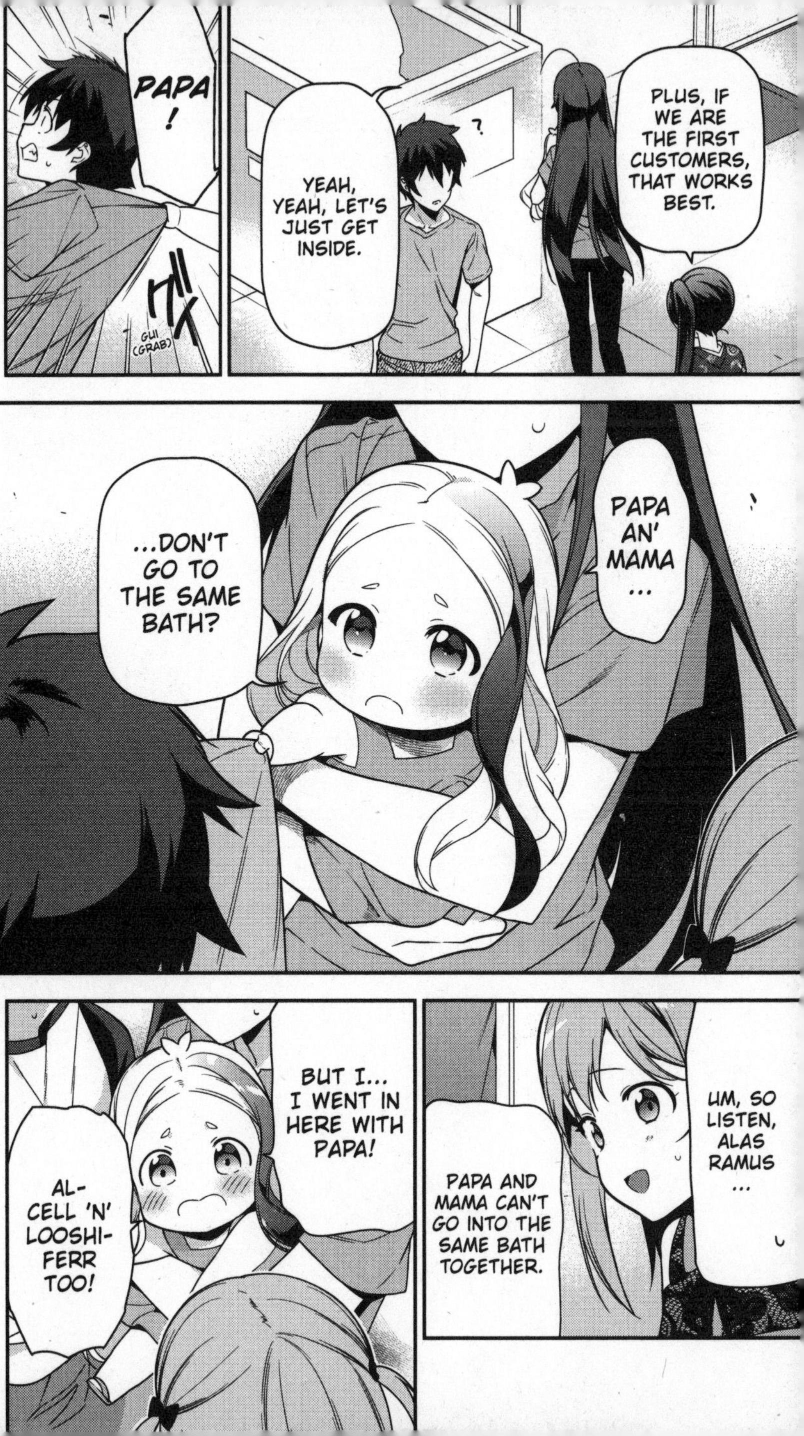
PLUS, IF WE ARE THE FIRST CUSTOMERS, THAT WORKS BEST.
?
YEAH, YEAH, LET'S JUST GET INSIDE.
PAPA!
GUI (GRAB)
PAPA AN' MAMA...
...DON'T GO TO THE SAME BATH?
UM, SO LISTEN, ALAS RAMUS...
PAPA AND MAMA CAN'T GO INTO THE SAME BATH TOGETHER.
BUT I... I WENT IN HERE WITH PAPA!
AL-CELL 'N' LOOSHI-FERR TOO!

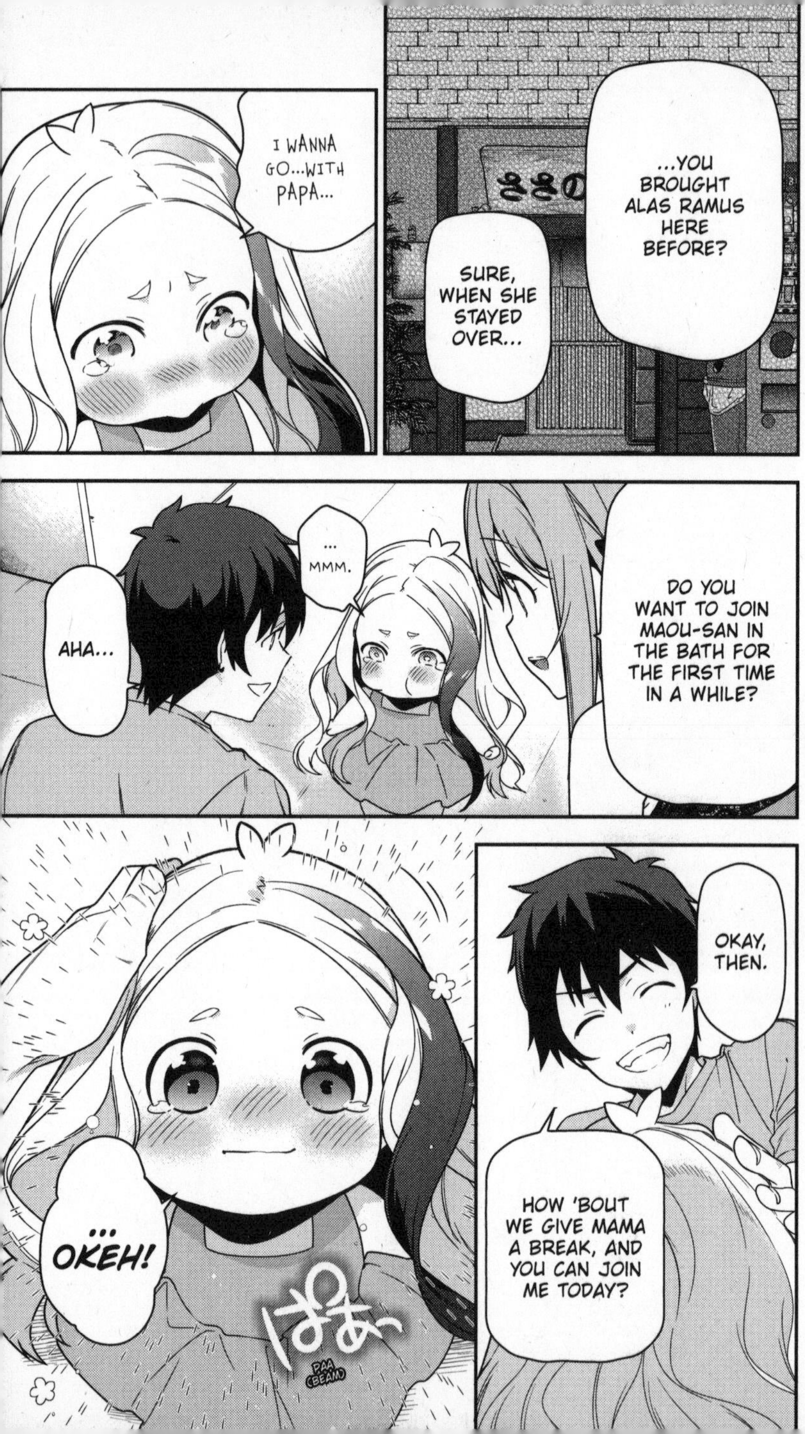
...YOU BROUGHT ALAS RAMUS HERE BEFORE?
SURE, WHEN SHE STAYED OVER...
I WANNA GO...WITH PAPA...
DO YOU WANT TO JOIN MAOU-SAN IN THE BATH FOR THE FIRST TIME IN A WHILE?
... MMM.
AHA...
OKAY, THEN.
HOW 'BOUT WE GIVE MAMA A BREAK, AND YOU CAN JOIN ME TODAY?
... OKEH!
ぱあ
PAA (BEAM)

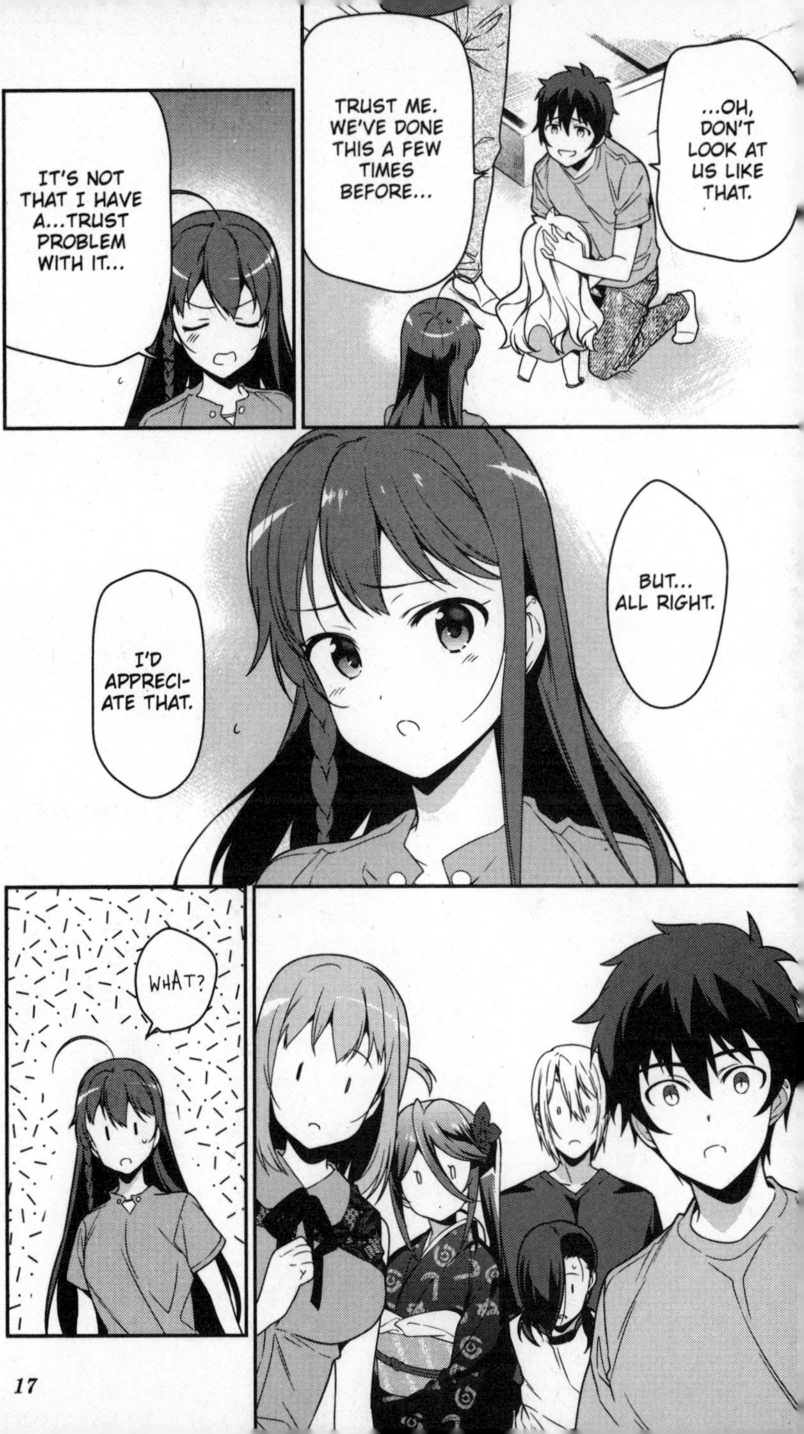
...OH, DON'T LOOK AT US LIKE THAT.
TRUST ME. WE'VE DONE THIS A FEW TIMES BEFORE...
IT'S NOT THAT I HAVE A...TRUST PROBLEM WITH IT...
BUT... ALL RIGHT.
I'D APPRECIATE THAT.
WHAT?

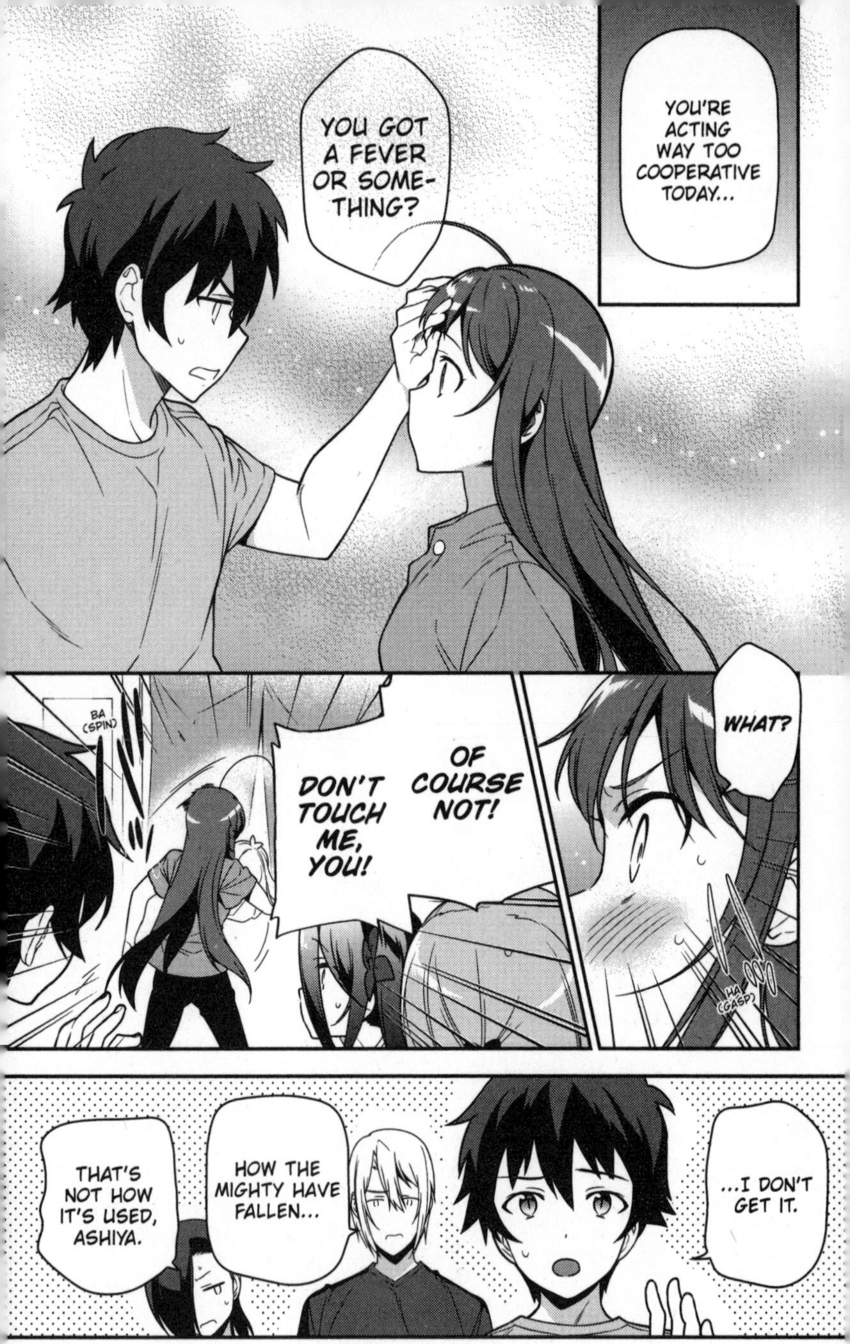
YOU'RE ACTING WAY TOO COOPERATIVE TODAY...
YOU GOT A FEVER OR SOME-THING?
WHAT?
HA (GASP)
OF COURSE NOT!
DON'T TOUCH ME, YOU!
BA (SPIN)
...I DON'T GET IT.
HOW THE MIGHTY HAVE FALLEN...
THAT'S NOT HOW IT'S USED, ASHIYA.

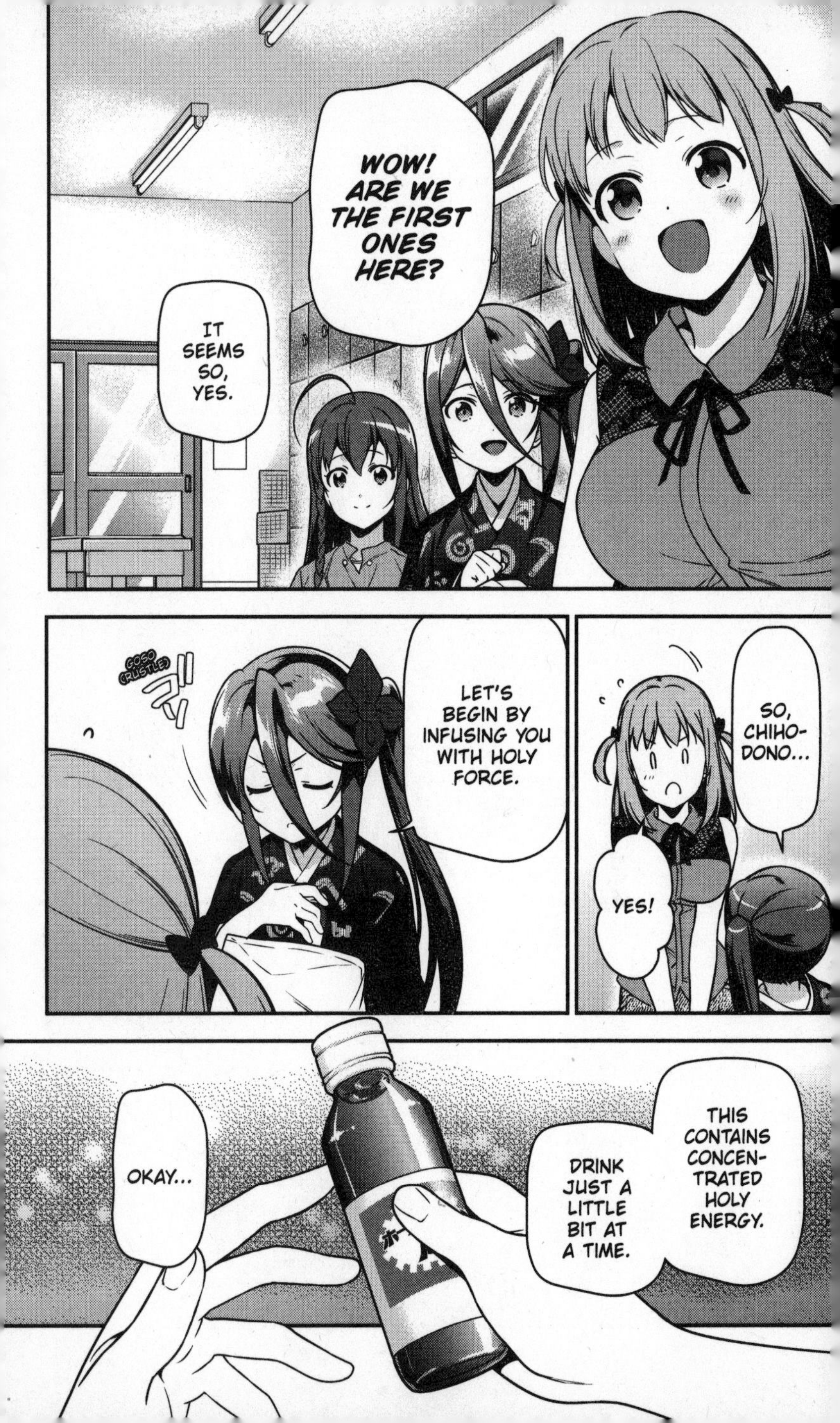
WOW! ARE WE THE FIRST ONES HERE?
IT SEEMS SO, YES.
SO, CHIHO-DONO...
YES!
LET'S BEGIN BY INFUSING YOU WITH HOLY FORCE.
GOSO (RUSTLE)
THIS CONTAINS CONCEN-TRATED HOLY ENERGY.
DRINK JUST A LITTLE BIT AT A TIME.
OKAY...

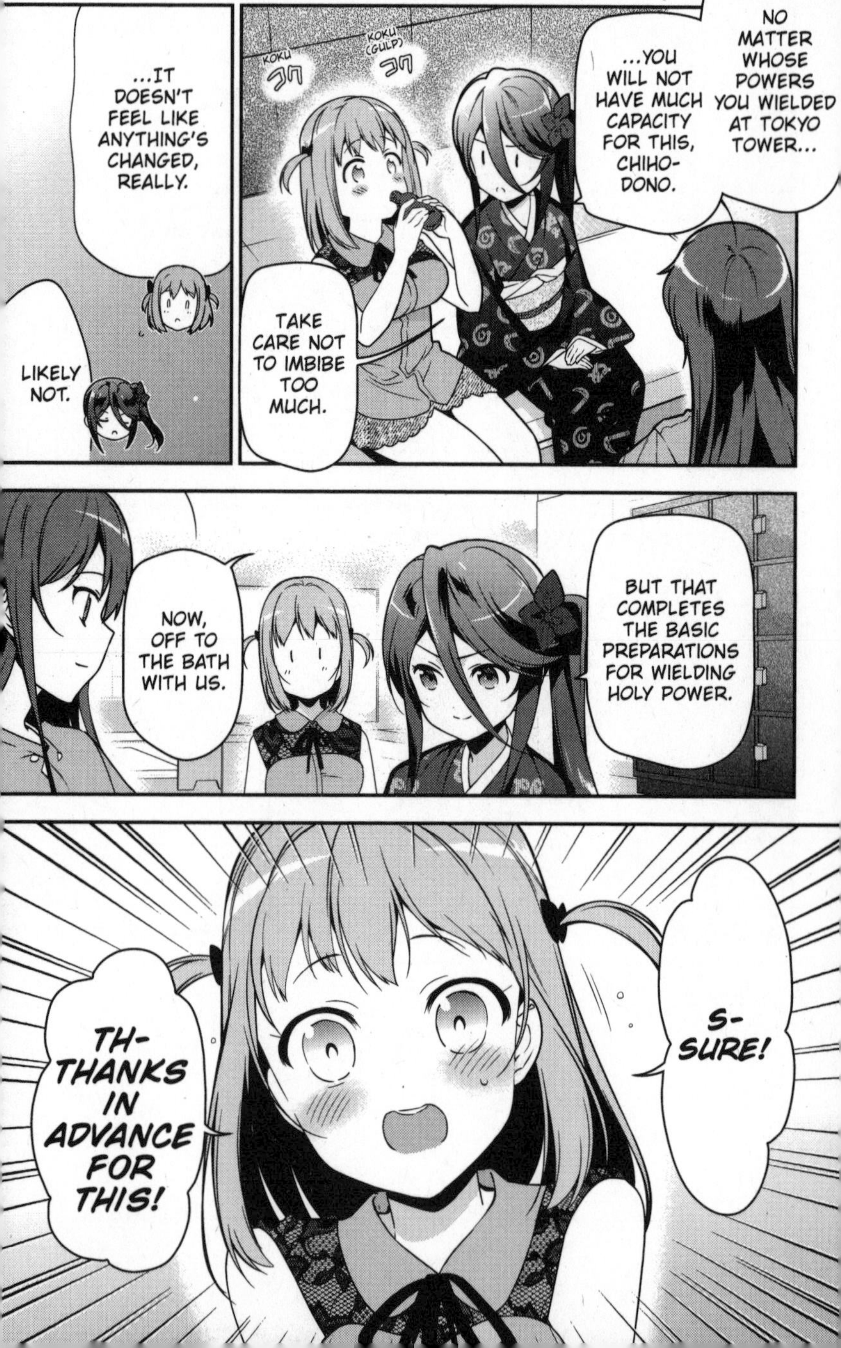
NO MATTER WHOSE POWERS YOU WIELDED AT TOKYO TOWER...
...YOU WILL NOT HAVE MUCH CAPACITY FOR THIS, CHIHO-DONO.
KOKU (GULP)
KOKU
TAKE CARE NOT TO IMBIBE TOO MUCH.
...IT DOESN'T FEEL LIKE ANYTHING'S CHANGED, REALLY.
LIKELY NOT.
BUT THAT COMPLETES THE BASIC PREPARATIONS FOR WIELDING HOLY POWER.
NOW, OFF TO THE BATH WITH US.
S-SURE!
TH-THANKS IN ADVANCE FOR THIS!

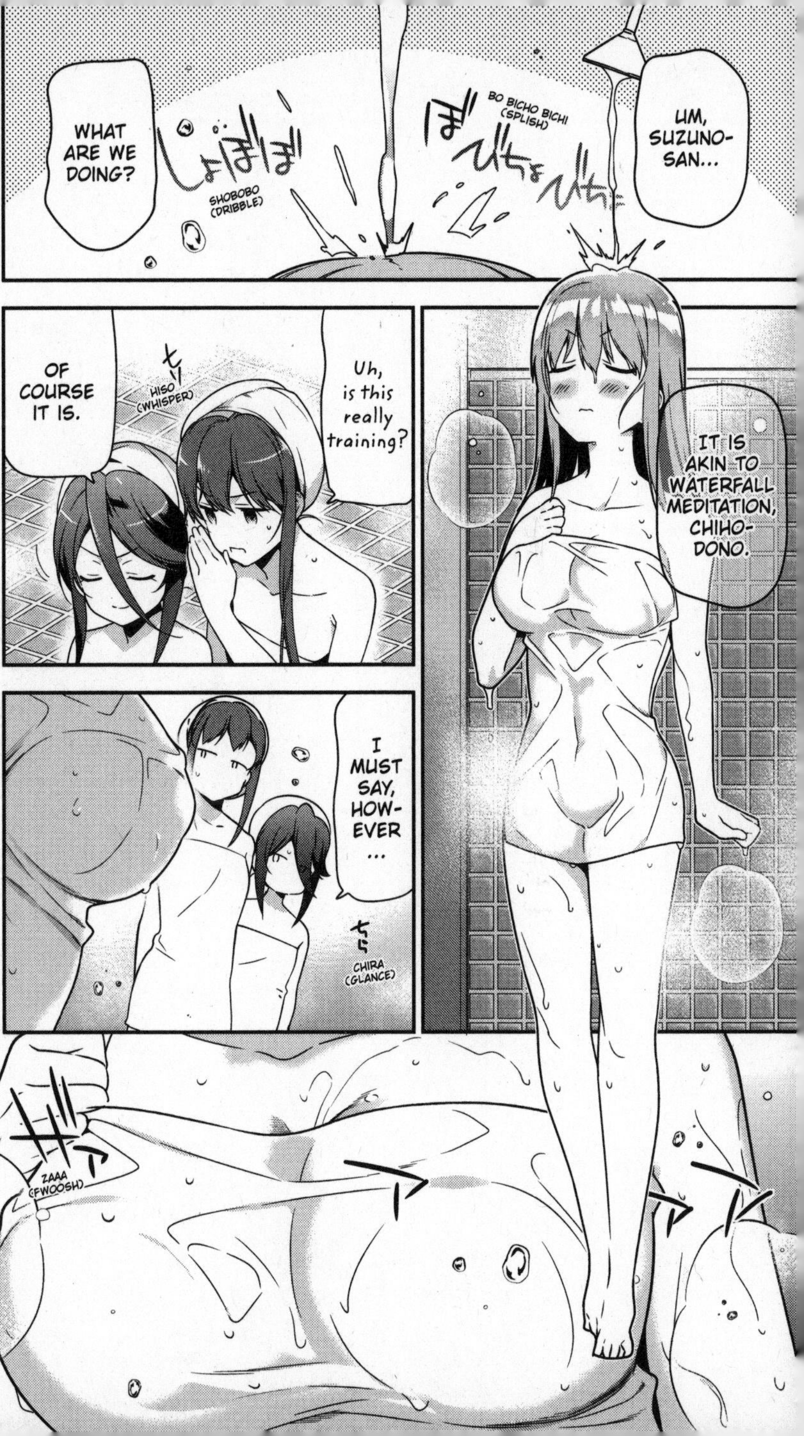
UM, SUZUNO-SAN...
BO BICHO BICHI (SPLISH)
SHOBOBO (DRIBBLE)
WHAT ARE WE DOING?
IT IS AKIN TO WATERFALL MEDITATION, CHIHO-DONO.
Uh, is this really training?
HISO (WHISPER)
OF COURSE IT IS.
I MUST SAY, HOWEVER ...
CHIRA (GLANCE)
ZAAA (FWOOSH)

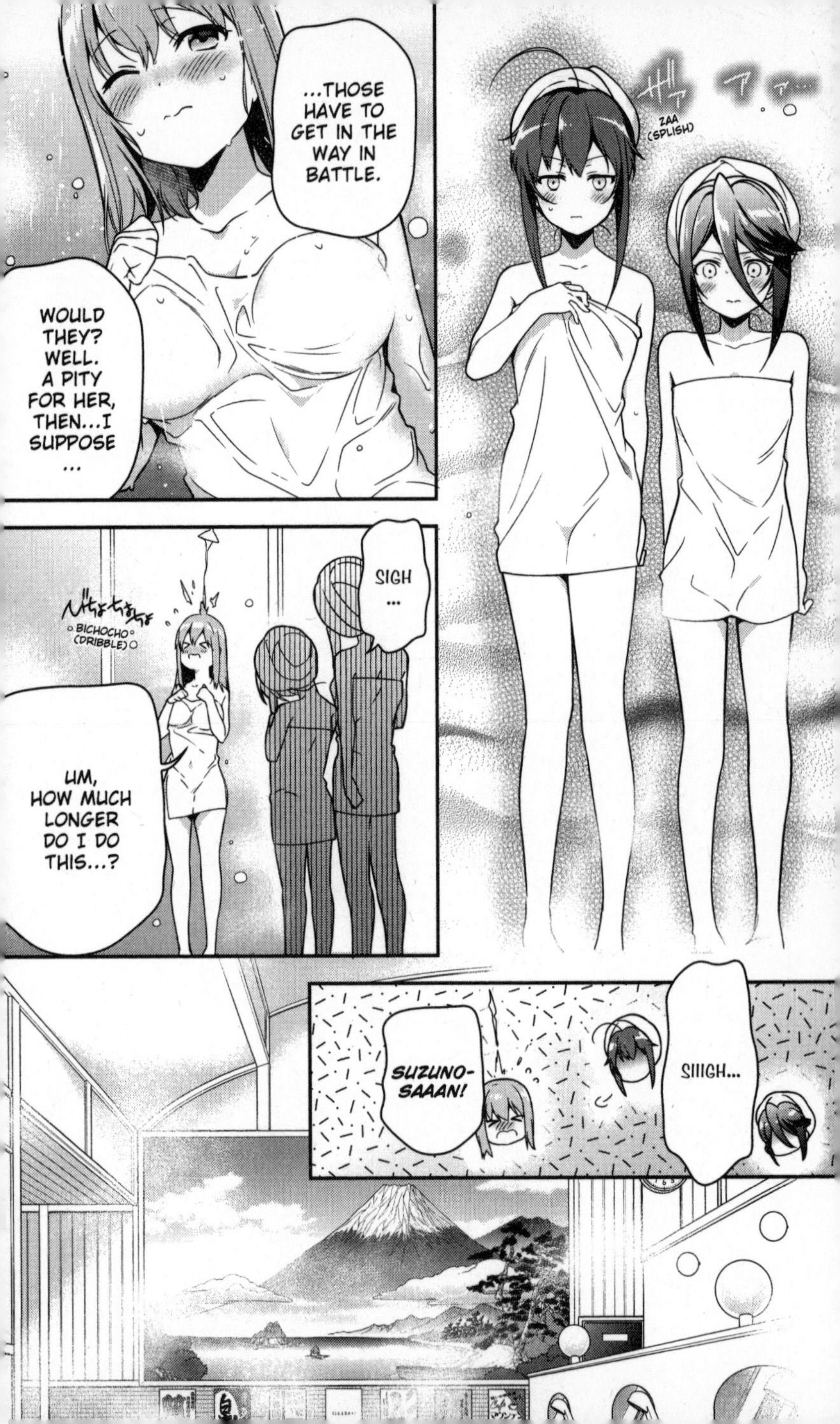

ZAA (SPLISH)
...THOSE HAVE TO GET IN THE WAY IN BATTLE.
WOULD THEY? WELL. A PITY FOR HER, THEN...I SUPPOSE...
SIGH...
BICHOCHO (DRIBBLE)
UM, HOW MUCH LONGER DO I DO THIS...?
SIIIGH...
SUZUNO-SAAAN!

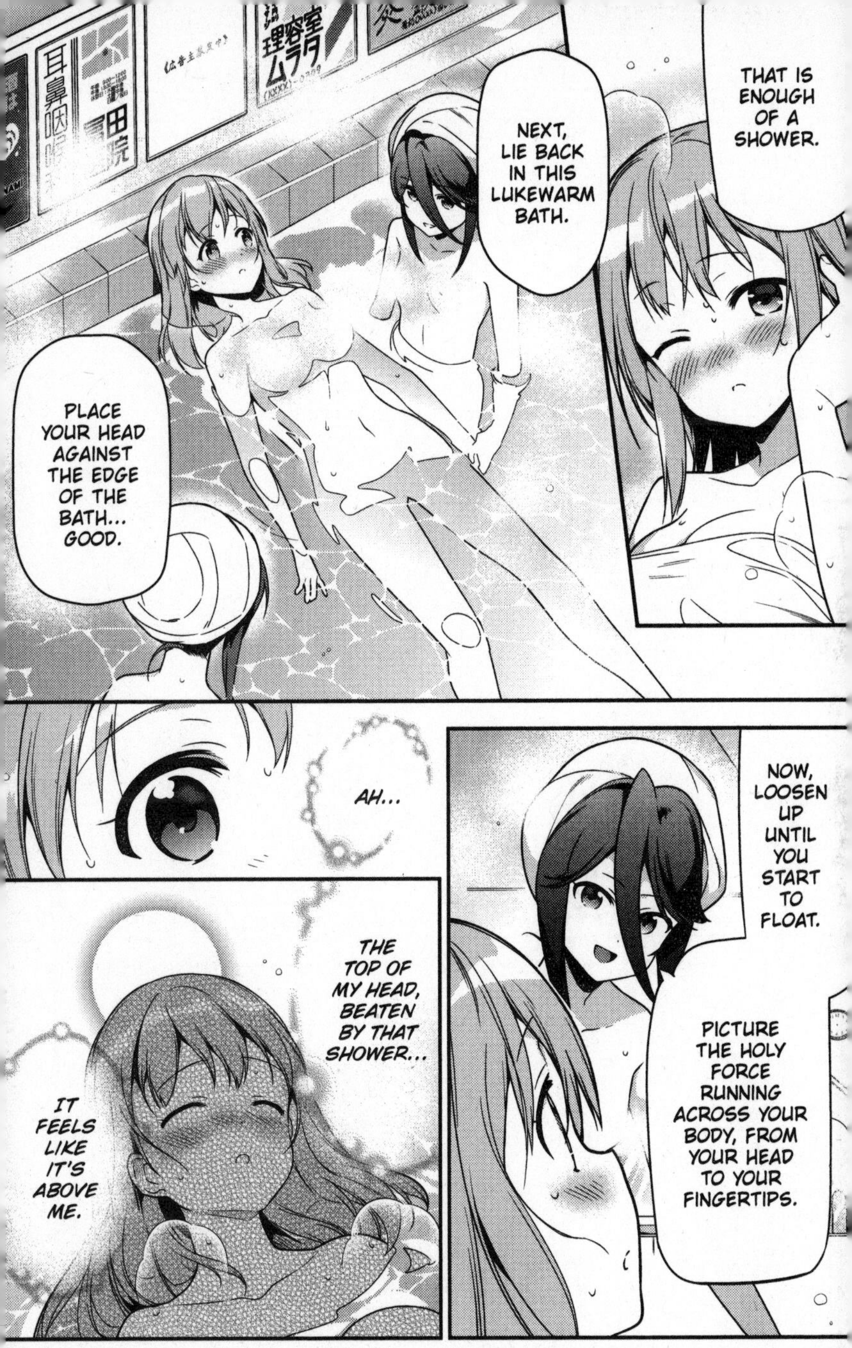
THAT IS ENOUGH OF A SHOWER.
NEXT, LIE BACK IN THIS LUKEWARM BATH.
PLACE YOUR HEAD AGAINST THE EDGE OF THE BATH... GOOD.
NOW, LOOSEN UP UNTIL YOU START TO FLOAT.
PICTURE THE HOLY FORCE RUNNING ACROSS YOUR BODY, FROM YOUR HEAD TO YOUR FINGERTIPS.
AH...
THE TOP OF MY HEAD, BEATEN BY THAT SHOWER...
IT FEELS LIKE IT'S ABOVE ME.

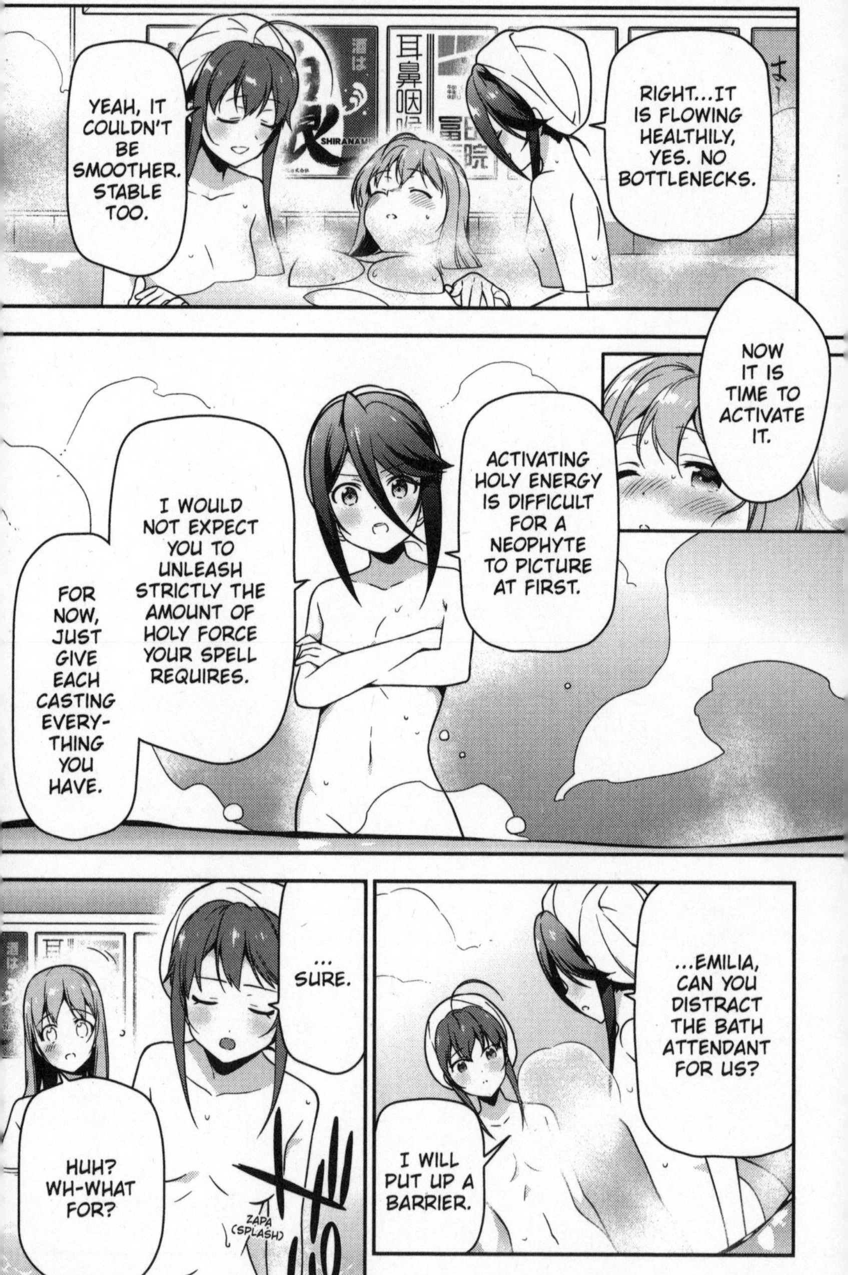
RIGHT...IT IS FLOWING HEALTHILY, YES. NO BOTTLENECKS.
耳鼻咽喉
SHIRANAMI
YEAH, IT COULDN'T BE SMOOTHER. STABLE TOO.
NOW IT IS TIME TO ACTIVATE IT.
ACTIVATING HOLY ENERGY IS DIFFICULT FOR A NEOPHYTE TO PICTURE AT FIRST.
I WOULD NOT EXPECT YOU TO UNLEASH STRICTLY THE AMOUNT OF HOLY FORCE YOUR SPELL REQUIRES.
FOR NOW, JUST GIVE EACH CASTING EVERYTHING YOU HAVE.
...EMILIA, CAN YOU DISTRACT THE BATH ATTENDANT FOR US?
I WILL PUT UP A BARRIER.
... SURE.
ZAPA (SPLASH)
HUH? WH-WHAT FOR?

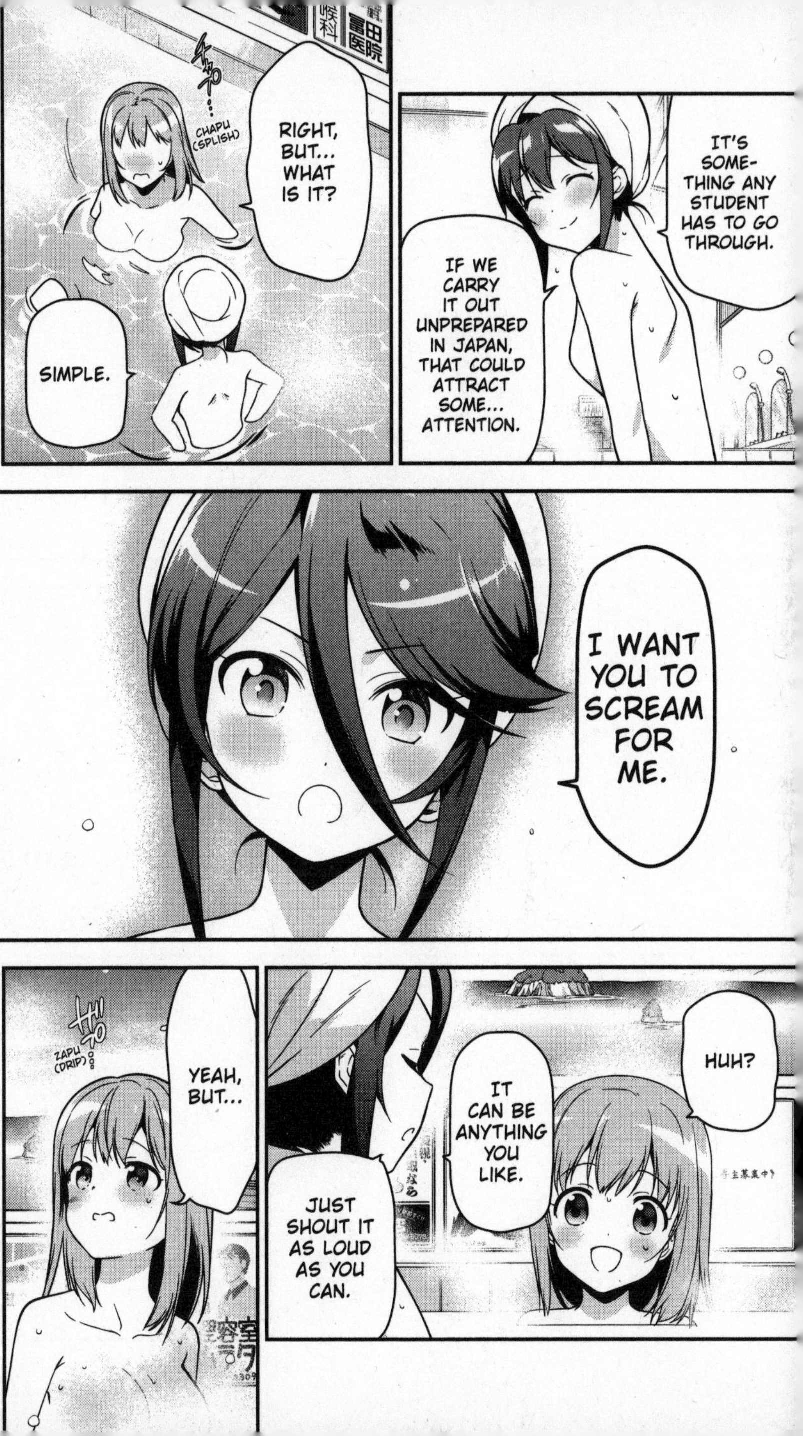

IT'S SOMETHING ANY STUDENT HAS TO GO THROUGH.
IF WE CARRY IT OUT UNPREPARED IN JAPAN, THAT COULD ATTRACT SOME... ATTENTION.
CHAPU (SPLISH)
RIGHT, BUT... WHAT IS IT?
SIMPLE.
I WANT YOU TO SCREAM FOR ME.
HUH?
IT CAN BE ANYTHING YOU LIKE.
JUST SHOUT IT AS LOUD AS YOU CAN.
ZAPU (DRIP)
YEAH, BUT...

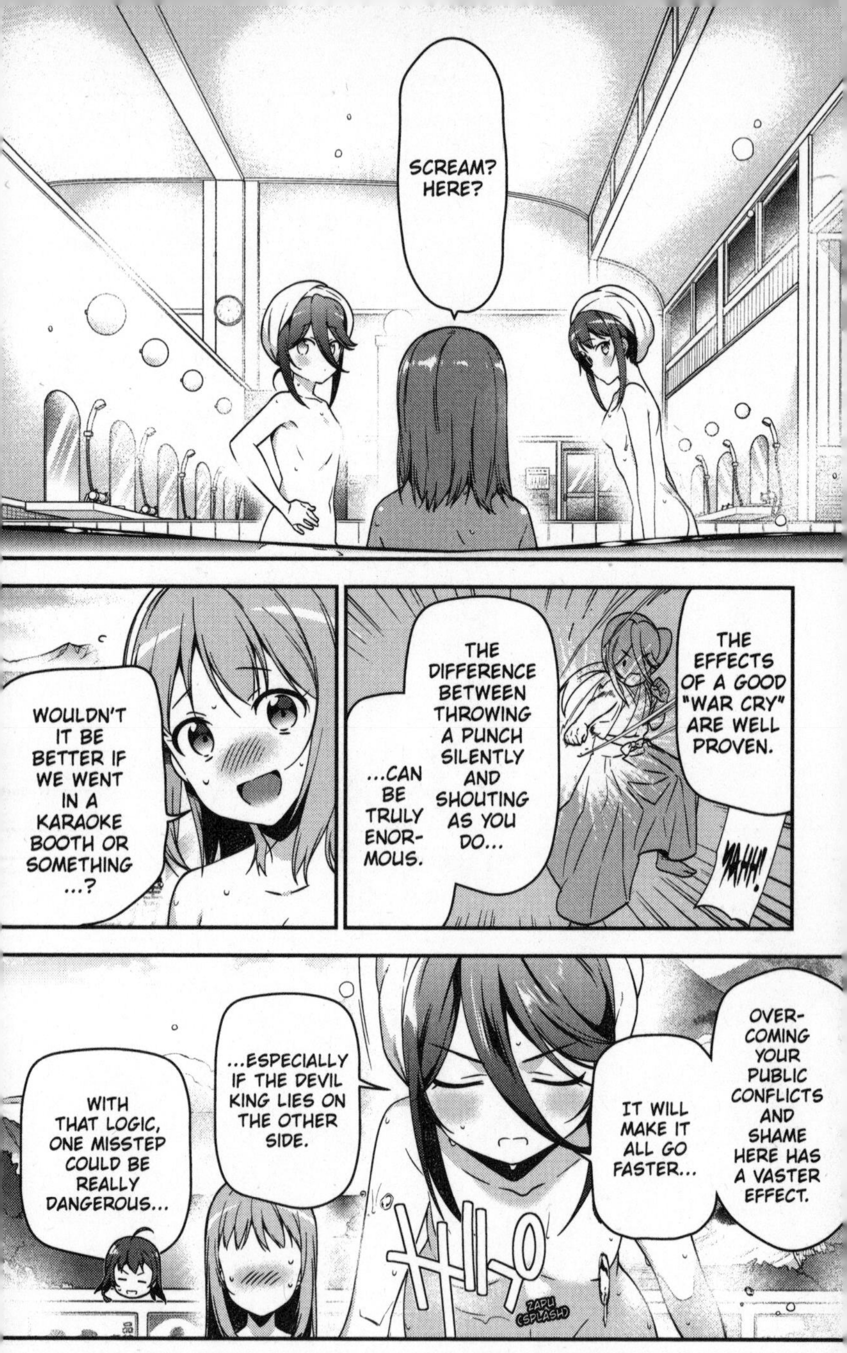
SCREAM? HERE?
THE EFFECTS OF A GOOD "WAR CRY" ARE WELL PROVEN.
THE DIFFERENCE BETWEEN THROWING A PUNCH SILENTLY AND SHOUTING AS YOU DO...
...CAN BE TRULY ENOR-MOUS.
YAHH!
WOULDN'T IT BE BETTER IF WE WENT IN A KARAOKE BOOTH OR SOMETHING...?
OVER-COMING YOUR PUBLIC CONFLICTS AND SHAME HERE HAS A VASTER EFFECT.
IT WILL MAKE IT ALL GO FASTER...
ZAPU (SPLASH)
...ESPECIALLY IF THE DEVIL KING LIES ON THE OTHER SIDE.
WITH THAT LOGIC, ONE MISSTEP COULD BE REALLY DANGEROUS...

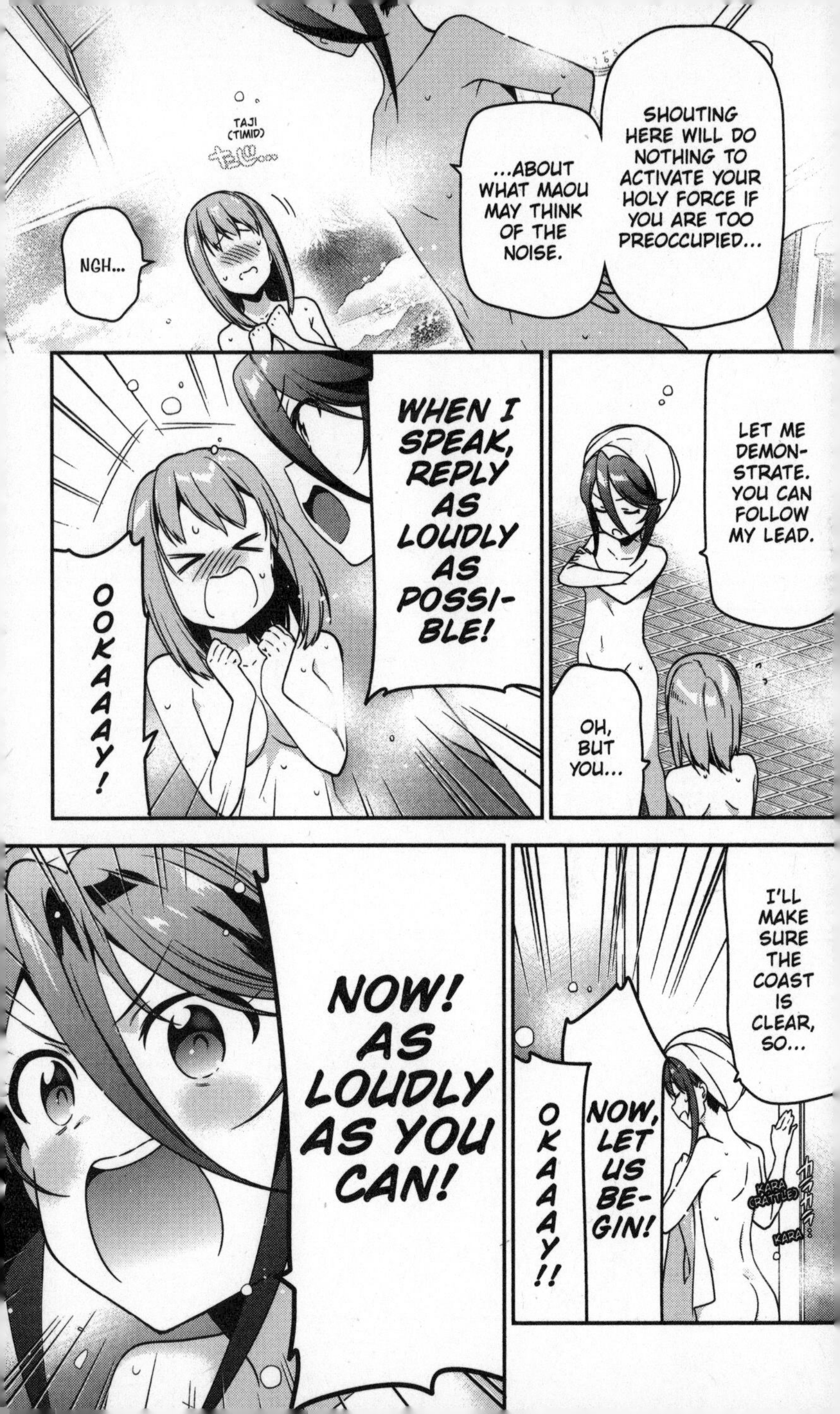
SHOUTING HERE WILL DO NOTHING TO ACTIVATE YOUR HOLY FORCE IF YOU ARE TOO PREOCCUPIED...
...ABOUT WHAT MAOU MAY THINK OF THE NOISE.
TAJI (TIMID)
NGH...
LET ME DEMON-STRATE. YOU CAN FOLLOW MY LEAD.
OH, BUT YOU...
WHEN I SPEAK, REPLY AS LOUDLY AS POSSI-BLE!
OOKAAAAY!
I'LL MAKE SURE THE COAST IS CLEAR, SO...
KARA (RATTLE)
KARA
NOW, LET US BE-GIN!
OKAAAAY!!
NOW! AS LOUDLY AS YOU CAN!

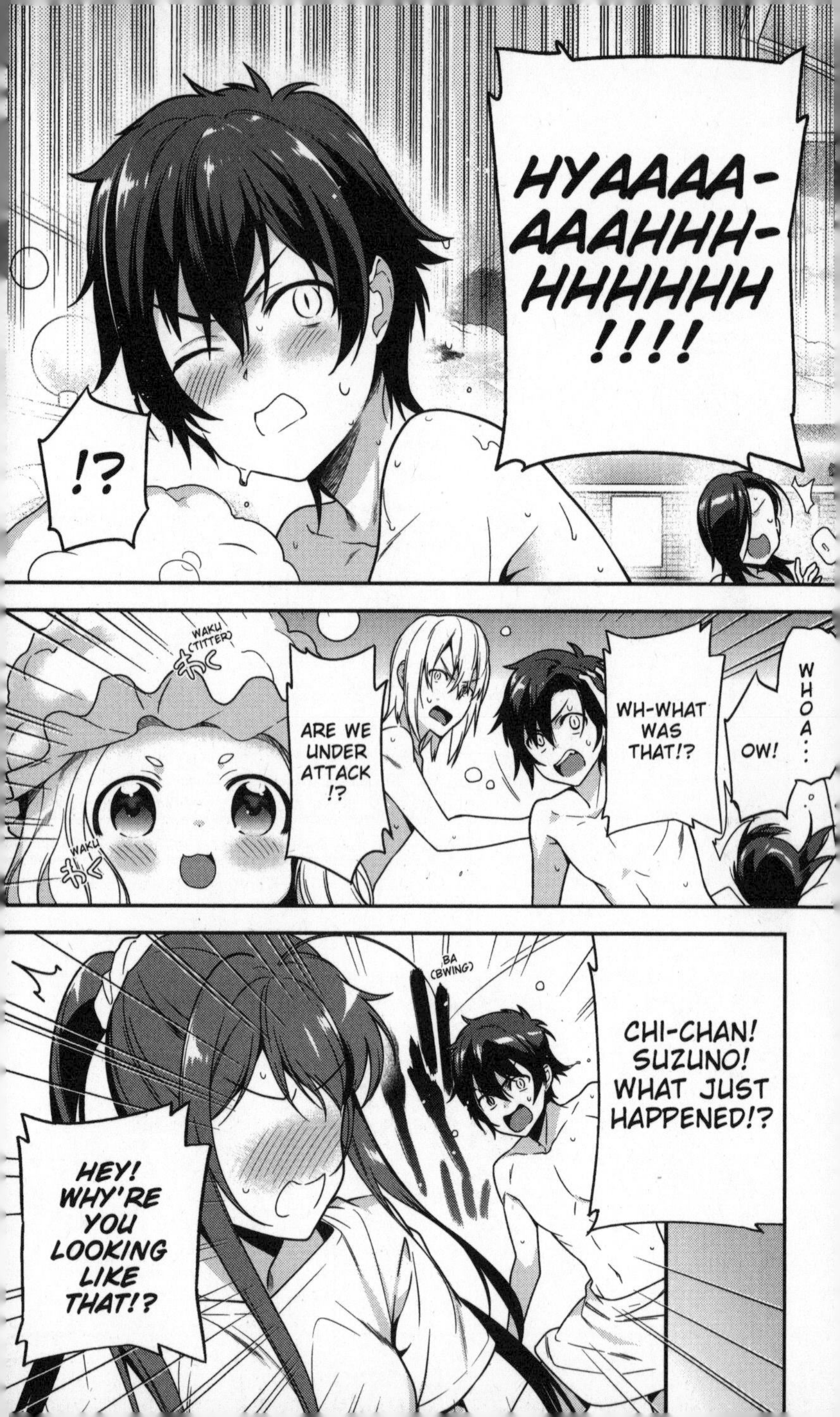
HYAAAA-AAAHHH-HHHHHH!!!!
!?
WHOA...
OW!
WH-WHAT WAS THAT!?
ARE WE UNDER ATTACK!?
WAKU (TITTER)
WAKU
BA (BWING)
CHI-CHAN! SUZUNO! WHAT JUST HAPPENED!?
HEY! WHY'RE YOU LOOKING LIKE THAT!?

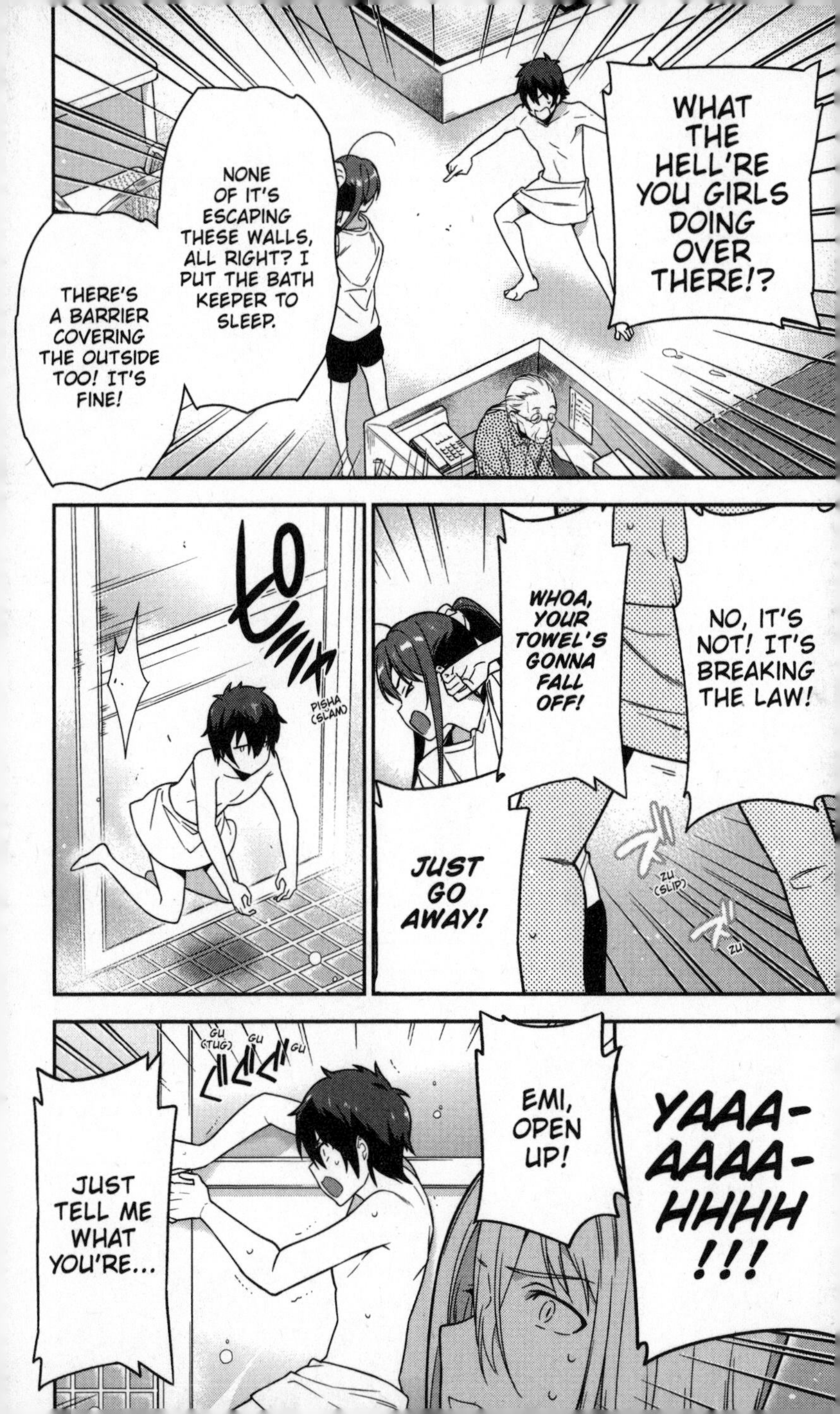
WHAT THE HELL'RE YOU GIRLS DOING OVER THERE!?
NONE OF IT'S ESCAPING THESE WALLS, ALL RIGHT? I PUT THE BATH KEEPER TO SLEEP.
THERE'S A BARRIER COVERING THE OUTSIDE TOO! IT'S FINE!
NO, IT'S NOT! IT'S BREAKING THE LAW!
WHOA, YOUR TOWEL'S GONNA FALL OFF!
ZU (SLIP)
ZU
JUST GO AWAY!
PISHA (SLAM)
YAAA-AAAA-HHHH!!!
EMI, OPEN UP!
GU (TUG) GU GU
JUST TELL ME WHAT YOU'RE...

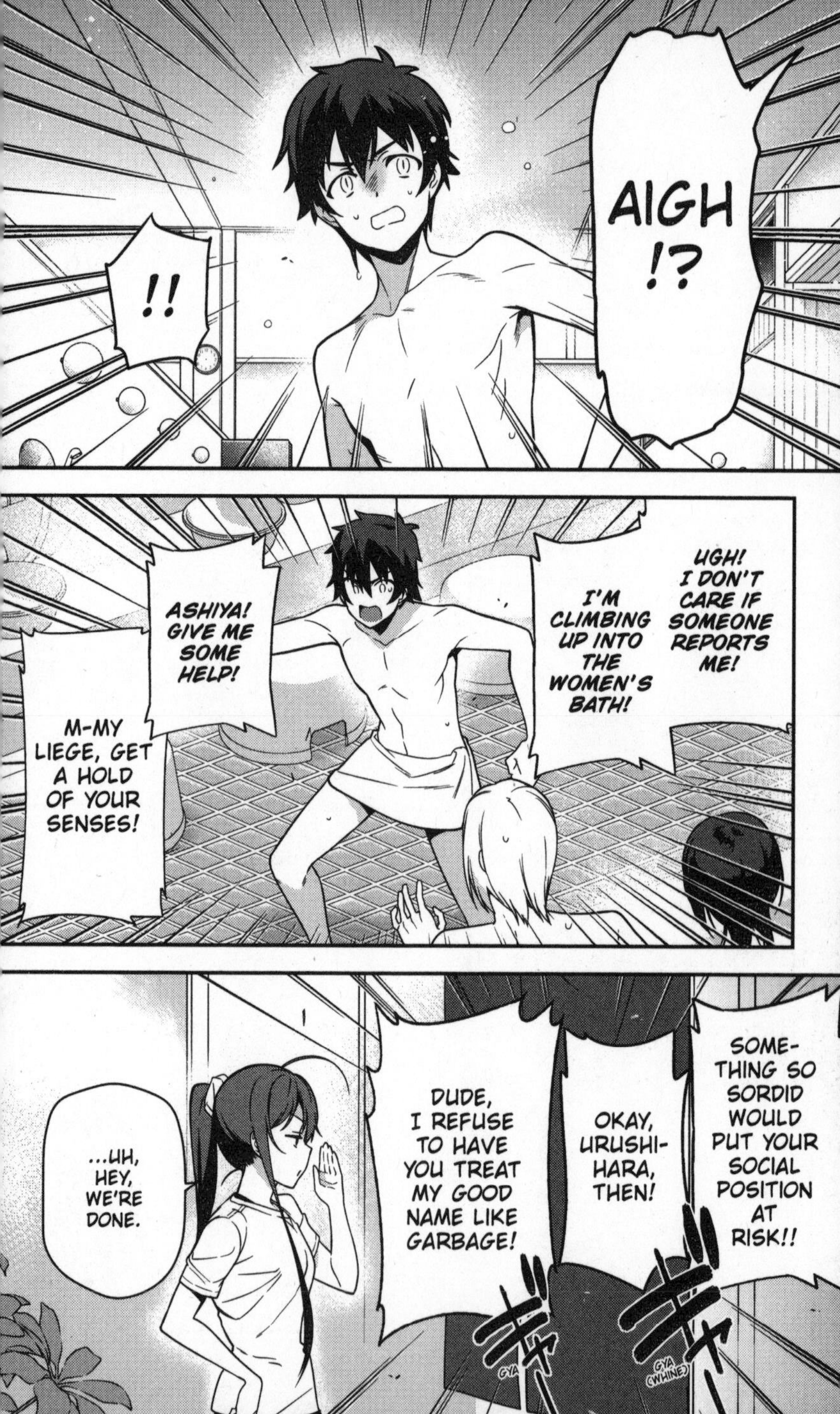
AIGH !?
!!
UGH! I DON'T CARE IF SOMEONE REPORTS ME!
I'M CLIMBING UP INTO THE WOMEN'S BATH!
ASHIYA! GIVE ME SOME HELP!
M-MY LIEGE, GET A HOLD OF YOUR SENSES!
SOME-THING SO SORDID WOULD PUT YOUR SOCIAL POSITION AT RISK!!
OKAY, URUSHI-HARA, THEN!
DUDE, I REFUSE TO HAVE YOU TREAT MY GOOD NAME LIKE GARBAGE!
GYA (WHINE)
GYA
...UH, HEY, WE'RE DONE.

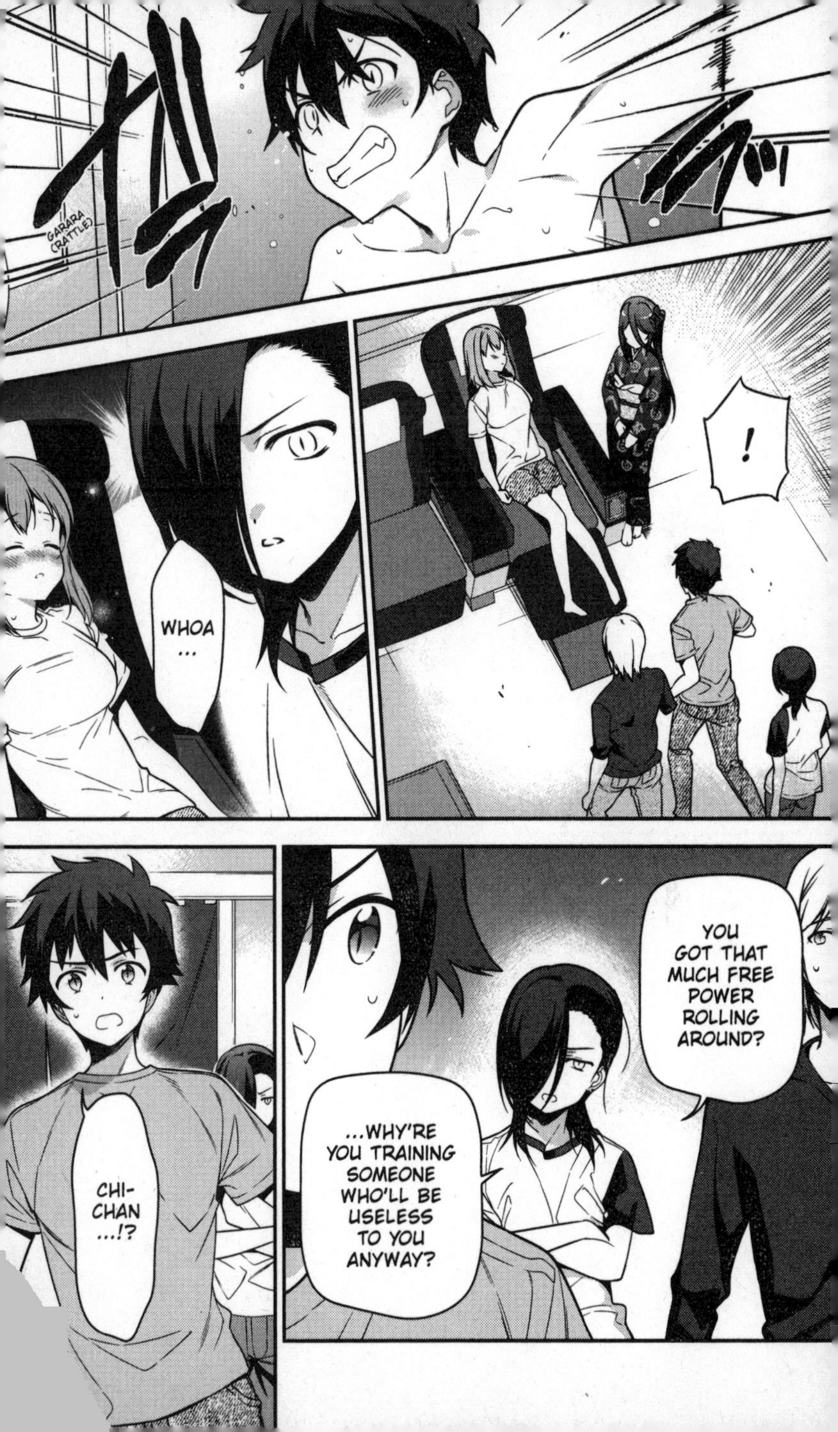
GARARA (RATTLE)
!
WHOA ...
YOU GOT THAT MUCH FREE POWER ROLLING AROUND?
...WHY'RE YOU TRAINING SOMEONE WHO'LL BE USELESS TO YOU ANYWAY?
CHI-CHAN ...!?

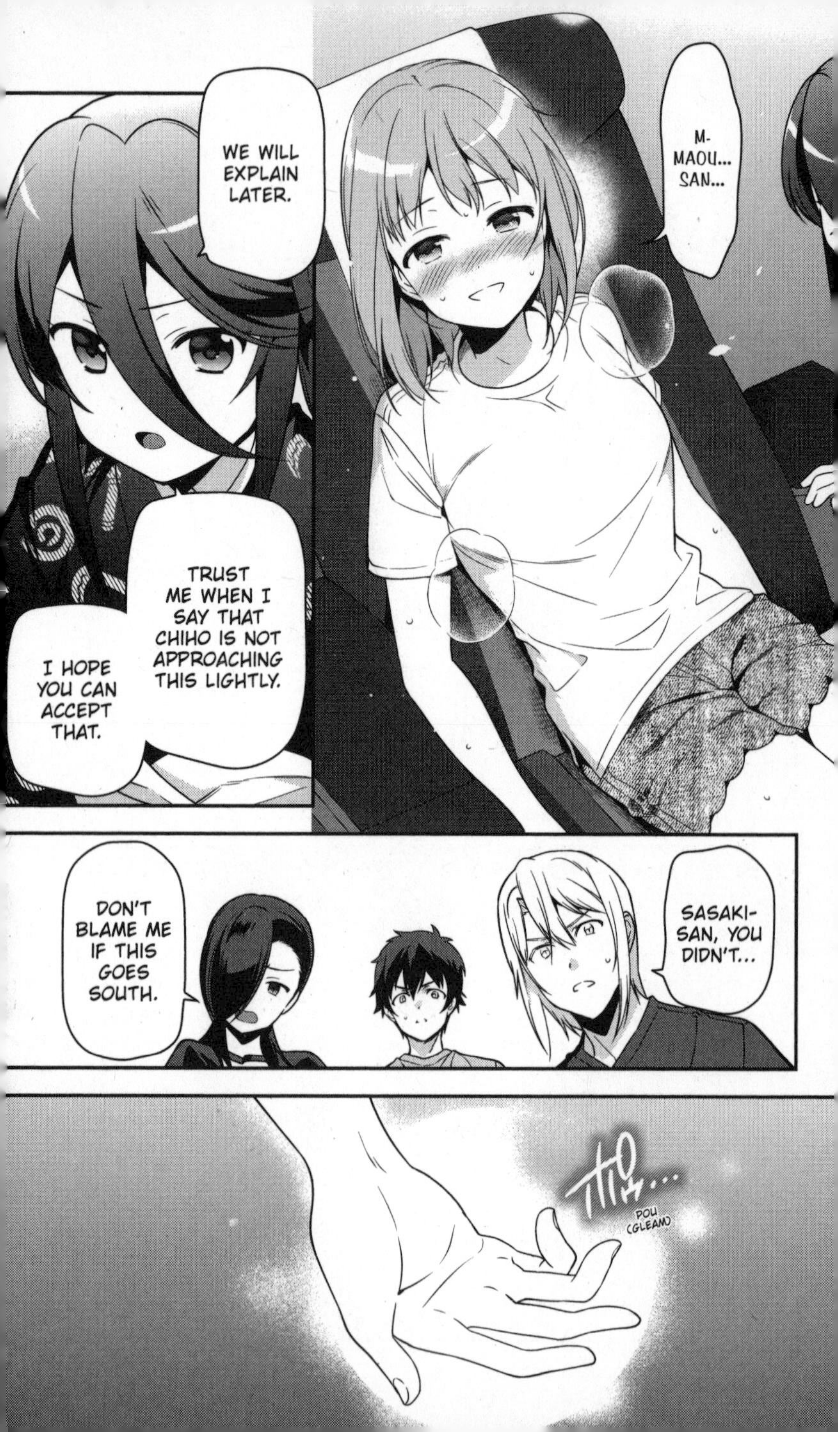
M-MAOU... SAN...
WE WILL EXPLAIN LATER.
TRUST ME WHEN I SAY THAT CHIHO IS NOT APPROACHING THIS LIGHTLY.
I HOPE YOU CAN ACCEPT THAT.
SASAKI-SAN, YOU DIDN'T...
DON'T BLAME ME IF THIS GOES SOUTH.
POU (GLEAM)

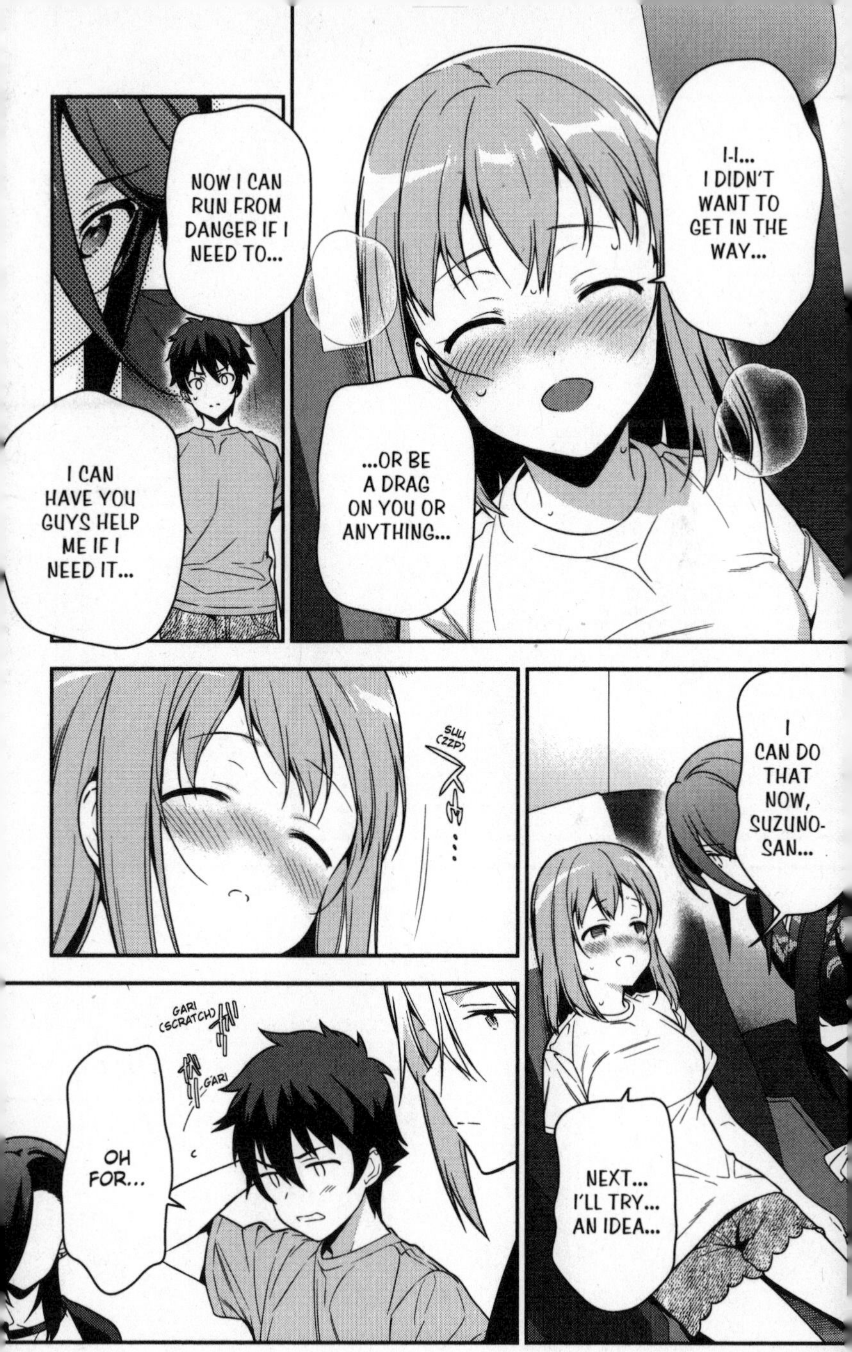
I-I... I DIDN'T WANT TO GET IN THE WAY...
...OR BE A DRAG ON YOU OR ANYTHING...
NOW I CAN RUN FROM DANGER IF I NEED TO...
I CAN HAVE YOU GUYS HELP ME IF I NEED IT...
I CAN DO THAT NOW, SUZUNO-SAN...
NEXT... I'LL TRY... AN IDEA...
SUU (ZZP)
GARI (SCRATCH)
GARI
OH FOR...

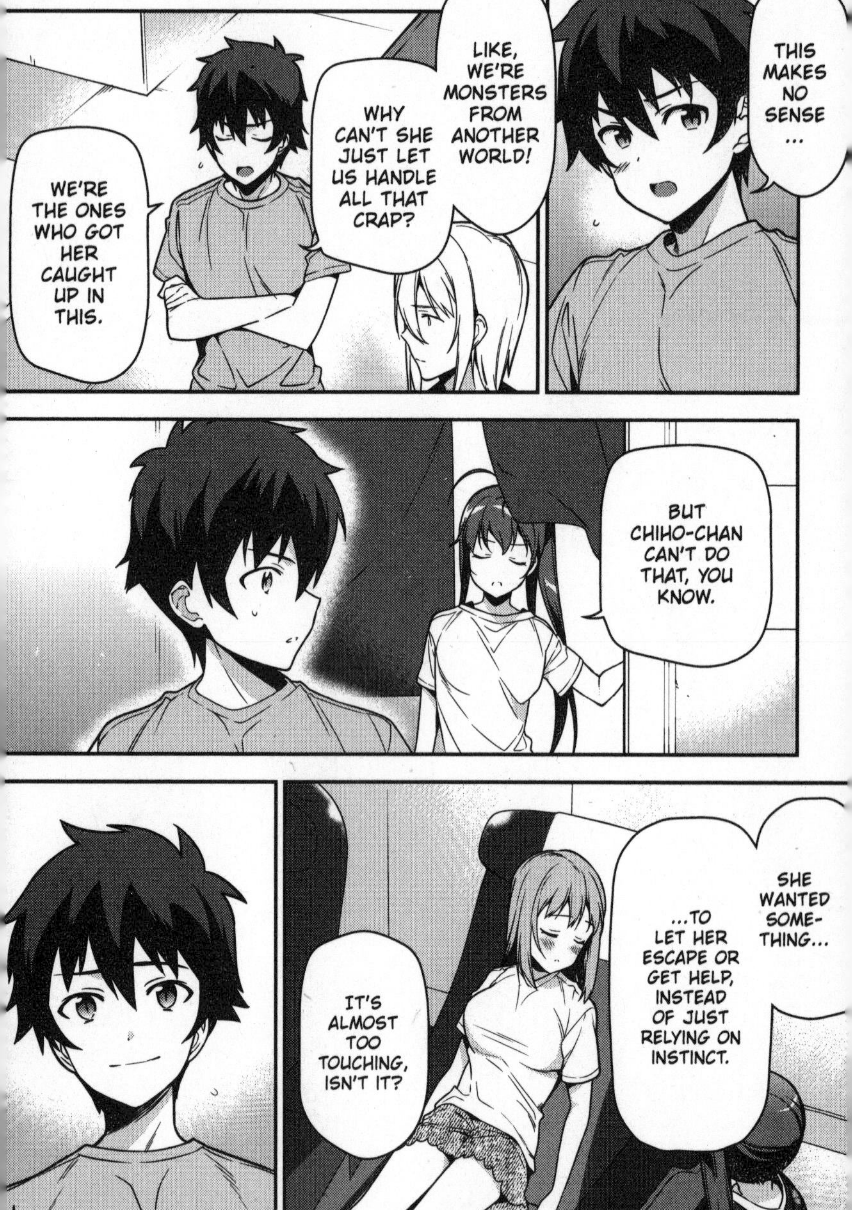
THIS MAKES NO SENSE...
LIKE, WE'RE MONSTERS FROM ANOTHER WORLD!
WHY CAN'T SHE JUST LET US HANDLE ALL THAT CRAP?
WE'RE THE ONES WHO GOT HER CAUGHT UP IN THIS.
BUT CHIHO-CHAN CAN'T DO THAT, YOU KNOW.
SHE WANTED SOME-THING...
...TO LET HER ESCAPE OR GET HELP, INSTEAD OF JUST RELYING ON INSTINCT.
IT'S ALMOST TOO TOUCHING, ISN'T IT?

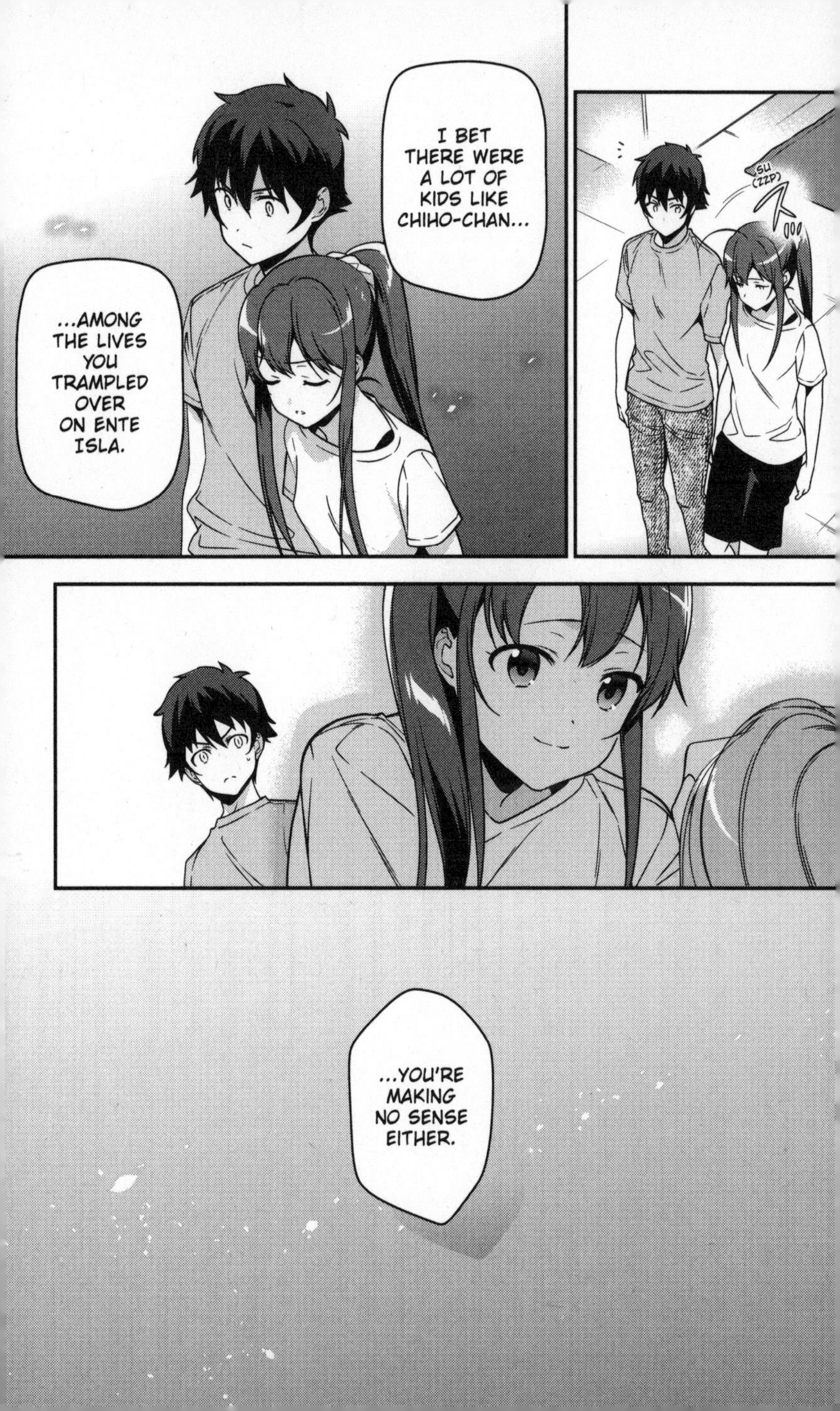
SU (ZZP)
I BET THERE WERE A LOT OF KIDS LIKE CHIHO-CHAN...
...AMONG THE LIVES YOU TRAMPLED OVER ON ENTE ISLA.
...YOU'RE MAKING NO SENSE EITHER.

THE DEVIL IS A PART-TIMER!

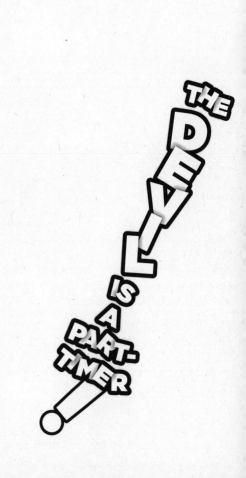

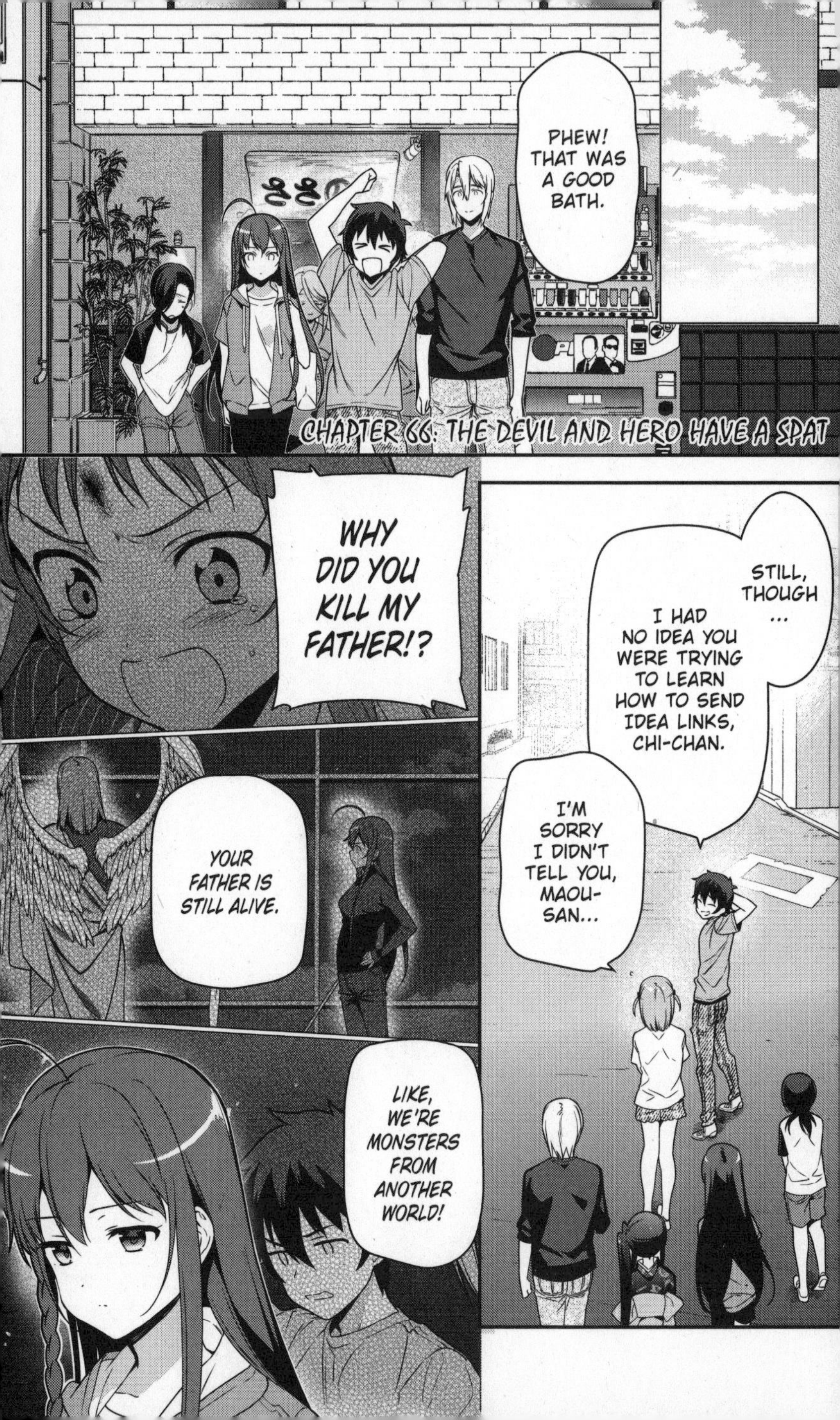
PHEW! THAT WAS A GOOD BATH.
CHAPTER 66: THE DEVIL AND HERO HAVE A SPAT
STILL, THOUGH ...
I HAD NO IDEA YOU WERE TRYING TO LEARN HOW TO SEND IDEA LINKS, CHI-CHAN.
I'M SORRY I DIDN'T TELL YOU, MAOU-SAN...
WHY DID YOU KILL MY FATHER!?
YOUR FATHER IS STILL ALIVE.
LIKE, WE'RE MONSTERS FROM ANOTHER WORLD!

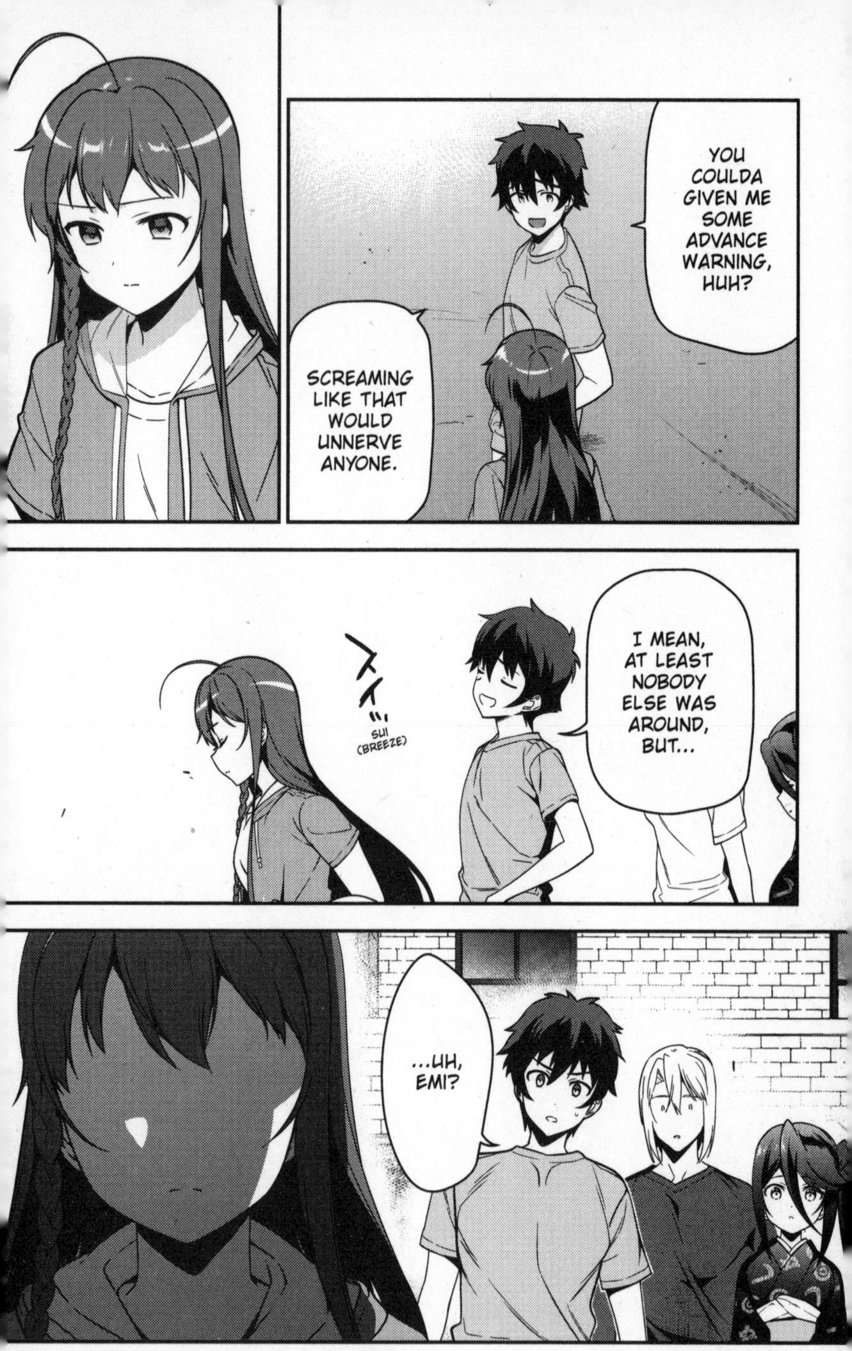
YOU COULDA GIVEN ME SOME ADVANCE WARNING, HUH?
SCREAMING LIKE THAT WOULD UNNERVE ANYONE.
I MEAN, AT LEAST NOBODY ELSE WAS AROUND, BUT...
SUI (BREEZE)
...UH, EMI?

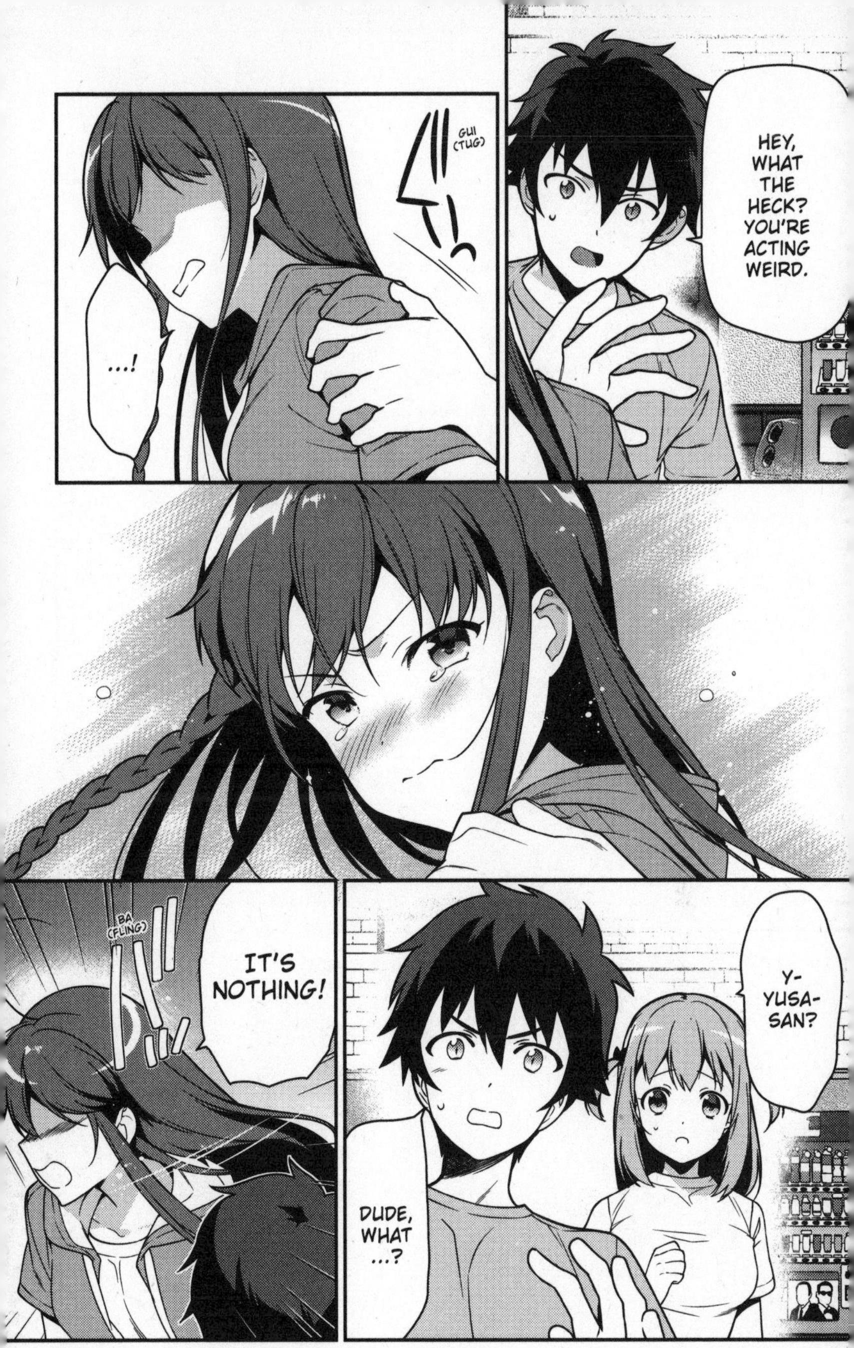
HEY, WHAT THE HECK? YOU'RE ACTING WEIRD.
GUI (TUG)
...!
Y-YUSA-SAN?
DUDE, WHAT ...?
BA (FLING)
IT'S NOTHING!

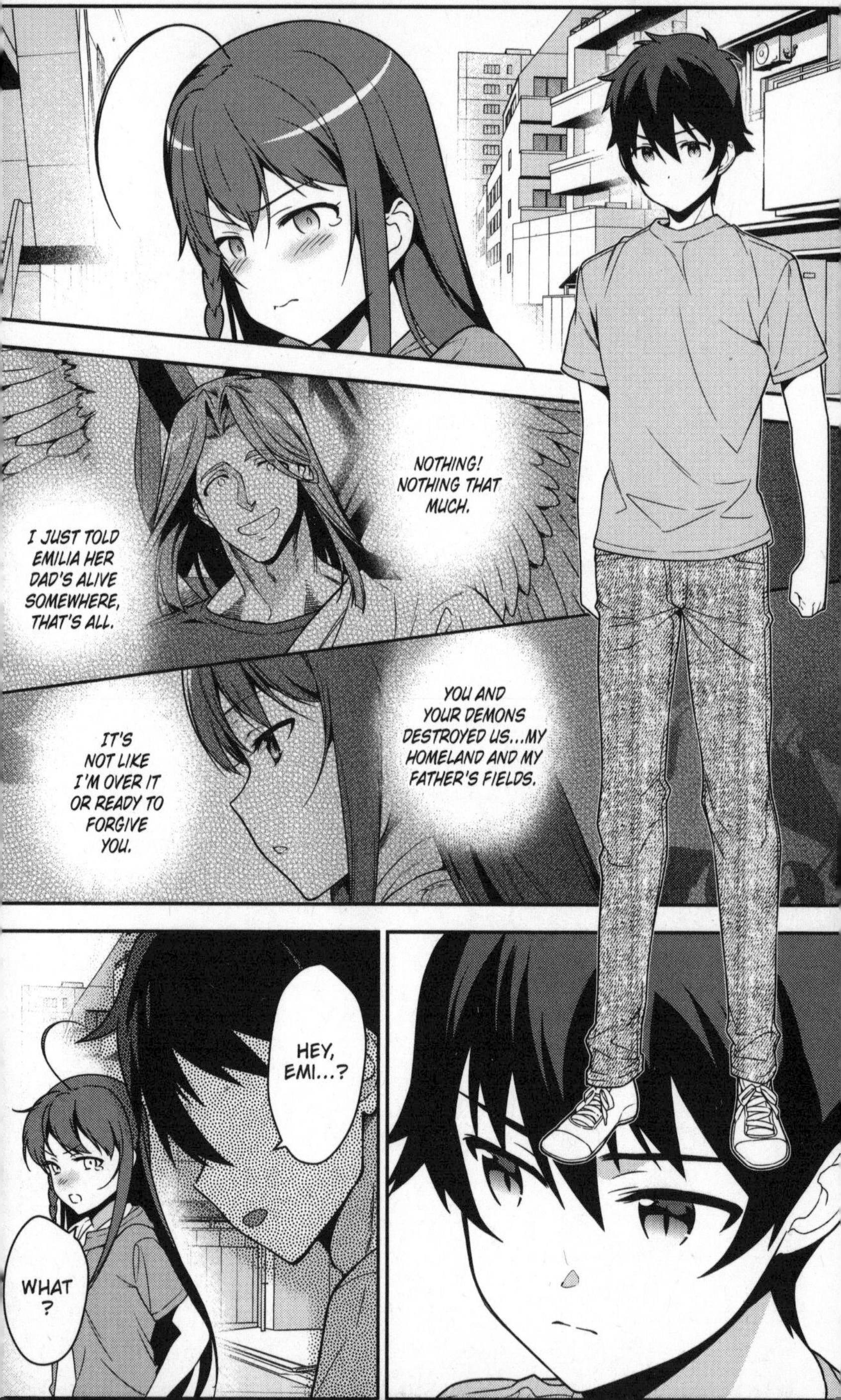
NOTHING! NOTHING THAT MUCH.
I JUST TOLD EMILIA HER DAD'S ALIVE SOMEWHERE, THAT'S ALL.
YOU AND YOUR DEMONS DESTROYED US...MY HOMELAND AND MY FATHER'S FIELDS.
IT'S NOT LIKE I'M OVER IT OR READY TO FORGIVE YOU.
HEY, EMI...?
WHAT?

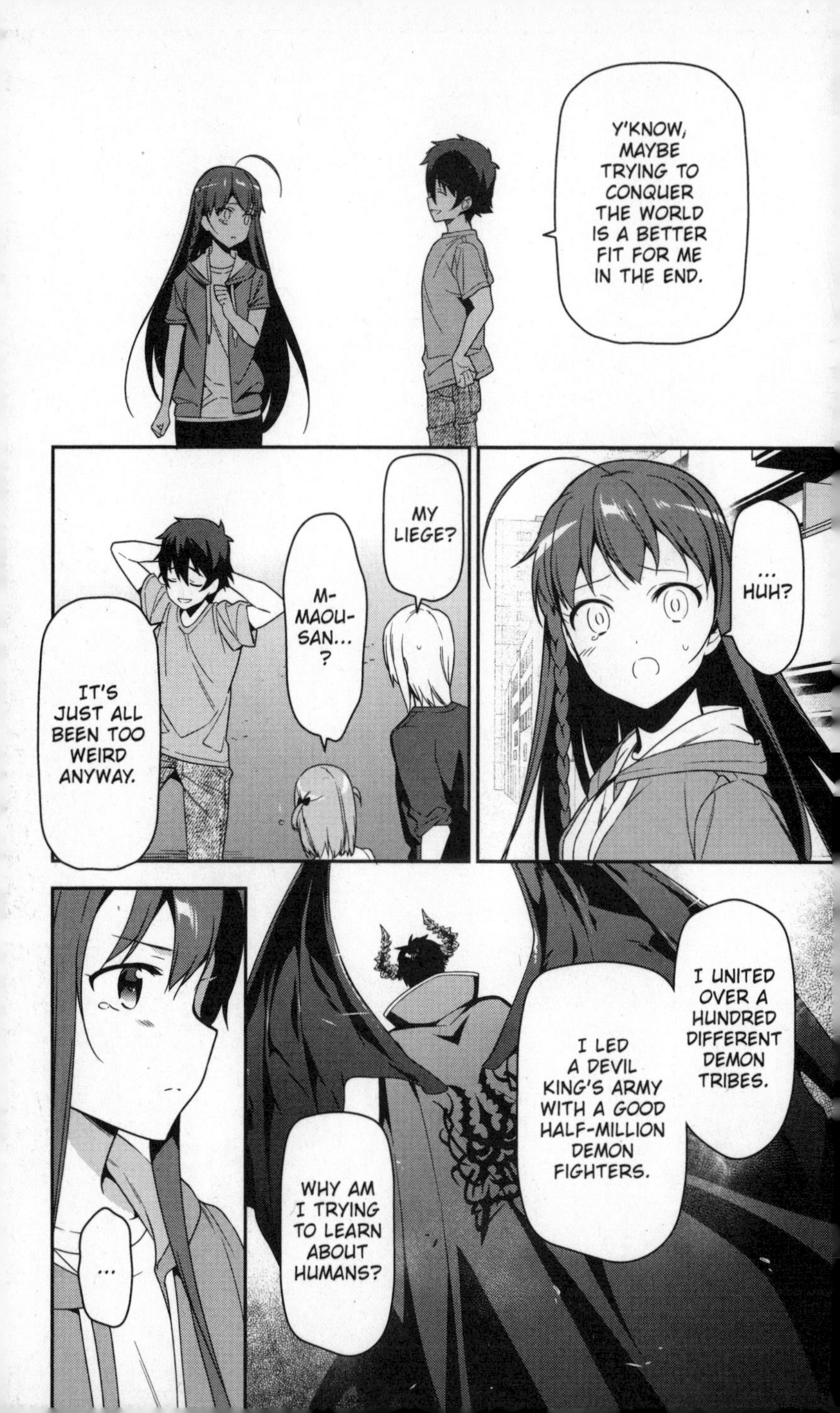

Y'KNOW, MAYBE TRYING TO CONQUER THE WORLD IS A BETTER FIT FOR ME IN THE END.
... HUH?
MY LIEGE?
M-MAOU-SAN... ?
IT'S JUST ALL BEEN TOO WEIRD ANYWAY.
I UNITED OVER A HUNDRED DIFFERENT DEMON TRIBES.
I LED A DEVIL KING'S ARMY WITH A GOOD HALF-MILLION DEMON FIGHTERS.
WHY AM I TRYING TO LEARN ABOUT HUMANS?
...

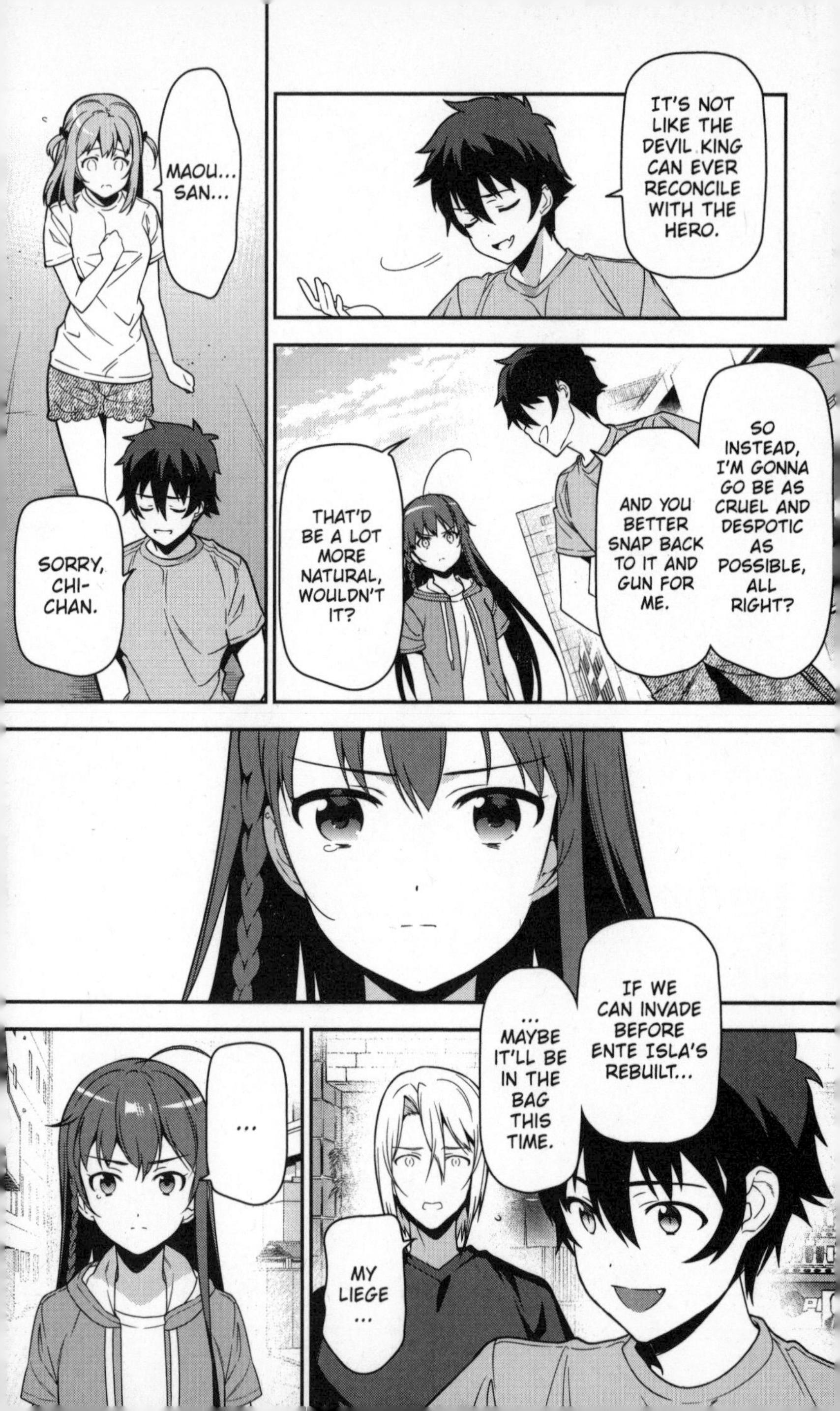
IT'S NOT LIKE THE DEVIL KING CAN EVER RECONCILE WITH THE HERO.
SO INSTEAD, I'M GONNA GO BE AS CRUEL AND DESPOTIC AS POSSIBLE, ALL RIGHT?
AND YOU BETTER SNAP BACK TO IT AND GUN FOR ME.
THAT'D BE A LOT MORE NATURAL, WOULDN'T IT?
MAOU... SAN...
SORRY, CHI-CHAN.
IF WE CAN INVADE BEFORE ENTE ISLA'S REBUILT...
... MAYBE IT'LL BE IN THE BAG THIS TIME.
MY LIEGE ...
...

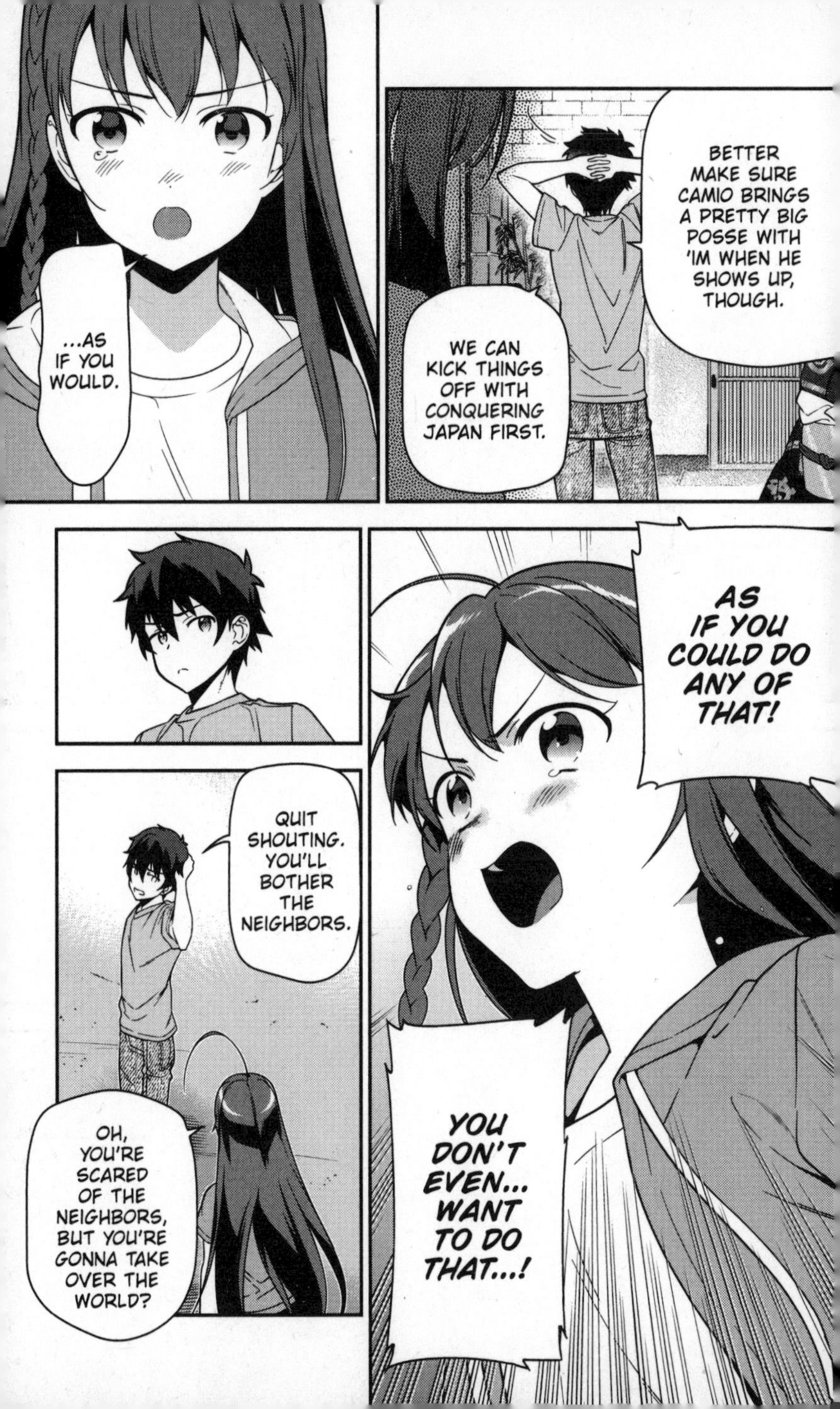
BETTER MAKE SURE CAMIO BRINGS A PRETTY BIG POSSE WITH 'IM WHEN HE SHOWS UP, THOUGH.
WE CAN KICK THINGS OFF WITH CONQUERING JAPAN FIRST.
...AS IF YOU WOULD.
AS IF YOU COULD DO ANY OF THAT!
YOU DON'T EVEN... WANT TO DO THAT...!
QUIT SHOUTING. YOU'LL BOTHER THE NEIGHBORS.
OH, YOU'RE SCARED OF THE NEIGHBORS, BUT YOU'RE GONNA TAKE OVER THE WORLD?

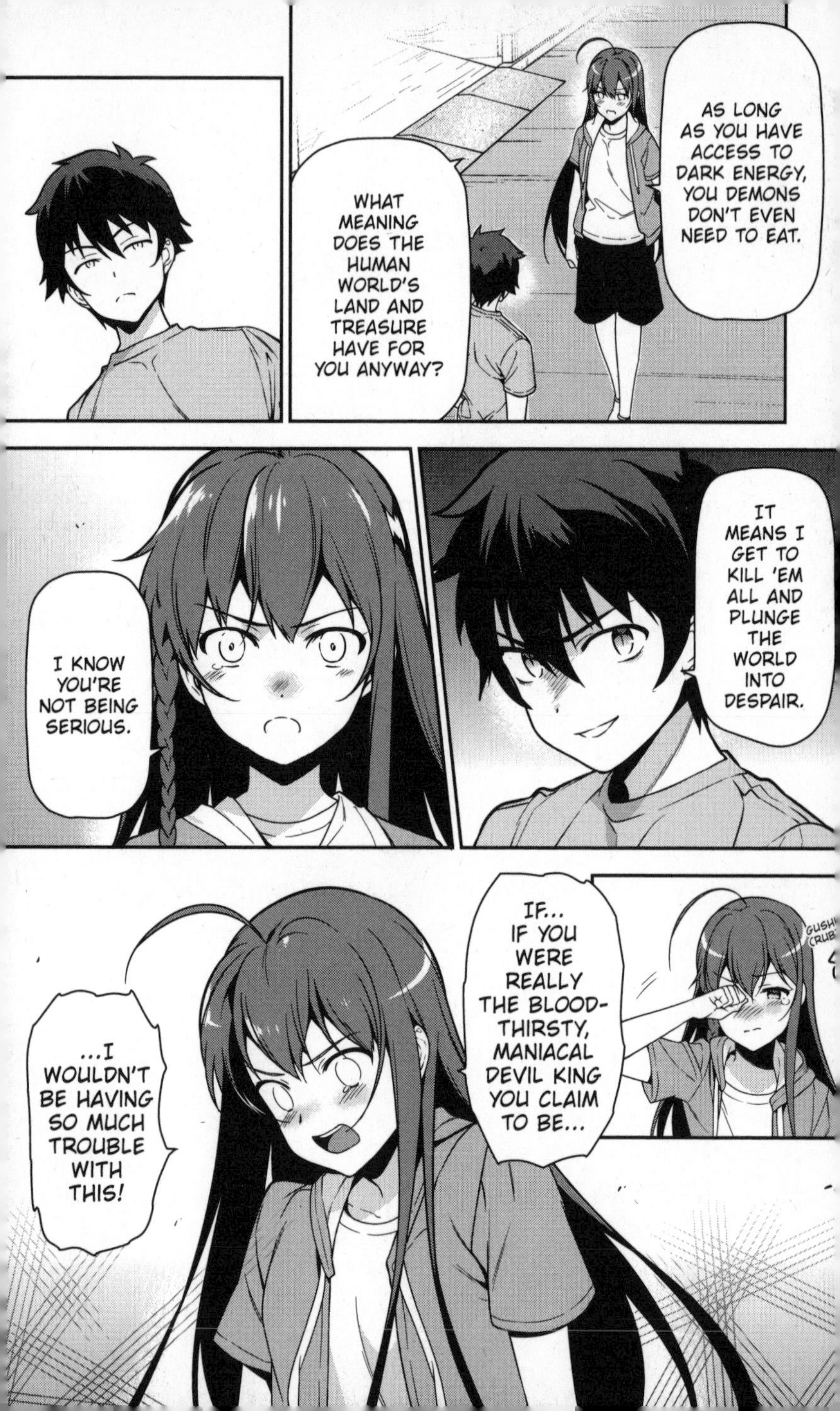
AS LONG AS YOU HAVE ACCESS TO DARK ENERGY, YOU DEMONS DON'T EVEN NEED TO EAT.
WHAT MEANING DOES THE HUMAN WORLD'S LAND AND TREASURE HAVE FOR YOU ANYWAY?
IT MEANS I GET TO KILL 'EM ALL AND PLUNGE THE WORLD INTO DESPAIR.
I KNOW YOU'RE NOT BEING SERIOUS.
IF... IF YOU WERE REALLY THE BLOOD-THIRSTY, MANIACAL DEVIL KING YOU CLAIM TO BE...
...I WOULDN'T BE HAVING SO MUCH TROUBLE WITH THIS!

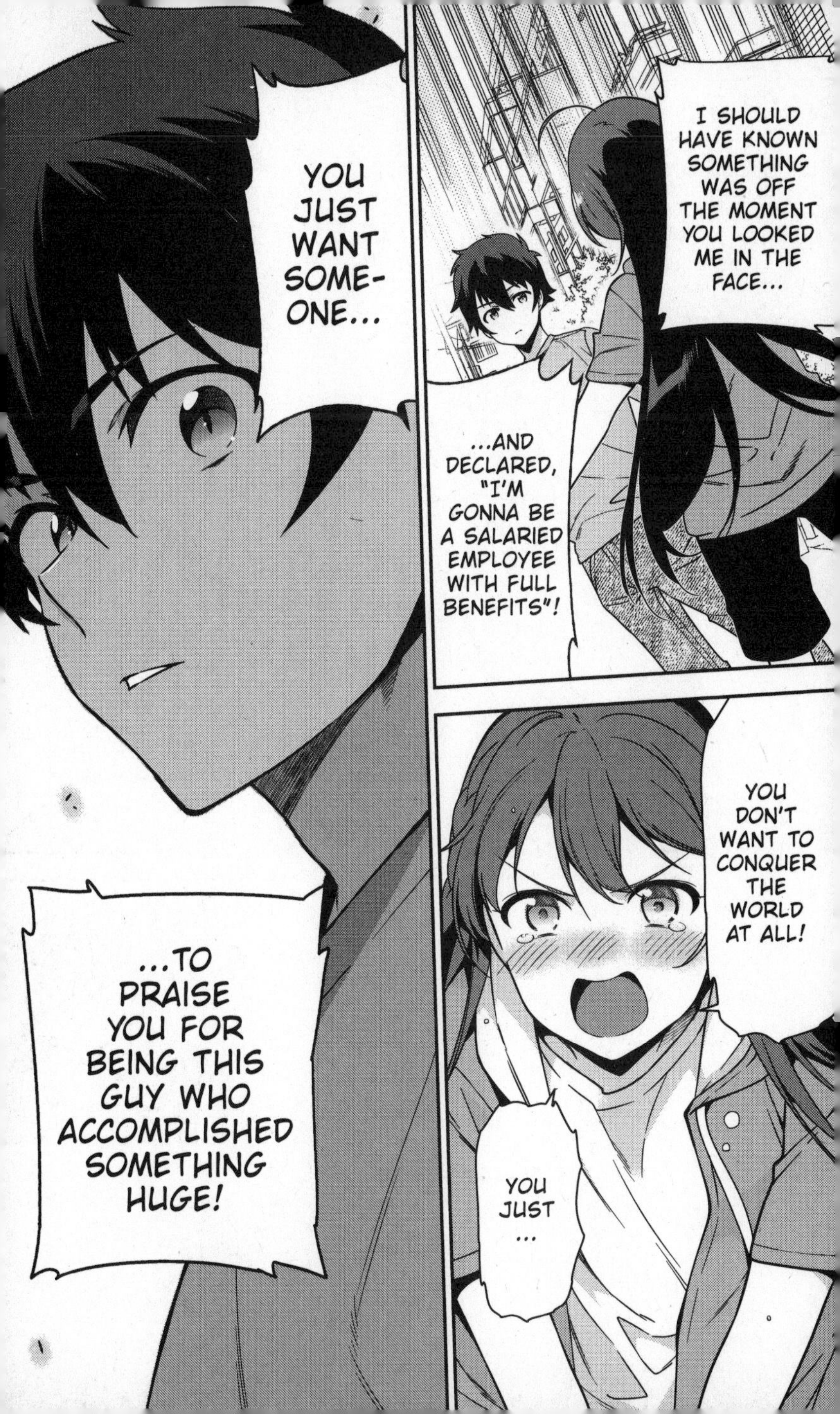
I SHOULD HAVE KNOWN SOMETHING WAS OFF THE MOMENT YOU LOOKED ME IN THE FACE...
...AND DECLARED, "I'M GONNA BE A SALARIED EMPLOYEE WITH FULL BENEFITS"!
YOU DON'T WANT TO CONQUER THE WORLD AT ALL!
YOU JUST...
YOU JUST WANT SOME-ONE...
...TO PRAISE YOU FOR BEING THIS GUY WHO ACCOMPLISHED SOMETHING HUGE!

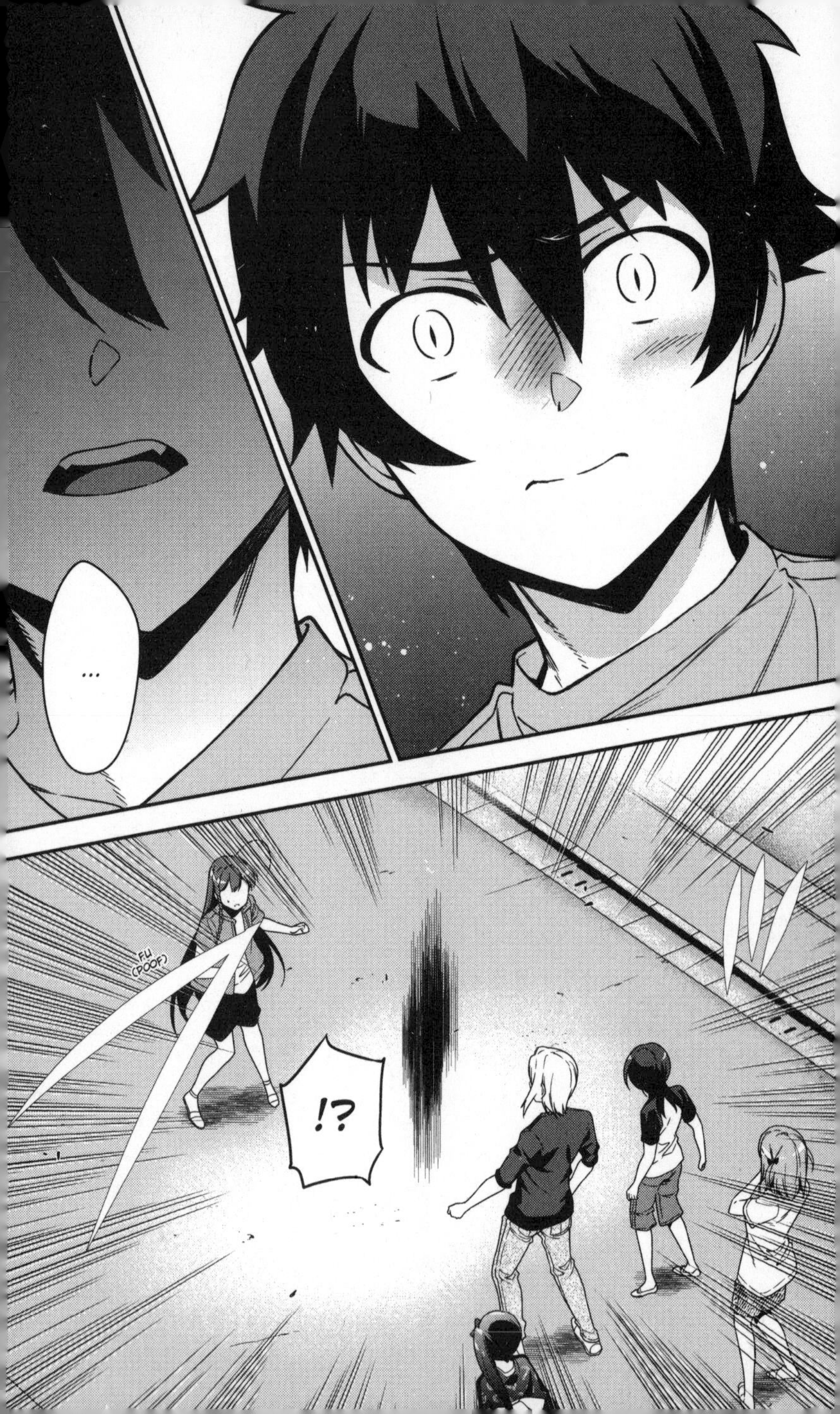
...
!?
FU (POOF)

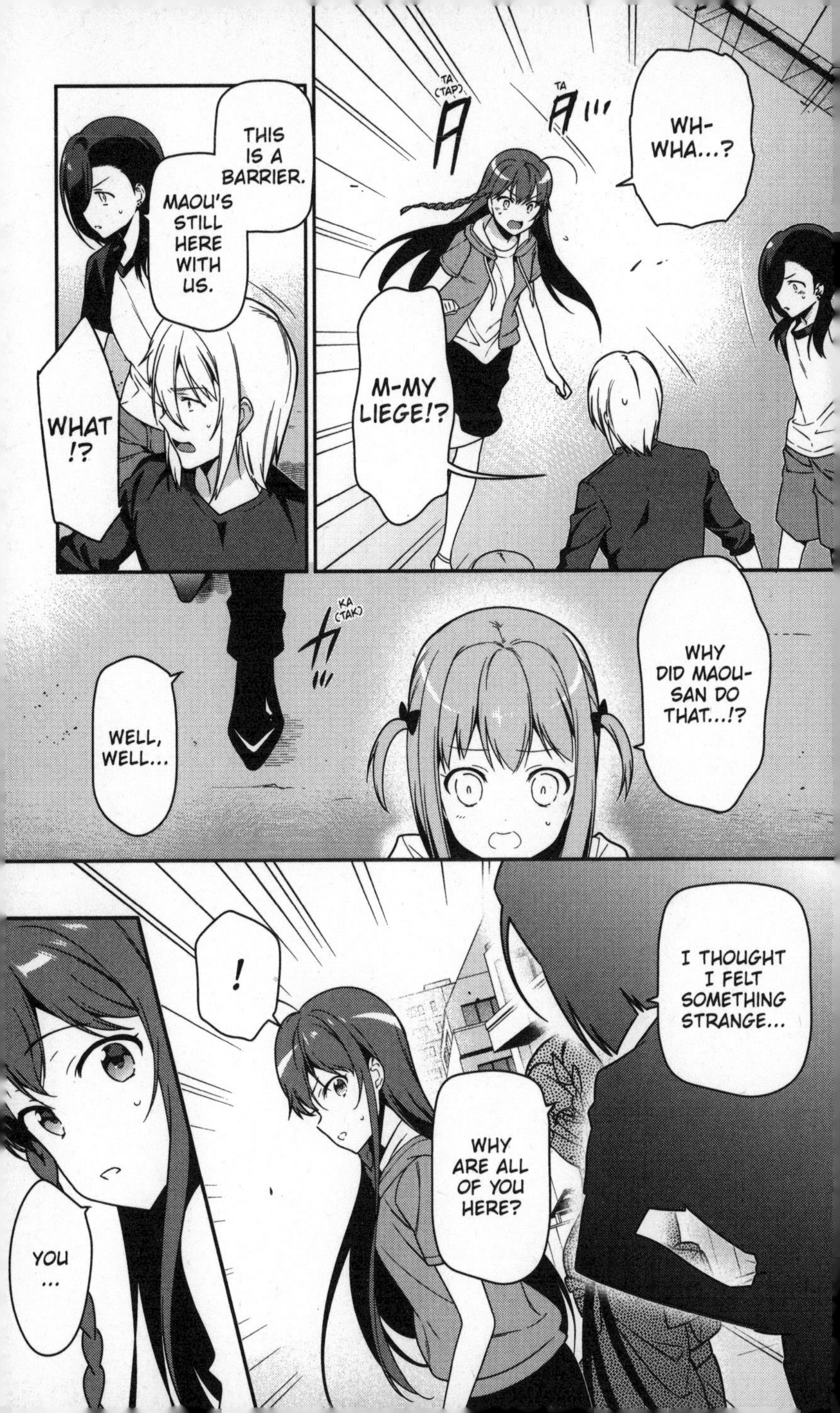
WH-WHA...?
TA
TA (TAP)
M-MY LIEGE!?
THIS IS A BARRIER.
MAOU'S STILL HERE WITH US.
WHAT!?
WHY DID MAOU-SAN DO THAT...!?
KA (TAK)
WELL, WELL...
I THOUGHT I FELT SOMETHING STRANGE...
WHY ARE ALL OF YOU HERE?
!
YOU ...

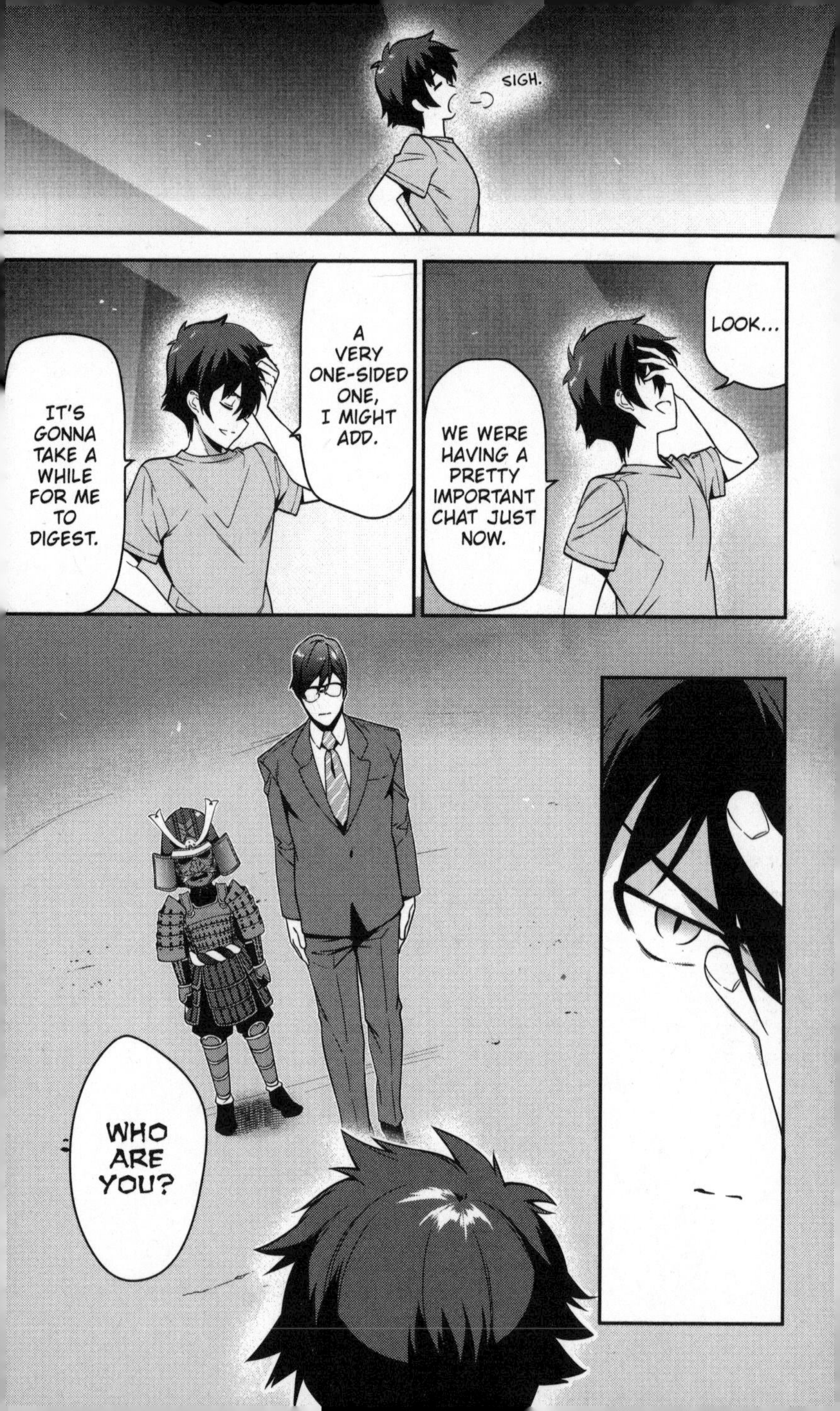
SIGH.
LOOK...
WE WERE HAVING A PRETTY IMPORTANT CHAT JUST NOW.
A VERY ONE-SIDED ONE, I MIGHT ADD.
IT'S GONNA TAKE A WHILE FOR ME TO DIGEST.
WHO ARE YOU?

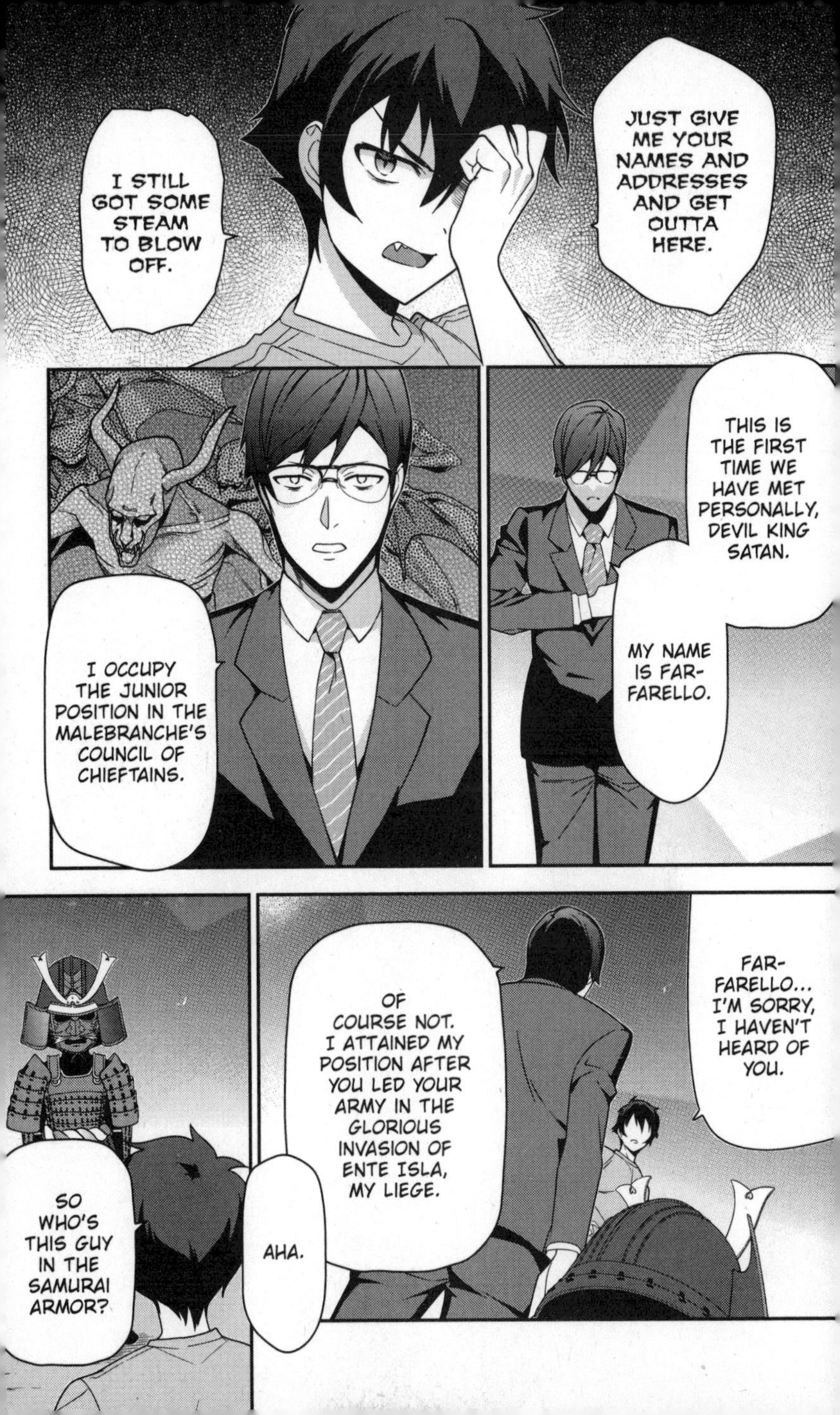
JUST GIVE ME YOUR NAMES AND ADDRESSES AND GET OUTTA HERE.
I STILL GOT SOME STEAM TO BLOW OFF.
THIS IS THE FIRST TIME WE HAVE MET PERSONALLY, DEVIL KING SATAN.
MY NAME IS FAR-FARELLO.
I OCCUPY THE JUNIOR POSITION IN THE MALEBRANCHE'S COUNCIL OF CHIEFTAINS.
FAR-FARELLO... I'M SORRY, I HAVEN'T HEARD OF YOU.
OF COURSE NOT. I ATTAINED MY POSITION AFTER YOU LED YOUR ARMY IN THE GLORIOUS INVASION OF ENTE ISLA, MY LIEGE.
AHA.
SO WHO'S THIS GUY IN THE SAMURAI ARMOR?

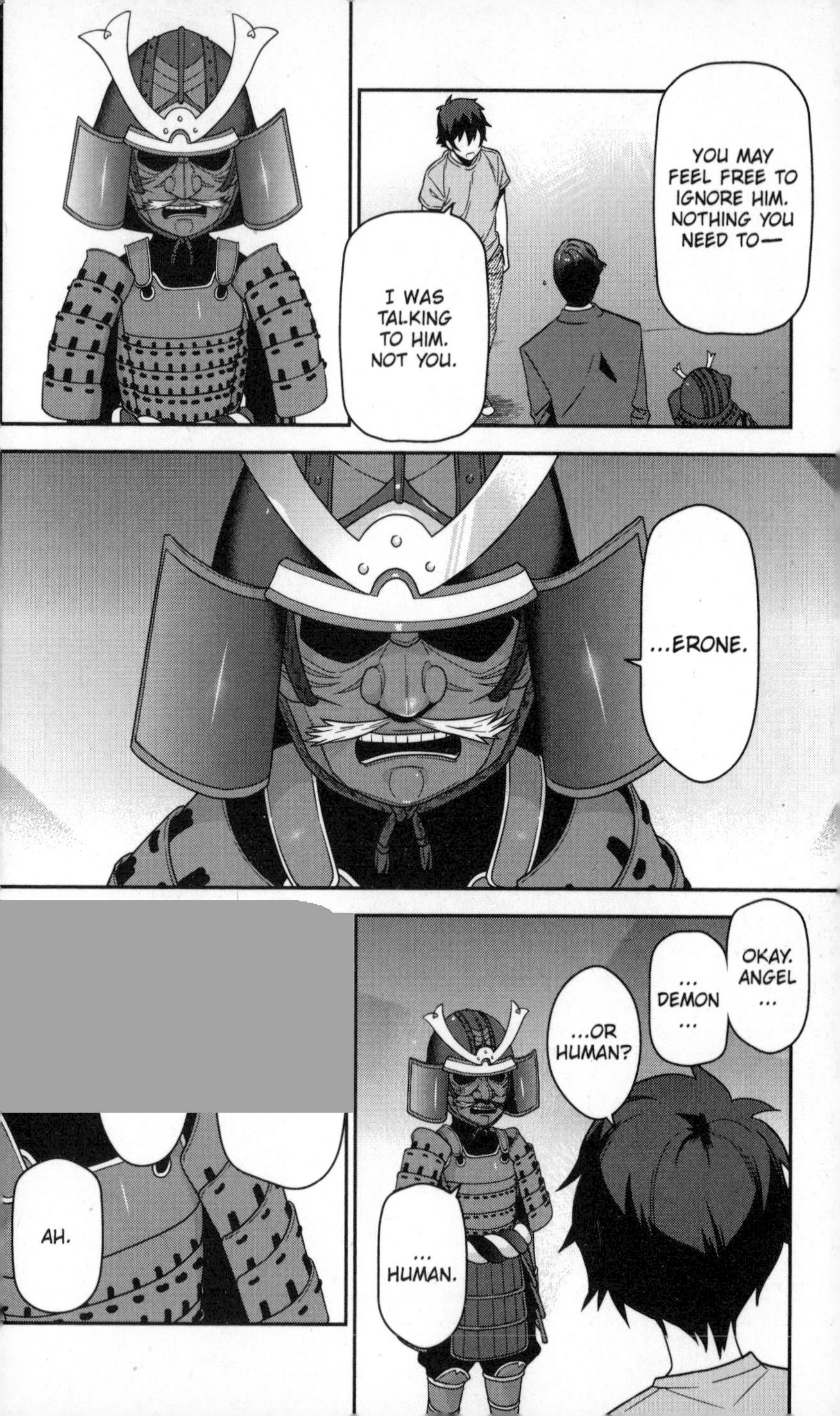
YOU MAY FEEL FREE TO IGNORE HIM. NOTHING YOU NEED TO—
I WAS TALKING TO HIM. NOT YOU.
...ERONE.
OKAY. ANGEL...
...DEMON...
...OR HUMAN?
...HUMAN.
AH.

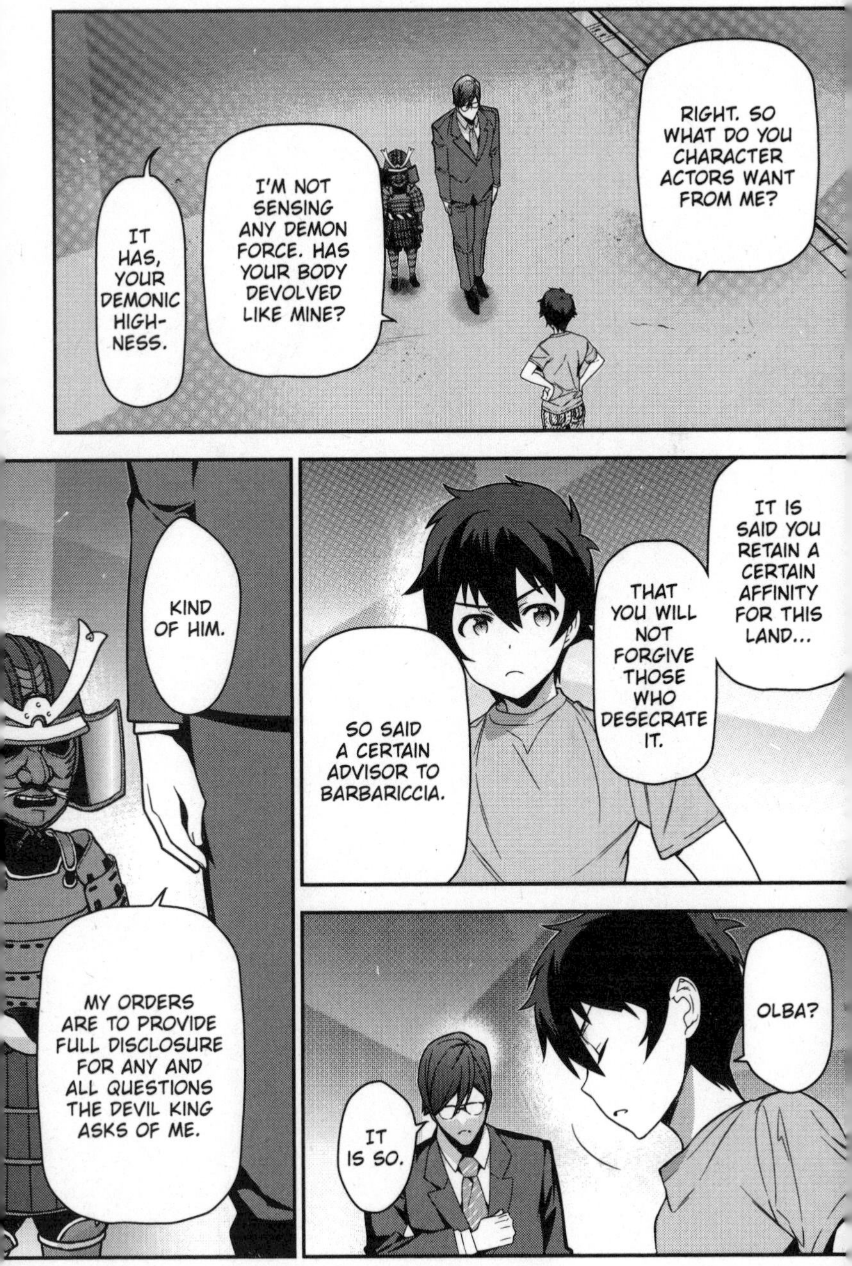
RIGHT. SO WHAT DO YOU CHARACTER ACTORS WANT FROM ME?
I'M NOT SENSING ANY DEMON FORCE. HAS YOUR BODY DEVOLVED LIKE MINE?
IT HAS, YOUR DEMONIC HIGH-NESS.
IT IS SAID YOU RETAIN A CERTAIN AFFINITY FOR THIS LAND...
THAT YOU WILL NOT FORGIVE THOSE WHO DESECRATE IT.
SO SAID A CERTAIN ADVISOR TO BARBARICCIA.
OLBA?
IT IS SO.
KIND OF HIM.
MY ORDERS ARE TO PROVIDE FULL DISCLOSURE FOR ANY AND ALL QUESTIONS THE DEVIL KING ASKS OF ME.

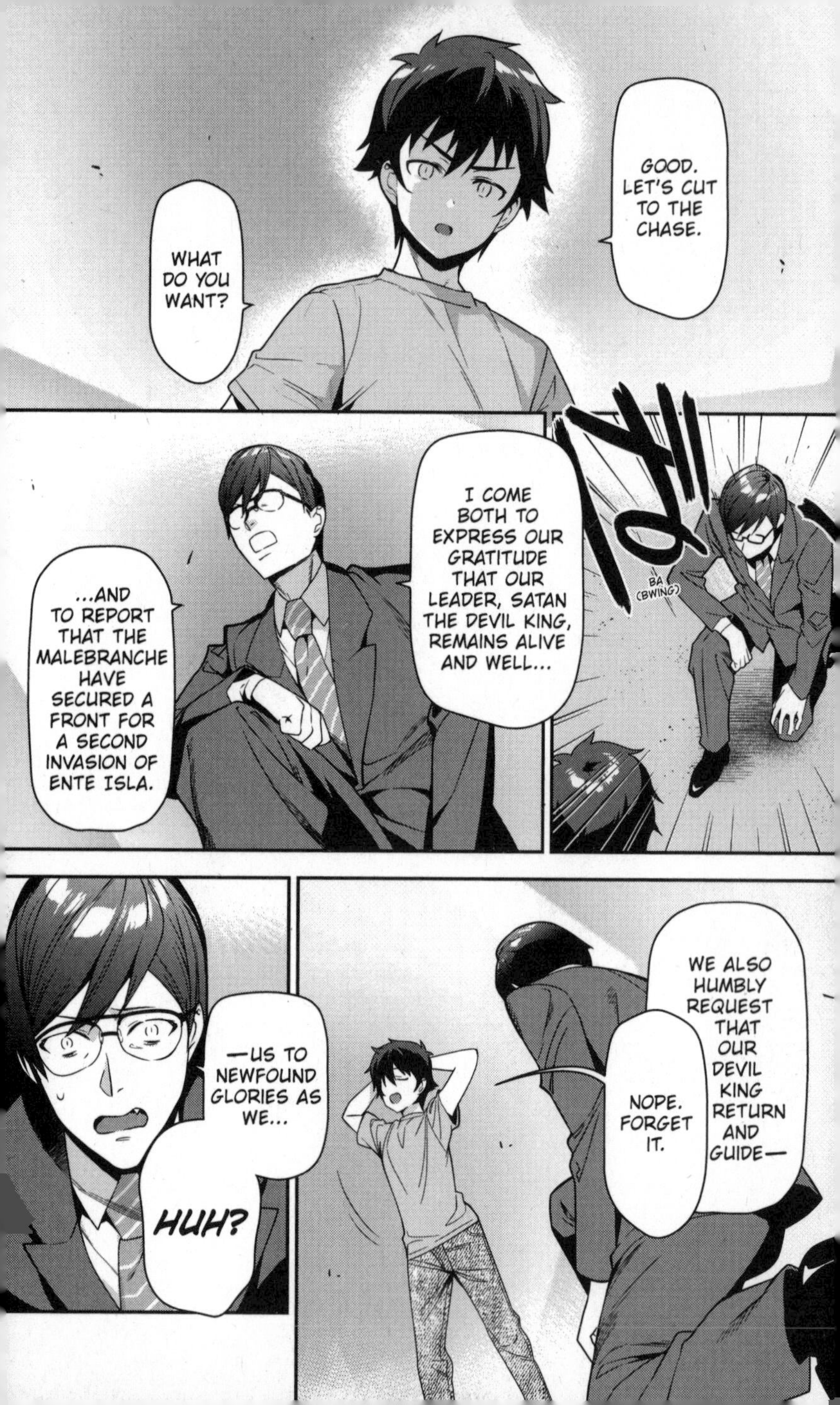
GOOD. LET'S CUT TO THE CHASE.
WHAT DO YOU WANT?
BA (BWING)
I COME BOTH TO EXPRESS OUR GRATITUDE THAT OUR LEADER, SATAN THE DEVIL KING, REMAINS ALIVE AND WELL...
...AND TO REPORT THAT THE MALEBRANCHE HAVE SECURED A FRONT FOR A SECOND INVASION OF ENTE ISLA.
WE ALSO HUMBLY REQUEST THAT OUR DEVIL KING RETURN AND GUIDE—
NOPE. FORGET IT.
—US TO NEWFOUND GLORIES AS WE...
HUH?

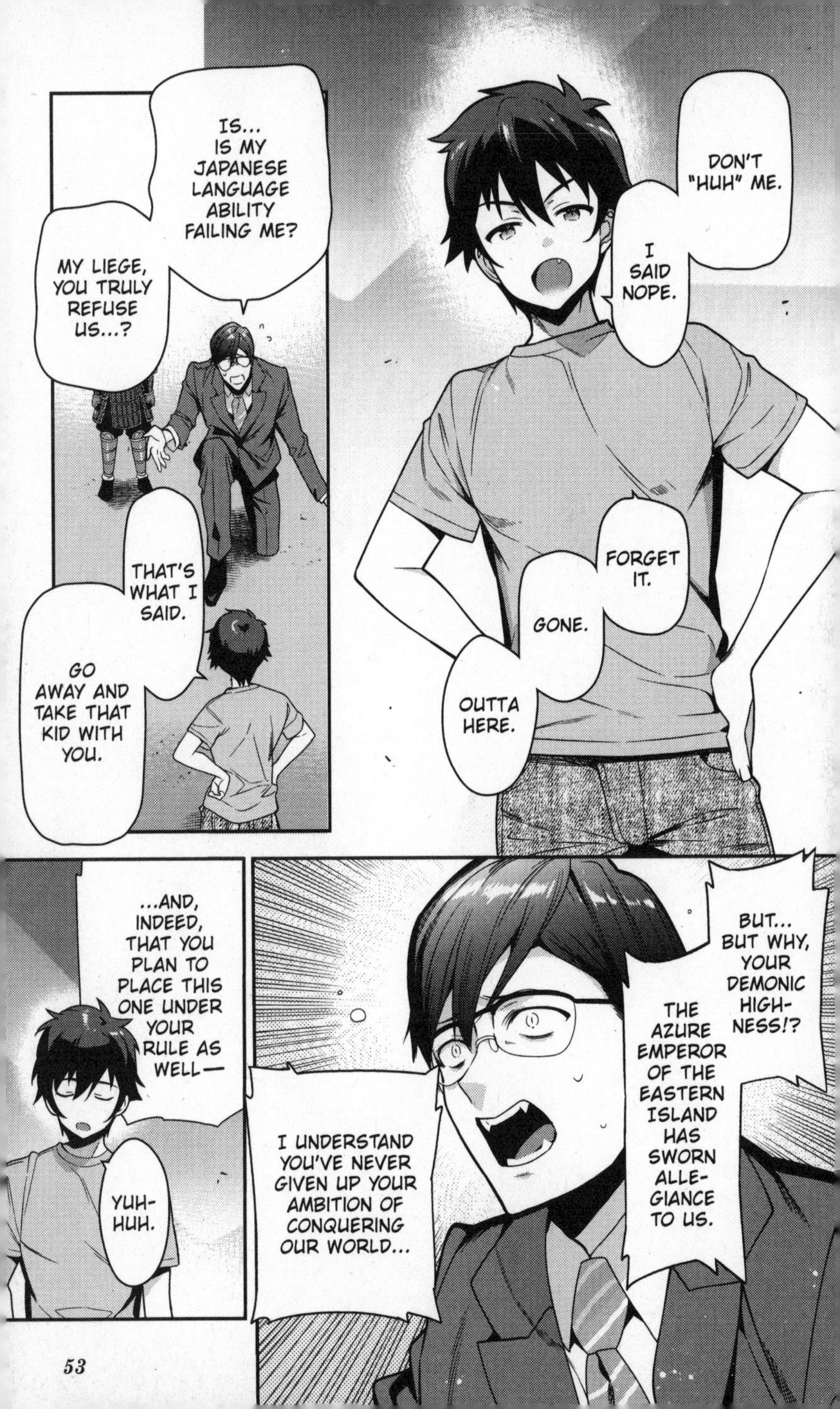
DON'T "HUH" ME.
I SAID NOPE.
FORGET IT.
GONE.
OUTTA HERE.
IS... IS MY JAPANESE LANGUAGE ABILITY FAILING ME?
MY LIEGE, YOU TRULY REFUSE US...?
THAT'S WHAT I SAID.
GO AWAY AND TAKE THAT KID WITH YOU.
BUT... BUT WHY, YOUR DEMONIC HIGH-NESS!?
THE AZURE EMPEROR OF THE EASTERN ISLAND HAS SWORN ALLE-GIANCE TO US.
I UNDERSTAND YOU'VE NEVER GIVEN UP YOUR AMBITION OF CONQUERING OUR WORLD...
...AND, INDEED, THAT YOU PLAN TO PLACE THIS ONE UNDER YOUR RULE AS WELL—
YUH-HUH.

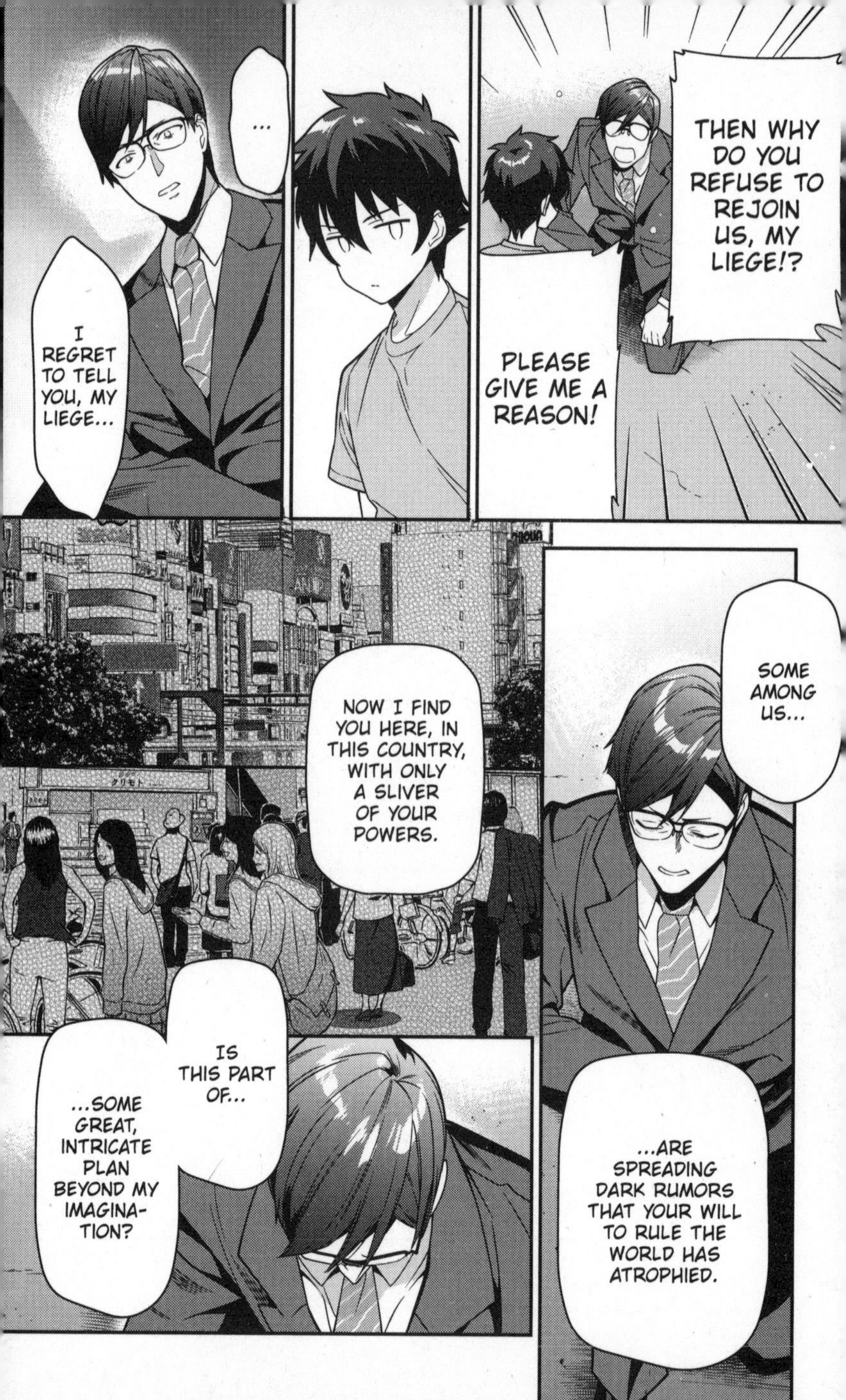
THEN WHY DO YOU REFUSE TO REJOIN US, MY LIEGE!?
PLEASE GIVE ME A REASON!
...
I REGRET TO TELL YOU, MY LIEGE...
SOME AMONG US...
...ARE SPREADING DARK RUMORS THAT YOUR WILL TO RULE THE WORLD HAS ATROPHIED.
NOW I FIND YOU HERE, IN THIS COUNTRY, WITH ONLY A SLIVER OF YOUR POWERS.
IS THIS PART OF...
...SOME GREAT, INTRICATE PLAN BEYOND MY IMAGINATION?

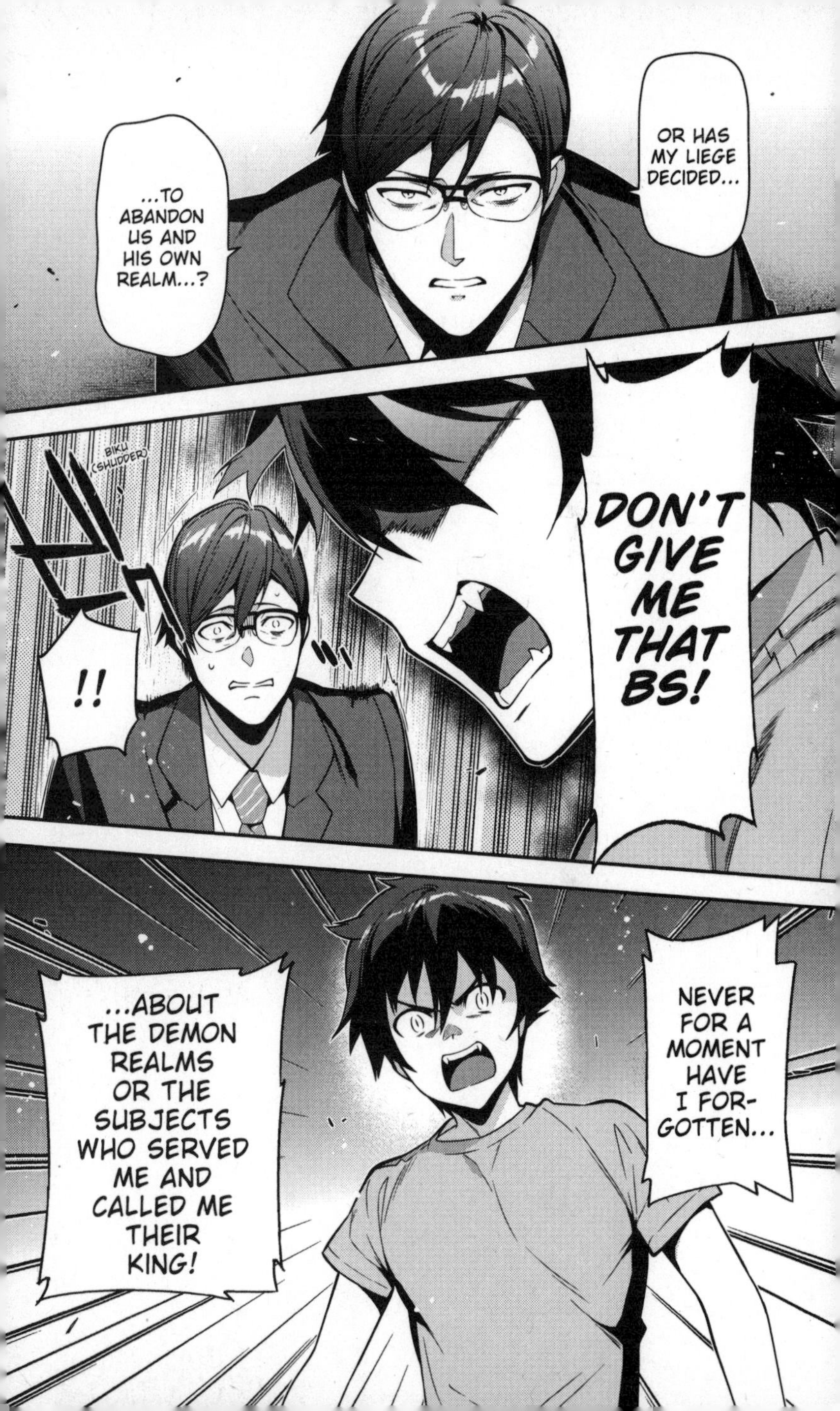
OR HAS MY LIEGE DECIDED...
...TO ABANDON US AND HIS OWN REALM...?
DON'T GIVE ME THAT BS!
BIKU (SHUDDER)
!!
NEVER FOR A MOMENT HAVE I FOR-GOTTEN...
...ABOUT THE DEMON REALMS OR THE SUBJECTS WHO SERVED ME AND CALLED ME THEIR KING!

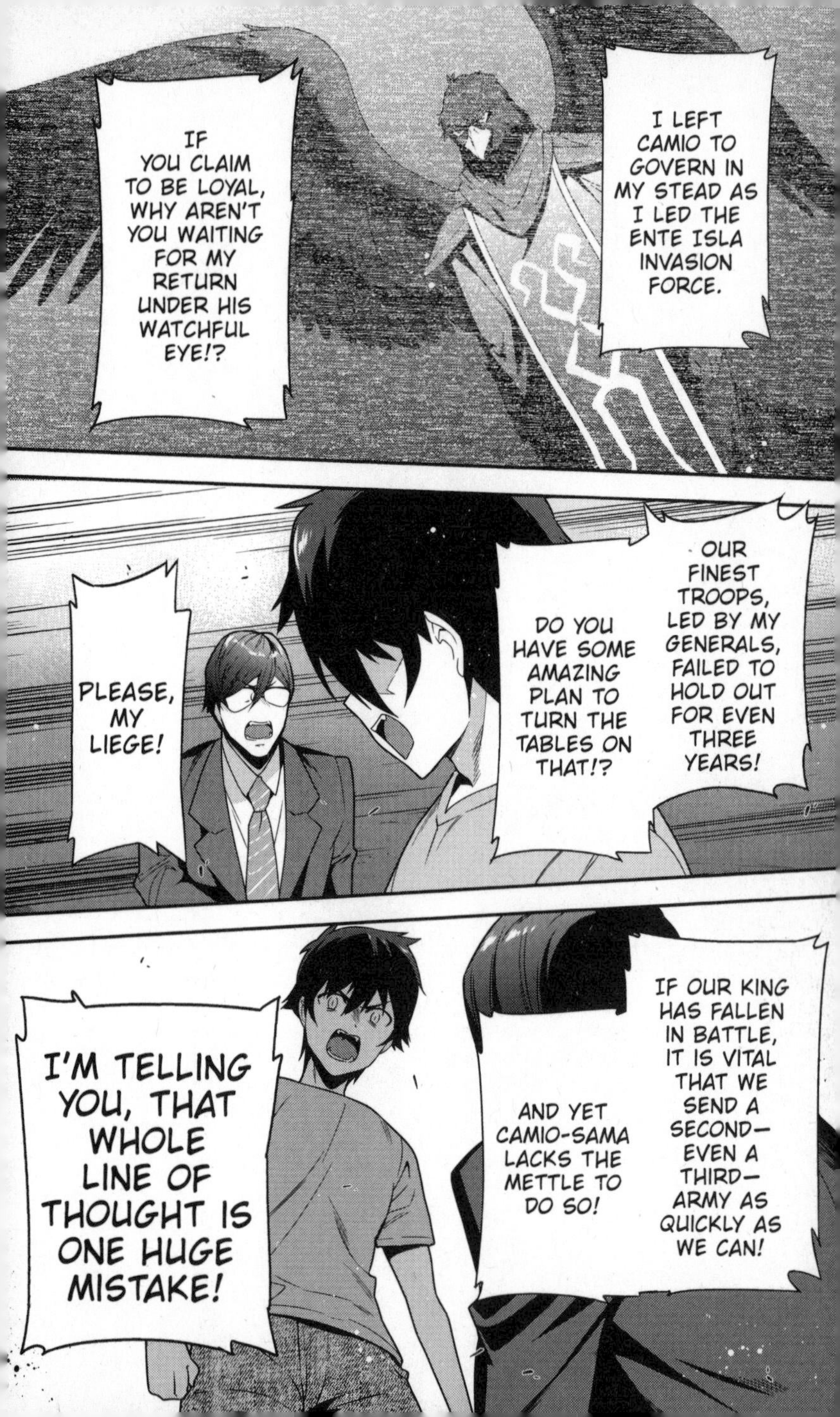
I LEFT CAMIO TO GOVERN IN MY STEAD AS I LED THE ENTE ISLA INVASION FORCE.
IF YOU CLAIM TO BE LOYAL, WHY AREN'T YOU WAITING FOR MY RETURN UNDER HIS WATCHFUL EYE!?
OUR FINEST TROOPS, LED BY MY GENERALS, FAILED TO HOLD OUT FOR EVEN THREE YEARS!
DO YOU HAVE SOME AMAZING PLAN TO TURN THE TABLES ON THAT!?
PLEASE, MY LIEGE!
IF OUR KING HAS FALLEN IN BATTLE, IT IS VITAL THAT WE SEND A SECOND—EVEN A THIRD—ARMY AS QUICKLY AS WE CAN!
AND YET CAMIO-SAMA LACKS THE METTLE TO DO SO!
I'M TELLING YOU, THAT WHOLE LINE OF THOUGHT IS ONE HUGE MISTAKE!

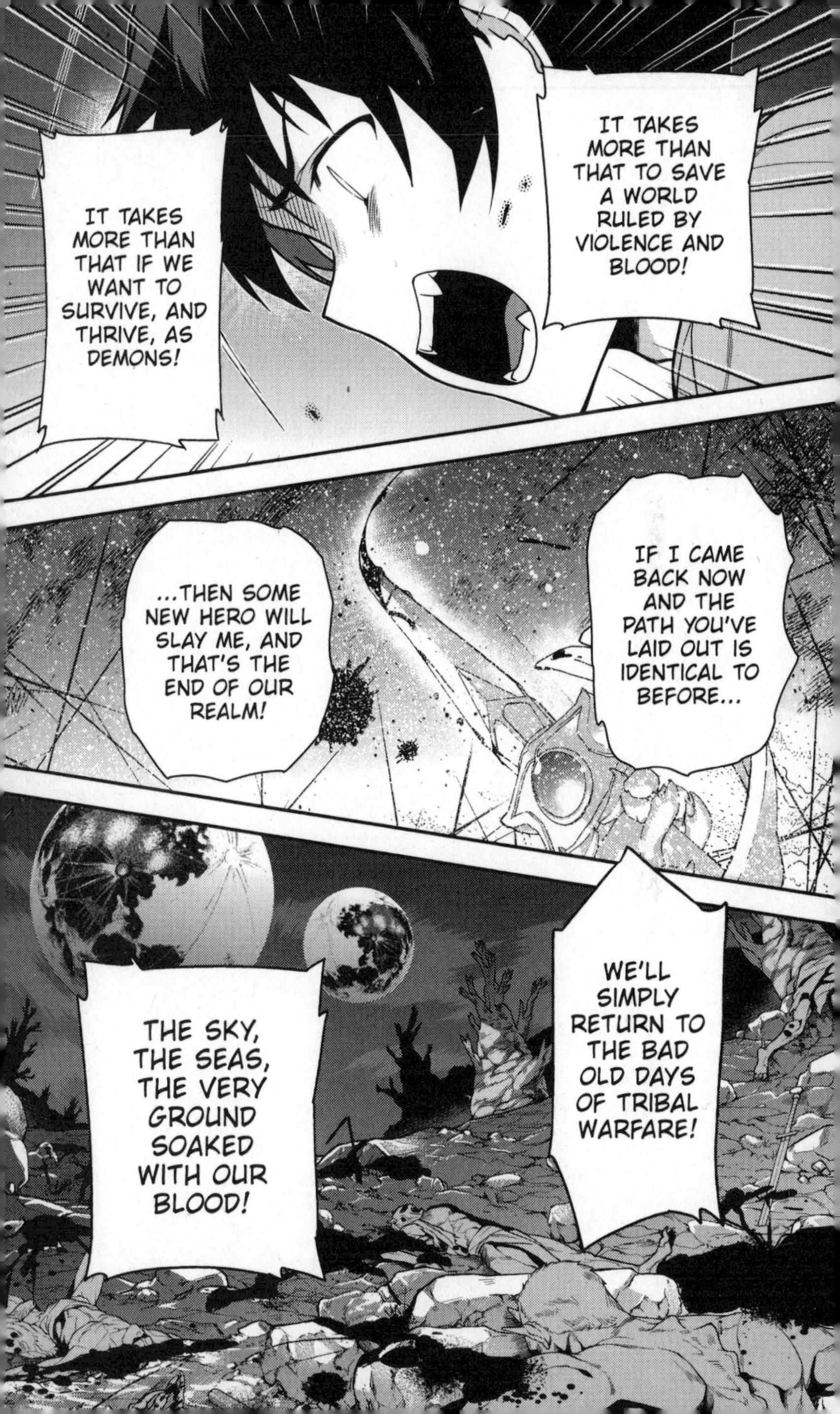
IT TAKES MORE THAN THAT TO SAVE A WORLD RULED BY VIOLENCE AND BLOOD!
IT TAKES MORE THAN THAT IF WE WANT TO SURVIVE, AND THRIVE, AS DEMONS!
IF I CAME BACK NOW AND THE PATH YOU'VE LAID OUT IS IDENTICAL TO BEFORE...
...THEN SOME NEW HERO WILL SLAY ME, AND THAT'S THE END OF OUR REALM!
WE'LL SIMPLY RETURN TO THE BAD OLD DAYS OF TRIBAL WARFARE!
THE SKY, THE SEAS, THE VERY GROUND SOAKED WITH OUR BLOOD!

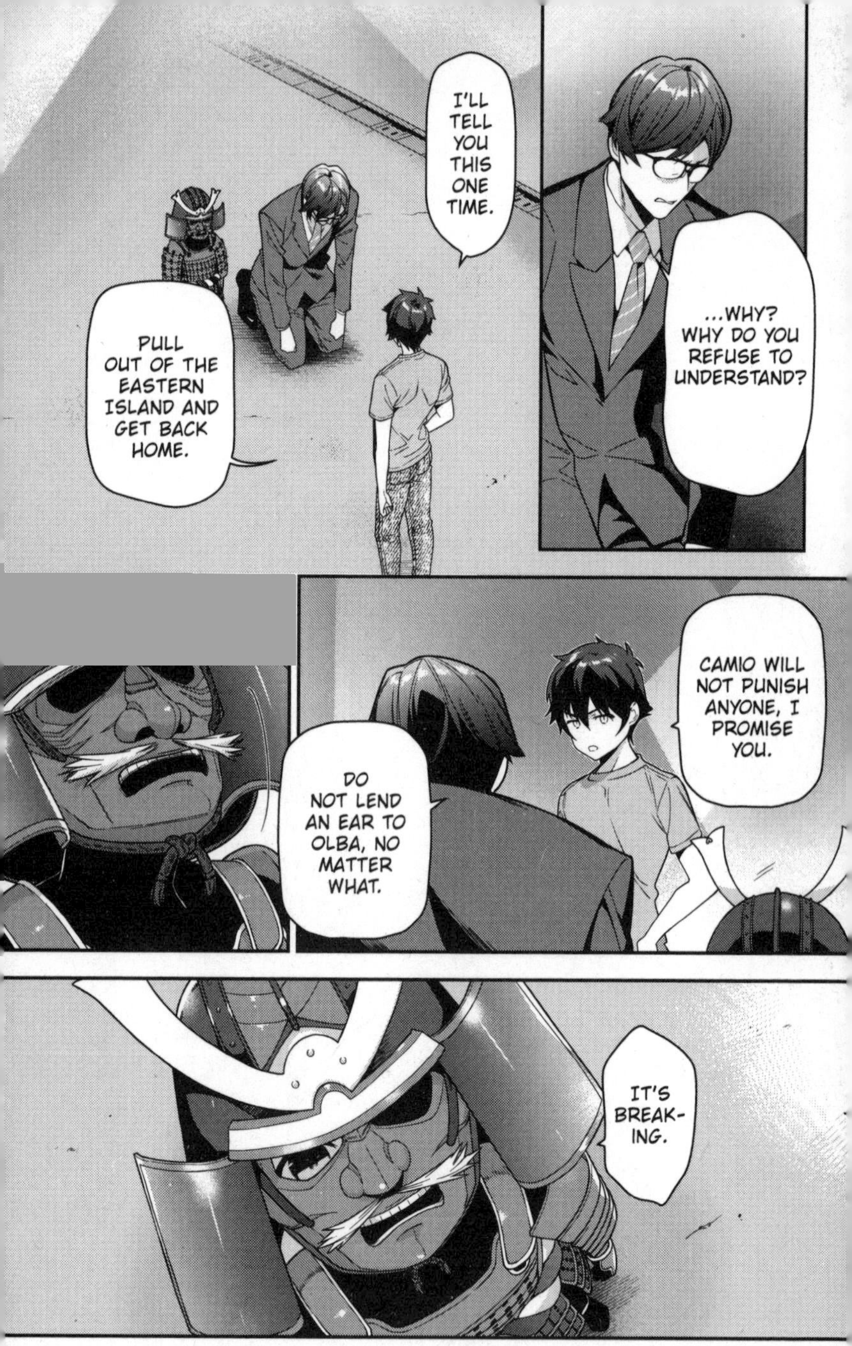
...WHY? WHY DO YOU REFUSE TO UNDERSTAND?
I'LL TELL YOU THIS ONE TIME.
PULL OUT OF THE EASTERN ISLAND AND GET BACK HOME.
CAMIO WILL NOT PUNISH ANYONE, I PROMISE YOU.
DO NOT LEND AN EAR TO OLBA, NO MATTER WHAT.
IT'S BREAK-ING.

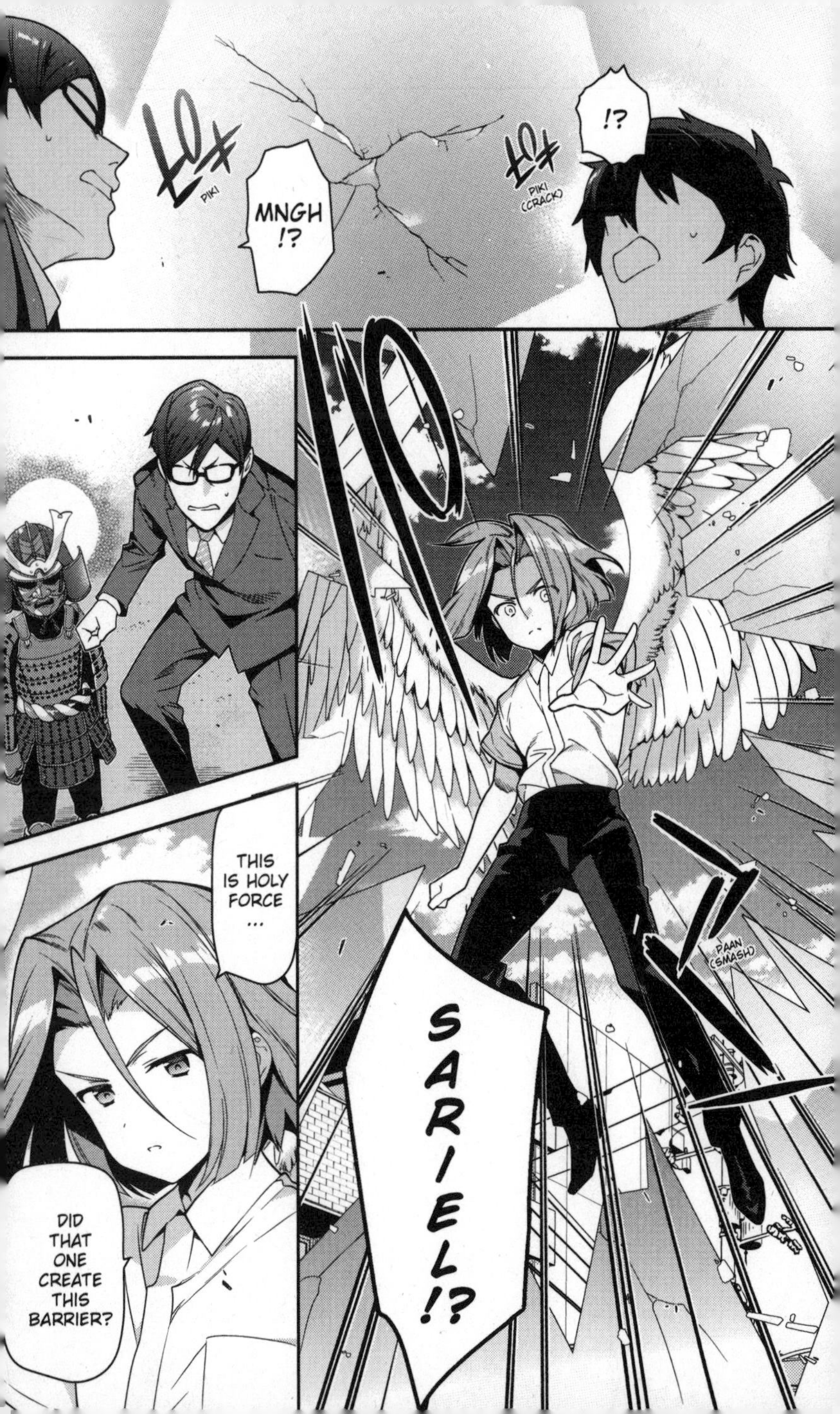
!?
PIKI (CRACK)
MNGH !?
PIKI
PAAN (SMASH)
SARIEL!?
THIS IS HOLY FORCE ...
DID THAT ONE CREATE THIS BARRIER?

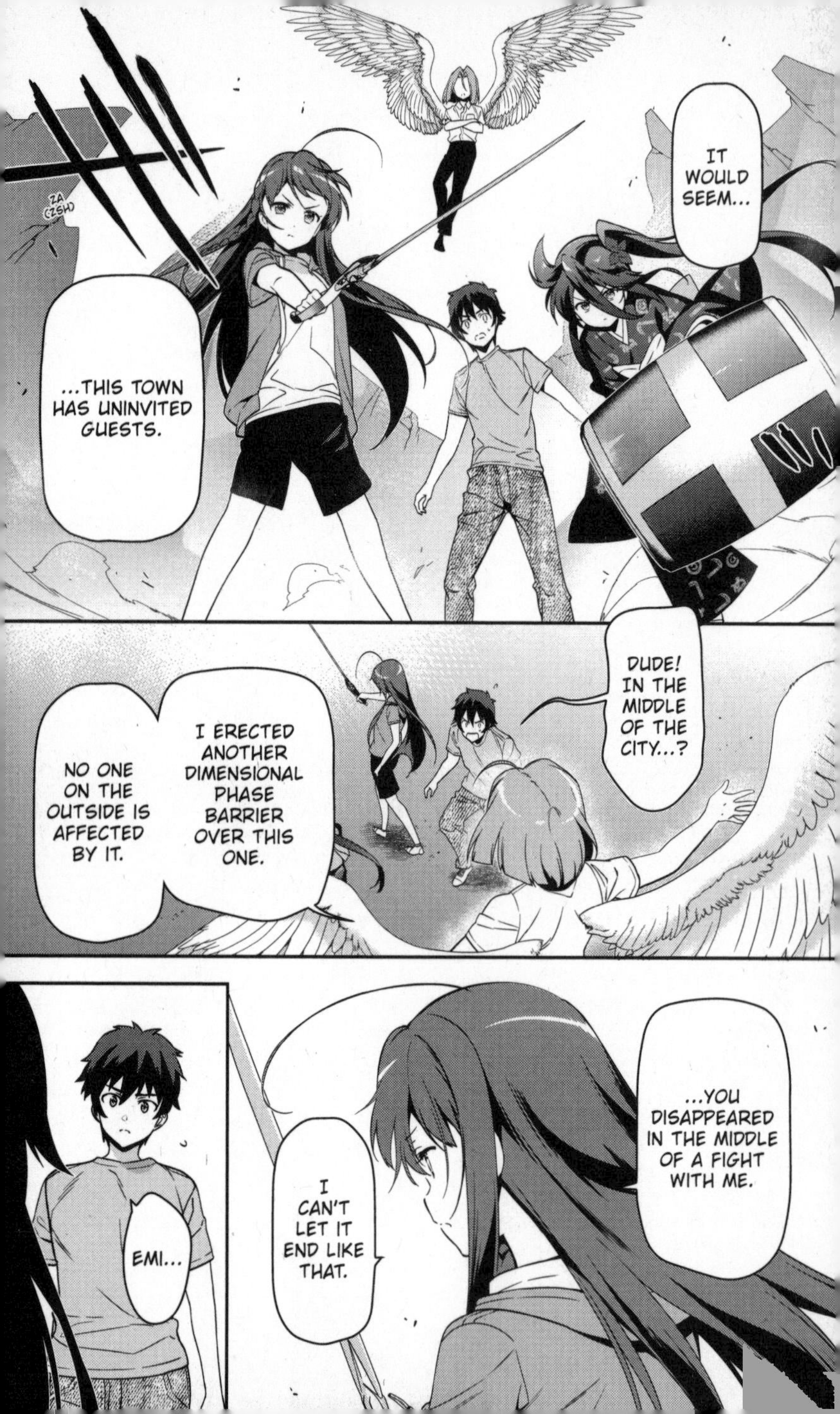
IT WOULD SEEM...
ZA (ZSH)
...THIS TOWN HAS UNINVITED GUESTS.
DUDE! IN THE MIDDLE OF THE CITY...?
I ERECTED ANOTHER DIMENSIONAL PHASE BARRIER OVER THIS ONE.
NO ONE ON THE OUTSIDE IS AFFECTED BY IT.
...YOU DISAPPEARED IN THE MIDDLE OF A FIGHT WITH ME.
I CAN'T LET IT END LIKE THAT.
EMI...

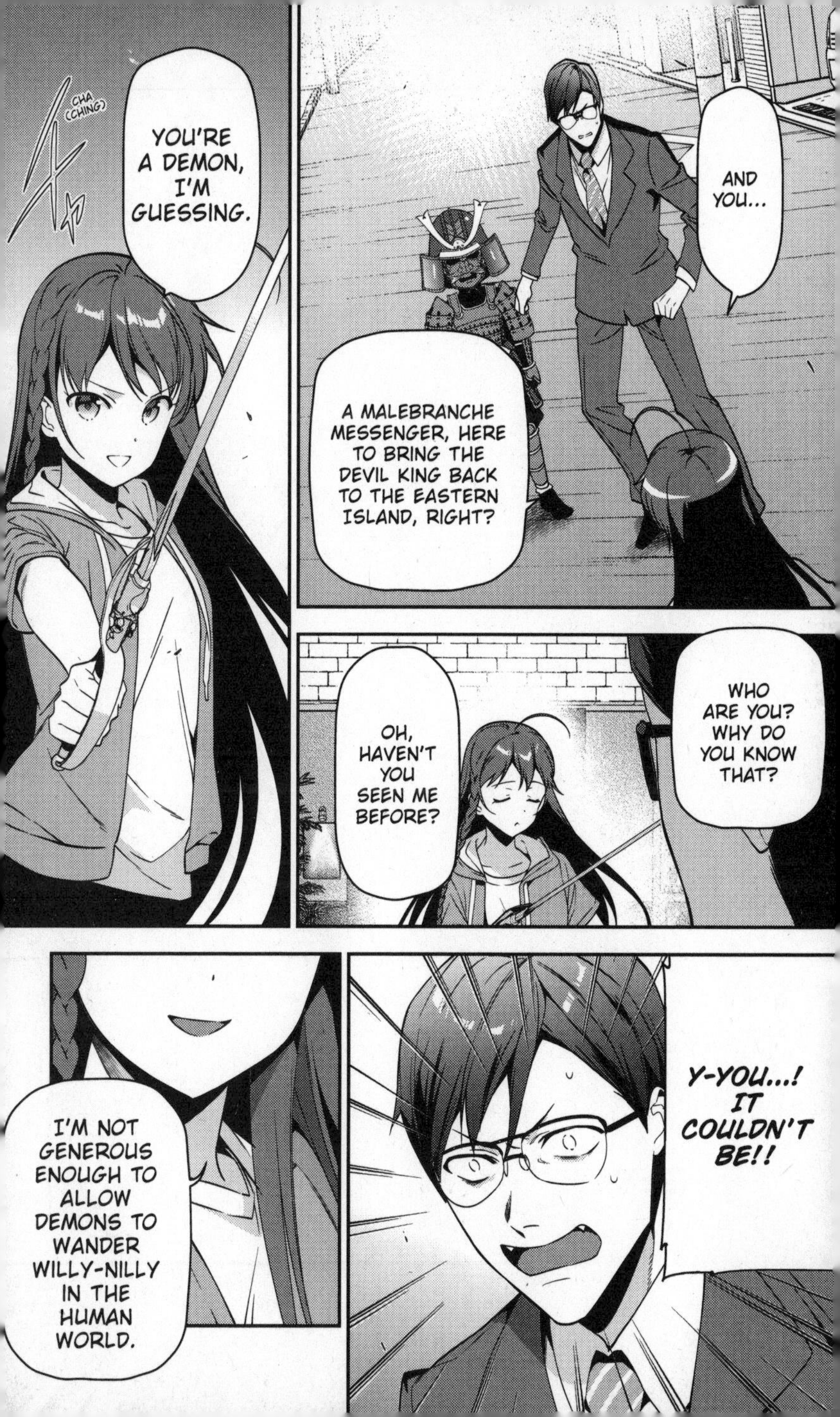
AND YOU...
A MALEBRANCHE MESSENGER, HERE TO BRING THE DEVIL KING BACK TO THE EASTERN ISLAND, RIGHT?
WHO ARE YOU? WHY DO YOU KNOW THAT?
OH, HAVEN'T YOU SEEN ME BEFORE?
CHA (CHING)
YOU'RE A DEMON, I'M GUESSING.
Y-YOU...! IT COULDN'T BE!!
I'M NOT GENEROUS ENOUGH TO ALLOW DEMONS TO WANDER WILLY-NILLY IN THE HUMAN WORLD.

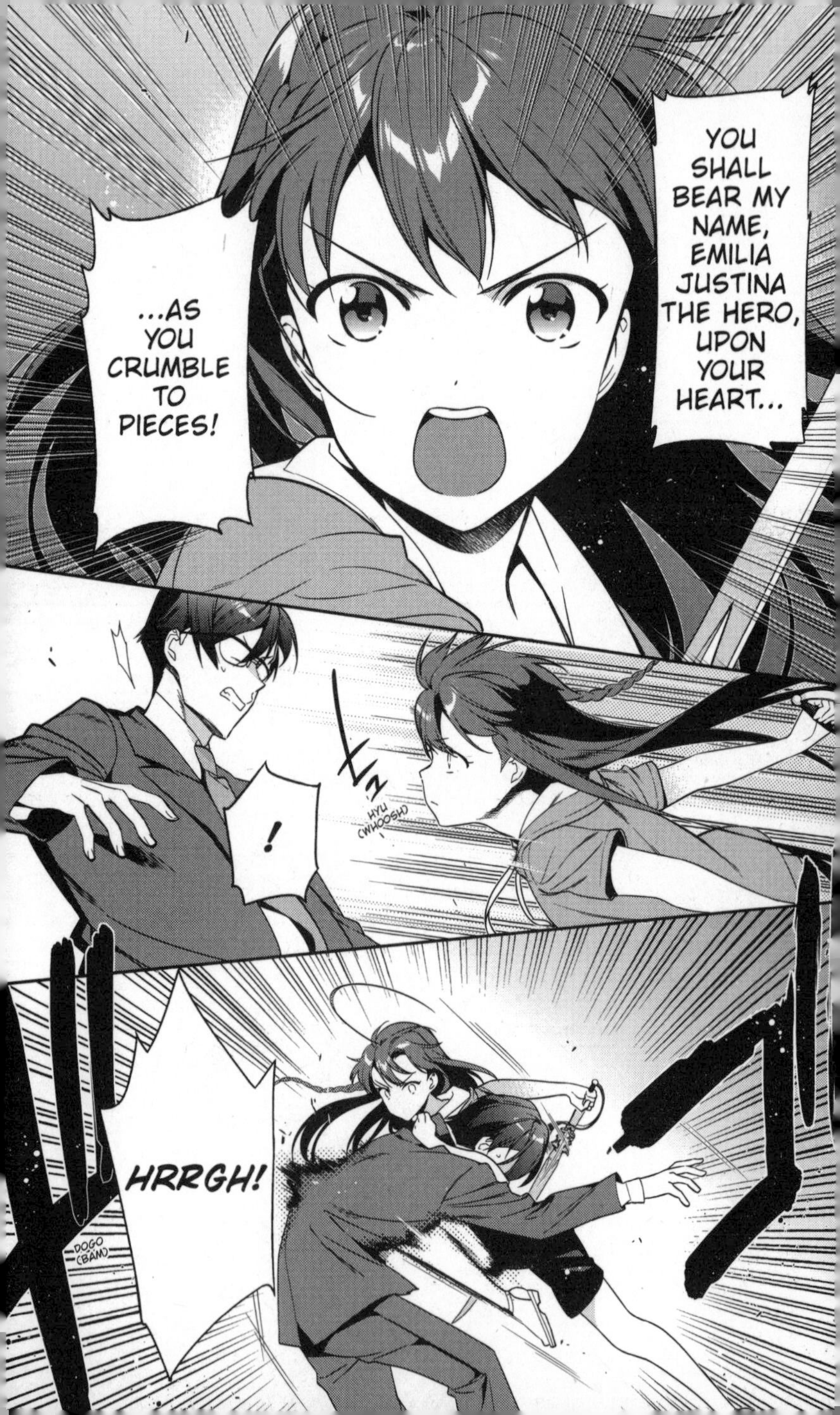
YOU SHALL BEAR MY NAME, EMILIA JUSTINA THE HERO, UPON YOUR HEART...
...AS YOU CRUMBLE TO PIECES!
HYU (WHOOSH)
!
HRRGH!
DOGO (BAM)

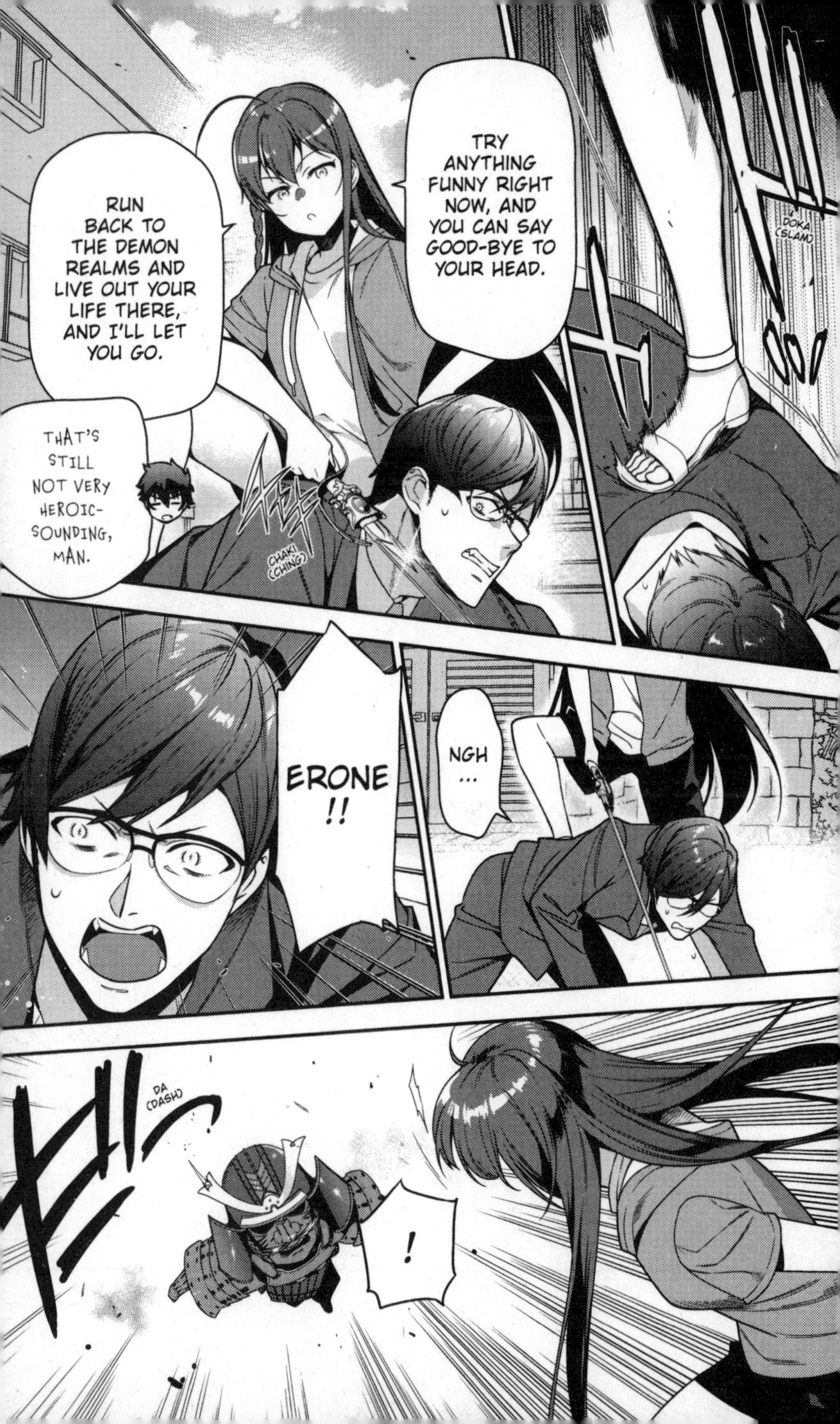
DOKA (SLAM)
TRY ANYTHING FUNNY RIGHT NOW, AND YOU CAN SAY GOOD-BYE TO YOUR HEAD.
RUN BACK TO THE DEMON REALMS AND LIVE OUT YOUR LIFE THERE, AND I'LL LET YOU GO.
CHAKI (CHING)
THAT'S STILL NOT VERY HEROIC-SOUNDING, MAN.
NGH ...
ERONE !!
!
DA (DASH)

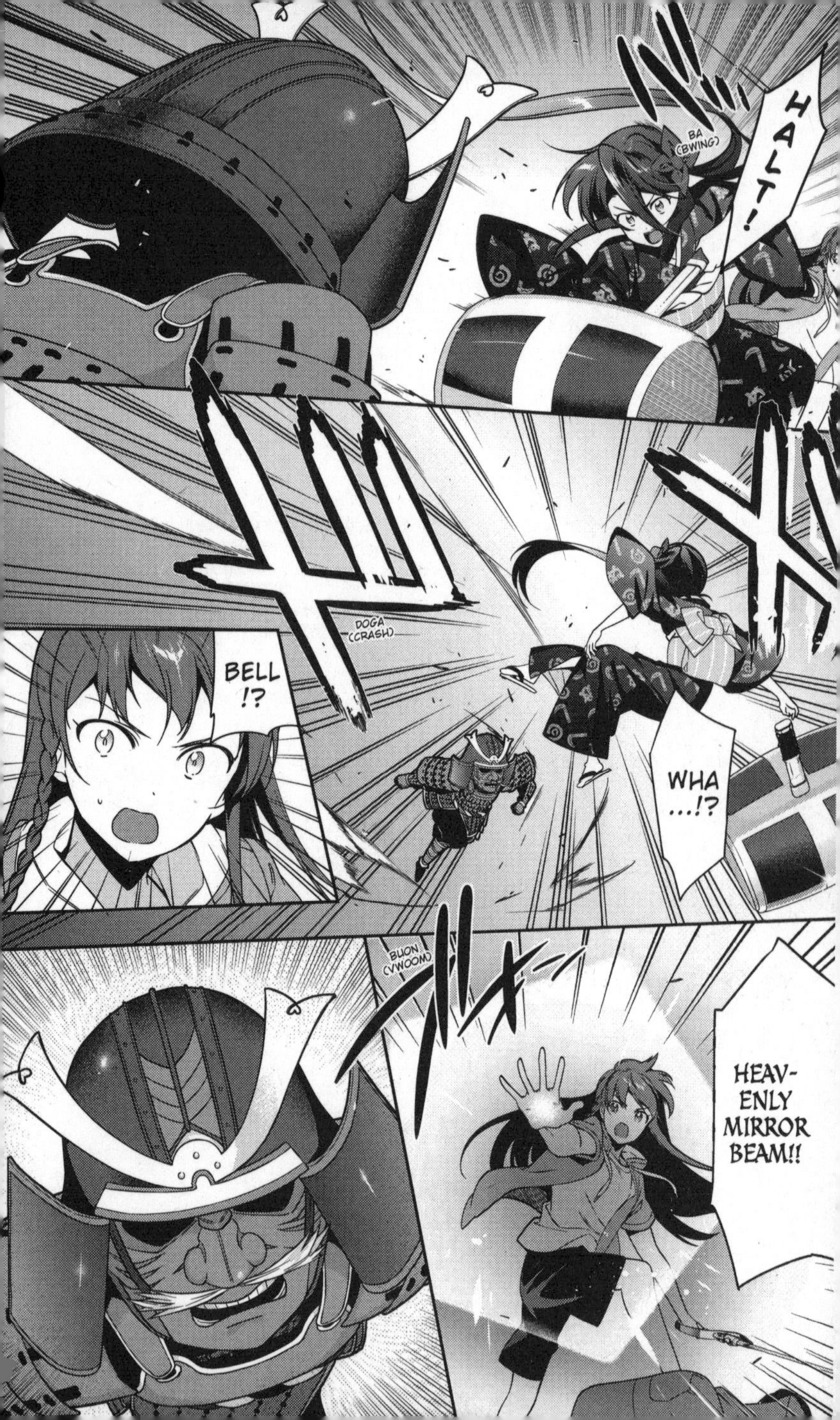
HALT!
BA (BWING)
DOGA (CRASH)
WHA ...!?
BELL !?
BUON (VWOOM)
HEAV-ENLY MIRROR BEAM!!

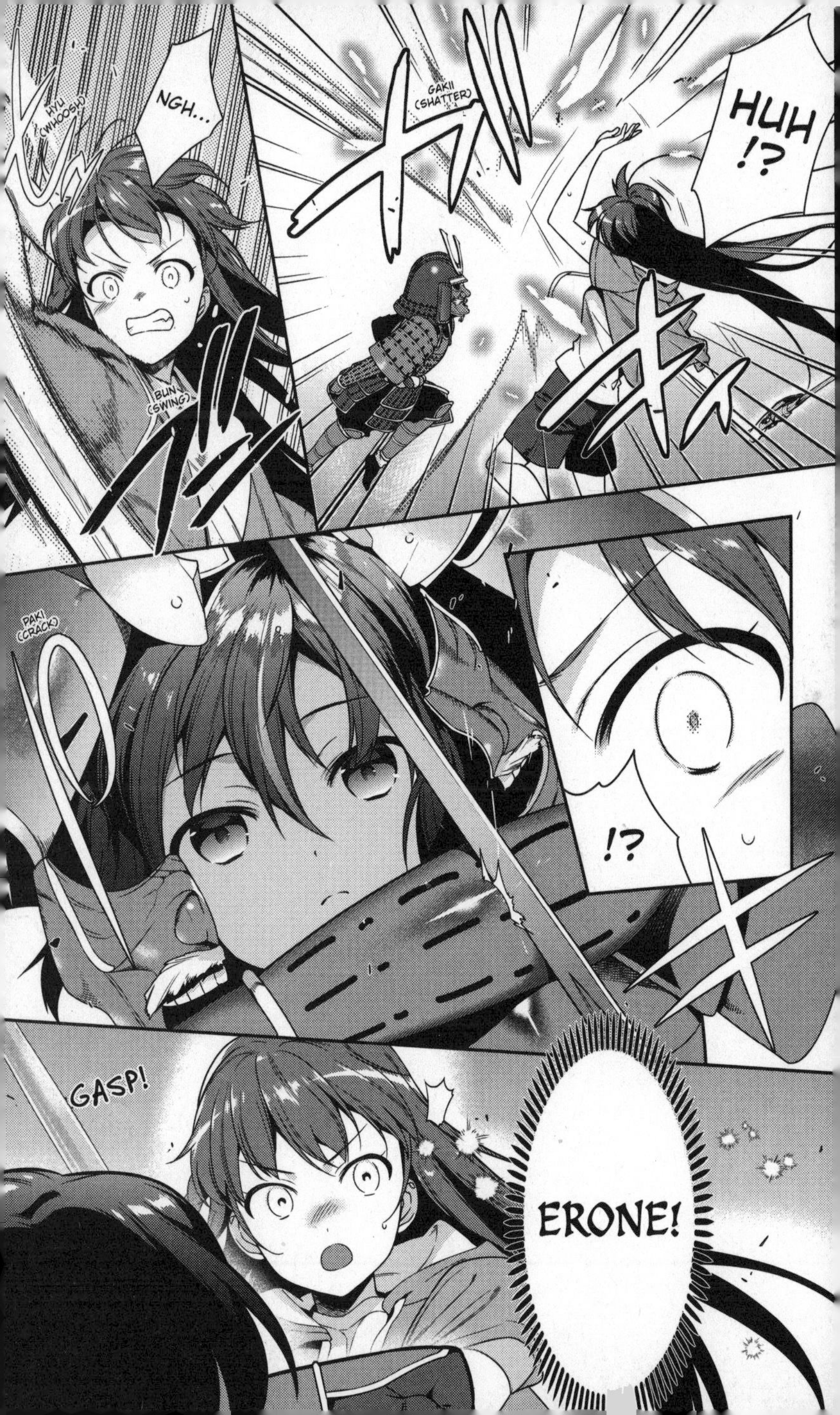
GAKII (SHATTER)
HUH !?
HYU (WHOOSH)
NGH...
BUN (SWING)
!?
PAKI (CRACK)
ERONE!
GASP!

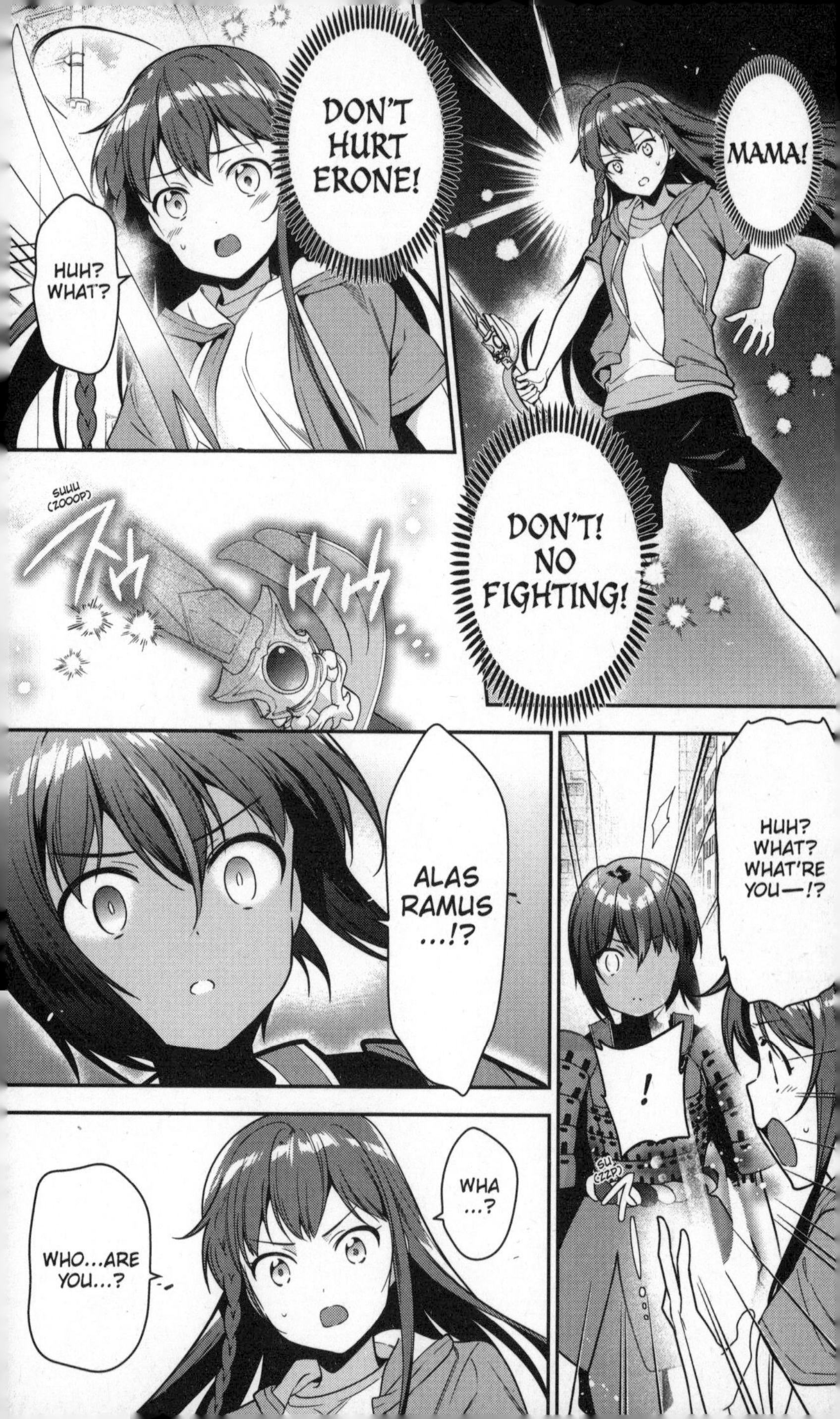
MAMA!
DON'T! NO FIGHTING!
DON'T HURT ERONE!
HUH? WHAT?
SUUU (ZOOOP)
HUH? WHAT? WHAT'RE YOU—!?
!
SU (ZZP)
ALAS RAMUS ...!?
WHA ...?
WHO...ARE YOU...?

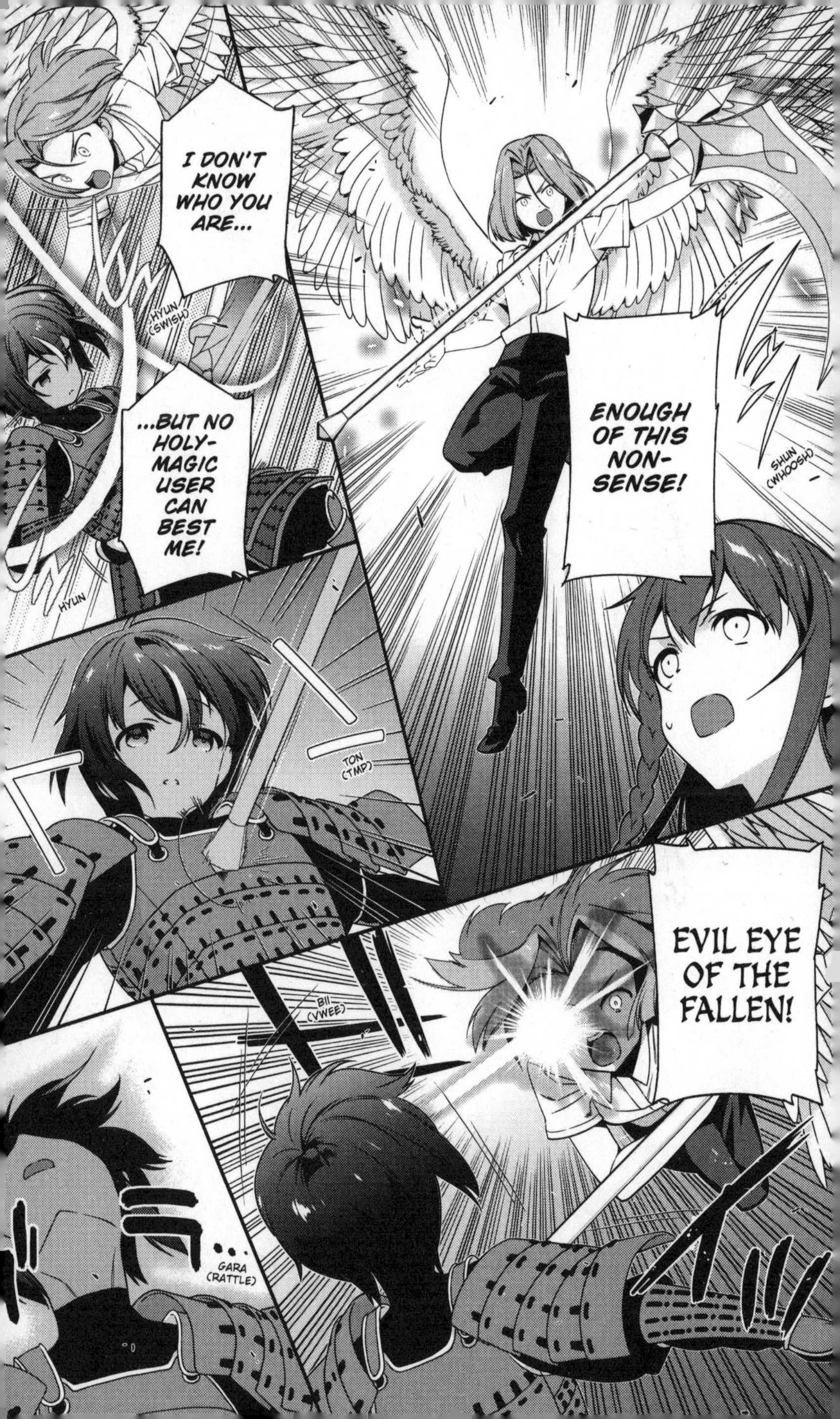

ENOUGH OF THIS NON-SENSE!
SHUN (WHOOSH)
I DON'T KNOW WHO YOU ARE...
HYUN (SWISH)
...BUT NO HOLY-MAGIC USER CAN BEST ME!
HYUN
TON (TMP)
EVIL EYE OF THE FALLEN!
BII (VWEE)
...
GARA (RATTLE)

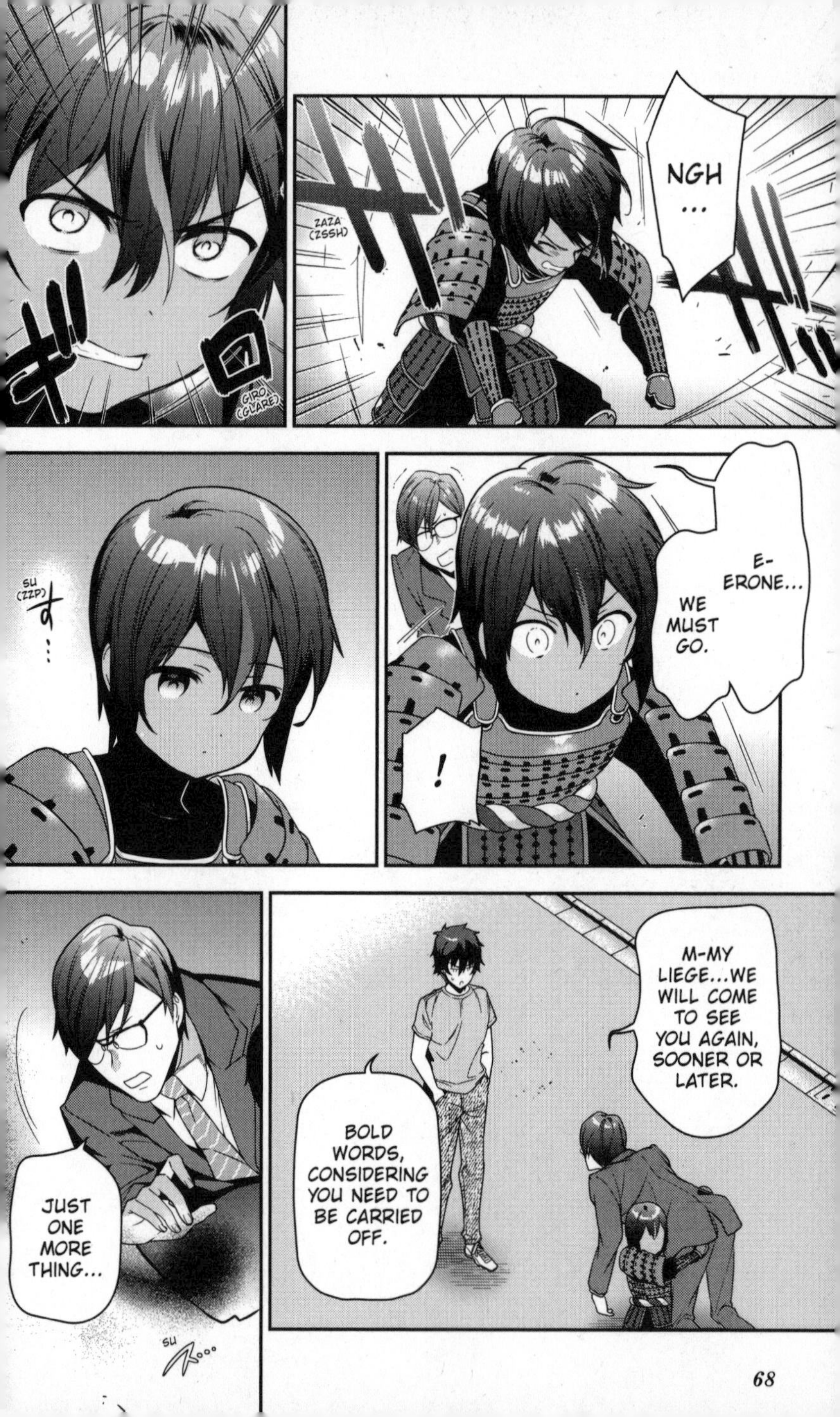
NGH...
ZAZA (ZSSH)
GIRO (GLARE)
E-ERONE...
WE MUST GO.
!
SU (ZZP)
M-MY LIEGE...WE WILL COME TO SEE YOU AGAIN, SOONER OR LATER.
BOLD WORDS, CONSIDERING YOU NEED TO BE CARRIED OFF.
JUST ONE MORE THING...
SU

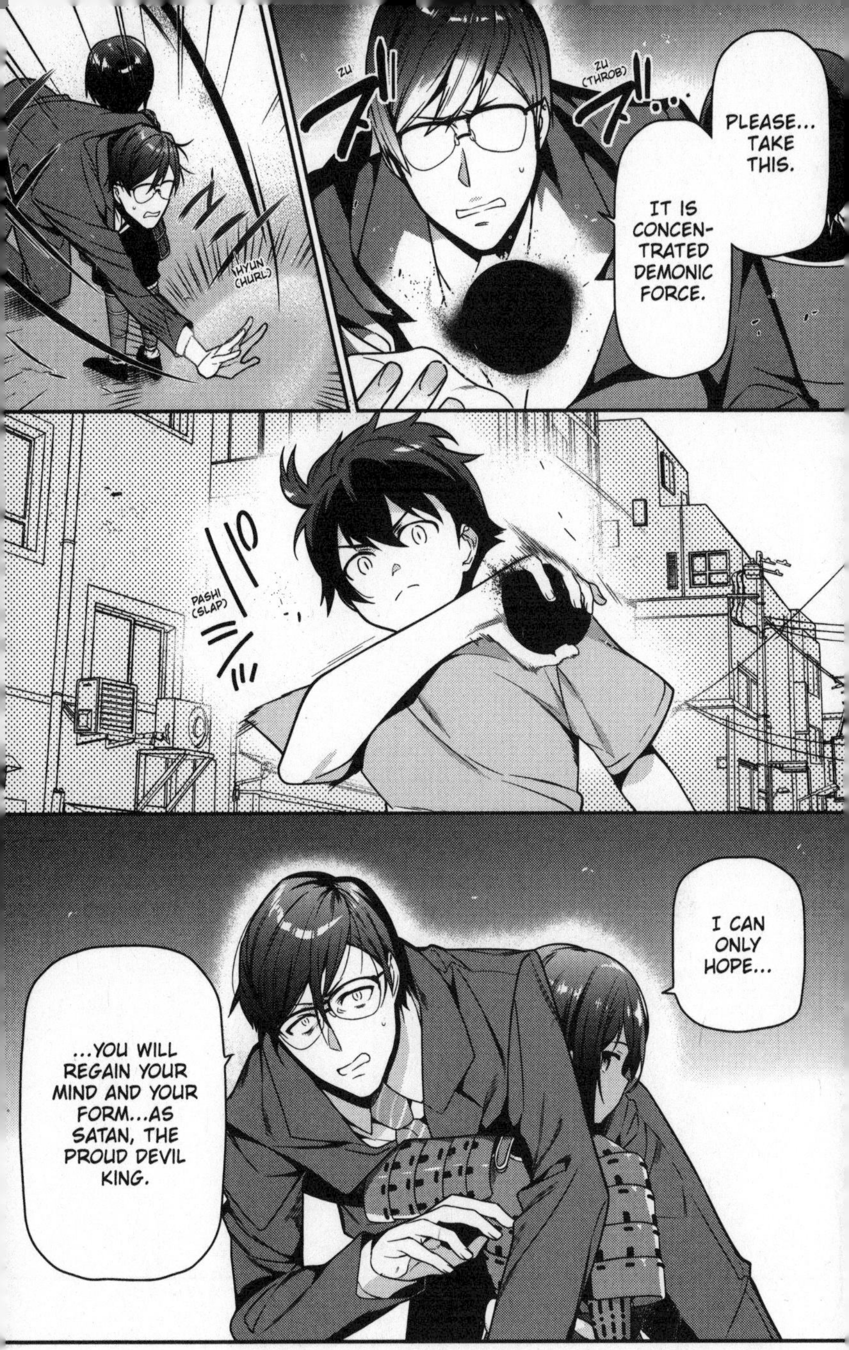
PLEASE... TAKE THIS.
IT IS CONCEN-TRATED DEMONIC FORCE.
ZU (THROB)
ZU
HYUN (HURL)
PASHI (SLAP)
I CAN ONLY HOPE...
...YOU WILL REGAIN YOUR MIND AND YOUR FORM...AS SATAN, THE PROUD DEVIL KING.

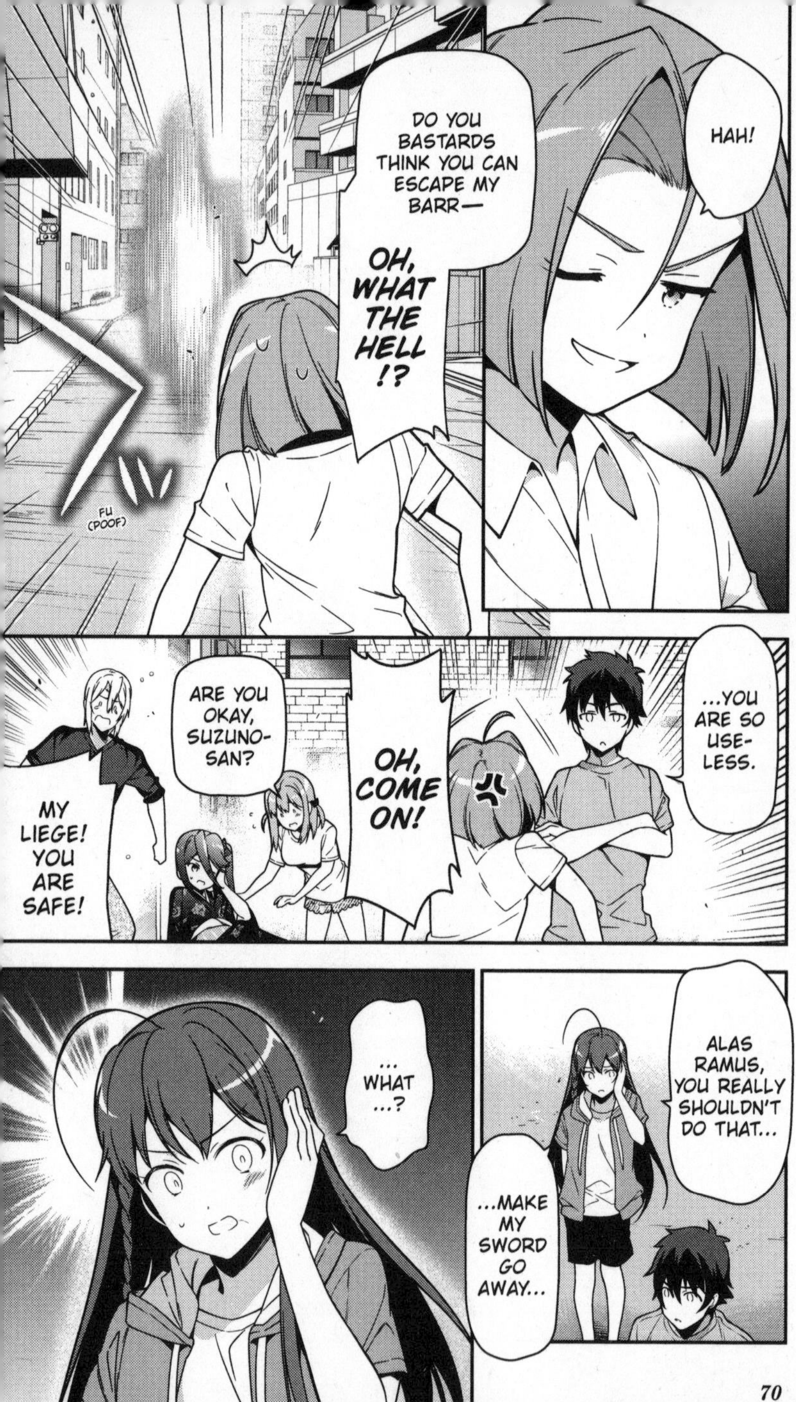
HAH!
DO YOU BASTARDS THINK YOU CAN ESCAPE MY BARR—
OH, WHAT THE HELL!?
FU (POOF)
...YOU ARE SO USE-LESS.
OH, COME ON!
ARE YOU OKAY, SUZUNO-SAN?
MY LIEGE! YOU ARE SAFE!
ALAS RAMUS, YOU REALLY SHOULDN'T DO THAT...
...MAKE MY SWORD GO AWAY...
... WHAT ...?

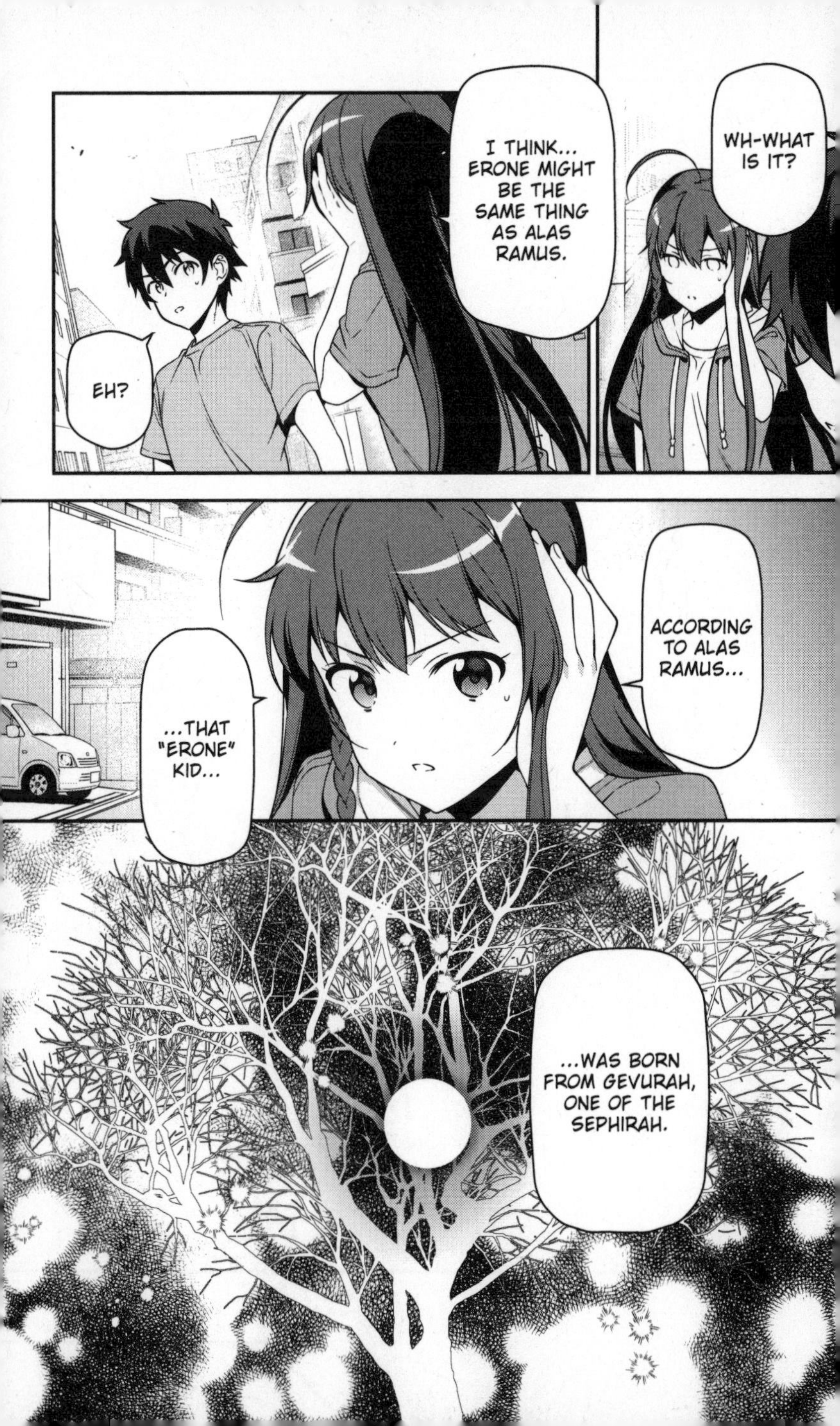
WH-WHAT IS IT?
I THINK... ERONE MIGHT BE THE SAME THING AS ALAS RAMUS.
EH?
ACCORDING TO ALAS RAMUS...
...THAT "ERONE" KID...
...WAS BORN FROM GEVURAH, ONE OF THE SEPHIRAH.

THE DEVIL IS A PART-TIMER!

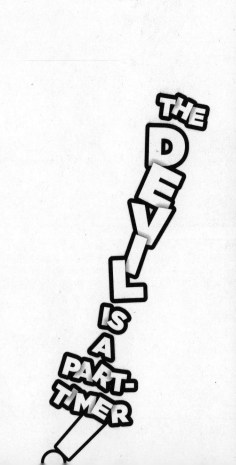

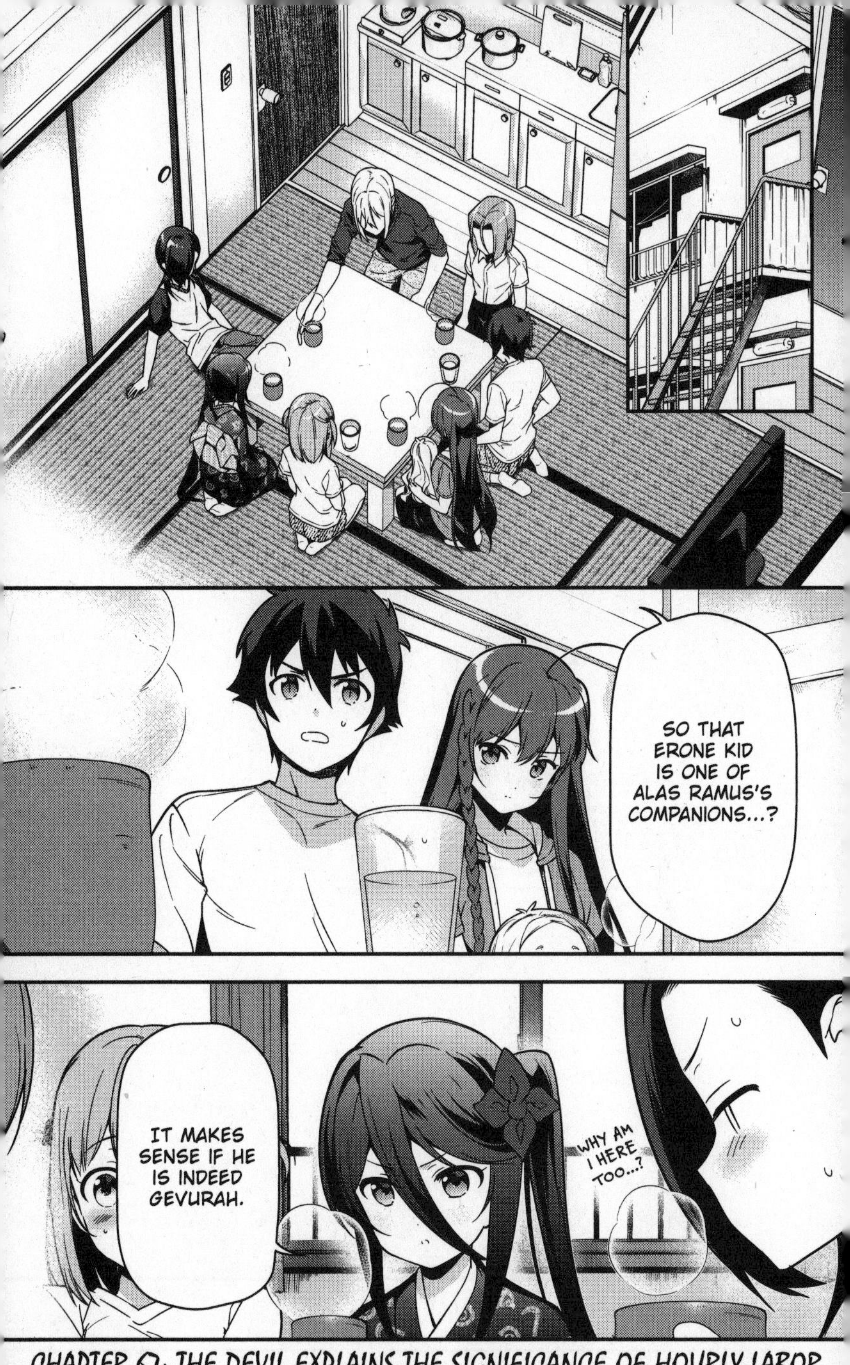
SO THAT ERONE KID IS ONE OF ALAS RAMUS'S COMPANIONS...?
WHY AM I HERE TOO...?
IT MAKES SENSE IF HE IS INDEED GEVURAH.

CHAPTER 67: THE DEVIL EXPLAINS THE SIGNIFICANCE OF HOURLY LABOR

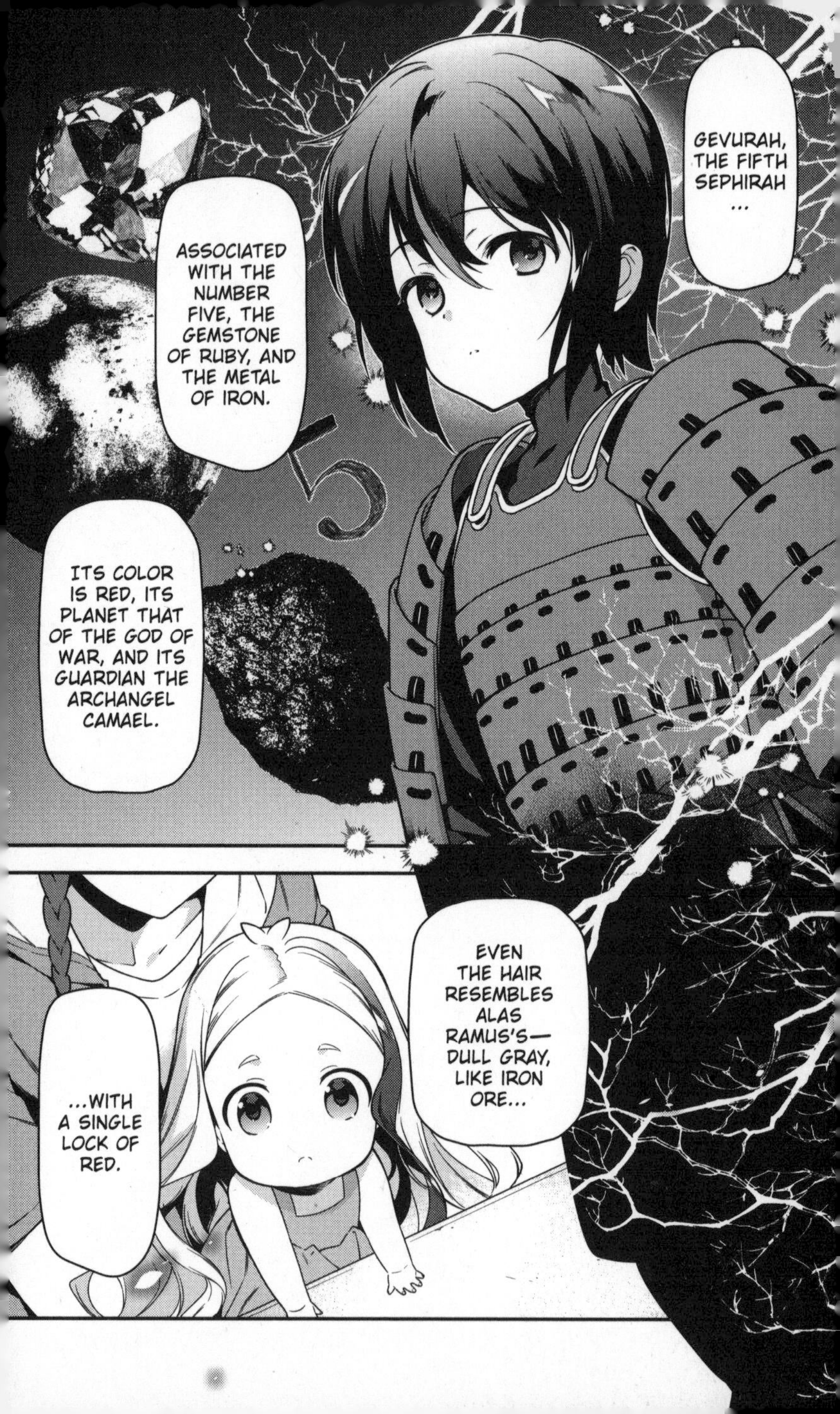
GEVURAH, THE FIFTH SEPHIRAH ...
ASSOCIATED WITH THE NUMBER FIVE, THE GEMSTONE OF RUBY, AND THE METAL OF IRON.
5
ITS COLOR IS RED, ITS PLANET THAT OF THE GOD OF WAR, AND ITS GUARDIAN THE ARCHANGEL CAMAEL.
EVEN THE HAIR RESEMBLES ALAS RAMUS'S—DULL GRAY, LIKE IRON ORE...
...WITH A SINGLE LOCK OF RED.

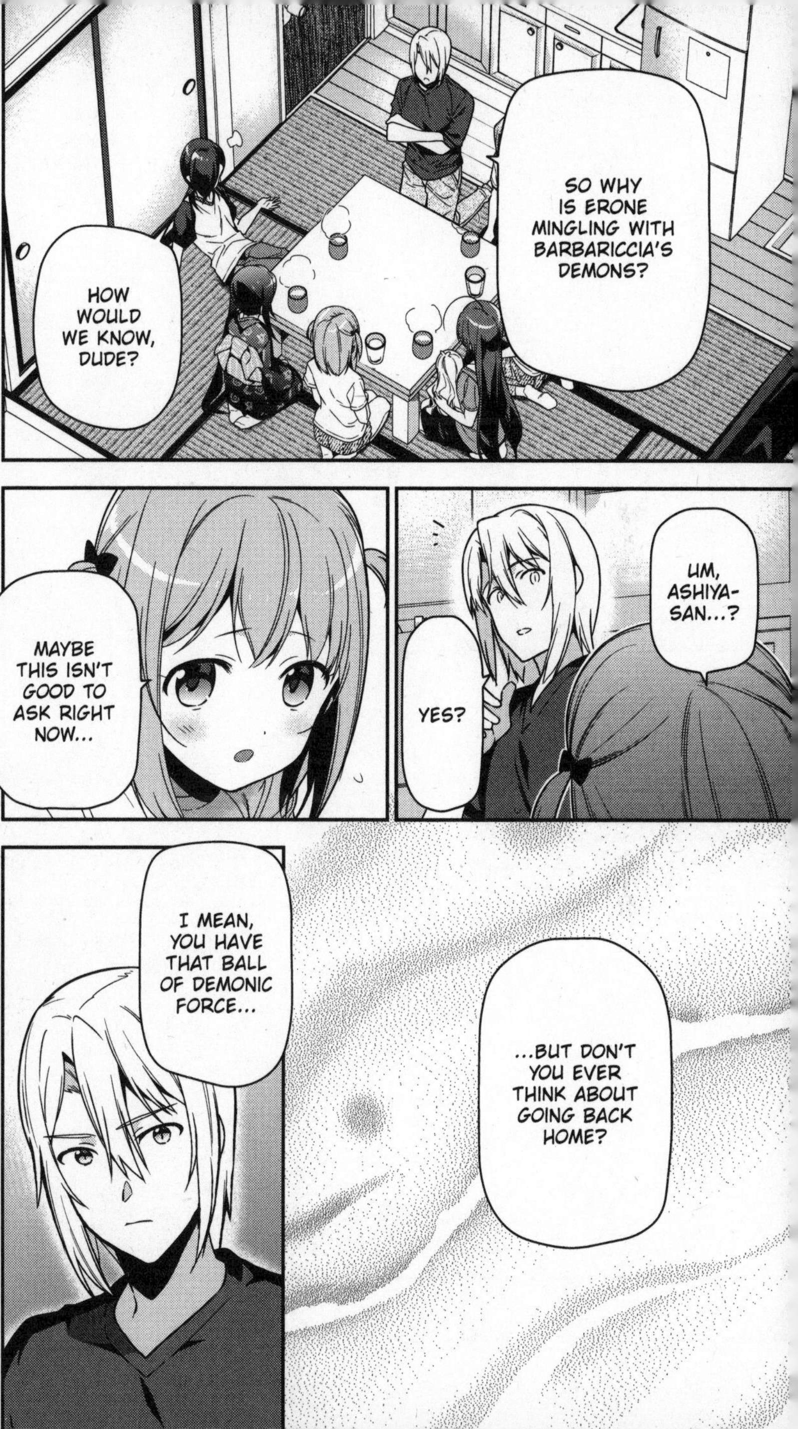
SO WHY IS ERONE MINGLING WITH BARBARICCIA'S DEMONS?
HOW WOULD WE KNOW, DUDE?
UM, ASHIYA-SAN...?
YES?
MAYBE THIS ISN'T GOOD TO ASK RIGHT NOW...
I MEAN, YOU HAVE THAT BALL OF DEMONIC FORCE...
...BUT DON'T YOU EVER THINK ABOUT GOING BACK HOME?

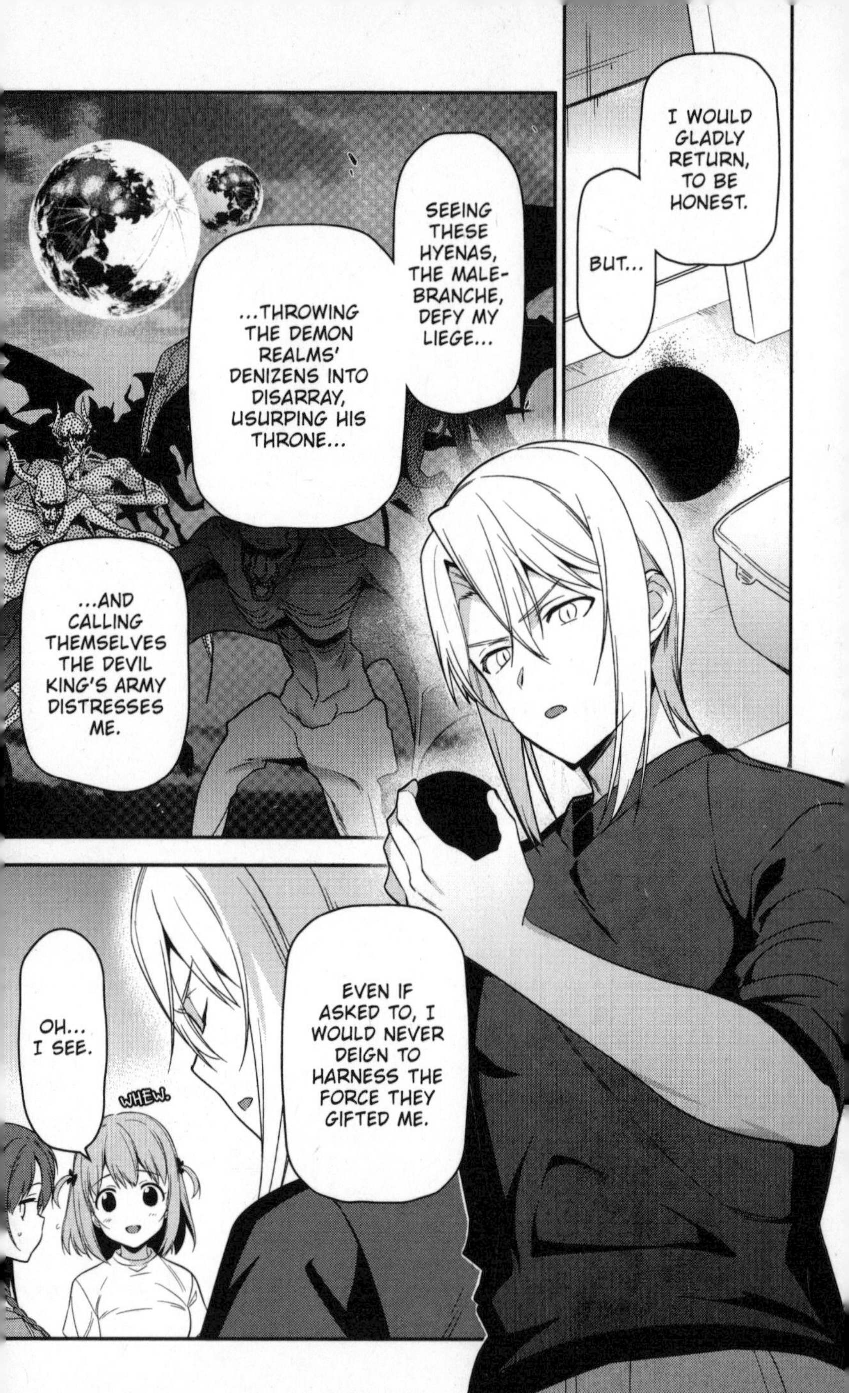
I WOULD GLADLY RETURN, TO BE HONEST.
BUT...
SEEING THESE HYENAS, THE MALE-BRANCHE, DEFY MY LIEGE...
...THROWING THE DEMON REALMS' DENIZENS INTO DISARRAY, USURPING HIS THRONE...
...AND CALLING THEMSELVES THE DEVIL KING'S ARMY DISTRESSES ME.
EVEN IF ASKED TO, I WOULD NEVER DEIGN TO HARNESS THE FORCE THEY GIFTED ME.
WHEW.
OH... I SEE.

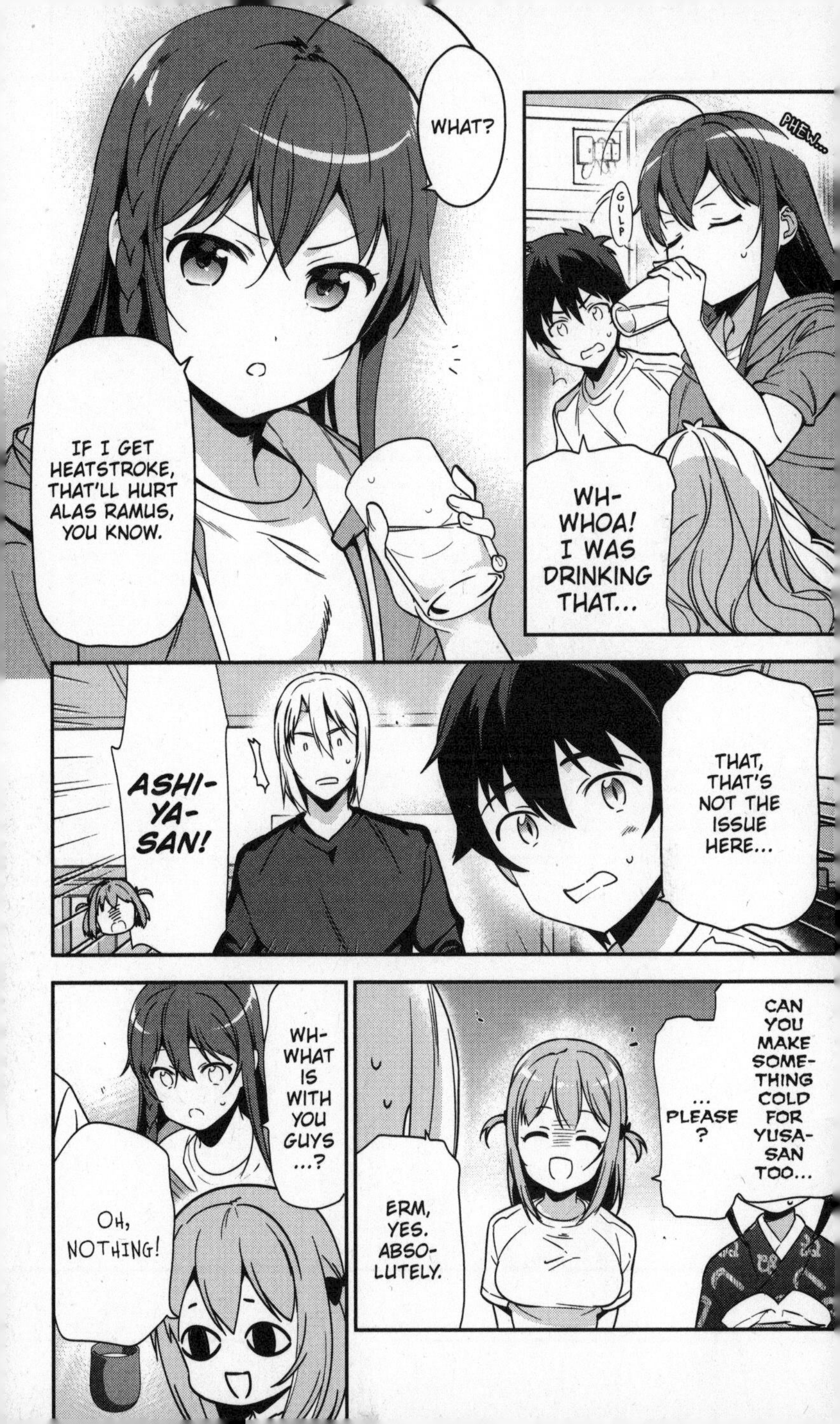
PHEW...
GULP
WH-WHOA! I WAS DRINKING THAT...
WHAT?
IF I GET HEATSTROKE, THAT'LL HURT ALAS RAMUS, YOU KNOW.
THAT, THAT'S NOT THE ISSUE HERE...
ASHIYA-SAN!
CAN YOU MAKE SOMETHING COLD FOR YUSA-SAN TOO...
...PLEASE?
ERM, YES. ABSOLUTELY.
WH-WHAT IS WITH YOU GUYS...?
OH, NOTHING!

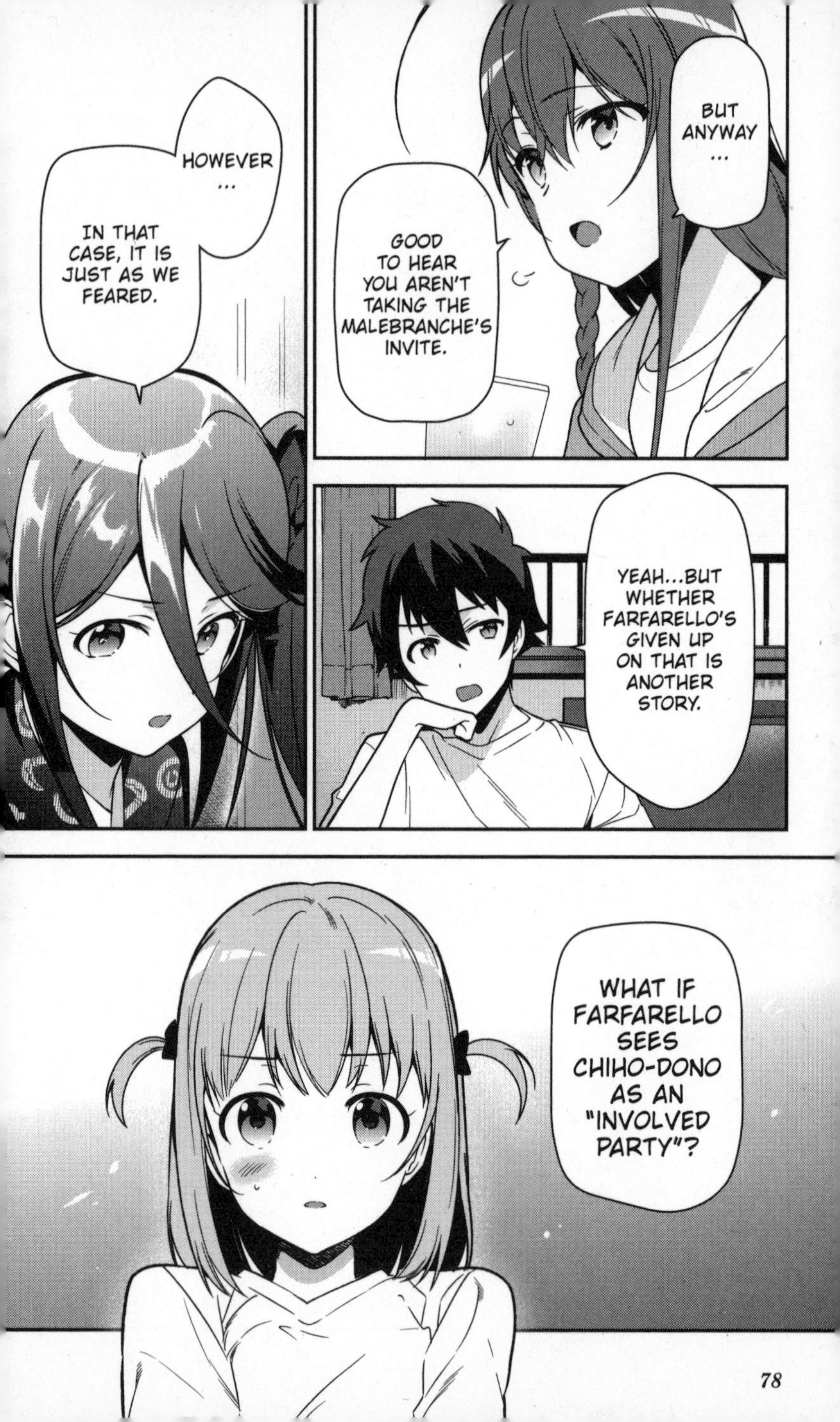
BUT ANYWAY ...
GOOD TO HEAR YOU AREN'T TAKING THE MALEBRANCHE'S INVITE.
YEAH...BUT WHETHER FARFARELLO'S GIVEN UP ON THAT IS ANOTHER STORY.
HOWEVER ...
IN THAT CASE, IT IS JUST AS WE FEARED.
WHAT IF FARFARELLO SEES CHIHO-DONO AS AN "INVOLVED PARTY"?

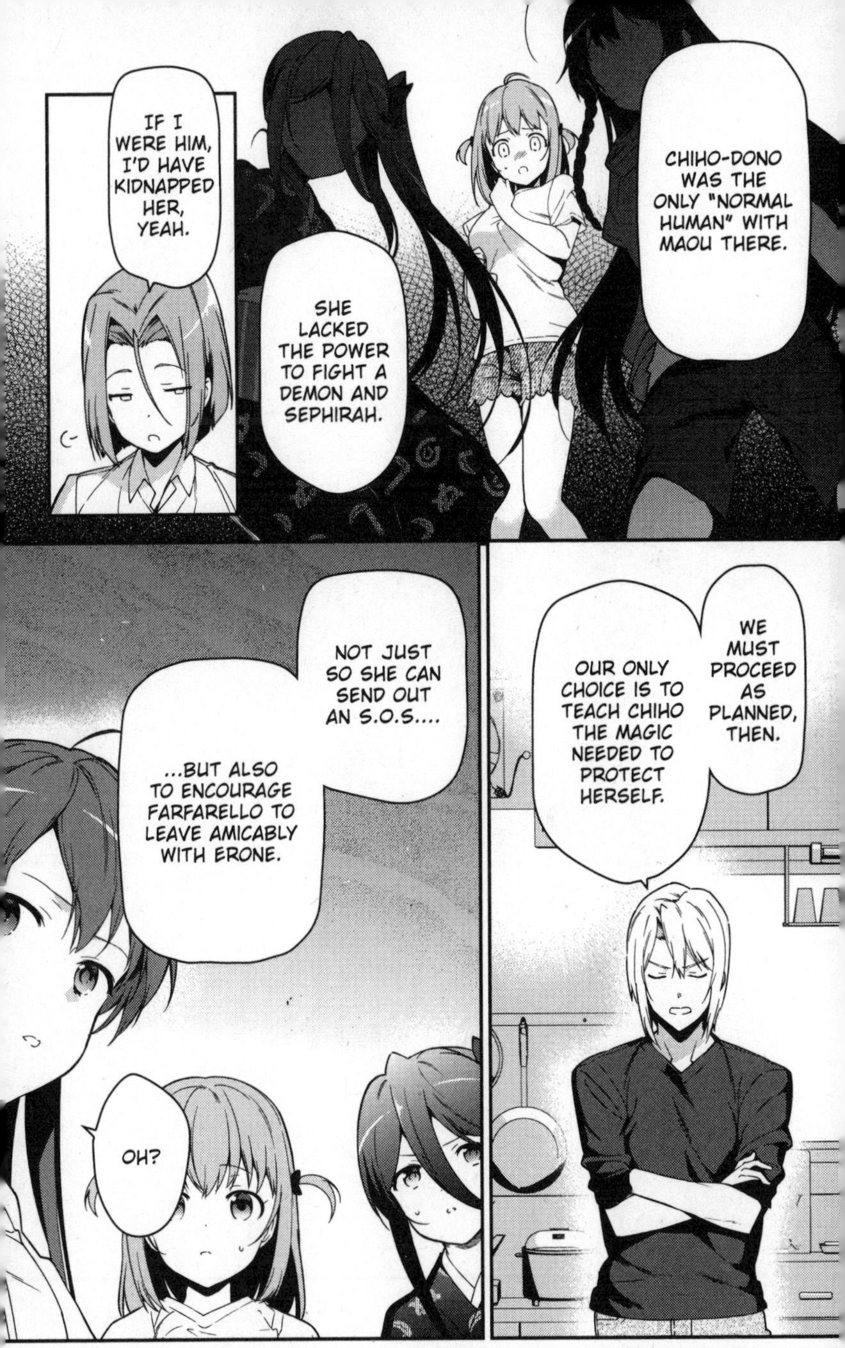
CHIHO-DONO WAS THE ONLY "NORMAL HUMAN" WITH MAOU THERE.
SHE LACKED THE POWER TO FIGHT A DEMON AND SEPHIRAH.
IF I WERE HIM, I'D HAVE KIDNAPPED HER, YEAH.
WE MUST PROCEED AS PLANNED, THEN.
OUR ONLY CHOICE IS TO TEACH CHIHO THE MAGIC NEEDED TO PROTECT HERSELF.
NOT JUST SO SHE CAN SEND OUT AN S.O.S....
...BUT ALSO TO ENCOURAGE FARFARELLO TO LEAVE AMICABLY WITH ERONE.
OH?

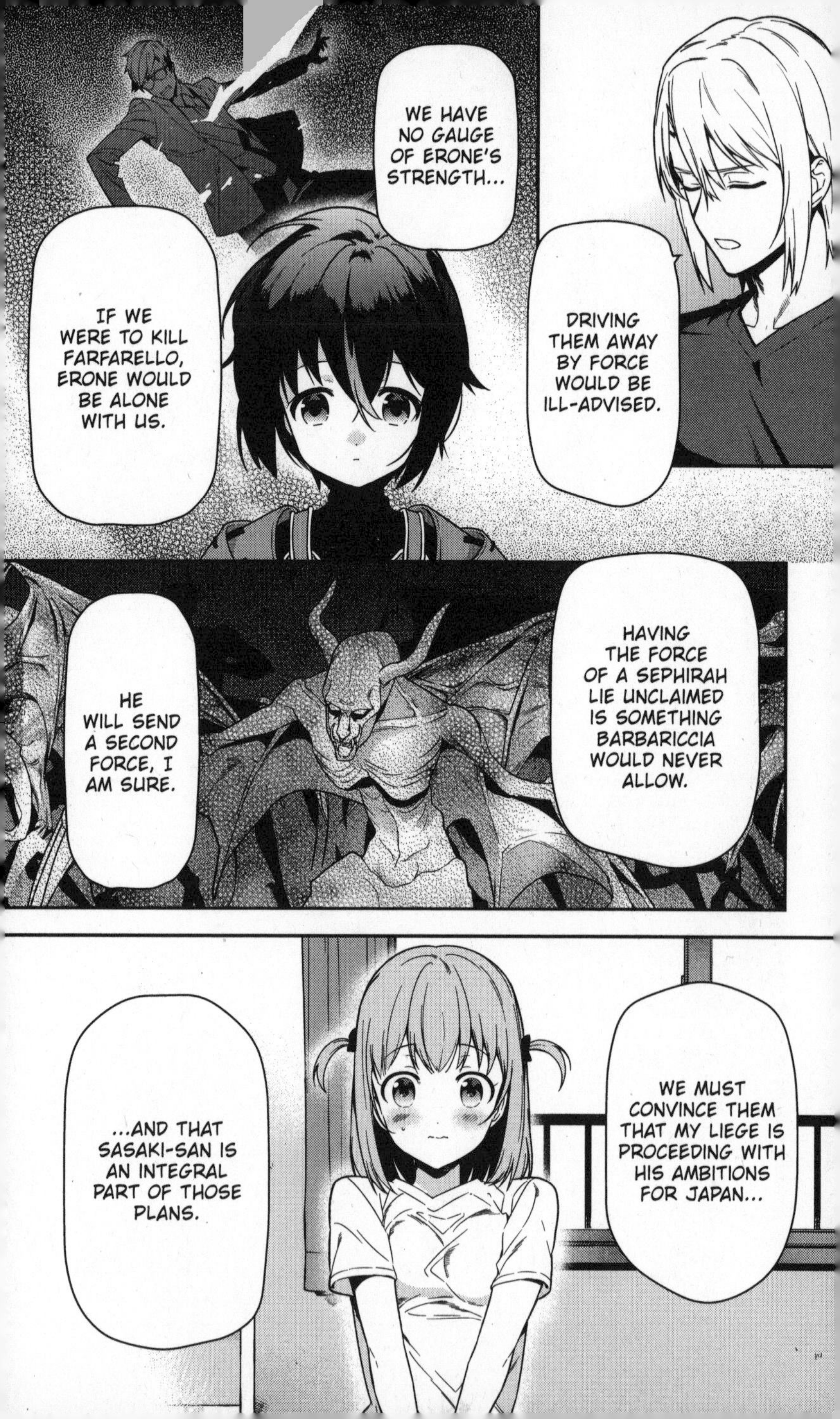
DRIVING THEM AWAY BY FORCE WOULD BE ILL-ADVISED.
WE HAVE NO GAUGE OF ERONE'S STRENGTH...
IF WE WERE TO KILL FARFARELLO, ERONE WOULD BE ALONE WITH US.
HAVING THE FORCE OF A SEPHIRAH LIE UNCLAIMED IS SOMETHING BARBARICCIA WOULD NEVER ALLOW.
HE WILL SEND A SECOND FORCE, I AM SURE.
WE MUST CONVINCE THEM THAT MY LIEGE IS PROCEEDING WITH HIS AMBITIONS FOR JAPAN...
...AND THAT SASAKI-SAN IS AN INTEGRAL PART OF THOSE PLANS.

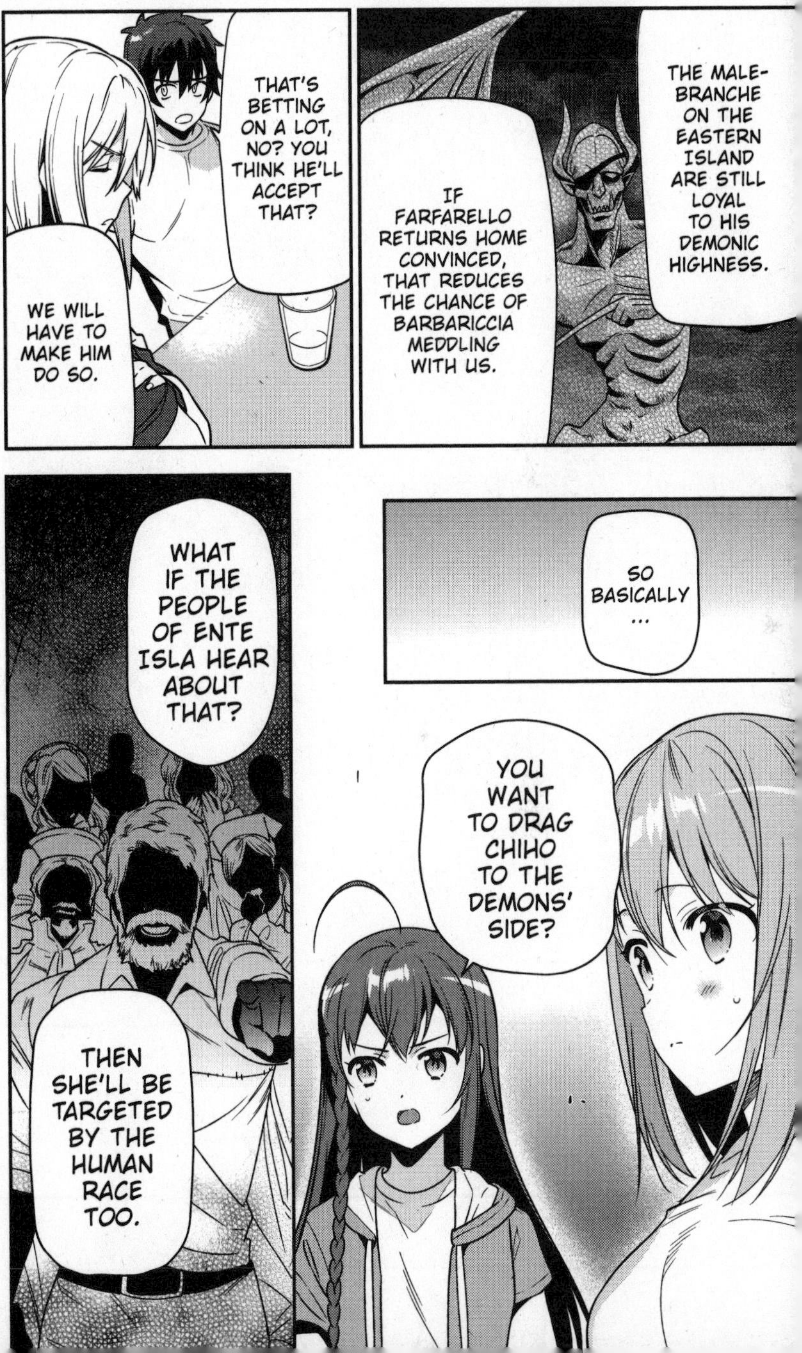
THE MALE-BRANCHE ON THE EASTERN ISLAND ARE STILL LOYAL TO HIS DEMONIC HIGHNESS.
IF FARFARELLO RETURNS HOME CONVINCED, THAT REDUCES THE CHANCE OF BARBARICCIA MEDDLING WITH US.
THAT'S BETTING ON A LOT, NO? YOU THINK HE'LL ACCEPT THAT?
WE WILL HAVE TO MAKE HIM DO SO.
SO BASICALLY...
YOU WANT TO DRAG CHIHO TO THE DEMONS' SIDE?
WHAT IF THE PEOPLE OF ENTE ISLA HEAR ABOUT THAT?
THEN SHE'LL BE TARGETED BY THE HUMAN RACE TOO.

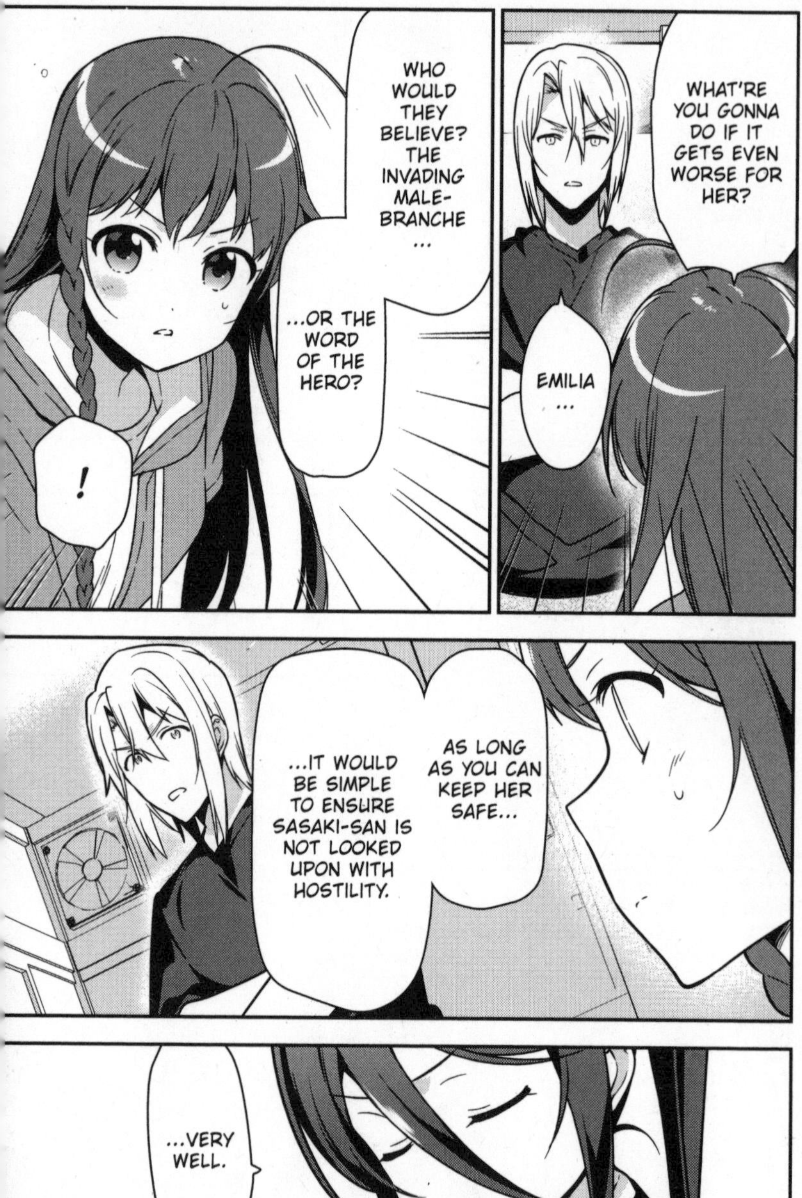
WHAT'RE YOU GONNA DO IF IT GETS EVEN WORSE FOR HER?
EMILIA...
WHO WOULD THEY BELIEVE? THE INVADING MALE-BRANCHE...
...OR THE WORD OF THE HERO?
!
AS LONG AS YOU CAN KEEP HER SAFE...
...IT WOULD BE SIMPLE TO ENSURE SASAKI-SAN IS NOT LOOKED UPON WITH HOSTILITY.
...VERY WELL.

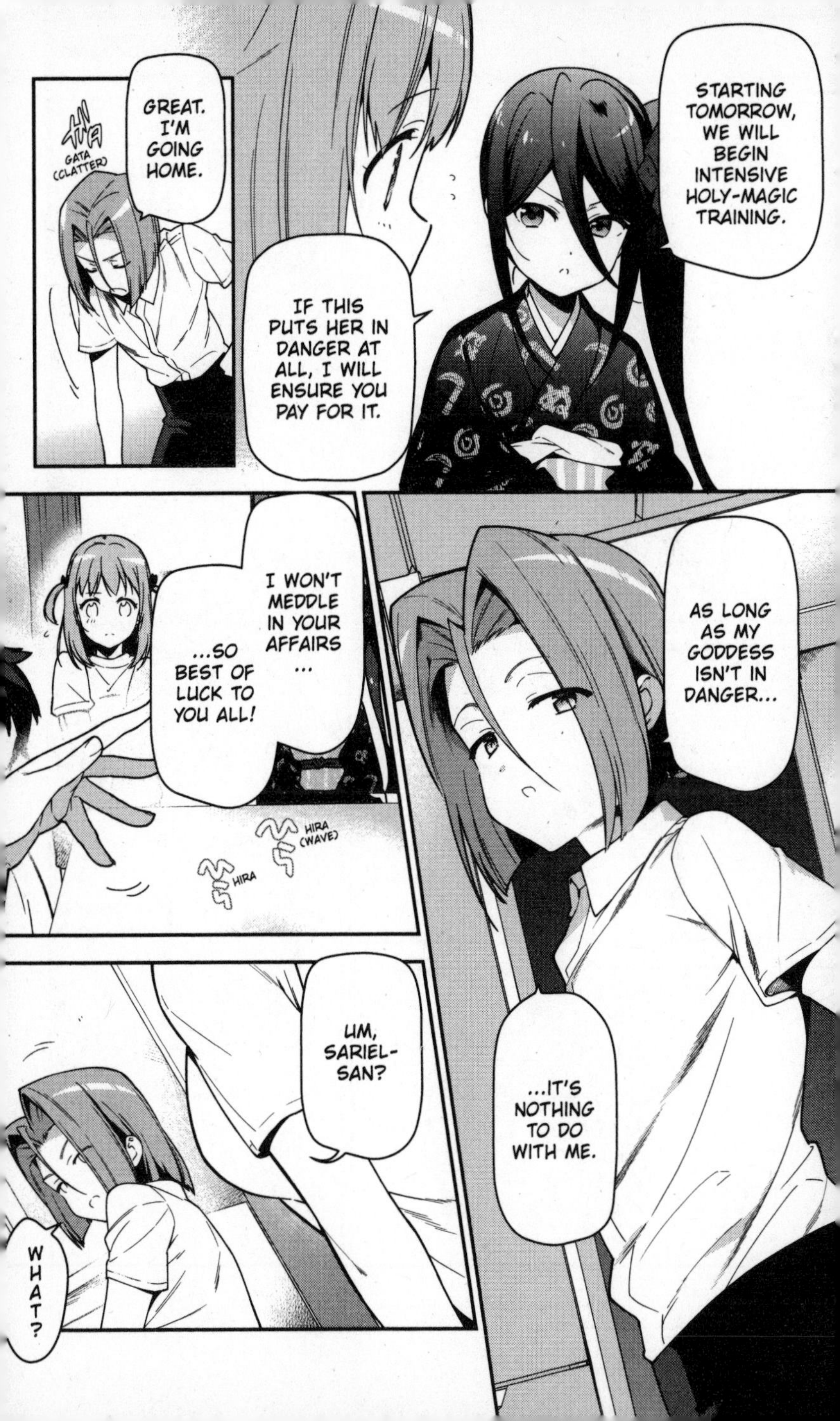
STARTING TOMORROW, WE WILL BEGIN INTENSIVE HOLY-MAGIC TRAINING.
IF THIS PUTS HER IN DANGER AT ALL, I WILL ENSURE YOU PAY FOR IT.
GATA (CLATTER)
GREAT. I'M GOING HOME.
AS LONG AS MY GODDESS ISN'T IN DANGER...
...IT'S NOTHING TO DO WITH ME.
I WON'T MEDDLE IN YOUR AFFAIRS...
...SO BEST OF LUCK TO YOU ALL!
HIRA (WAVE)
HIRA
UM, SARIEL-SAN?
WHAT?

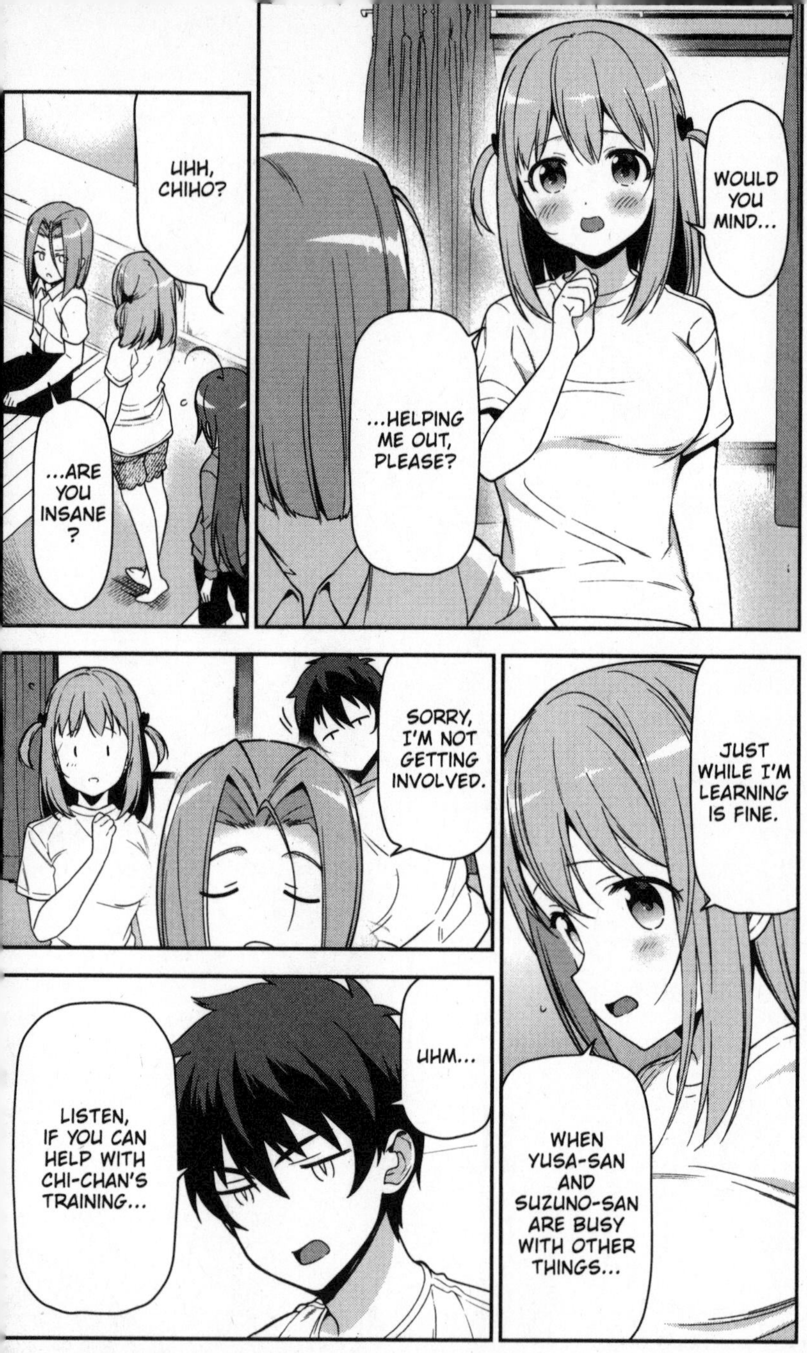
WOULD YOU MIND...
...HELPING ME OUT, PLEASE?
UHH, CHIHO?
...ARE YOU INSANE?
JUST WHILE I'M LEARNING IS FINE.
WHEN YUSA-SAN AND SUZUNO-SAN ARE BUSY WITH OTHER THINGS...
SORRY, I'M NOT GETTING INVOLVED.
UHM...
LISTEN, IF YOU CAN HELP WITH CHI-CHAN'S TRAINING...

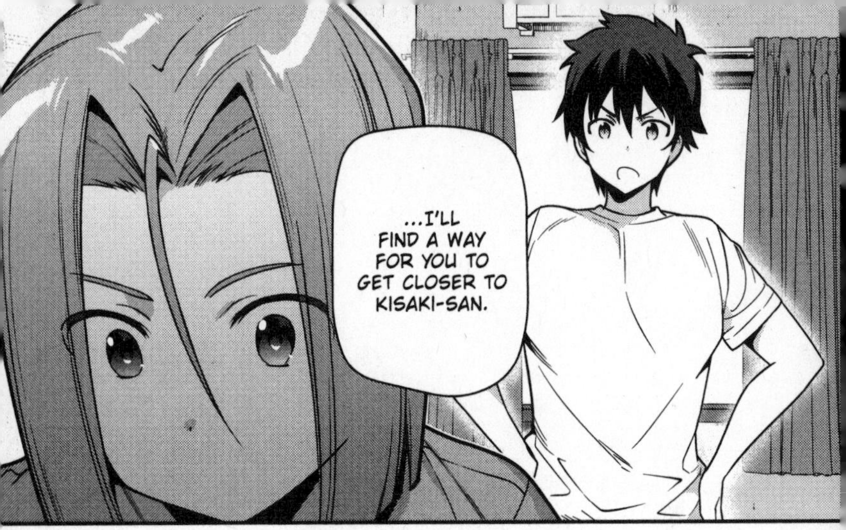
...I'LL FIND A WAY FOR YOU TO GET CLOSER TO KISAKI-SAN.

SIGN: SASAZUKA SPORTS CENTER

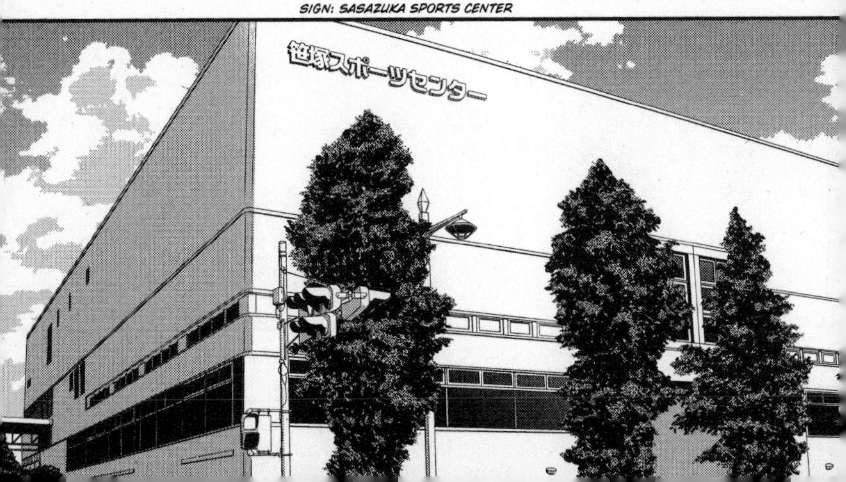
笹塚スポーツセンター

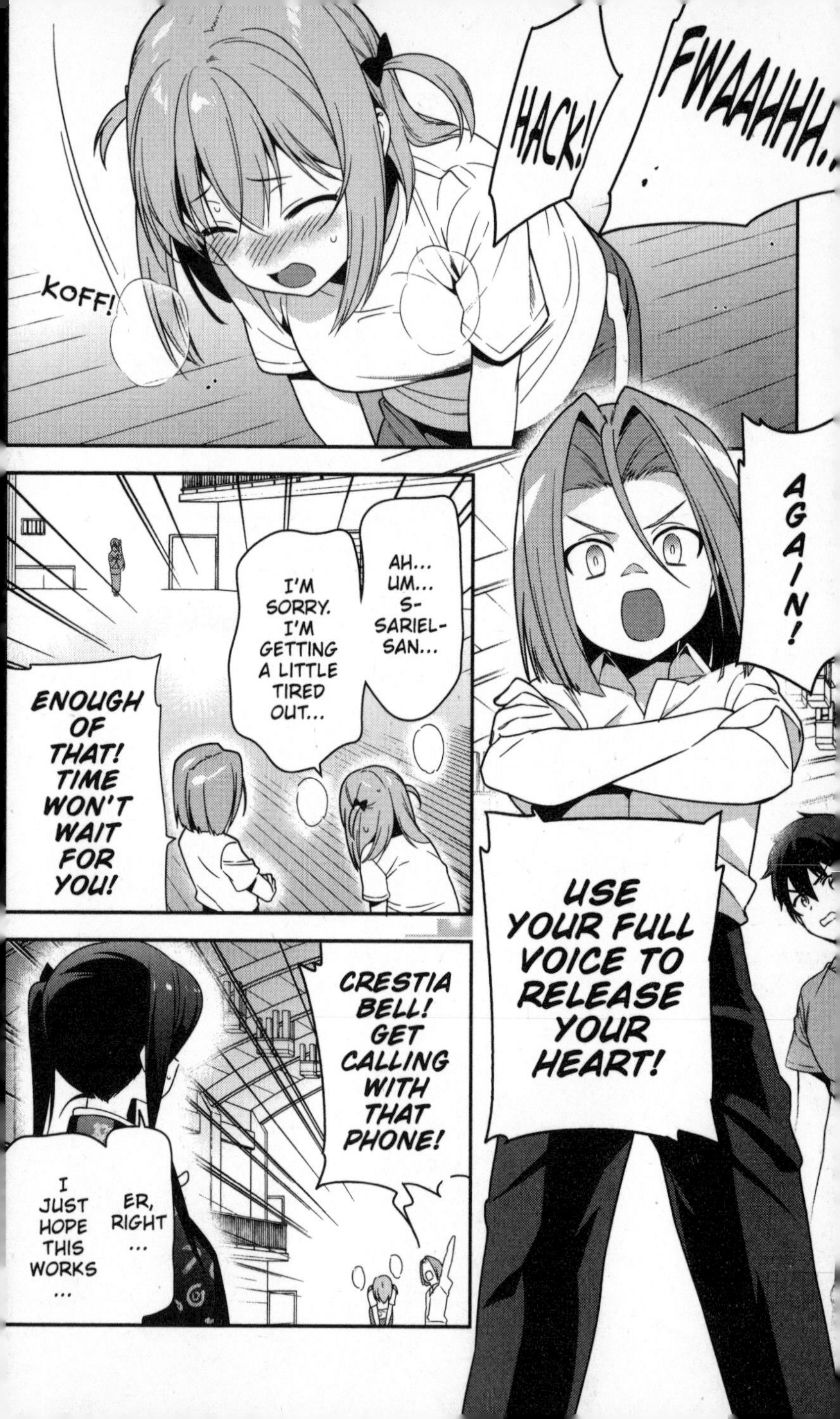
FWAAHHH...
HACK!
KOFF!
AGAIN!
USE YOUR FULL VOICE TO RELEASE YOUR HEART!
AH... UM... S-SARIEL-SAN...
I'M SORRY. I'M GETTING A LITTLE TIRED OUT...
ENOUGH OF THAT! TIME WON'T WAIT FOR YOU!
CRESTIA BELL! GET CALLING WITH THAT PHONE!
ER, RIGHT...
I JUST HOPE THIS WORKS...

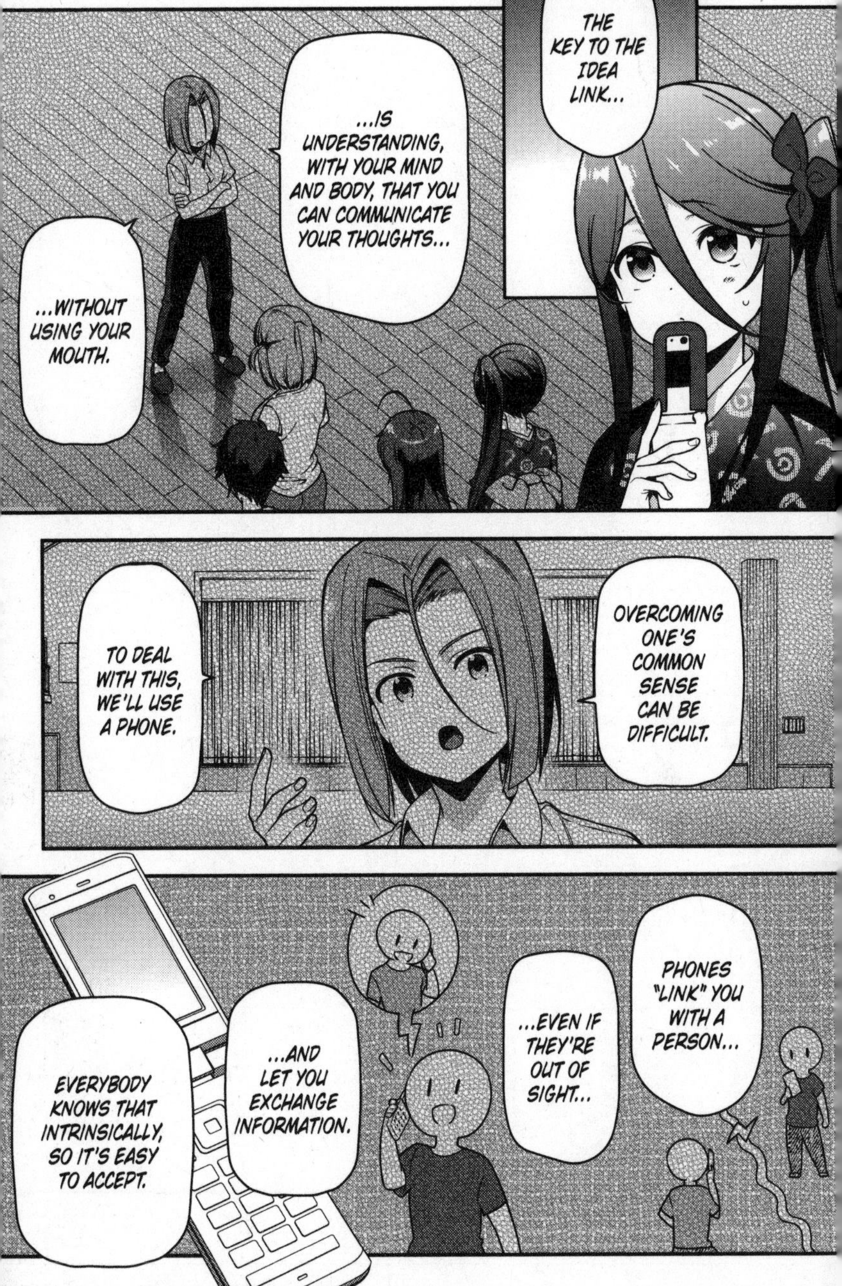
THE KEY TO THE IDEA LINK...
...IS UNDERSTANDING, WITH YOUR MIND AND BODY, THAT YOU CAN COMMUNICATE YOUR THOUGHTS...
...WITHOUT USING YOUR MOUTH.
OVERCOMING ONE'S COMMON SENSE CAN BE DIFFICULT.
TO DEAL WITH THIS, WE'LL USE A PHONE.
PHONES "LINK" YOU WITH A PERSON...
...EVEN IF THEY'RE OUT OF SIGHT...
...AND LET YOU EXCHANGE INFORMATION.
EVERYBODY KNOWS THAT INTRINSICALLY, SO IT'S EASY TO ACCEPT.

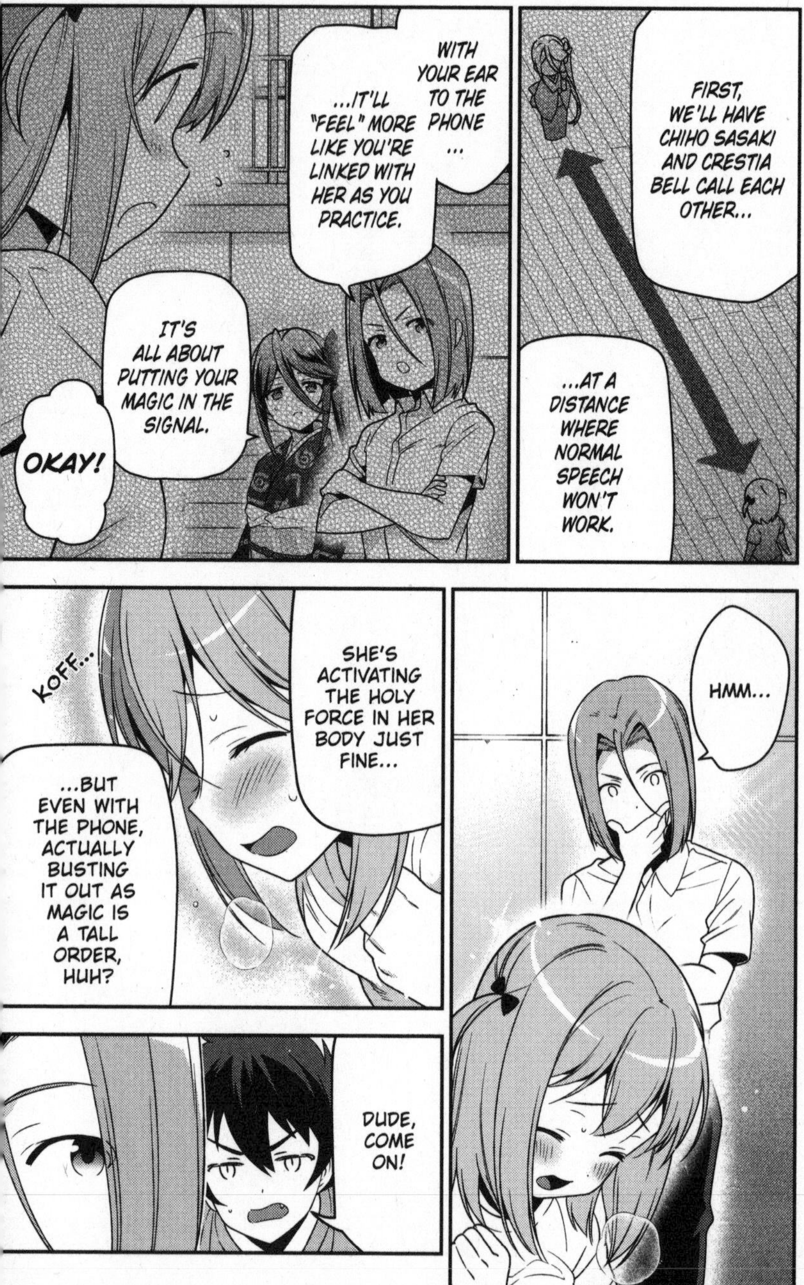
FIRST, WE'LL HAVE CHIHO SASAKI AND CRESTIA BELL CALL EACH OTHER...
...AT A DISTANCE WHERE NORMAL SPEECH WON'T WORK.
WITH YOUR EAR TO THE PHONE...
..IT'LL "FEEL" MORE LIKE YOU'RE LINKED WITH HER AS YOU PRACTICE.
IT'S ALL ABOUT PUTTING YOUR MAGIC IN THE SIGNAL.
OKAY!
HMM...
SHE'S ACTIVATING THE HOLY FORCE IN HER BODY JUST FINE...
...BUT EVEN WITH THE PHONE, ACTUALLY BUSTING IT OUT AS MAGIC IS A TALL ORDER, HUH?
KOFF...
DUDE, COME ON!

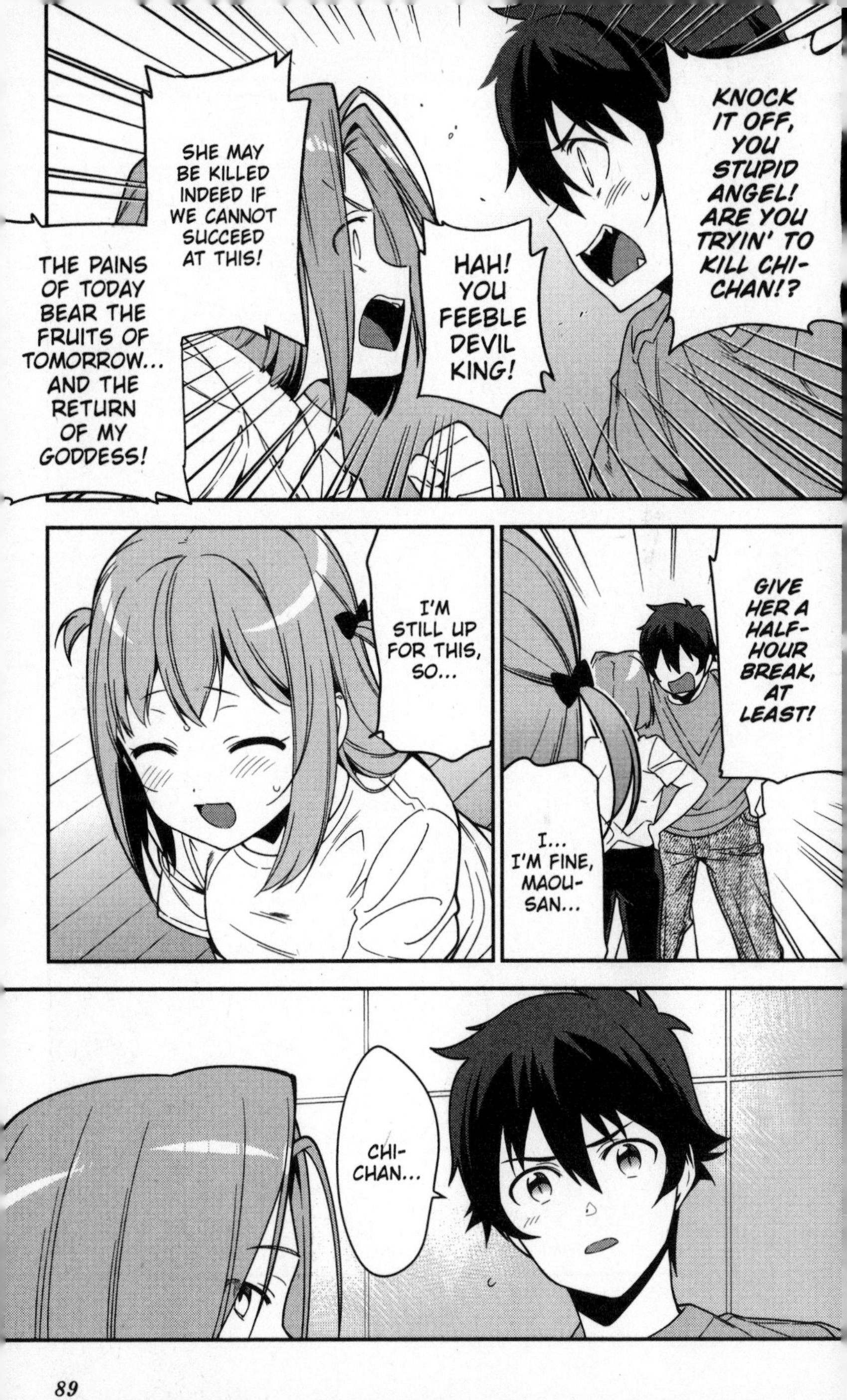
KNOCK IT OFF, YOU STUPID ANGEL! ARE YOU TRYIN' TO KILL CHI-CHAN!?
HAH! YOU FEEBLE DEVIL KING!
SHE MAY BE KILLED INDEED IF WE CANNOT SUCCEED AT THIS!
THE PAINS OF TODAY BEAR THE FRUITS OF TOMORROW... AND THE RETURN OF MY GODDESS!
GIVE HER A HALF-HOUR BREAK, AT LEAST!
I... I'M FINE, MAOU-SAN...
I'M STILL UP FOR THIS, SO...
CHI-CHAN...

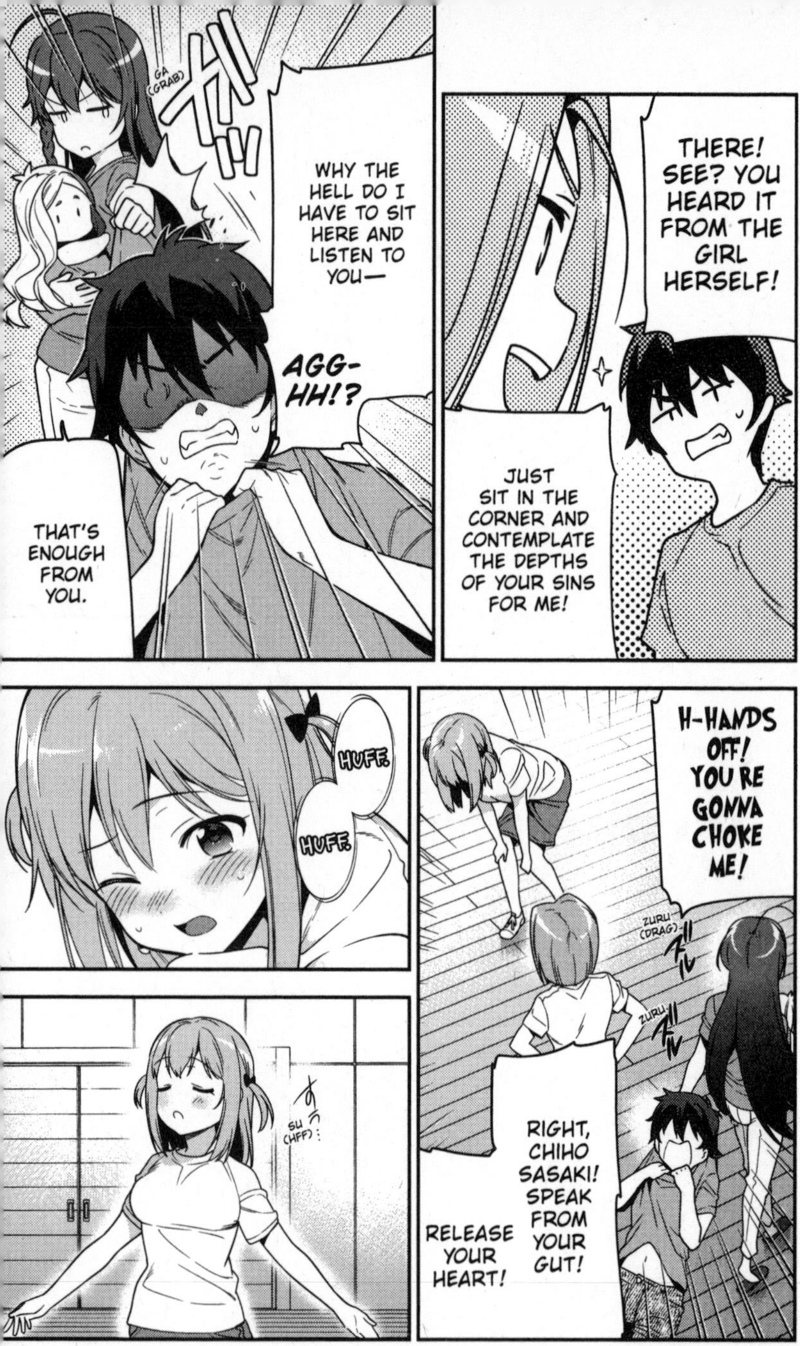

THERE! SEE? YOU HEARD IT FROM THE GIRL HERSELF!
JUST SIT IN THE CORNER AND CONTEMPLATE THE DEPTHS OF YOUR SINS FOR ME!
GA (GRAB)
WHY THE HELL DO I HAVE TO SIT HERE AND LISTEN TO YOU—
AGG-HH!?
THAT'S ENOUGH FROM YOU.
H-HANDS OFF! YOU'RE GONNA CHOKE ME!
ZURU (DRAG)
ZURU
RIGHT, CHIHO SASAKI! SPEAK FROM YOUR GUT!
RELEASE YOUR HEART!
HUFF.
HUFF.
SU (HFF)

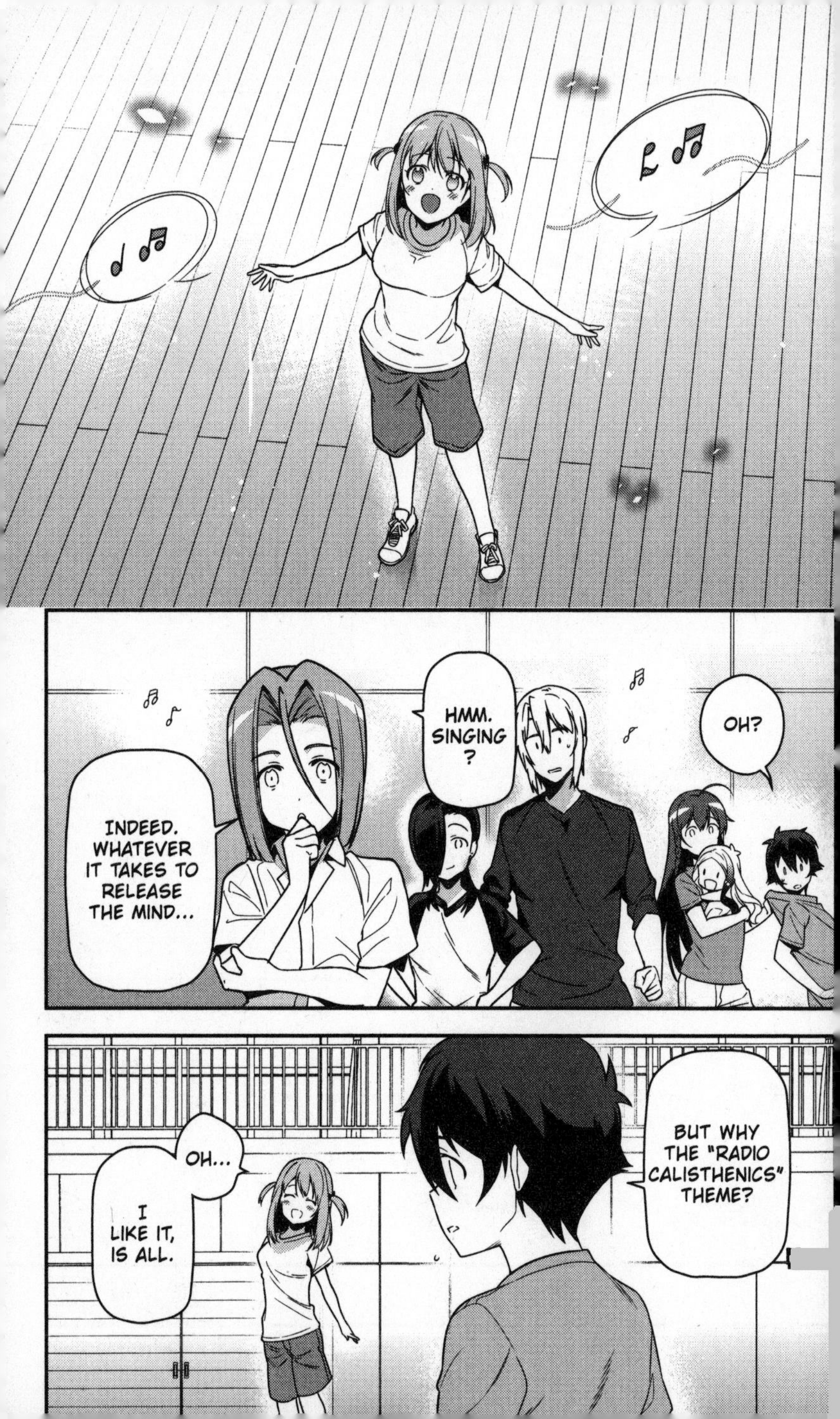
OH?
HMM. SINGING?
INDEED. WHATEVER IT TAKES TO RELEASE THE MIND...
BUT WHY THE "RADIO CALISTHENICS" THEME?
OH...
I LIKE IT, IS ALL.

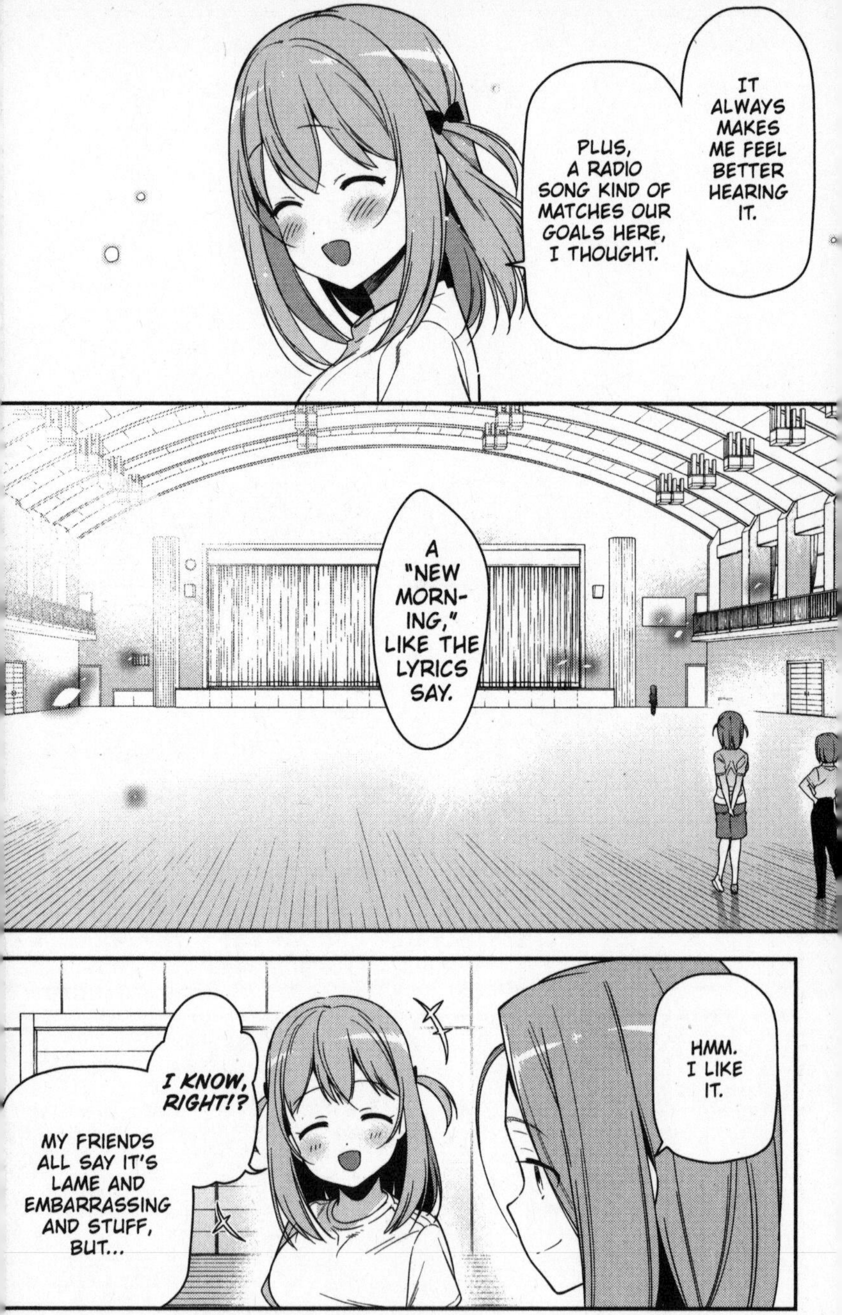
IT ALWAYS MAKES ME FEEL BETTER HEARING IT.
PLUS, A RADIO SONG KIND OF MATCHES OUR GOALS HERE, I THOUGHT.
A "NEW MORNING," LIKE THE LYRICS SAY.
HMM. I LIKE IT.
I KNOW, RIGHT!?
MY FRIENDS ALL SAY IT'S LAME AND EMBARRASSING AND STUFF, BUT...

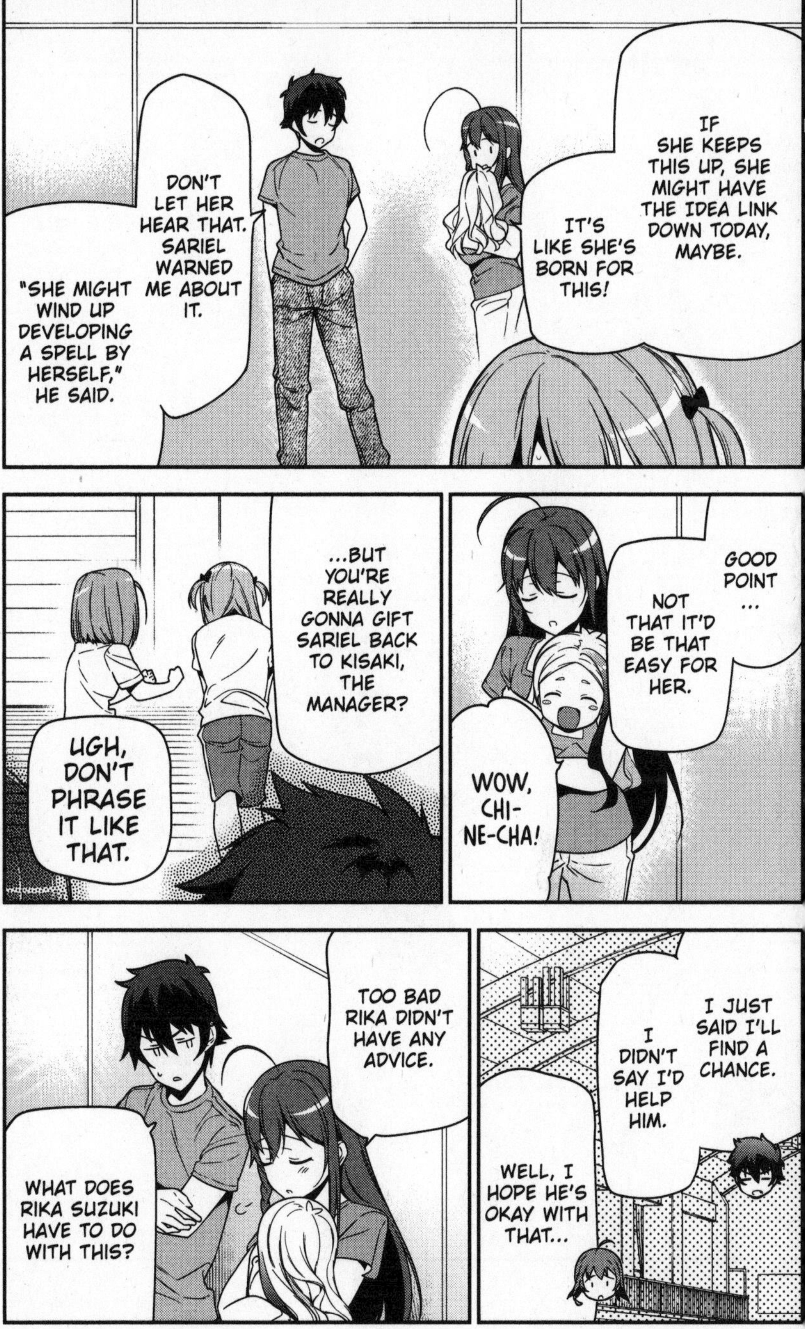
IF SHE KEEPS THIS UP, SHE MIGHT HAVE THE IDEA LINK DOWN TODAY, MAYBE.
IT'S LIKE SHE'S BORN FOR THIS!
DON'T LET HER HEAR THAT. SARIEL WARNED ME ABOUT IT.
"SHE MIGHT WIND UP DEVELOPING A SPELL BY HERSELF," HE SAID.
GOOD POINT ...
NOT THAT IT'D BE THAT EASY FOR HER.
WOW, CHI-NE-CHA!
...BUT YOU'RE REALLY GONNA GIFT SARIEL BACK TO KISAKI, THE MANAGER?
UGH, DON'T PHRASE IT LIKE THAT.
I JUST SAID I'LL FIND A CHANCE.
I DIDN'T SAY I'D HELP HIM.
WELL, I HOPE HE'S OKAY WITH THAT...
TOO BAD RIKA DIDN'T HAVE ANY ADVICE.
WHAT DOES RIKA SUZUKI HAVE TO DO WITH THIS?

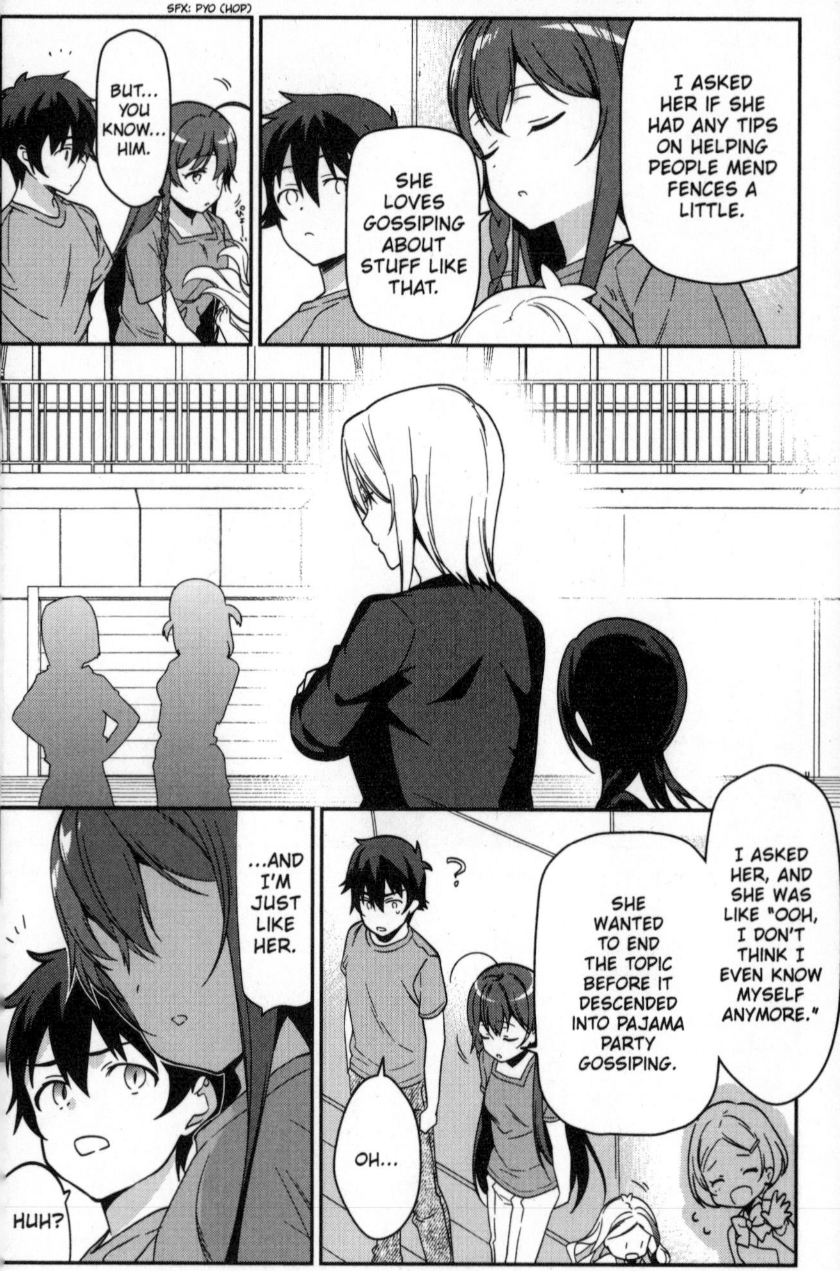
I ASKED HER IF SHE HAD ANY TIPS ON HELPING PEOPLE MEND FENCES A LITTLE.
SHE LOVES GOSSIPING ABOUT STUFF LIKE THAT.
BUT... YOU KNOW... HIM.
SFX: PYO (HOP)
I ASKED HER, AND SHE WAS LIKE "OOH, I DON'T THINK I EVEN KNOW MYSELF ANYMORE."
SHE WANTED TO END THE TOPIC BEFORE IT DESCENDED INTO PAJAMA PARTY GOSSIPING.
OH...
...AND I'M JUST LIKE HER.
HUH?

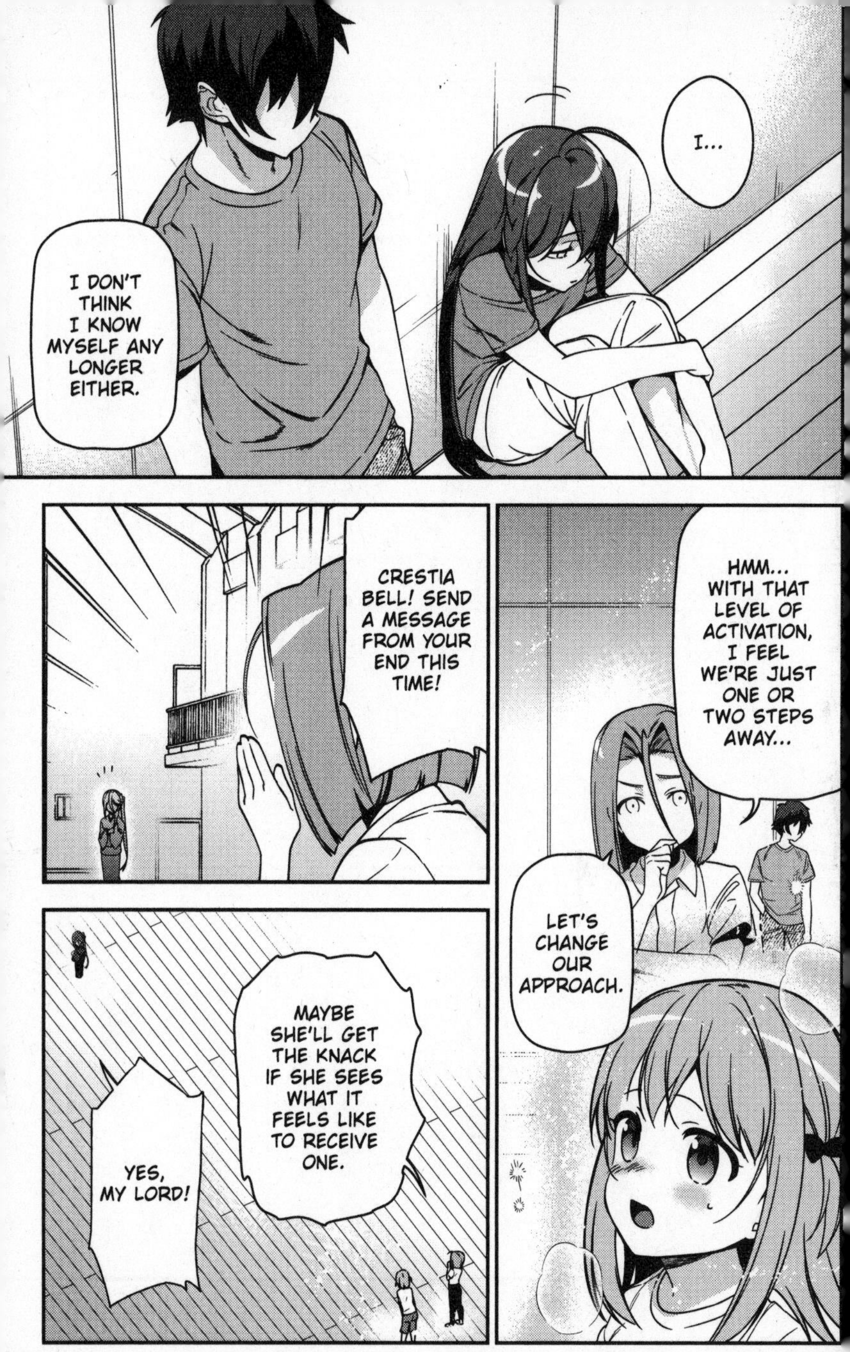
I...
I DON'T THINK I KNOW MYSELF ANY LONGER EITHER.
HMM... WITH THAT LEVEL OF ACTIVATION, I FEEL WE'RE JUST ONE OR TWO STEPS AWAY...
LET'S CHANGE OUR APPROACH.
CRESTIA BELL! SEND A MESSAGE FROM YOUR END THIS TIME!
MAYBE SHE'LL GET THE KNACK IF SHE SEES WHAT IT FEELS LIKE TO RECEIVE ONE.
YES, MY LORD!

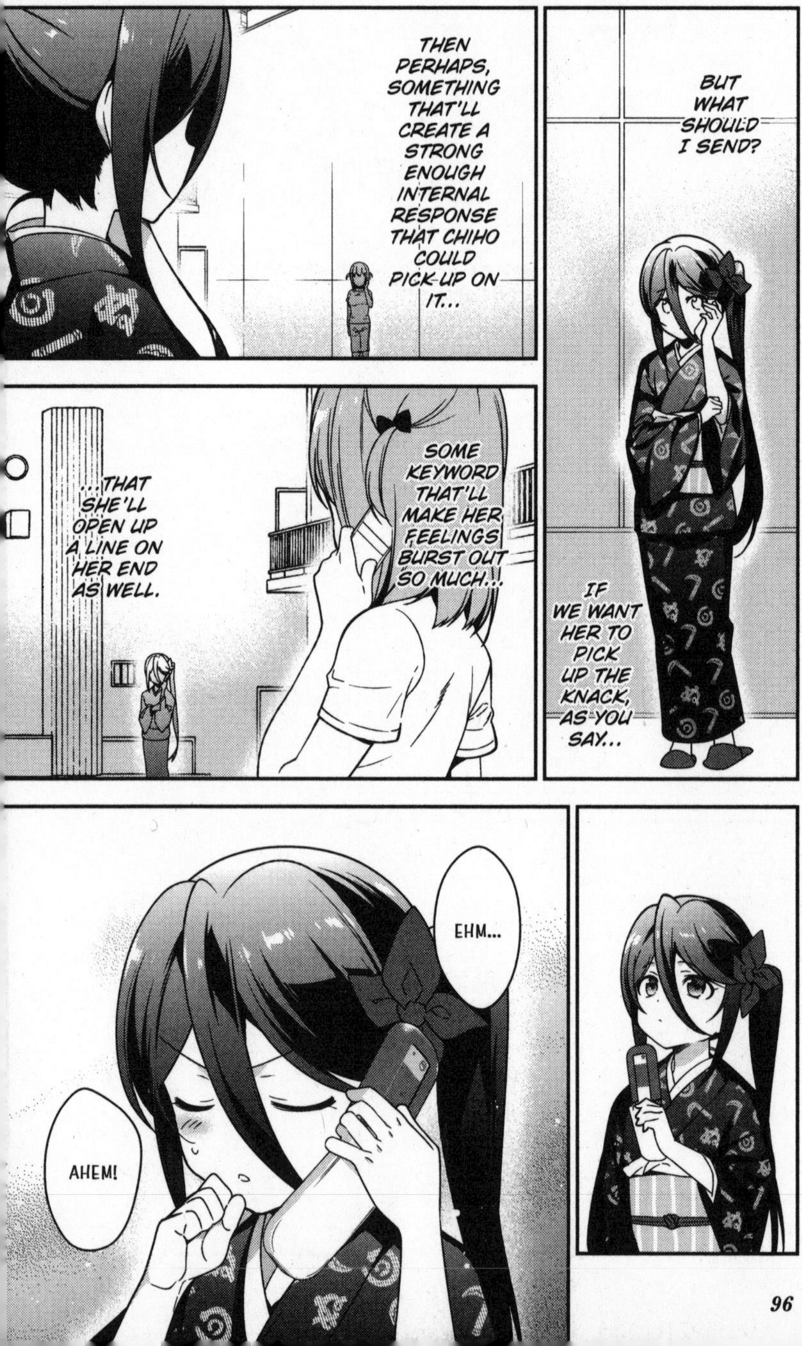
BUT WHAT SHOULD I SEND?
IF WE WANT HER TO PICK UP THE KNACK, AS YOU SAY...
THEN PERHAPS, SOMETHING THAT'LL CREATE A STRONG ENOUGH INTERNAL RESPONSE THAT CHIHO COULD PICK UP ON IT...
SOME KEYWORD THAT'LL MAKE HER FEELINGS BURST OUT SO MUCH...
...THAT SHE'LL OPEN UP A LINE ON HER END AS WELL.
EHM...
AHEM!

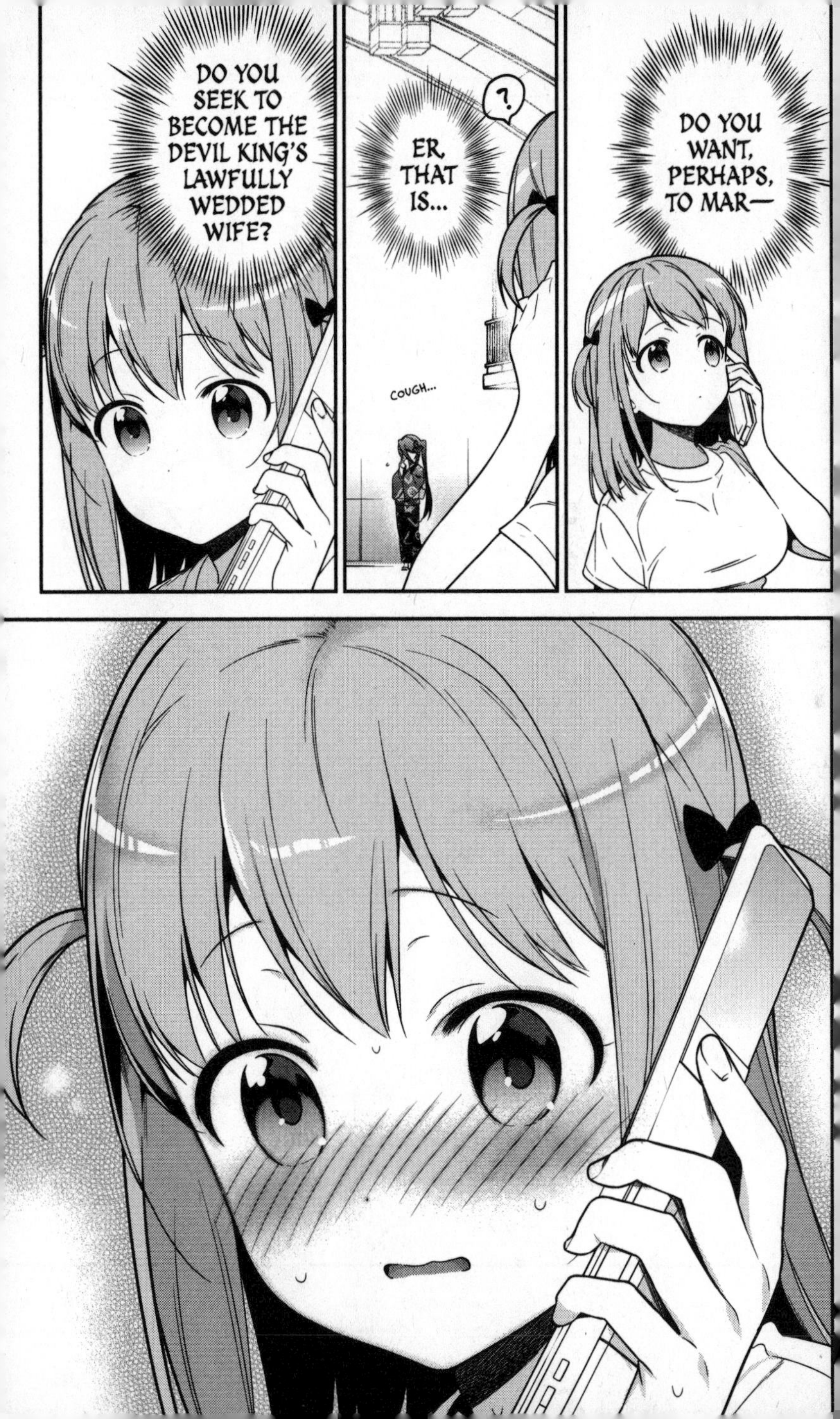
DO YOU WANT, PERHAPS, TO MAR—
?
ER, THAT IS...
COUGH...
DO YOU SEEK TO BECOME THE DEVIL KING'S LAWFULLY WEDDED WIFE?

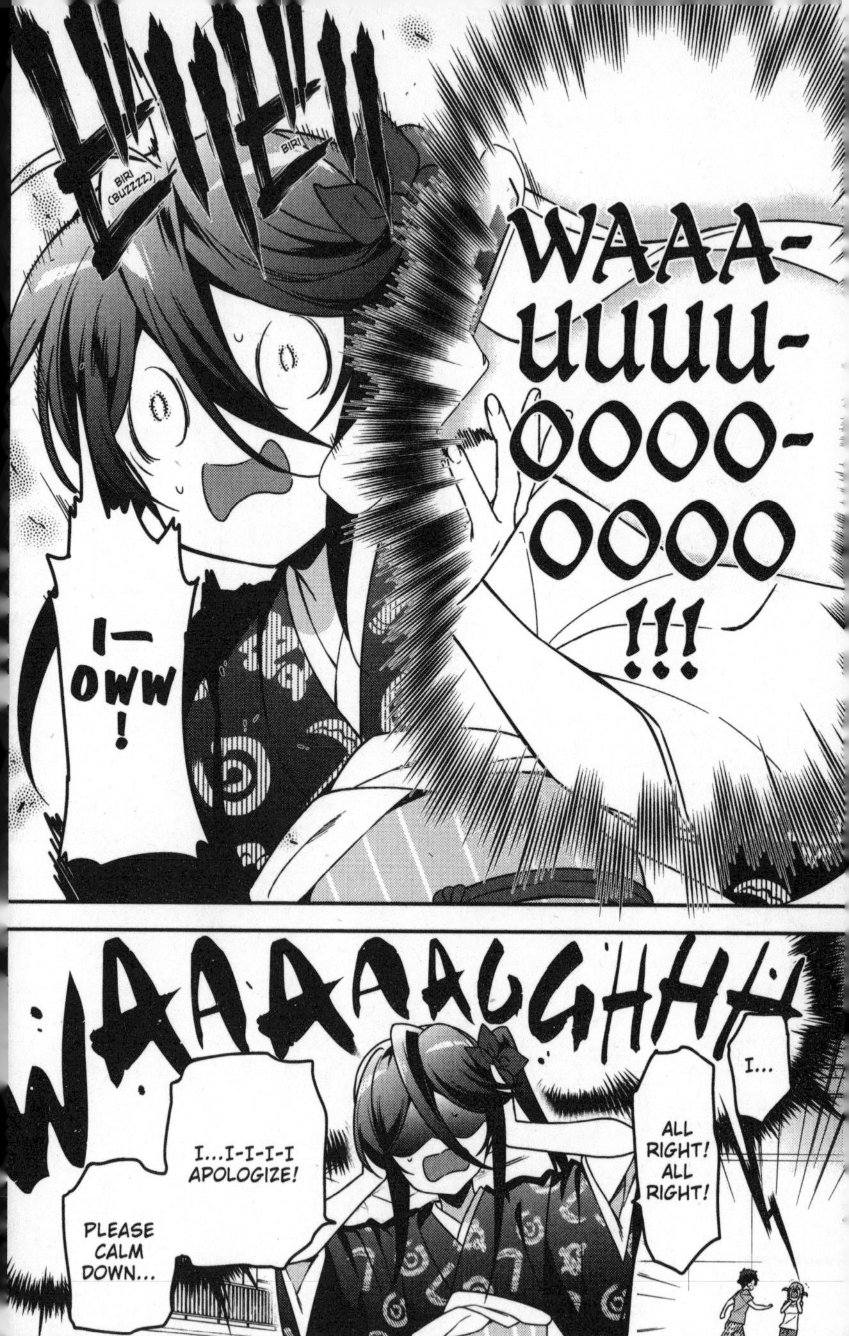
WAAA-UUUU-OOOO-OOOO!!!
BIRI
BIRI (BUZZZZ)
I— OWW!
WAAAAAGHHH
I...
ALL RIGHT! ALL RIGHT!
I...I-I-I-I APOLOGIZE!
PLEASE CALM DOWN...

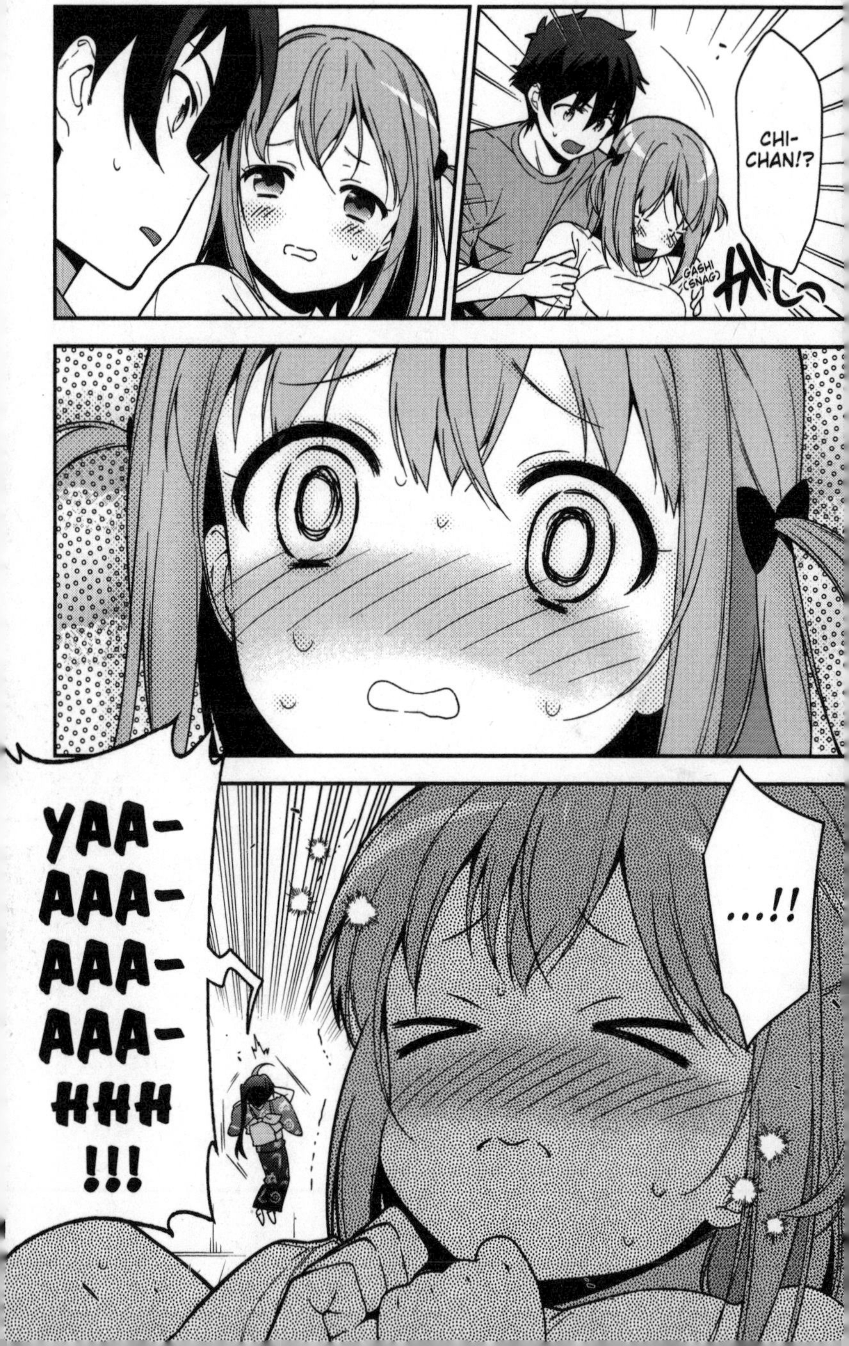
CHI-CHAN!?
GASHI (SNAG)
...!!
YAA-AAA-AAA-AAA-HHH!!!

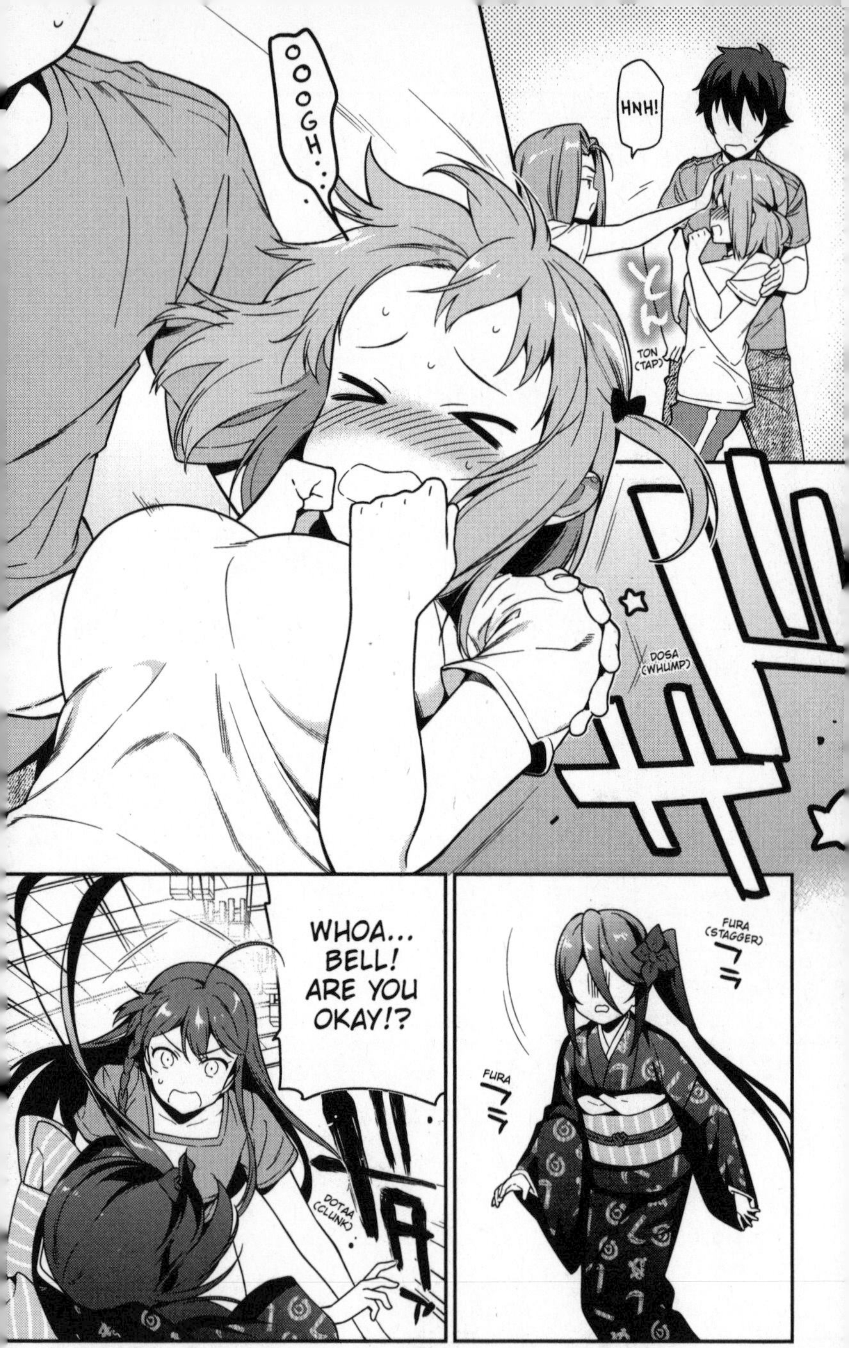
HNH!
とん
TON (TAP)
OOOGH...
DOSA (WHUMP)
FURA (STAGGER)
FURA
WHOA... BELL! ARE YOU OKAY!?
DOTAA (CLUNK)

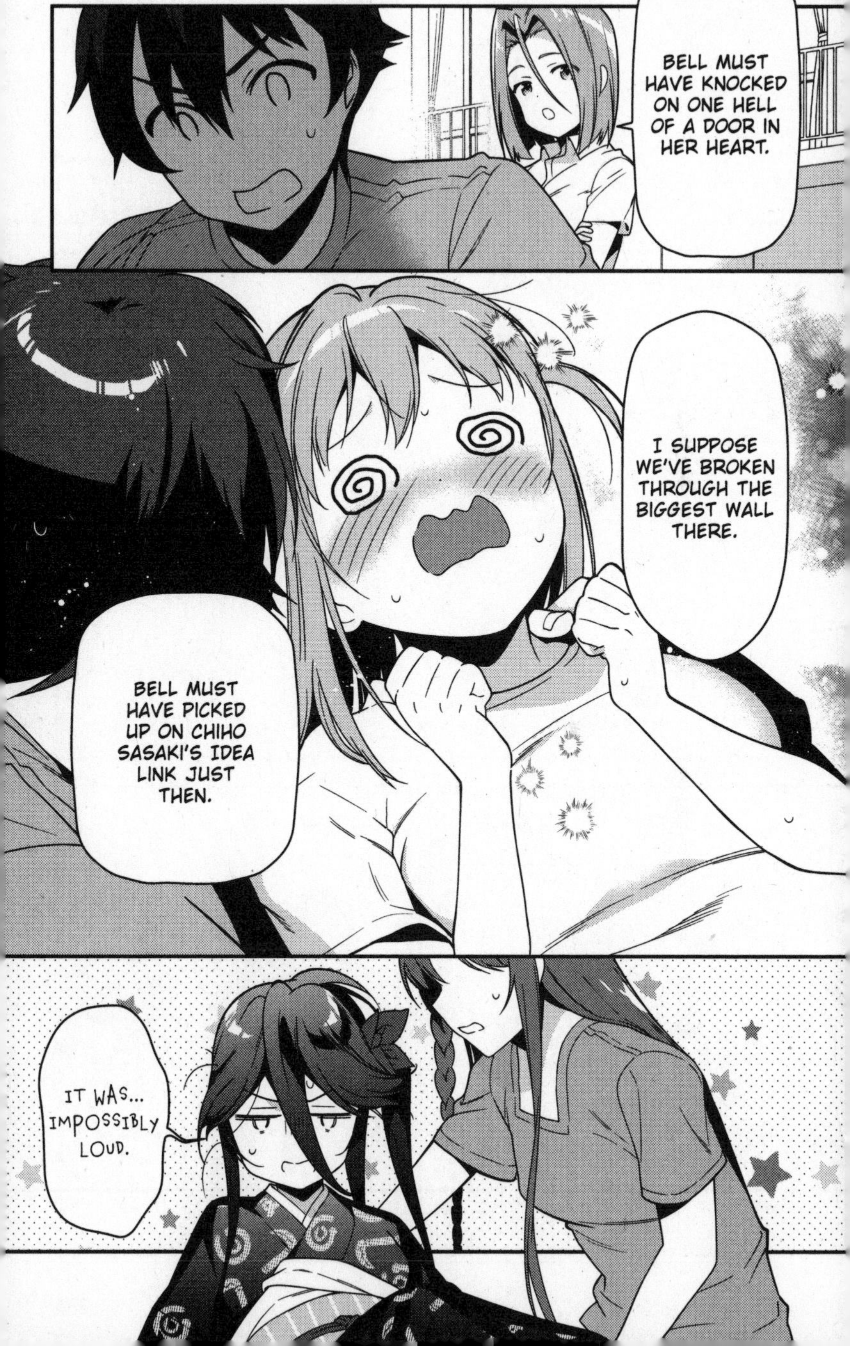
BELL MUST HAVE KNOCKED ON ONE HELL OF A DOOR IN HER HEART.
I SUPPOSE WE'VE BROKEN THROUGH THE BIGGEST WALL THERE.
BELL MUST HAVE PICKED UP ON CHIHO SASAKI'S IDEA LINK JUST THEN.
IT WAS... IMPOSSIBLY LOUD.

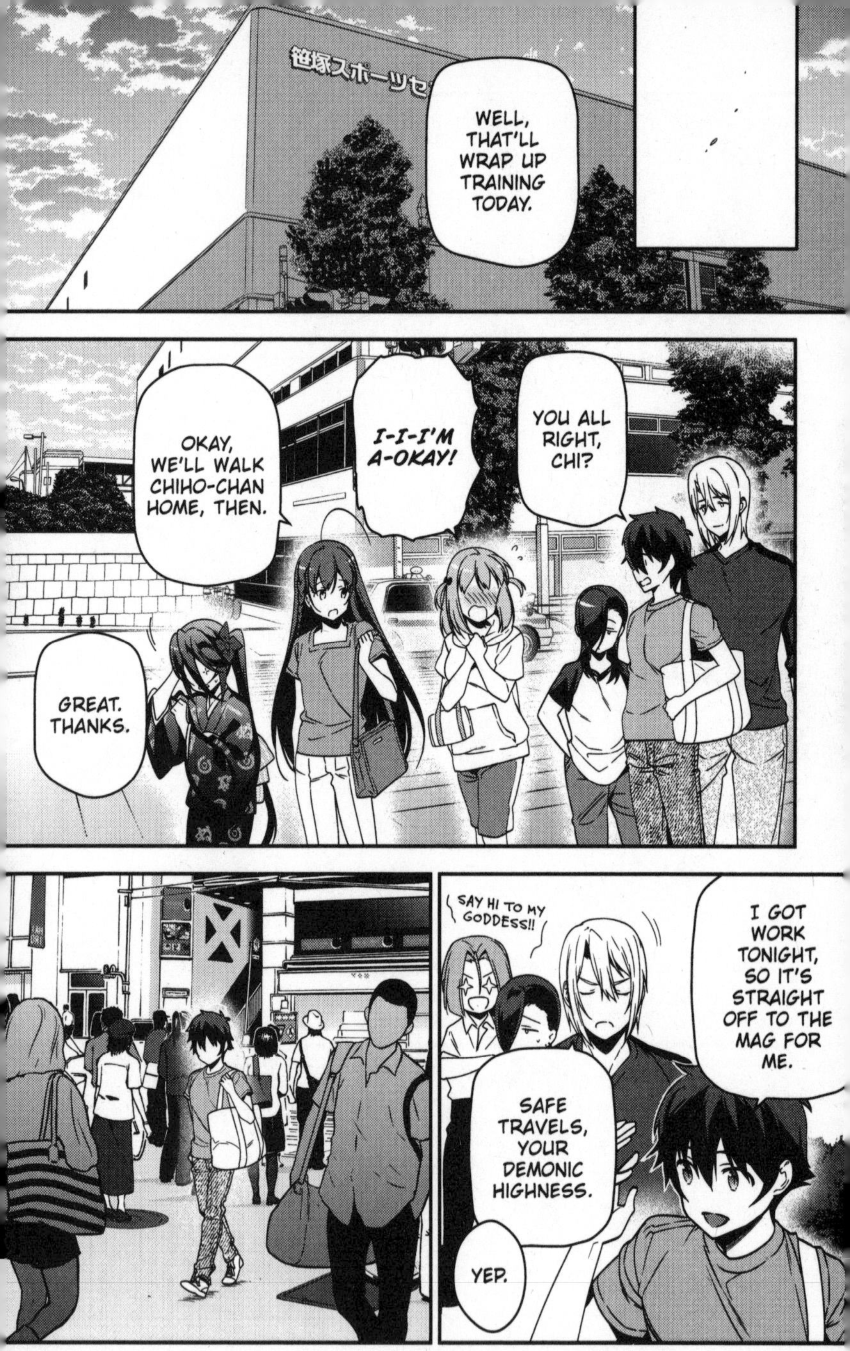
笹塚スポーツセ
WELL, THAT'LL WRAP UP TRAINING TODAY.
YOU ALL RIGHT, CHI?
I-I-I'M A-OKAY!
OKAY, WE'LL WALK CHIHO-CHAN HOME, THEN.
GREAT. THANKS.
I GOT WORK TONIGHT, SO IT'S STRAIGHT OFF TO THE MAG FOR ME.
SAY HI TO MY GODDESS!!
SAFE TRAVELS, YOUR DEMONIC HIGHNESS.
YEP.

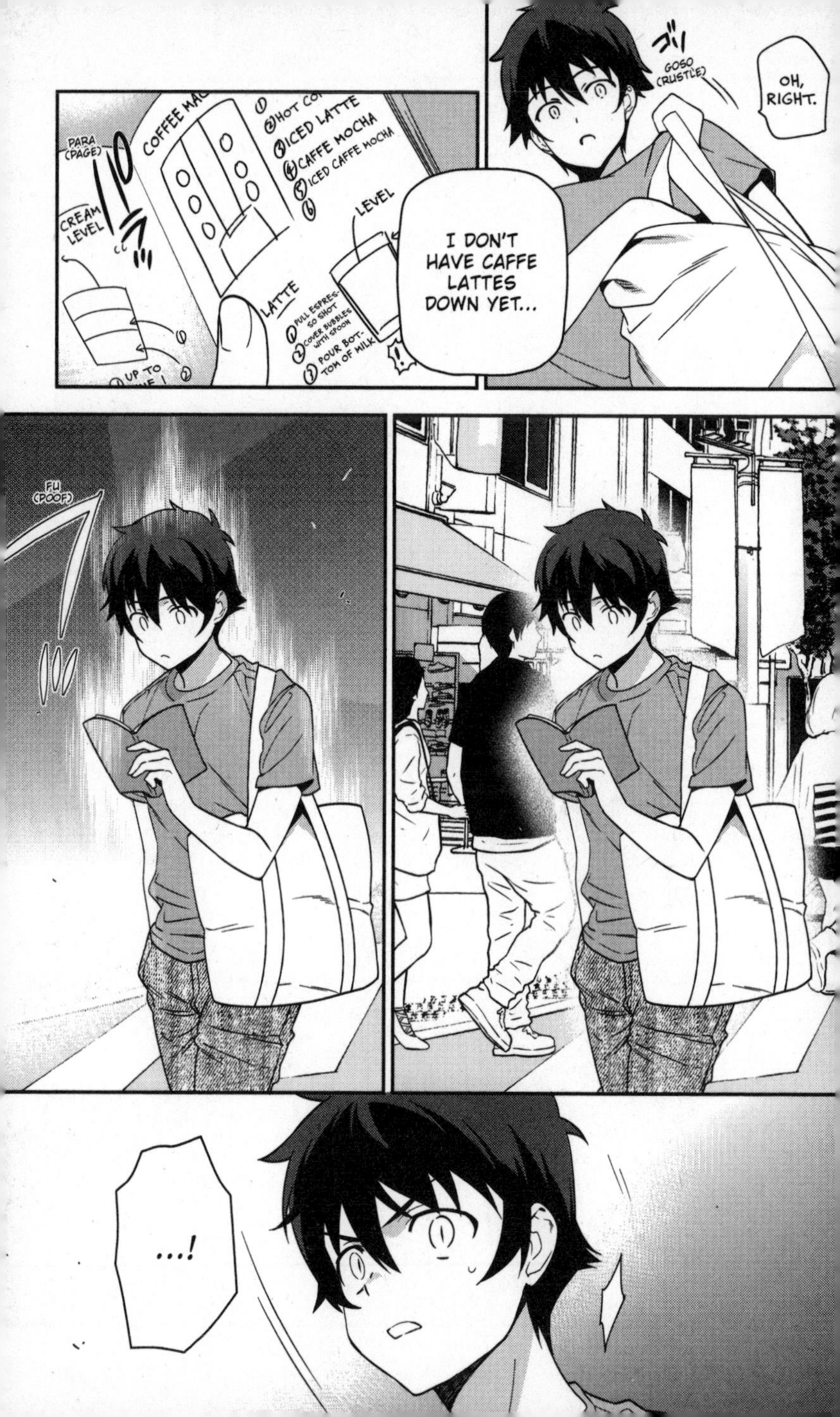
GOSO (RUSTLE)
OH, RIGHT.
I DON'T HAVE CAFFE LATTES DOWN YET...
COFFEE MA
1
2 HOT CO
3 ICED LATTE
4 CAFFE MOCHA
5 ICED CAFFE MOCHA
6
LEVEL
PARA (PAGE)
CREAM LEVEL
LATTE
1 PULL ESPRESSO SHOT
2 COVER BUBBLES WITH SPOON
3 POUR BOTTOM OF MILK
1 UP TO
FU (POOF)
...!

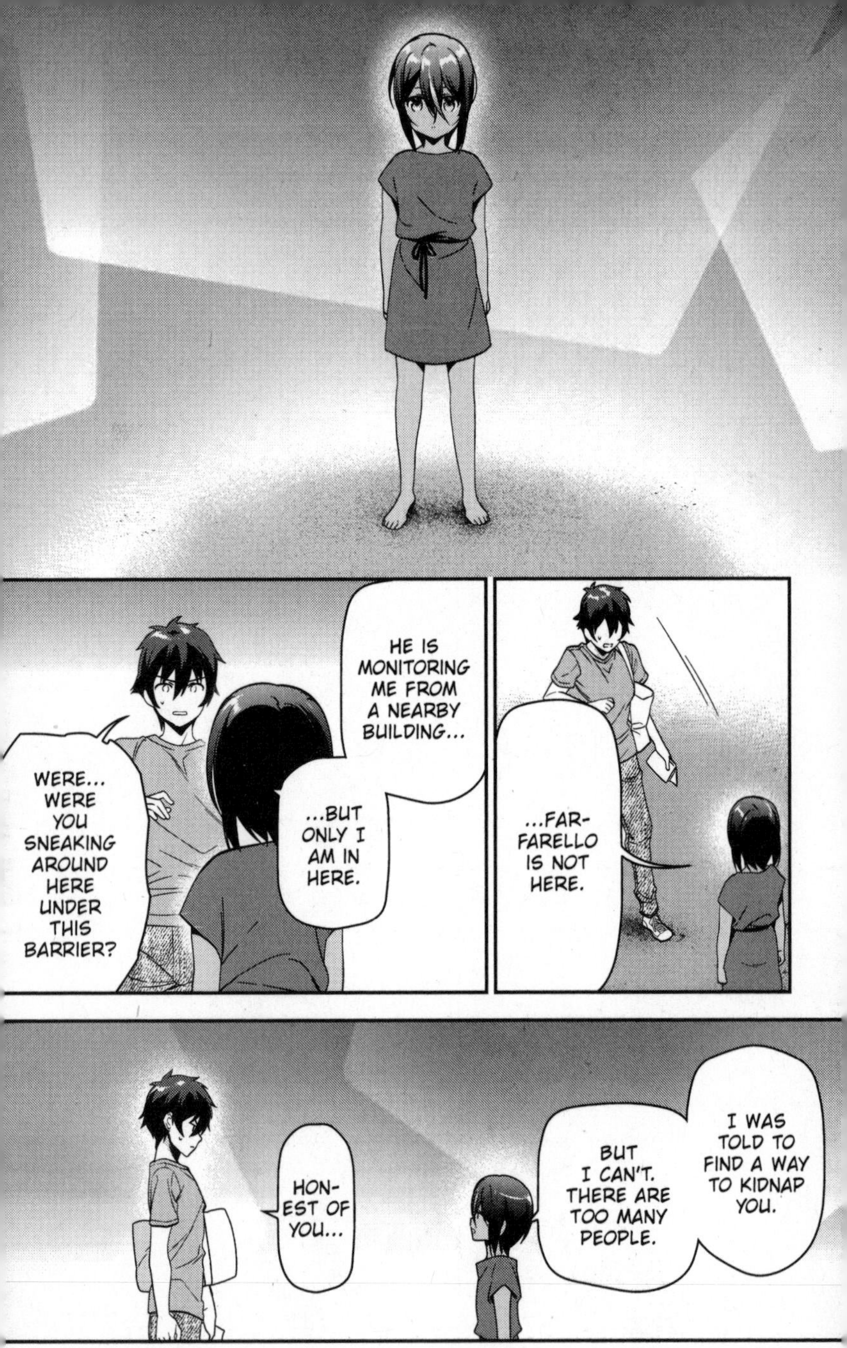
...FAR-FARELLO IS NOT HERE.
HE IS MONITORING ME FROM A NEARBY BUILDING...
...BUT ONLY I AM IN HERE.
WERE... WERE YOU SNEAKING AROUND HERE UNDER THIS BARRIER?
I WAS TOLD TO FIND A WAY TO KIDNAP YOU.
BUT I CAN'T. THERE ARE TOO MANY PEOPLE.
HON-EST OF YOU...

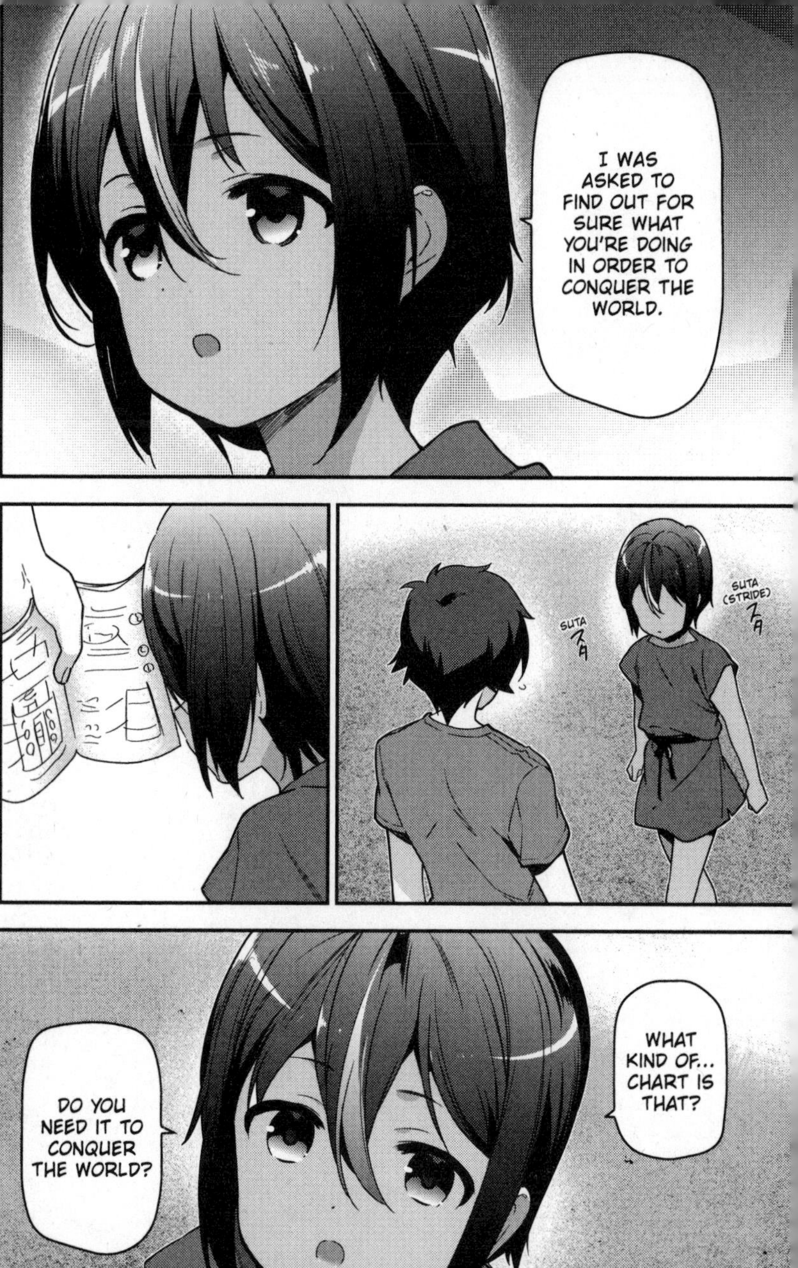
I WAS ASKED TO FIND OUT FOR SURE WHAT YOU'RE DOING IN ORDER TO CONQUER THE WORLD.
SUTA (STRIDE)
SUTA
WHAT KIND OF... CHART IS THAT?
DO YOU NEED IT TO CONQUER THE WORLD?

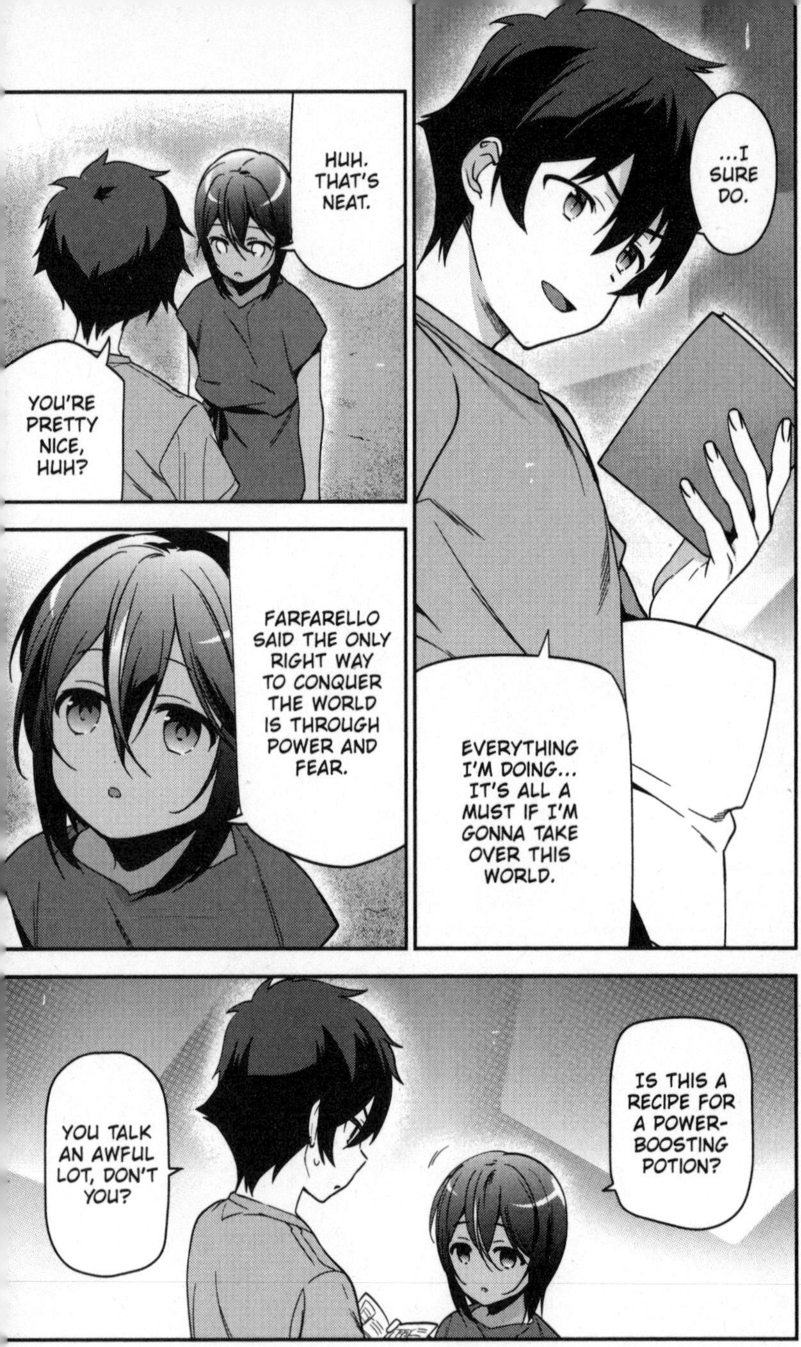
...I SURE DO.
EVERYTHING I'M DOING... IT'S ALL A MUST IF I'M GONNA TAKE OVER THIS WORLD.
HUH. THAT'S NEAT.
YOU'RE PRETTY NICE, HUH?
FARFARELLO SAID THE ONLY RIGHT WAY TO CONQUER THE WORLD IS THROUGH POWER AND FEAR.
IS THIS A RECIPE FOR A POWER-BOOSTING POTION?
YOU TALK AN AWFUL LOT, DON'T YOU?

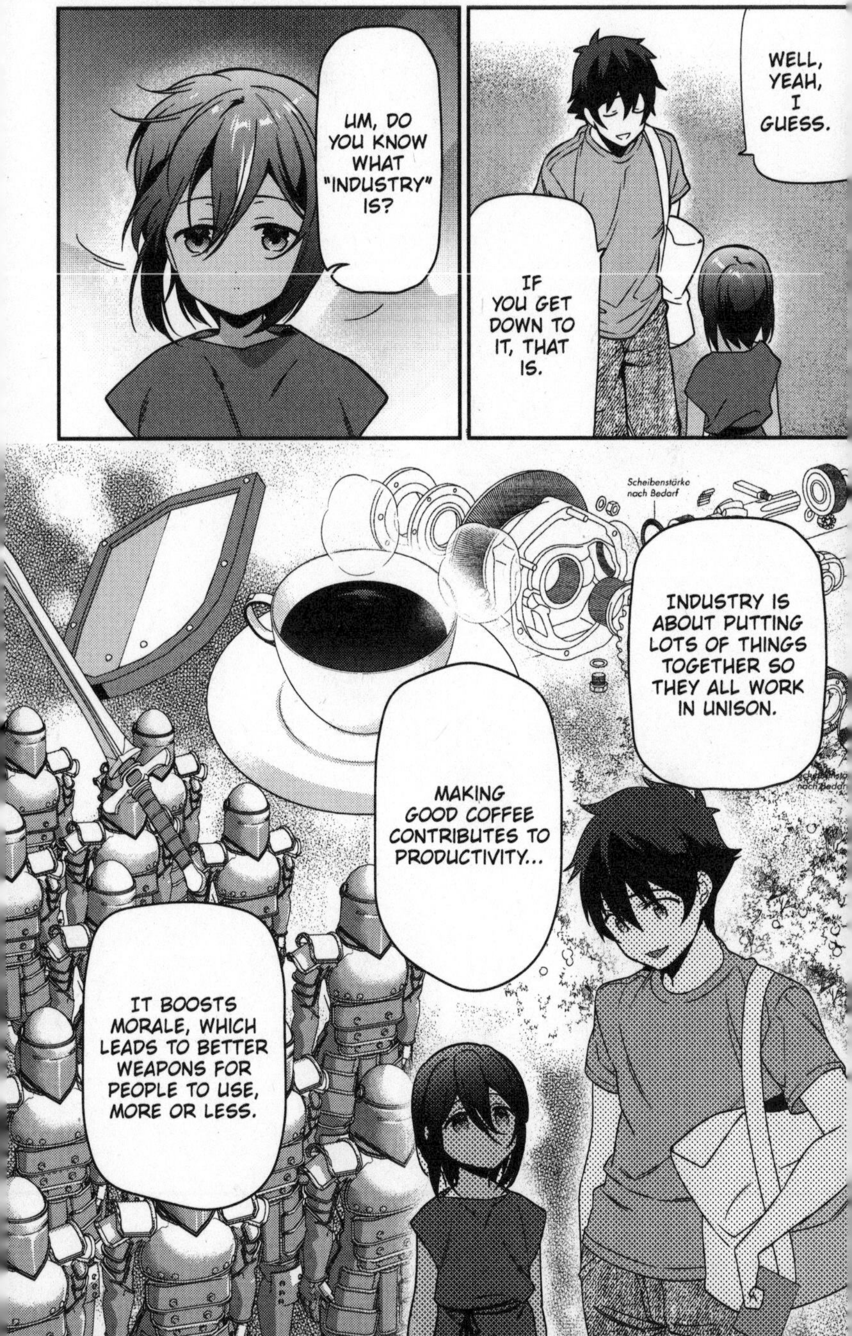
WELL, YEAH, I GUESS.
IF YOU GET DOWN TO IT, THAT IS.
UM, DO YOU KNOW WHAT "INDUSTRY" IS?
Scheibenstärke nach Bedarf
INDUSTRY IS ABOUT PUTTING LOTS OF THINGS TOGETHER SO THEY ALL WORK IN UNISON.
MAKING GOOD COFFEE CONTRIBUTES TO PRODUCTIVITY...
IT BOOSTS MORALE, WHICH LEADS TO BETTER WEAPONS FOR PEOPLE TO USE, MORE OR LESS.

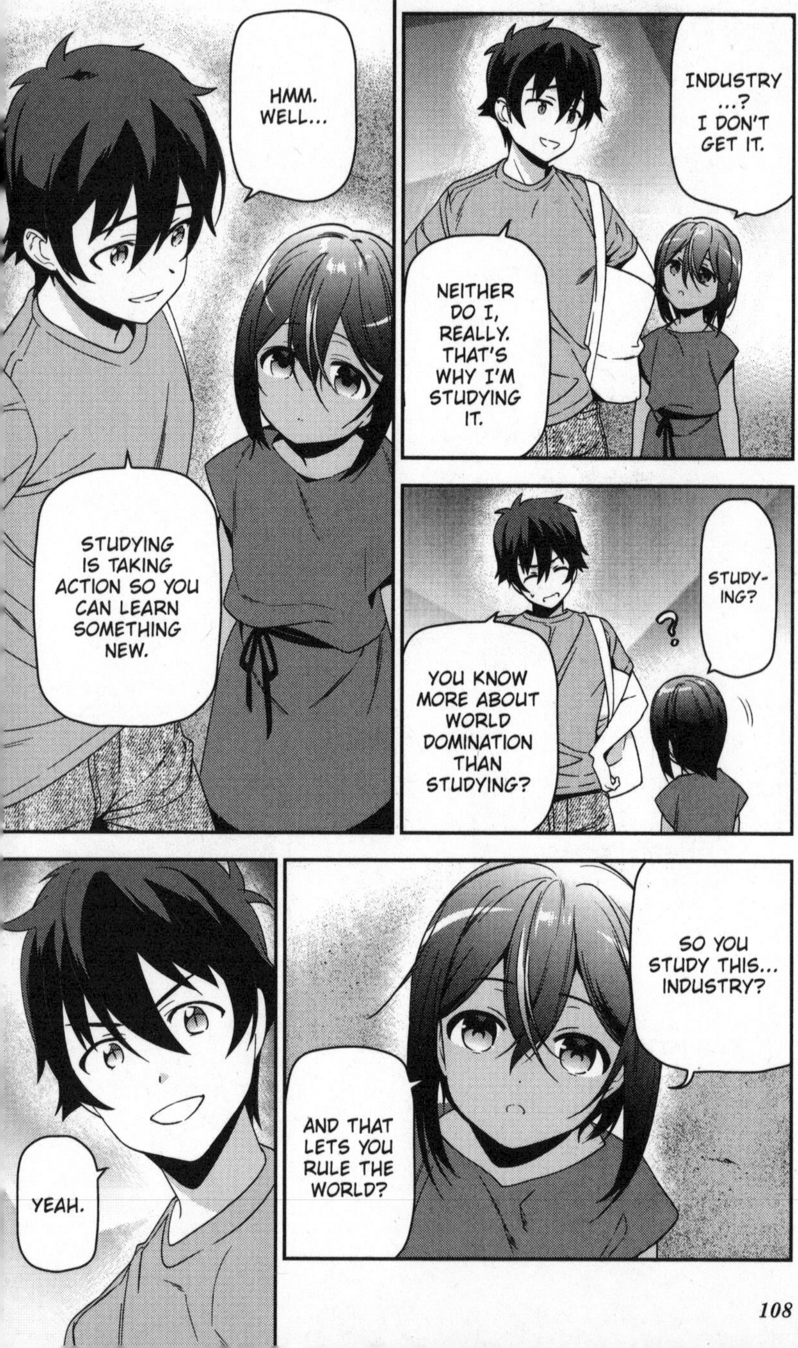
INDUSTRY ...? I DON'T GET IT.
NEITHER DO I, REALLY. THAT'S WHY I'M STUDYING IT.
STUDY-ING?
YOU KNOW MORE ABOUT WORLD DOMINATION THAN STUDYING?
HMM. WELL...
STUDYING IS TAKING ACTION SO YOU CAN LEARN SOMETHING NEW.
SO YOU STUDY THIS... INDUSTRY?
AND THAT LETS YOU RULE THE WORLD?
YEAH.

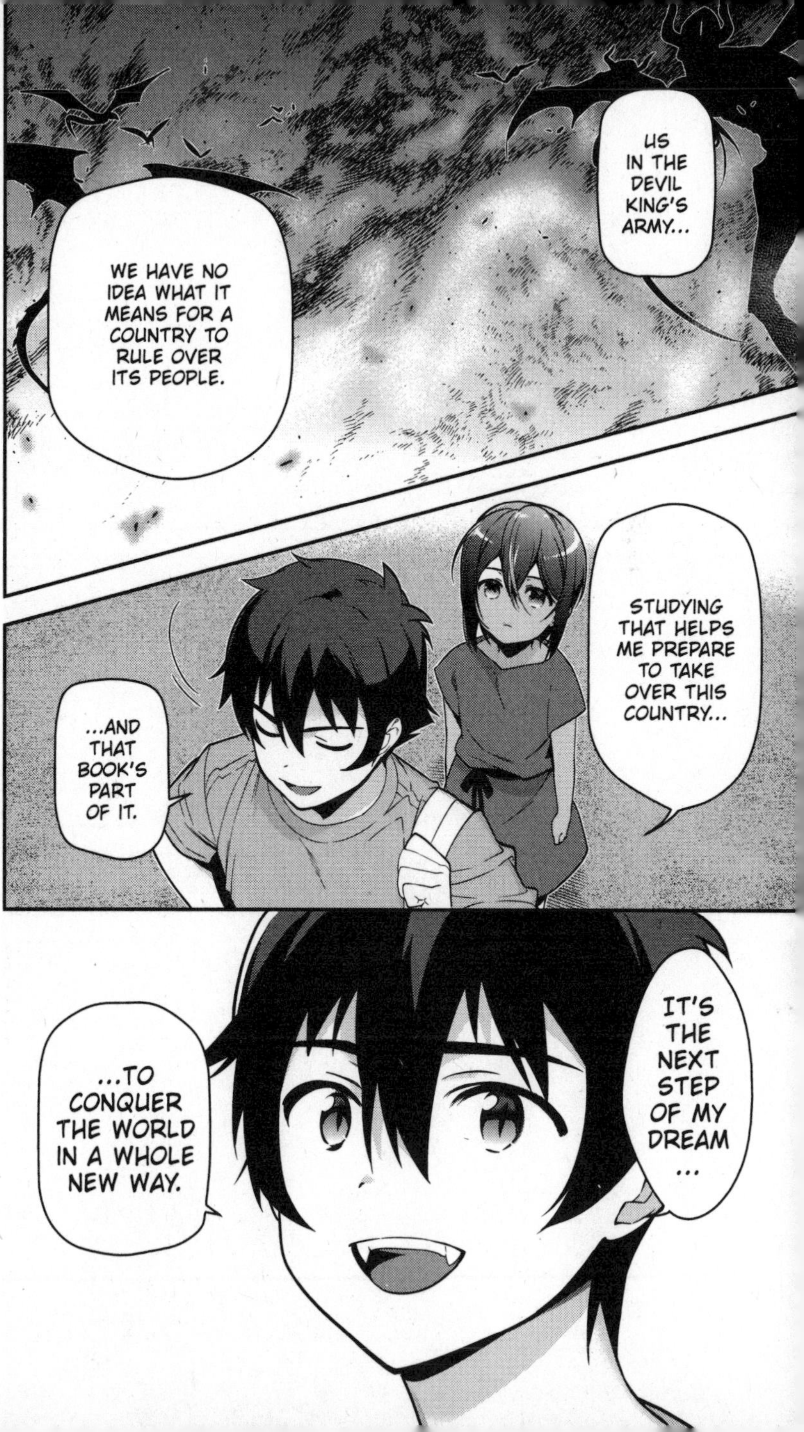
US IN THE DEVIL KING'S ARMY...
WE HAVE NO IDEA WHAT IT MEANS FOR A COUNTRY TO RULE OVER ITS PEOPLE.
STUDYING THAT HELPS ME PREPARE TO TAKE OVER THIS COUNTRY...
...AND THAT BOOK'S PART OF IT.
IT'S THE NEXT STEP OF MY DREAM ...
...TO CONQUER THE WORLD IN A WHOLE NEW WAY.

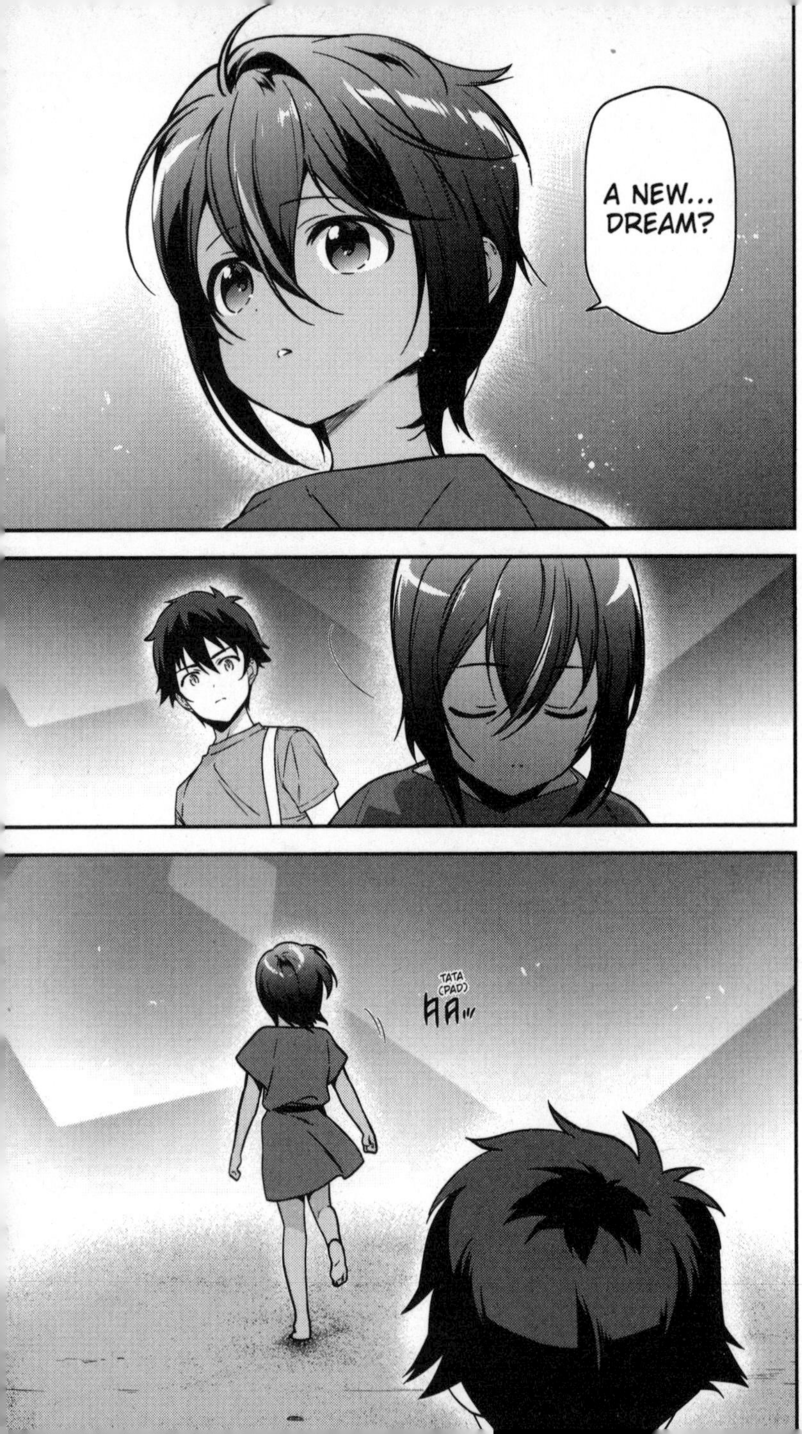
A NEW... DREAM?
TATA (PAD)

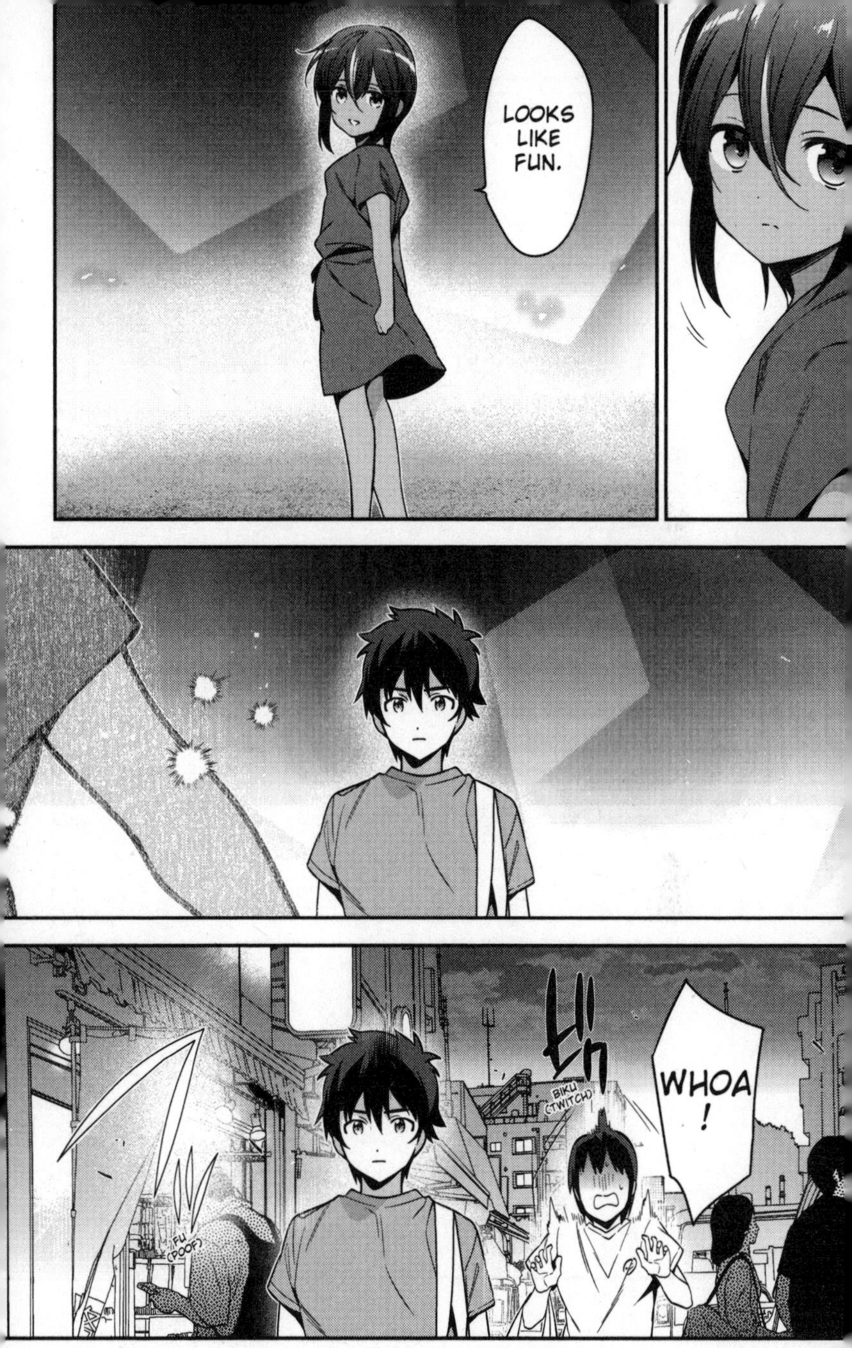
LOOKS LIKE FUN.
WHOA!
BIKU (TWITCH)
FU (POOF)

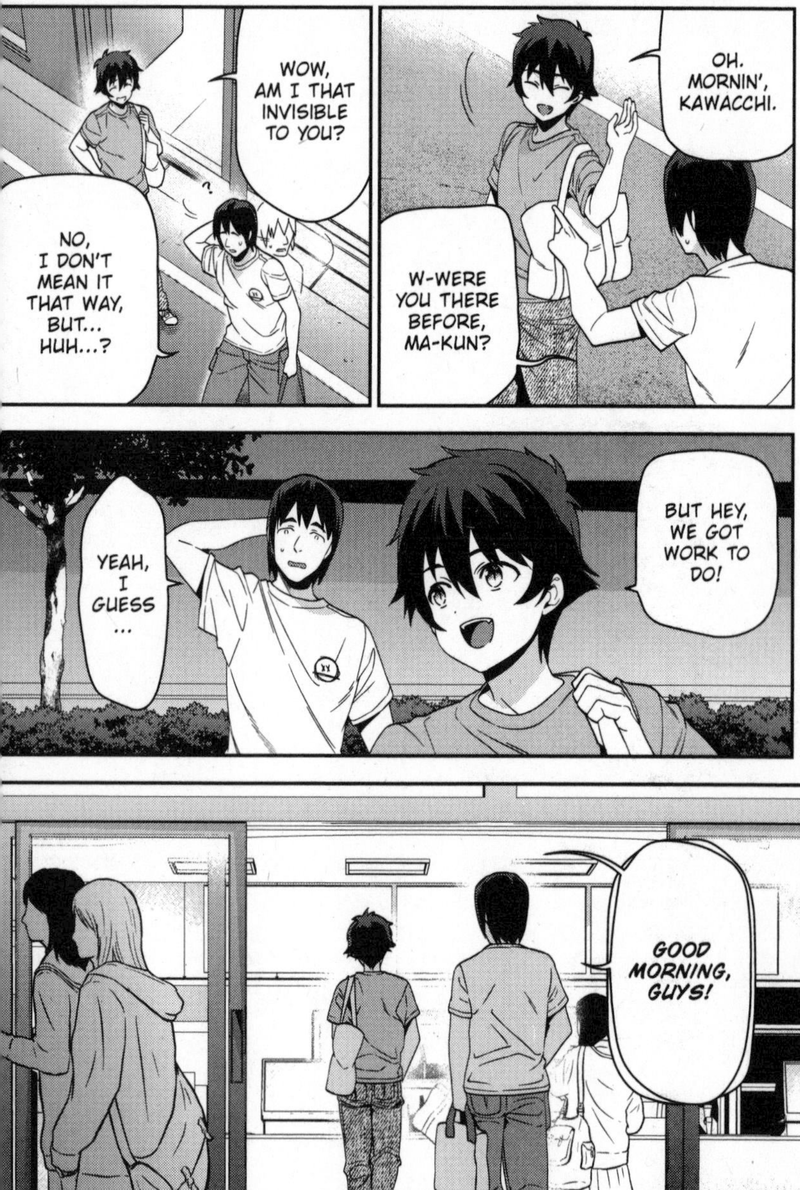
OH. MORNIN', KAWACCHI.
W-WERE YOU THERE BEFORE, MA-KUN?
WOW, AM I THAT INVISIBLE TO YOU?
NO, I DON'T MEAN IT THAT WAY, BUT... HUH...?
BUT HEY, WE GOT WORK TO DO!
YEAH, I GUESS ...
GOOD MORNING, GUYS!

Iron

THE DEVIL IS A PART-TIMER!

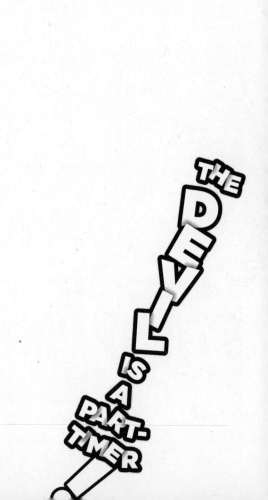

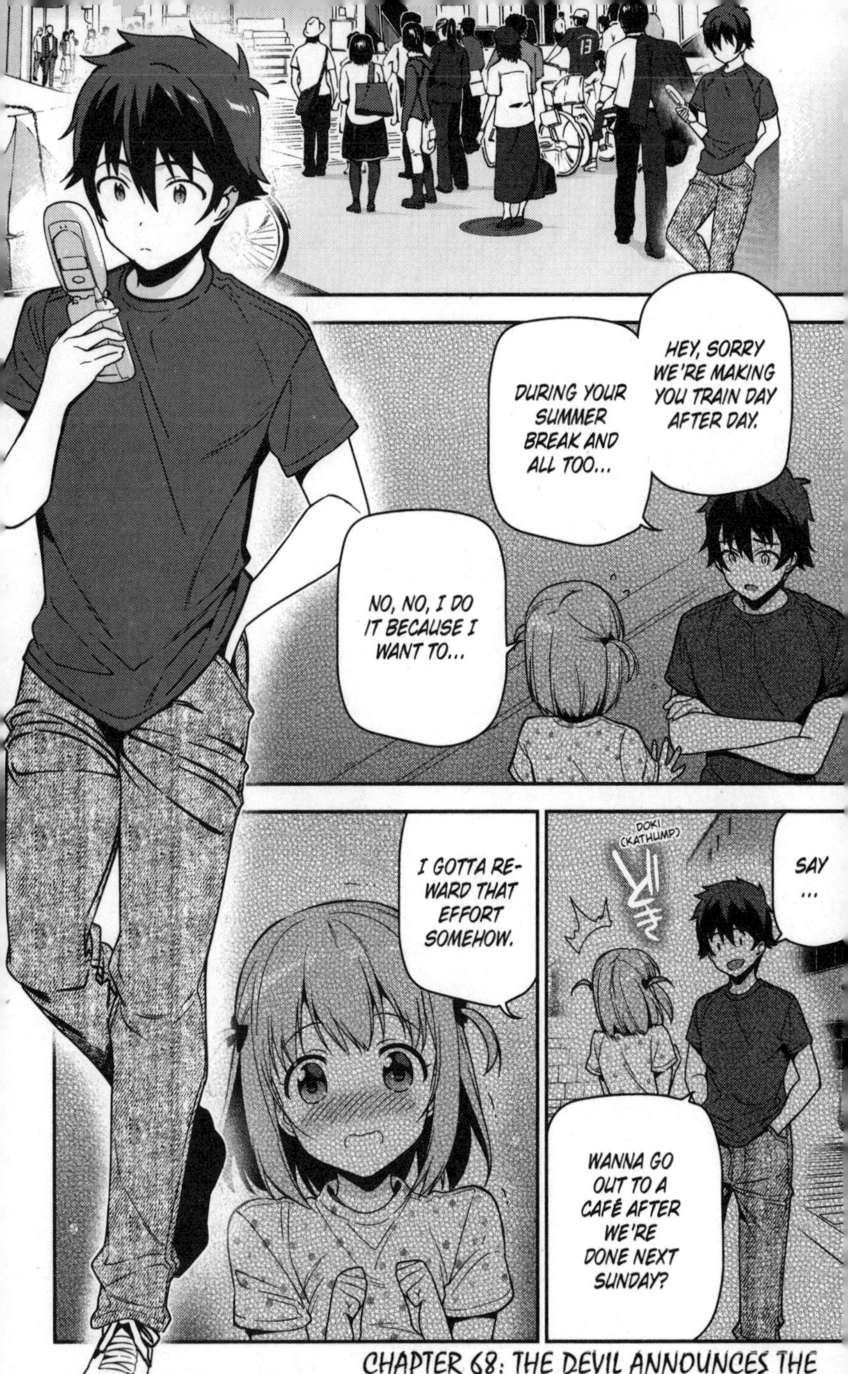
HEY, SORRY WE'RE MAKING YOU TRAIN DAY AFTER DAY.
DURING YOUR SUMMER BREAK AND ALL TOO...
NO, NO, I DO IT BECAUSE I WANT TO...
SAY ...
DOKI (KATHUMP)
WANNA GO OUT TO A CAFÉ AFTER WE'RE DONE NEXT SUNDAY?
I GOTTA RE-WARD THAT EFFORT SOMEHOW.

CHAPTER 68: THE DEVIL ANNOUNCES THE NEW DEVIL KING'S ARMY

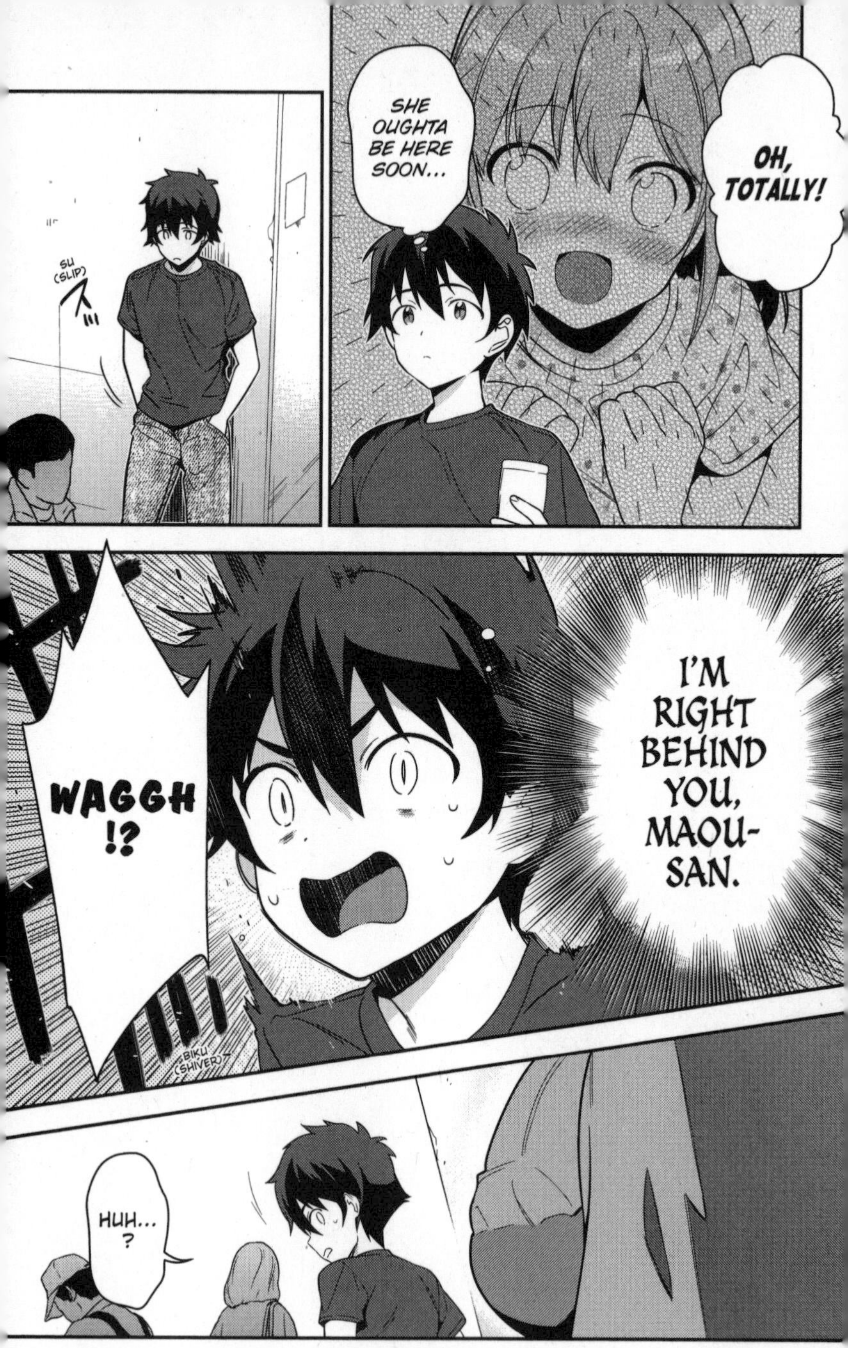

SHE OUGHTA BE HERE SOON...
OH, TOTALLY!
SU (SLIP)
I'M RIGHT BEHIND YOU, MAOU-SAN.
WAGGH !?
BIKU (SHIVER)
HUH... ?

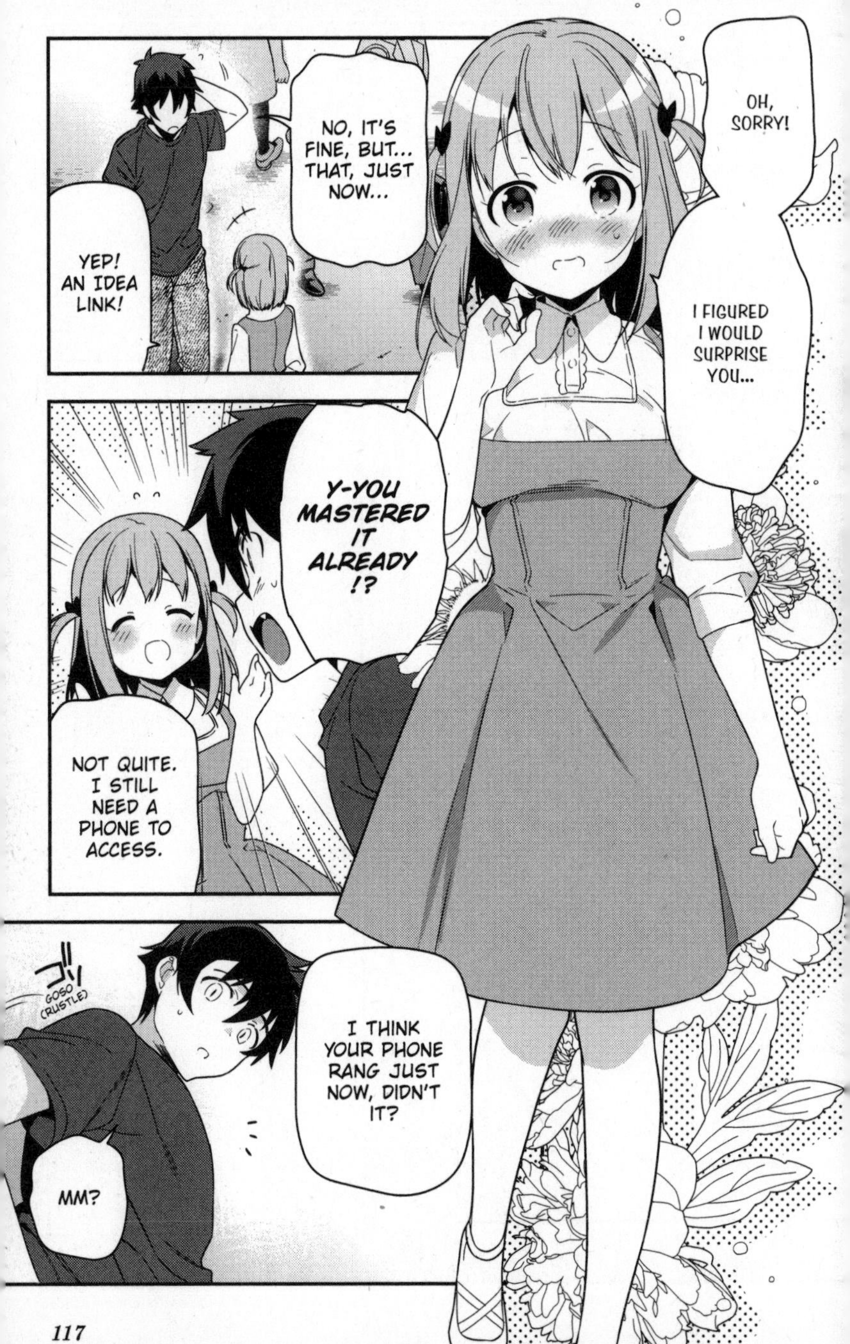
OH, SORRY!
I FIGURED I WOULD SURPRISE YOU...
NO, IT'S FINE, BUT... THAT, JUST NOW...
YEP! AN IDEA LINK!
Y-YOU MASTERED IT ALREADY!?
NOT QUITE. I STILL NEED A PHONE TO ACCESS.
I THINK YOUR PHONE RANG JUST NOW, DIDN'T IT?
GOSO (RUSTLE)
MM?

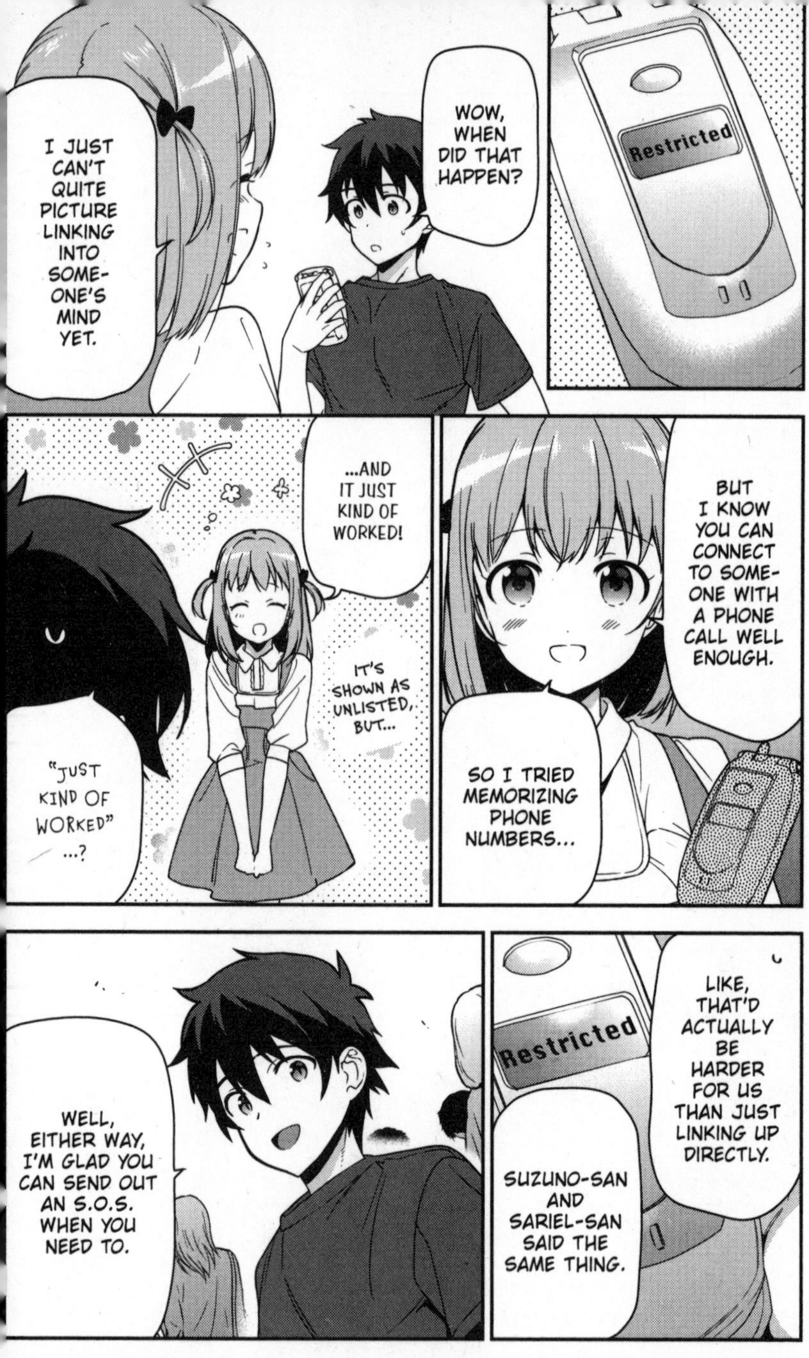
Restricted
WOW, WHEN DID THAT HAPPEN?
I JUST CAN'T QUITE PICTURE LINKING INTO SOME-ONE'S MIND YET.
BUT I KNOW YOU CAN CONNECT TO SOME-ONE WITH A PHONE CALL WELL ENOUGH.
SO I TRIED MEMORIZING PHONE NUMBERS...
...AND IT JUST KIND OF WORKED!
IT'S SHOWN AS UNLISTED, BUT...
"JUST KIND OF WORKED" ...?
Restricted
LIKE, THAT'D ACTUALLY BE HARDER FOR US THAN JUST LINKING UP DIRECTLY.
SUZUNO-SAN AND SARIEL-SAN SAID THE SAME THING.
WELL, EITHER WAY, I'M GLAD YOU CAN SEND OUT AN S.O.S. WHEN YOU NEED TO.

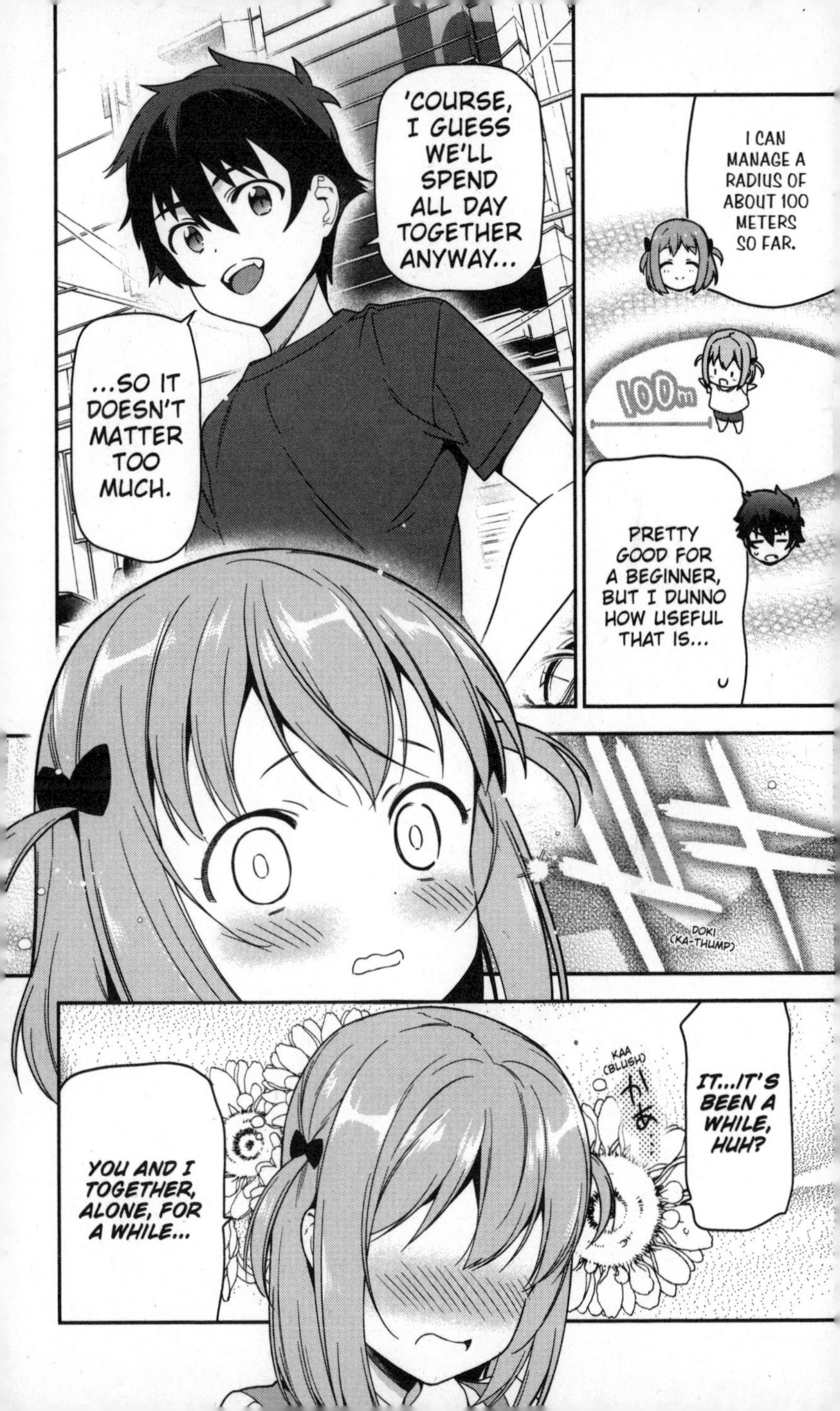
I CAN MANAGE A RADIUS OF ABOUT 100 METERS SO FAR.
100m
PRETTY GOOD FOR A BEGINNER, BUT I DUNNO HOW USEFUL THAT IS...
'COURSE, I GUESS WE'LL SPEND ALL DAY TOGETHER ANYWAY...
...SO IT DOESN'T MATTER TOO MUCH.
DOKI (KA-THUMP)
KAA (BLUSH)
IT...IT'S BEEN A WHILE, HUH?
YOU AND I TOGETHER, ALONE, FOR A WHILE...

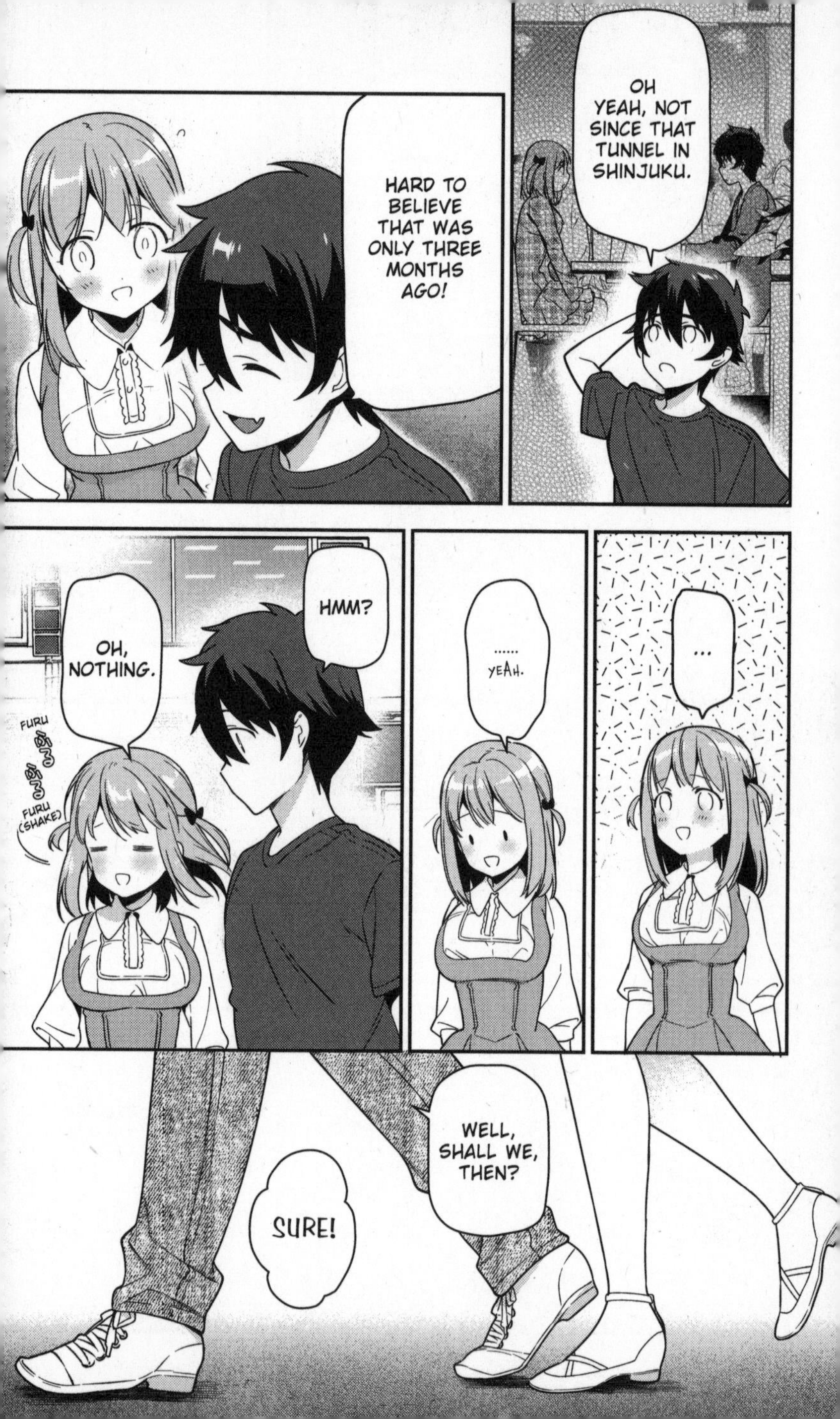
OH YEAH, NOT SINCE THAT TUNNEL IN SHINJUKU.
HARD TO BELIEVE THAT WAS ONLY THREE MONTHS AGO!
...
...... YEAH.
HMM?
OH, NOTHING.
FURU ふる ふる FURU (SHAKE)
WELL, SHALL WE, THEN?
SURE!

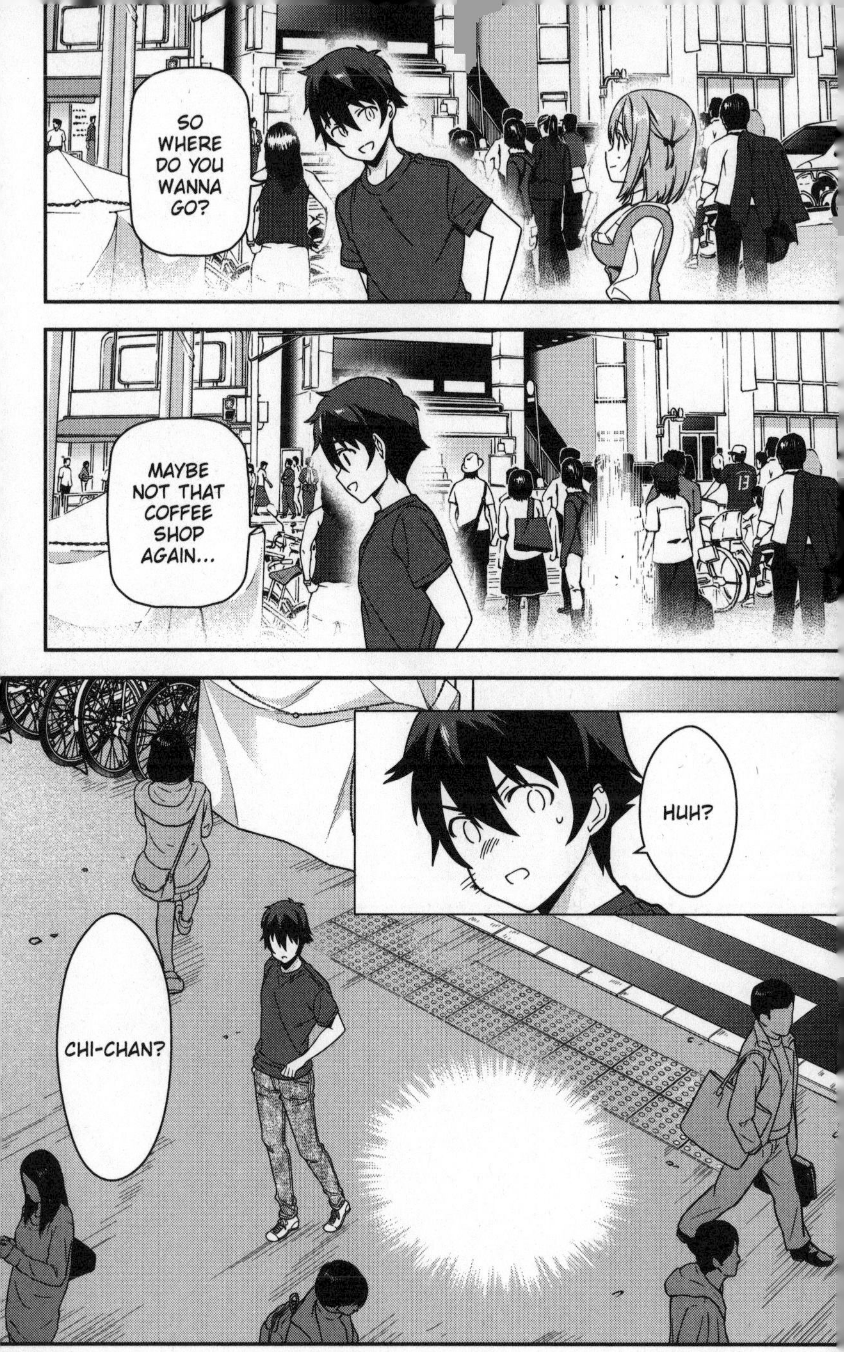
SO WHERE DO YOU WANNA GO?
MAYBE NOT THAT COFFEE SHOP AGAIN...
HUH?
CHI-CHAN?

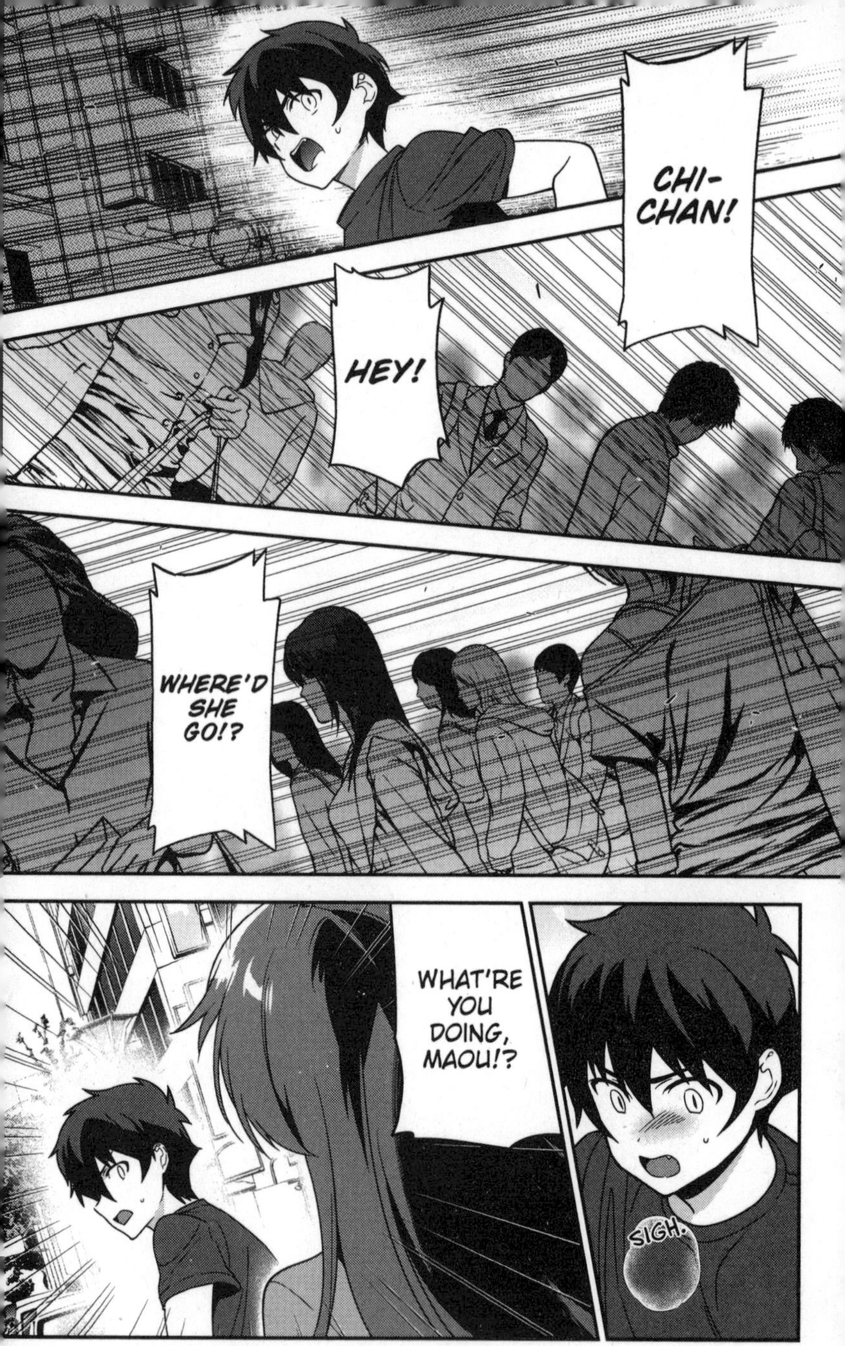
CHI-CHAN!
HEY!
WHERE'D SHE GO!?
WHAT'RE YOU DOING, MAOU!?
SIGH.

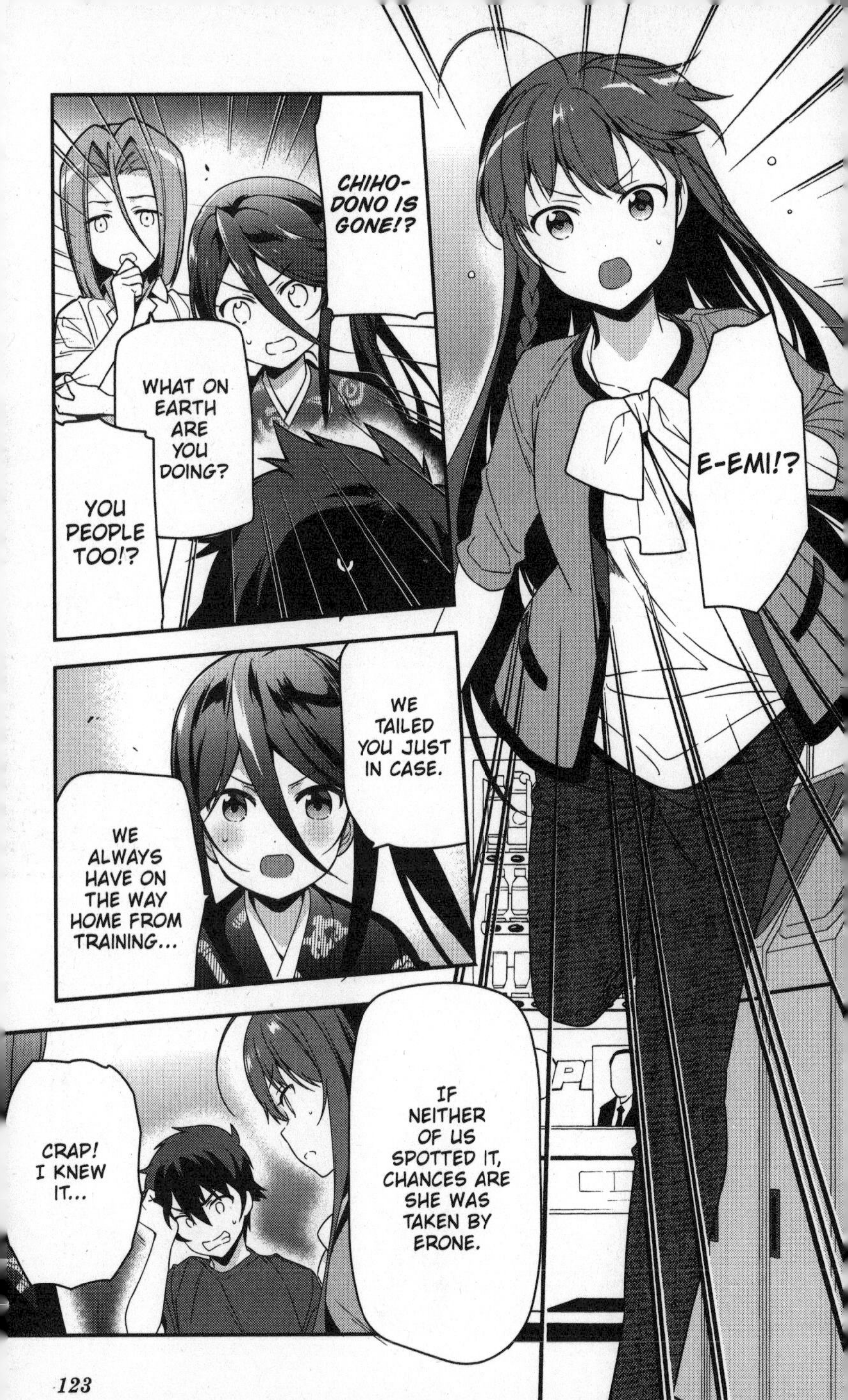
E-EMI!?
CHIHO-DONO IS GONE!?
WHAT ON EARTH ARE YOU DOING?
YOU PEOPLE TOO!?
WE TAILED YOU JUST IN CASE.
WE ALWAYS HAVE ON THE WAY HOME FROM TRAINING...
IF NEITHER OF US SPOTTED IT, CHANCES ARE SHE WAS TAKEN BY ERONE.
CRAP! I KNEW IT...

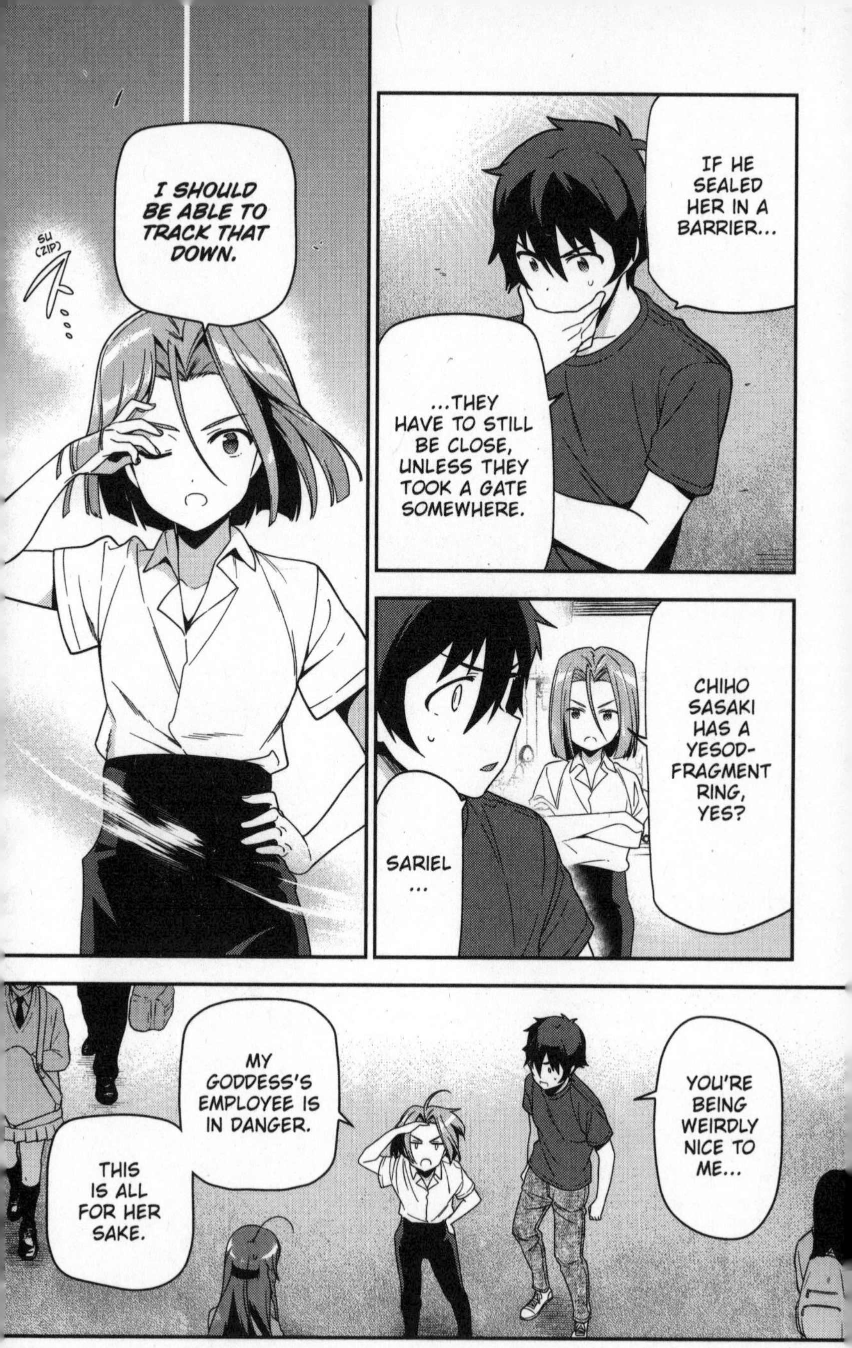
IF HE SEALED HER IN A BARRIER...
...THEY HAVE TO STILL BE CLOSE, UNLESS THEY TOOK A GATE SOMEWHERE.
CHIHO SASAKI HAS A YESOD-FRAGMENT RING, YES?
SARIEL...
I SHOULD BE ABLE TO TRACK THAT DOWN.
SU (ZIP)
YOU'RE BEING WEIRDLY NICE TO ME...
MY GODDESS'S EMPLOYEE IS IN DANGER.
THIS IS ALL FOR HER SAKE.

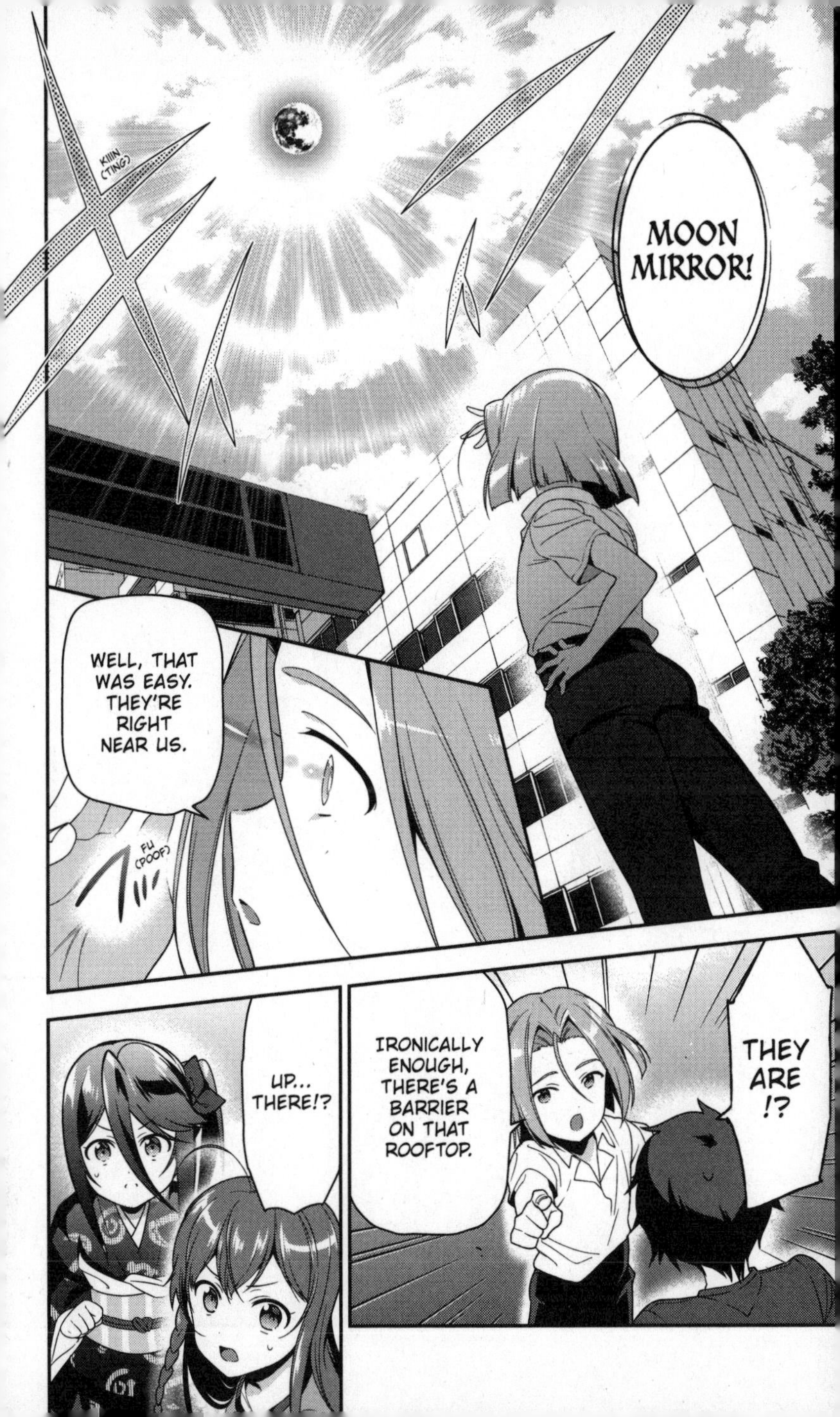
MOON MIRROR!
KIIIN (TING)
WELL, THAT WAS EASY. THEY'RE RIGHT NEAR US.
FU (POOF)
THEY ARE!?
IRONICALLY ENOUGH, THERE'S A BARRIER ON THAT ROOFTOP.
UP... THERE!?

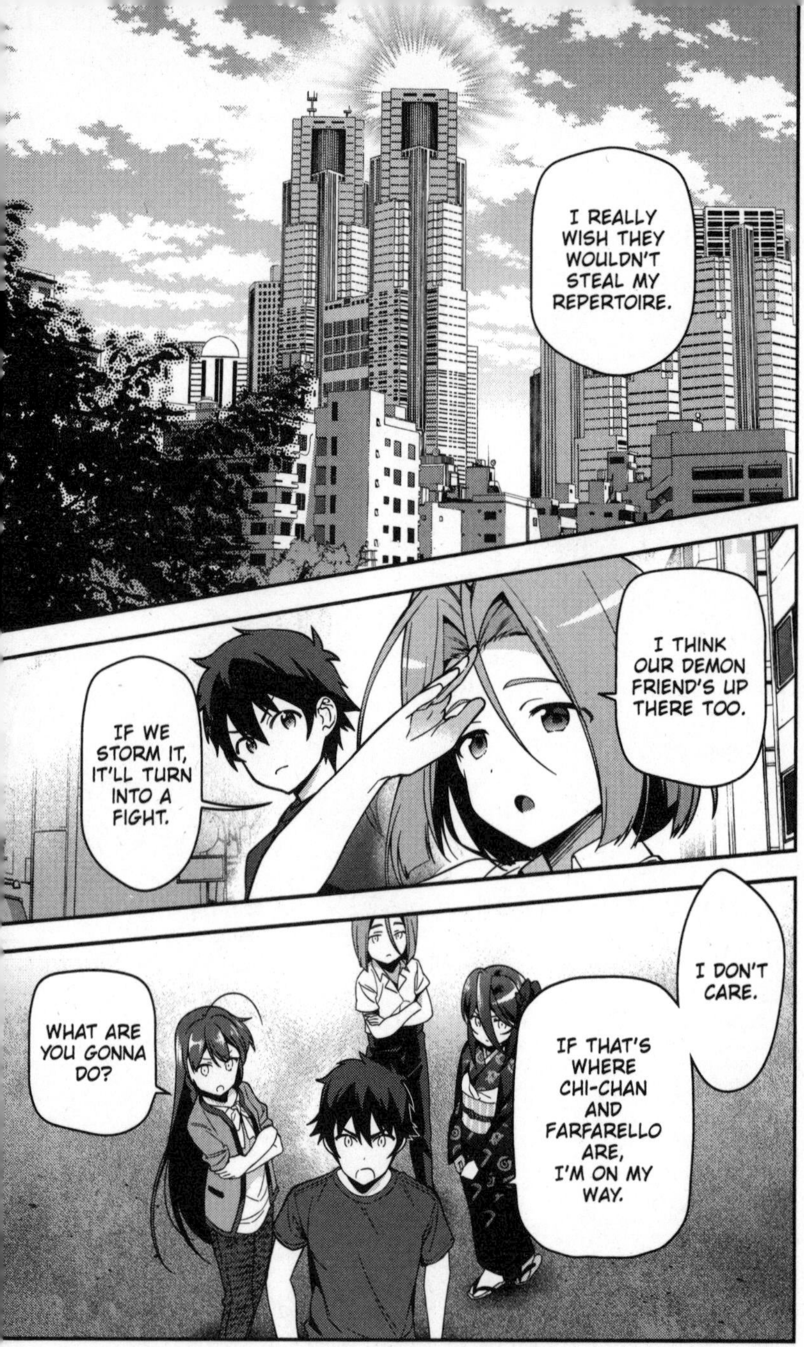
I REALLY WISH THEY WOULDN'T STEAL MY REPERTOIRE.
I THINK OUR DEMON FRIEND'S UP THERE TOO.
IF WE STORM IT, IT'LL TURN INTO A FIGHT.
I DON'T CARE.
IF THAT'S WHERE CHI-CHAN AND FARFARELLO ARE, I'M ON MY WAY.
WHAT ARE YOU GONNA DO?

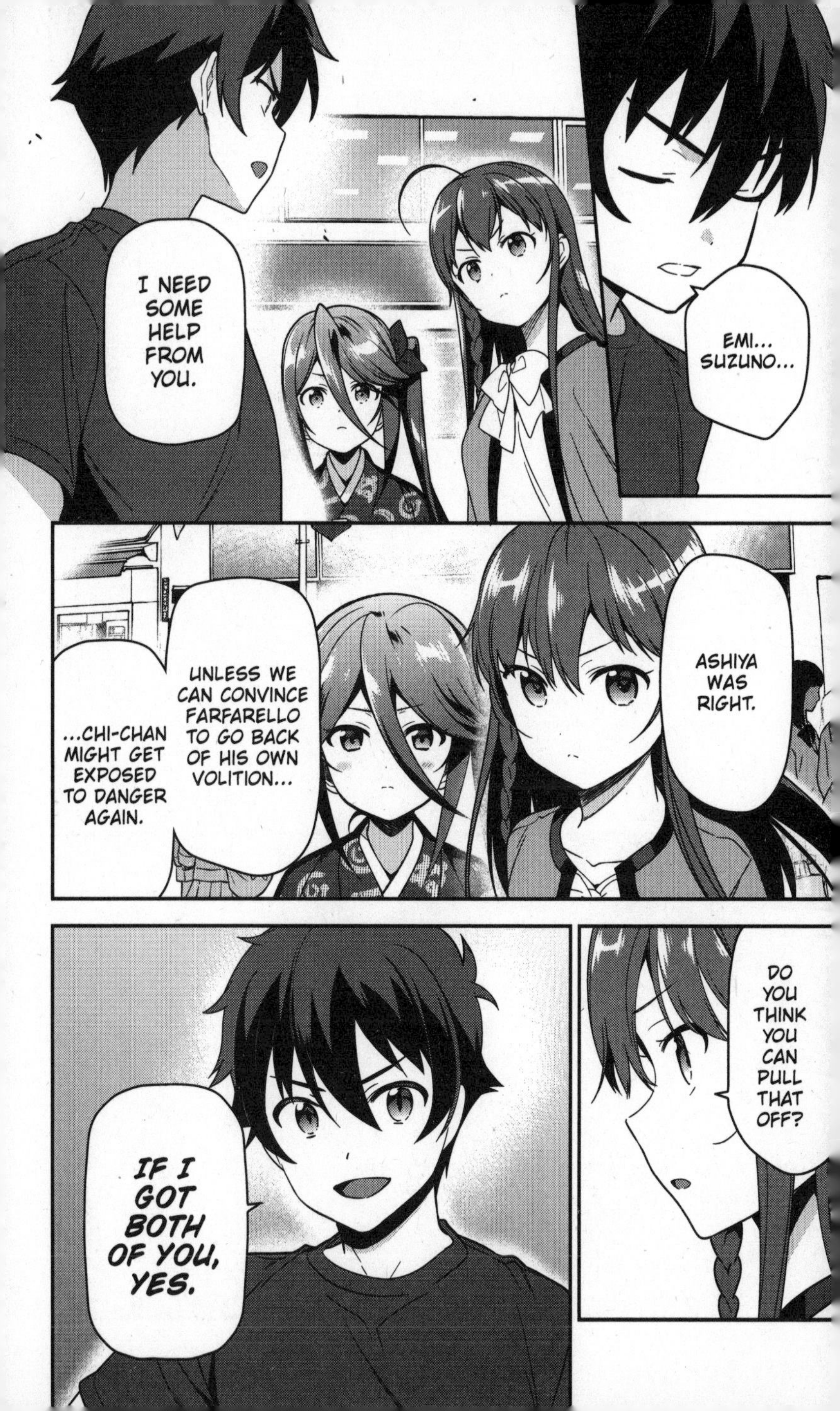
EMI... SUZUNO...
I NEED SOME HELP FROM YOU.
ASHIYA WAS RIGHT.
UNLESS WE CAN CONVINCE FARFARELLO TO GO BACK OF HIS OWN VOLITION...
...CHI-CHAN MIGHT GET EXPOSED TO DANGER AGAIN.
DO YOU THINK YOU CAN PULL THAT OFF?
IF I GOT BOTH OF YOU, YES.

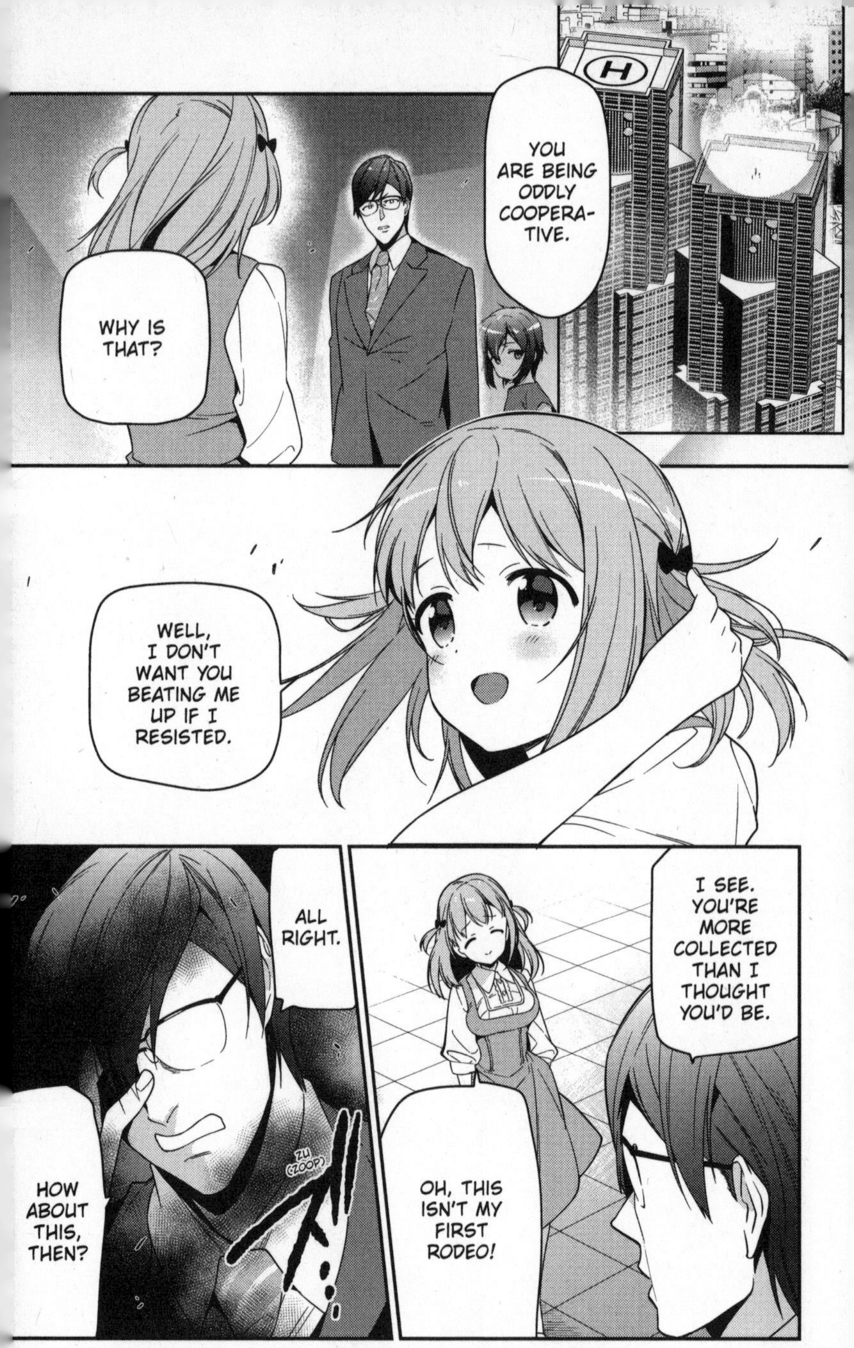
YOU ARE BEING ODDLY COOPERA-TIVE.
WHY IS THAT?
WELL, I DON'T WANT YOU BEATING ME UP IF I RESISTED.
I SEE. YOU'RE MORE COLLECTED THAN I THOUGHT YOU'D BE.
OH, THIS ISN'T MY FIRST RODEO!
ALL RIGHT.
ZU (ZOOP)
HOW ABOUT THIS, THEN?

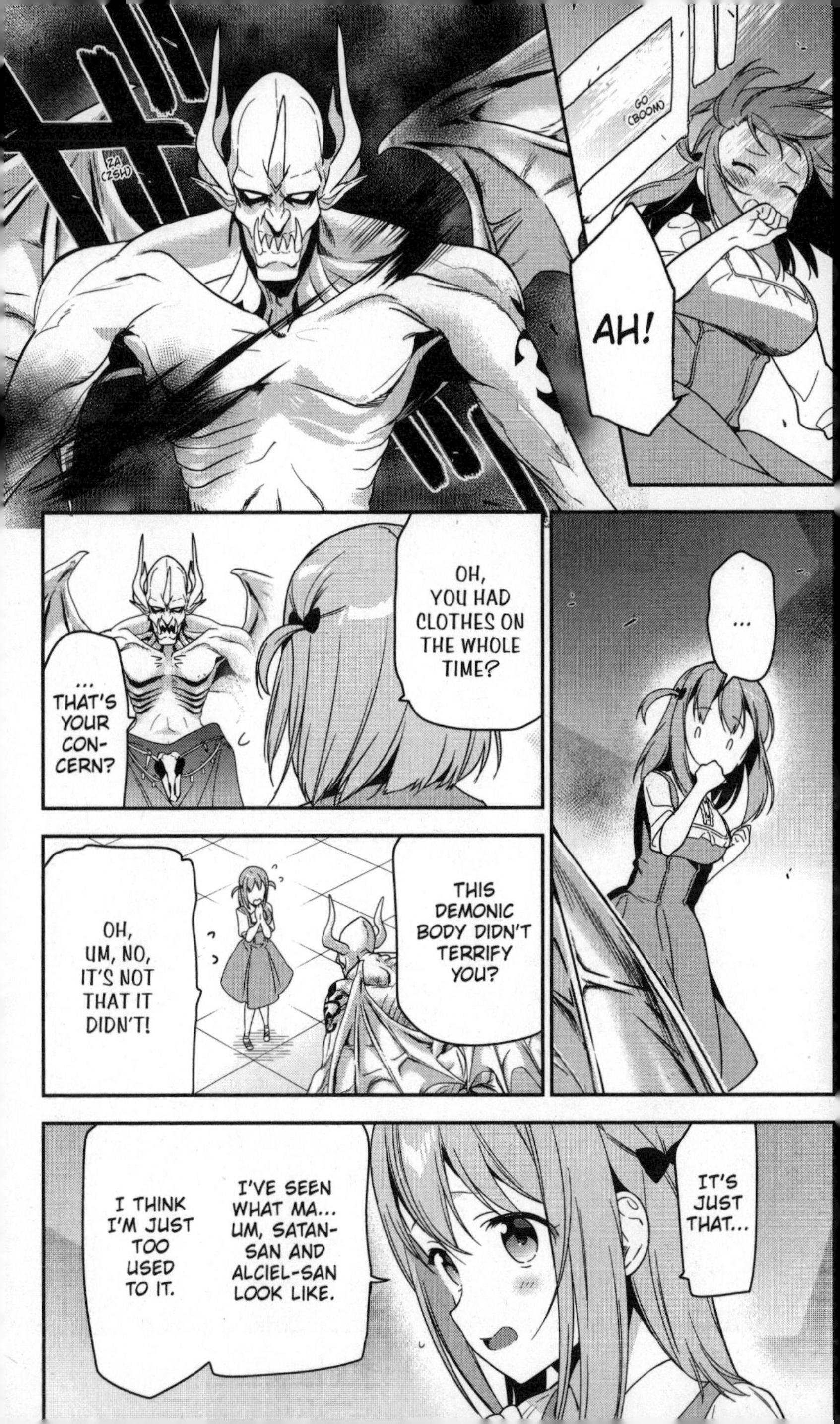
GO (BOOM)
AH!
ZA (ZSH)
...
OH, YOU HAD CLOTHES ON THE WHOLE TIME?
... THAT'S YOUR CON-CERN?
THIS DEMONIC BODY DIDN'T TERRIFY YOU?
OH, UM, NO, IT'S NOT THAT IT DIDN'T!
IT'S JUST THAT...
I'VE SEEN WHAT MA... UM, SATAN-SAN AND ALCIEL-SAN LOOK LIKE.
I THINK I'M JUST TOO USED TO IT.

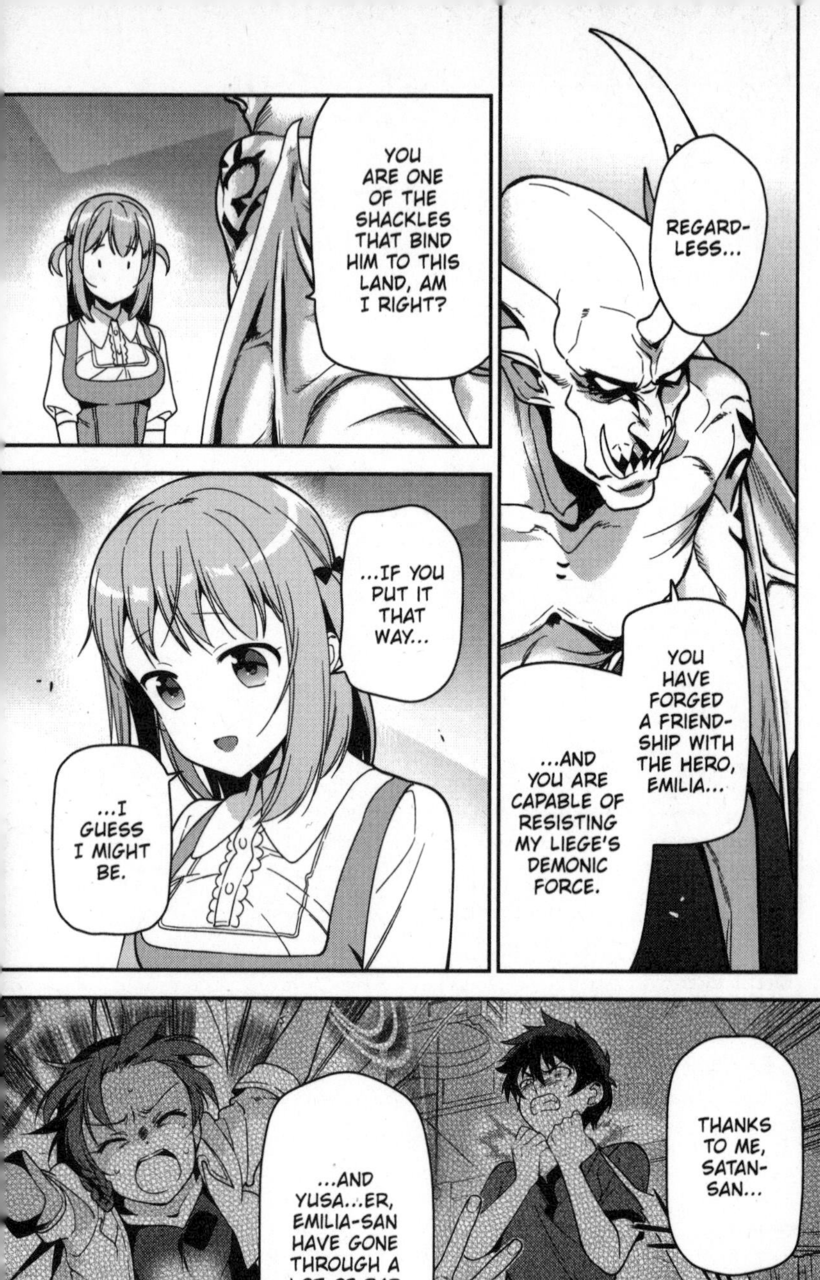
REGARDLESS...
YOU HAVE FORGED A FRIENDSHIP WITH THE HERO, EMILIA...
...AND YOU ARE CAPABLE OF RESISTING MY LIEGE'S DEMONIC FORCE.
YOU ARE ONE OF THE SHACKLES THAT BIND HIM TO THIS LAND, AM I RIGHT?
...IF YOU PUT IT THAT WAY...
...I GUESS I MIGHT BE.
THANKS TO ME, SATAN-SAN...
...AND YUSA...ER, EMILIA-SAN HAVE GONE THROUGH A LOT OF BAD STUFF.

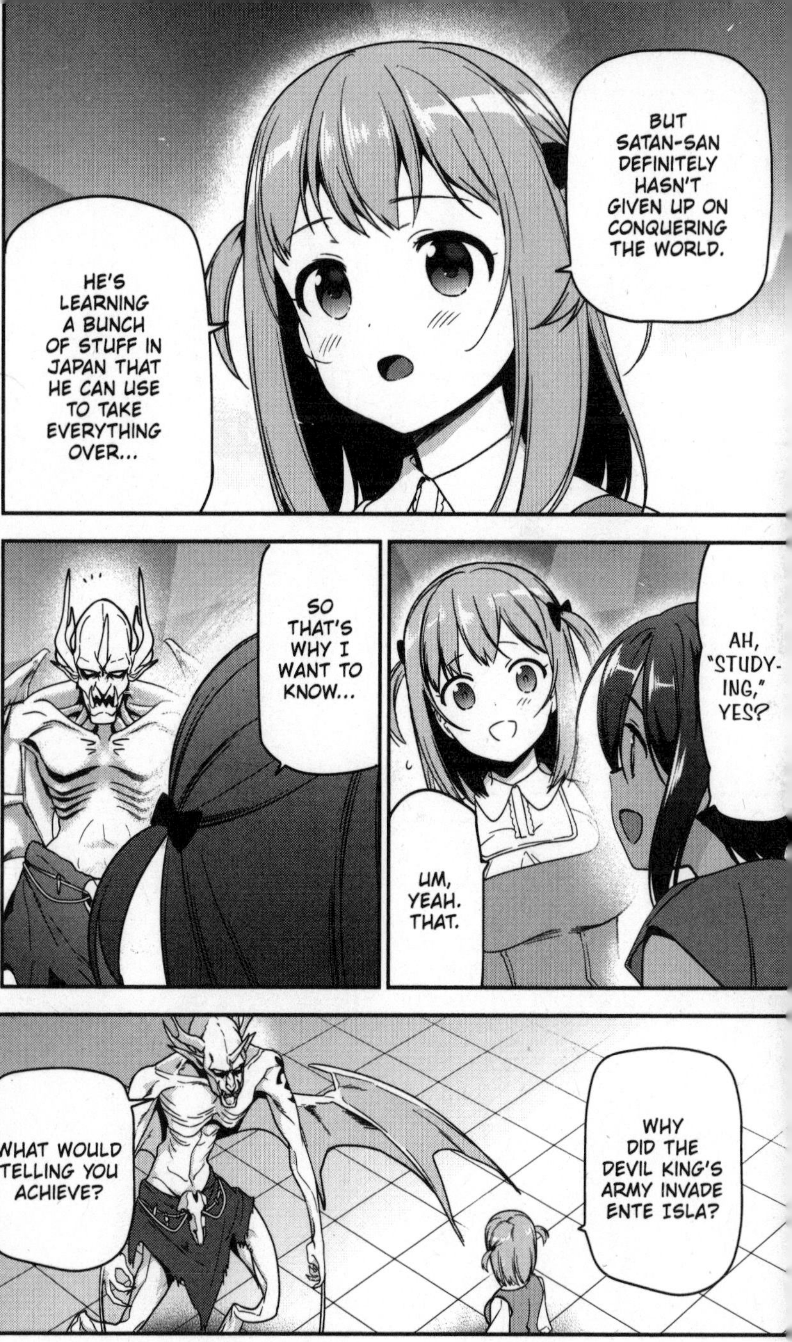
BUT SATAN-SAN DEFINITELY HASN'T GIVEN UP ON CONQUERING THE WORLD.
HE'S LEARNING A BUNCH OF STUFF IN JAPAN THAT HE CAN USE TO TAKE EVERYTHING OVER...
AH, "STUDY-ING," YES?
UM, YEAH. THAT.
SO THAT'S WHY I WANT TO KNOW...
WHY DID THE DEVIL KING'S ARMY INVADE ENTE ISLA?
WHAT WOULD TELLING YOU ACHIEVE?

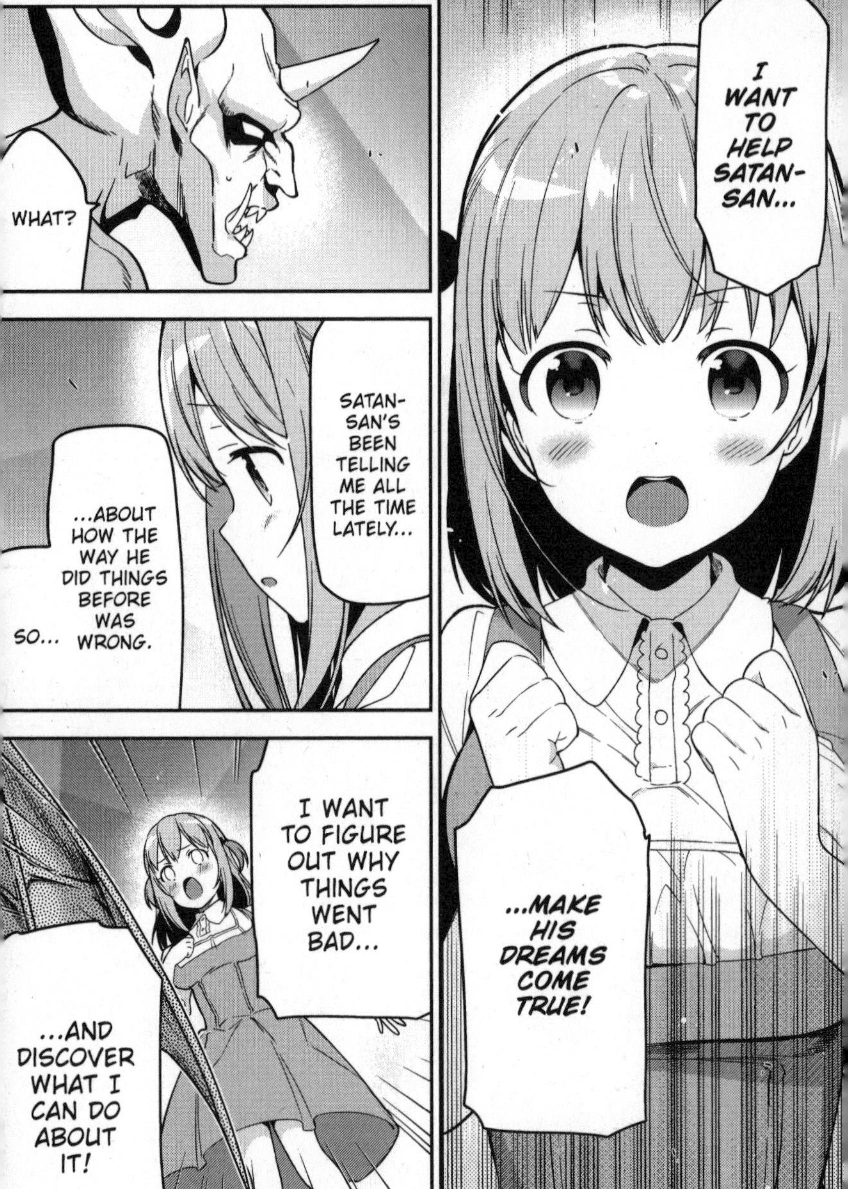
I WANT TO HELP SATAN-SAN...
...MAKE HIS DREAMS COME TRUE!
WHAT?
SATAN-SAN'S BEEN TELLING ME ALL THE TIME LATELY...
...ABOUT HOW THE WAY HE DID THINGS BEFORE WAS WRONG.
SO...
I WANT TO FIGURE OUT WHY THINGS WENT BAD...
...AND DISCOVER WHAT I CAN DO ABOUT IT!

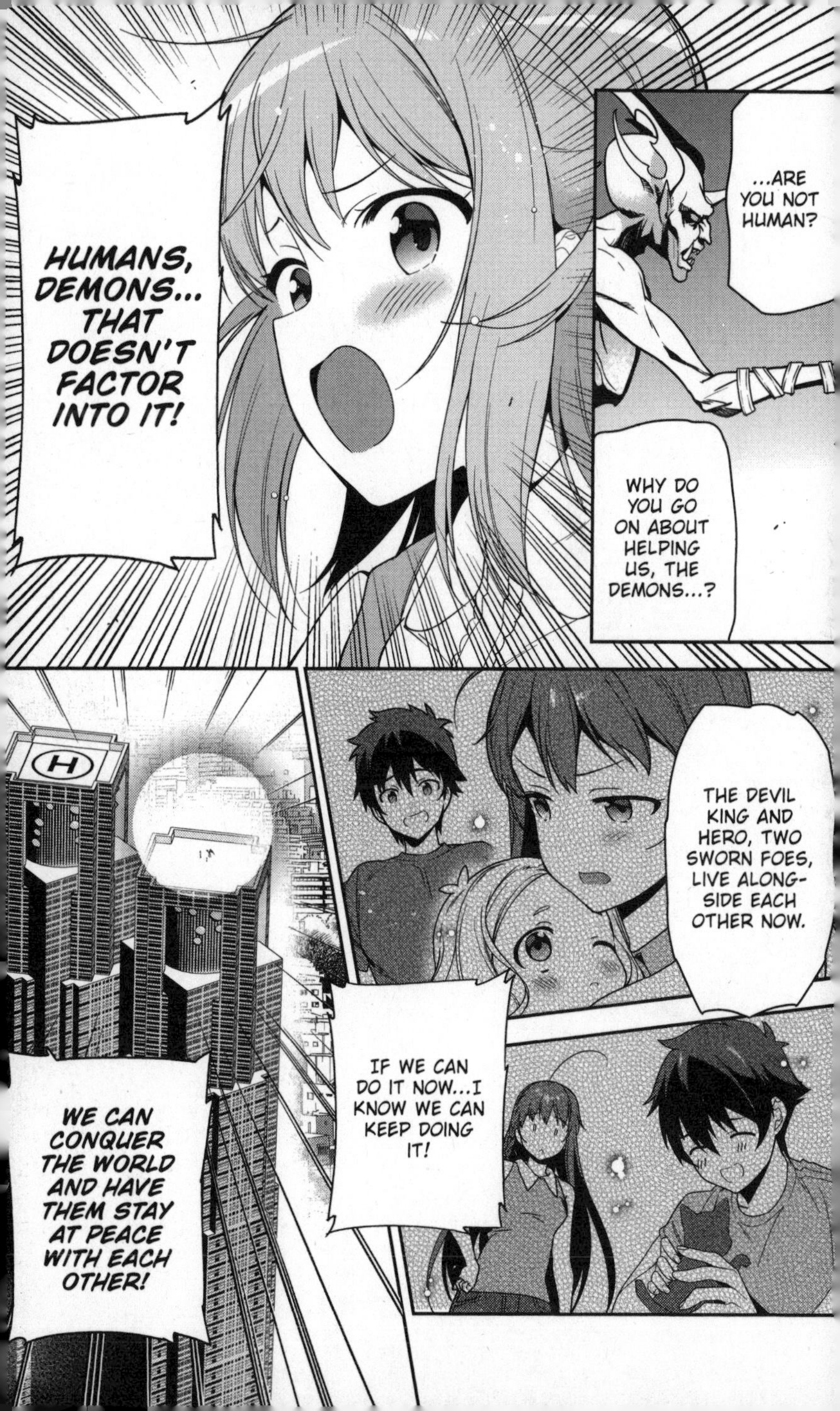
...ARE YOU NOT HUMAN?
WHY DO YOU GO ON ABOUT HELPING US, THE DEMONS...?
HUMANS, DEMONS... THAT DOESN'T FACTOR INTO IT!
THE DEVIL KING AND HERO, TWO SWORN FOES, LIVE ALONG-SIDE EACH OTHER NOW.
IF WE CAN DO IT NOW...I KNOW WE CAN KEEP DOING IT!
WE CAN CONQUER THE WORLD AND HAVE THEM STAY AT PEACE WITH EACH OTHER!

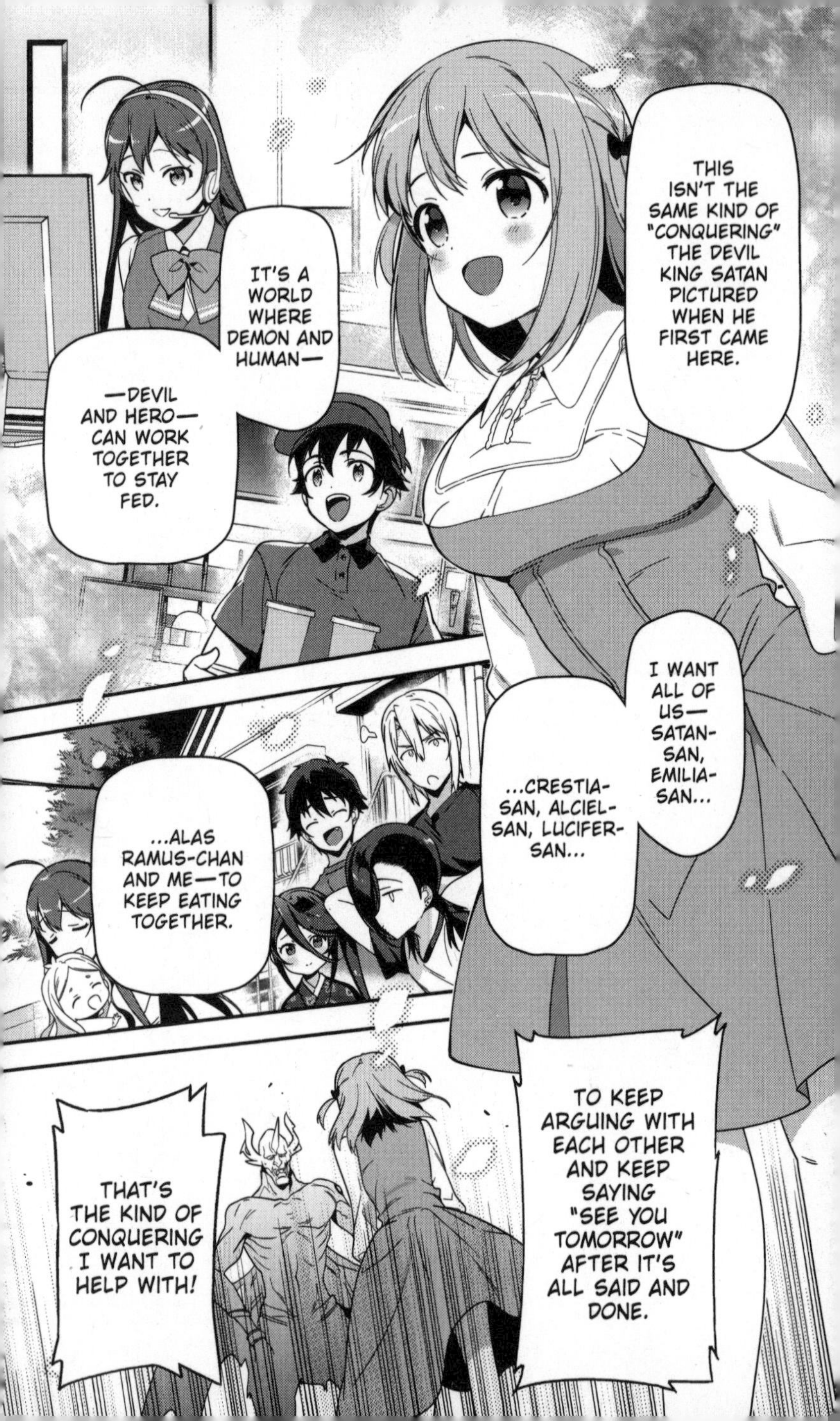
THIS ISN'T THE SAME KIND OF "CONQUERING" THE DEVIL KING SATAN PICTURED WHEN HE FIRST CAME HERE.
IT'S A WORLD WHERE DEMON AND HUMAN—
—DEVIL AND HERO—CAN WORK TOGETHER TO STAY FED.
I WANT ALL OF US—SATAN-SAN, EMILIA-SAN...
...CRESTIA-SAN, ALCIEL-SAN, LUCIFER-SAN...
...ALAS RAMUS-CHAN AND ME—TO KEEP EATING TOGETHER.
TO KEEP ARGUING WITH EACH OTHER AND KEEP SAYING "SEE YOU TOMORROW" AFTER IT'S ALL SAID AND DONE.
THAT'S THE KIND OF CONQUERING I WANT TO HELP WITH!

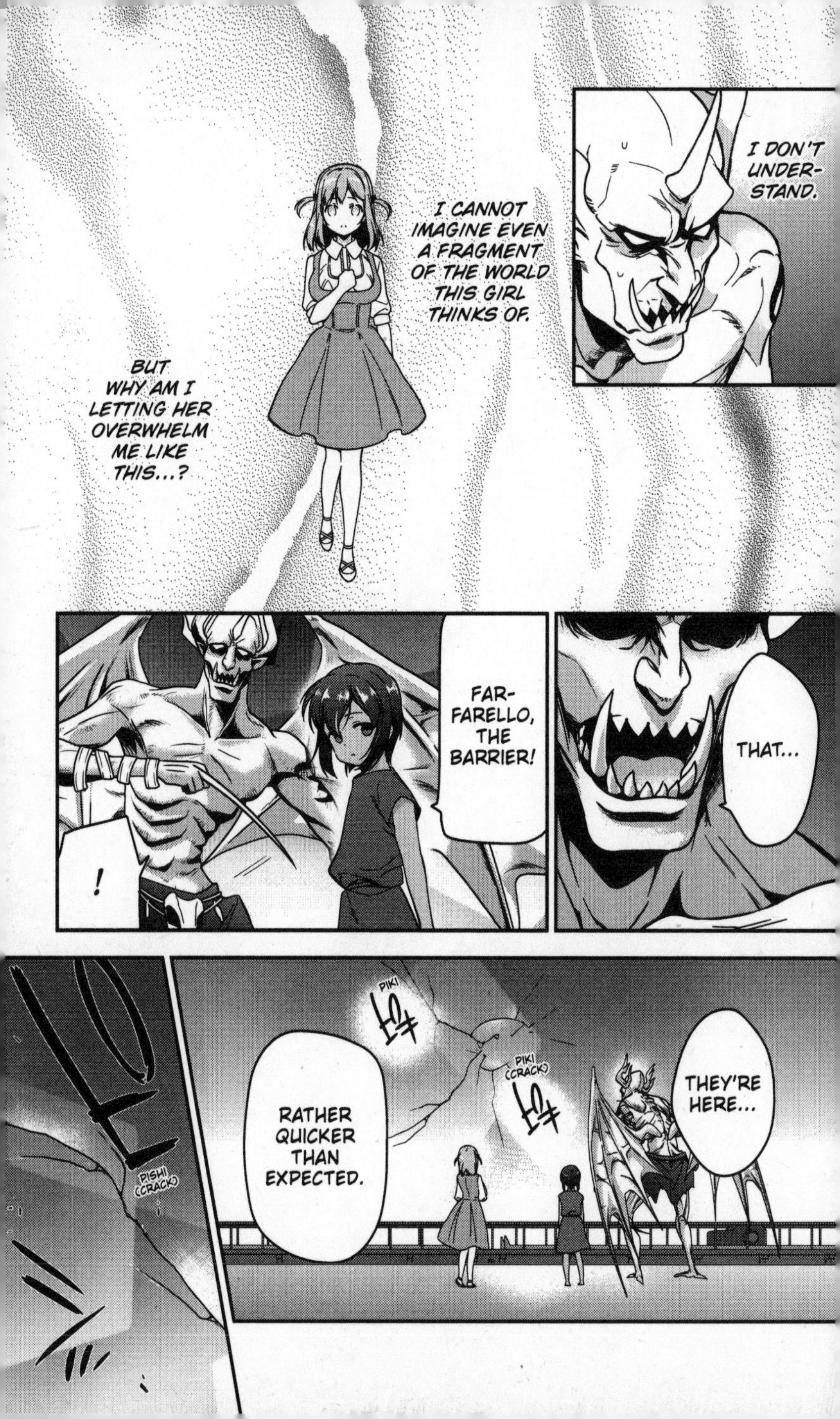
I DON'T UNDER-STAND.
I CANNOT IMAGINE EVEN A FRAGMENT OF THE WORLD THIS GIRL THINKS OF.
BUT WHY AM I LETTING HER OVERWHELM ME LIKE THIS...?
THAT...
FAR-FARELLO, THE BARRIER!
!
THEY'RE HERE...
PIKI (CRACK)
PIKI
RATHER QUICKER THAN EXPECTED.
PISHI (CRACK)

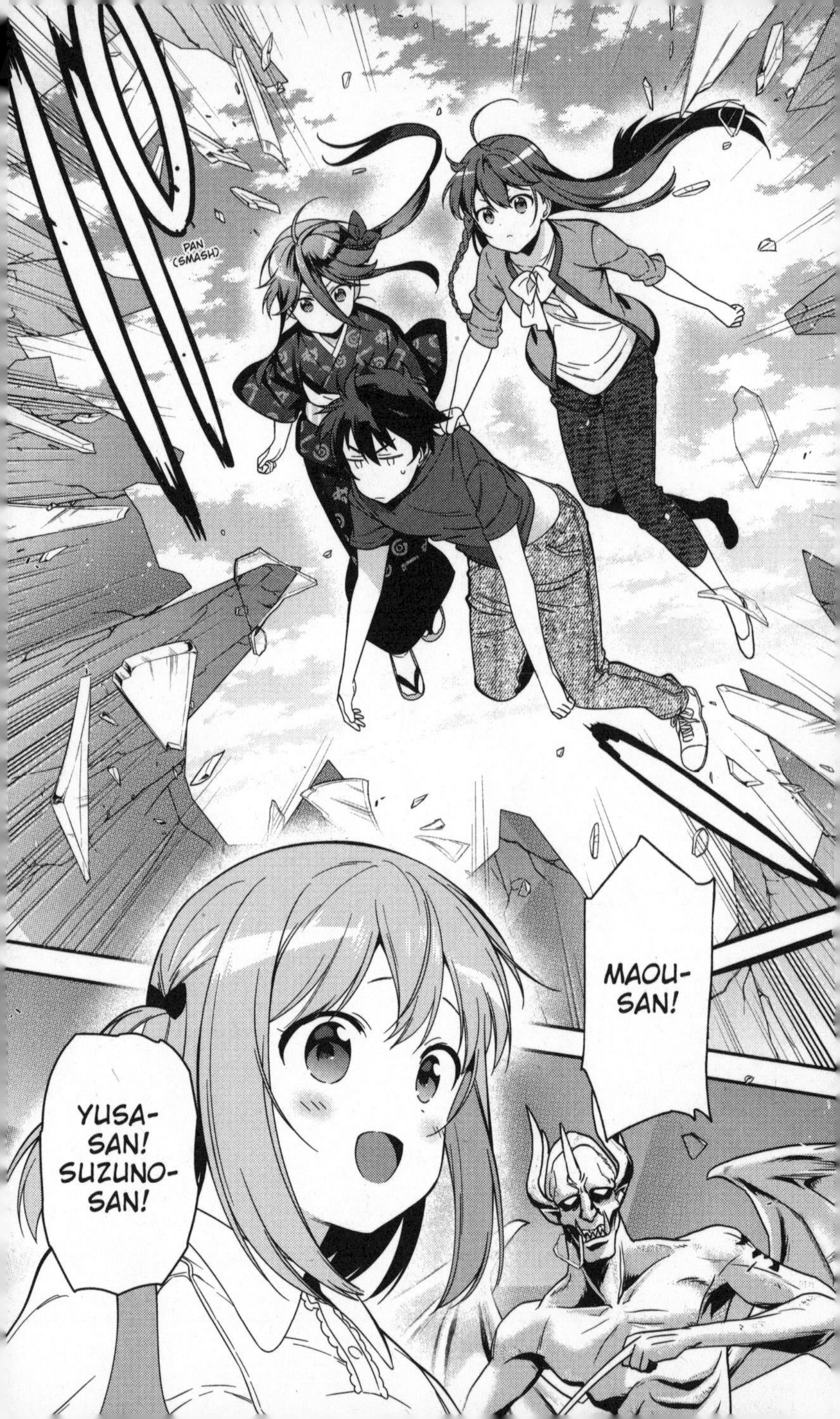
PAN
(SMASH)
MAOU-SAN!
YUSA-SAN! SUZUNO-SAN!

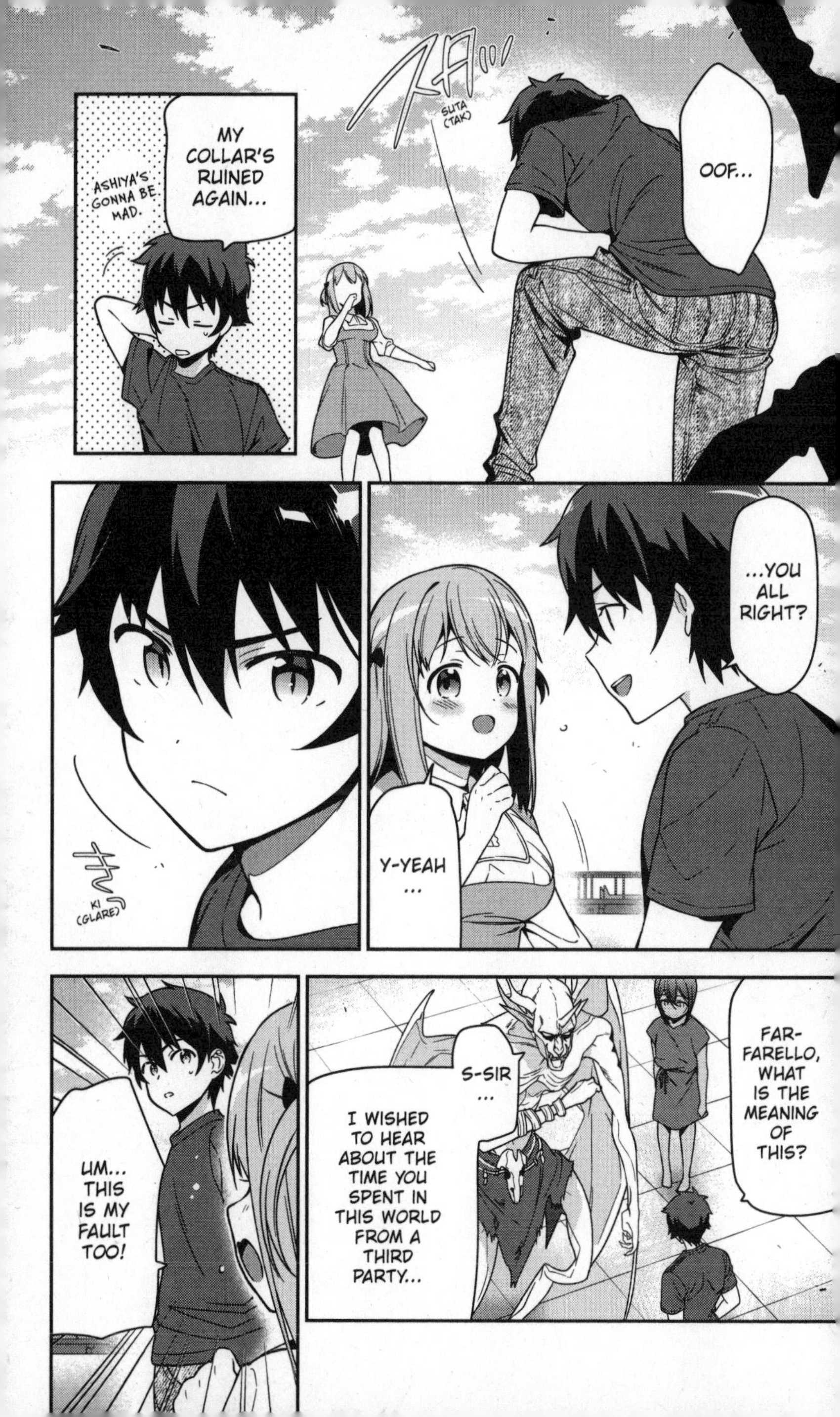
OOF...
SUTA (TAK)
MY COLLAR'S RUINED AGAIN...
ASHIYA'S GONNA BE MAD.
...YOU ALL RIGHT?
Y-YEAH ...
KI (GLARE)
FAR-FARELLO, WHAT IS THE MEANING OF THIS?
S-SIR ...
I WISHED TO HEAR ABOUT THE TIME YOU SPENT IN THIS WORLD FROM A THIRD PARTY...
UM... THIS IS MY FAULT TOO!

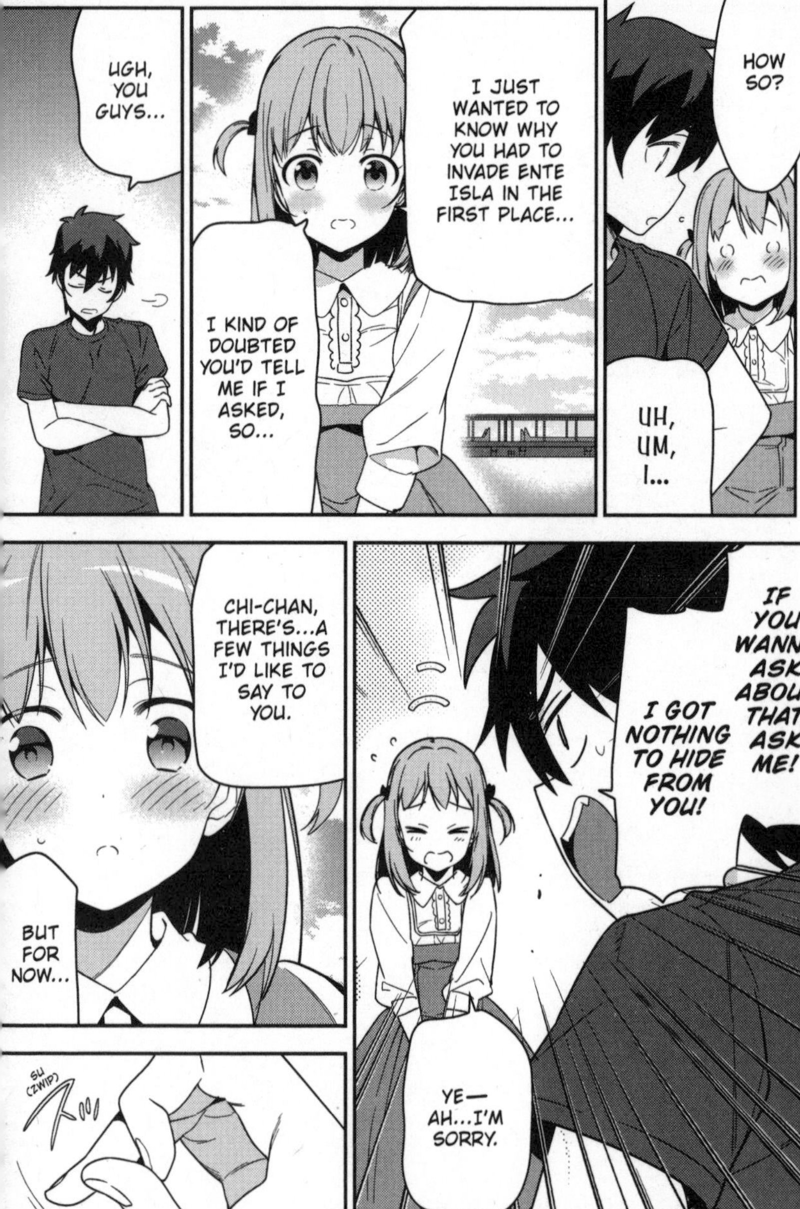
HOW SO?
UH, UM, I...
I JUST WANTED TO KNOW WHY YOU HAD TO INVADE ENTE ISLA IN THE FIRST PLACE...
I KIND OF DOUBTED YOU'D TELL ME IF I ASKED, SO...
UGH, YOU GUYS...
IF YOU WANNA ASK ABOUT THAT, ASK ME!
I GOT NOTHING TO HIDE FROM YOU!
YE—AH...I'M SORRY.
CHI-CHAN, THERE'S...A FEW THINGS I'D LIKE TO SAY TO YOU.
BUT FOR NOW...
SU (ZWIP)

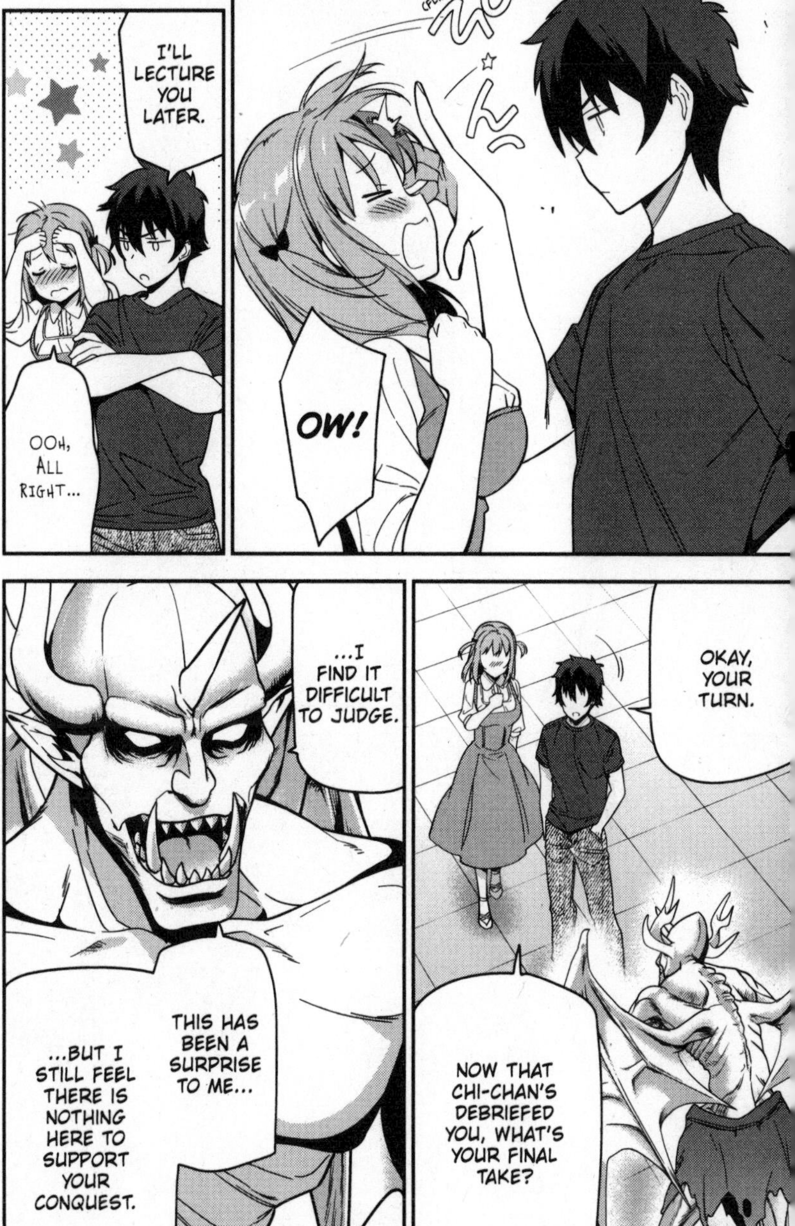
PIN (FLICK)
OW!
I'LL LECTURE YOU LATER.
OOH, ALL RIGHT...
OKAY, YOUR TURN.
NOW THAT CHI-CHAN'S DEBRIEFED YOU, WHAT'S YOUR FINAL TAKE?
...I FIND IT DIFFICULT TO JUDGE.
THIS HAS BEEN A SURPRISE TO ME...
...BUT I STILL FEEL THERE IS NOTHING HERE TO SUPPORT YOUR CONQUEST.

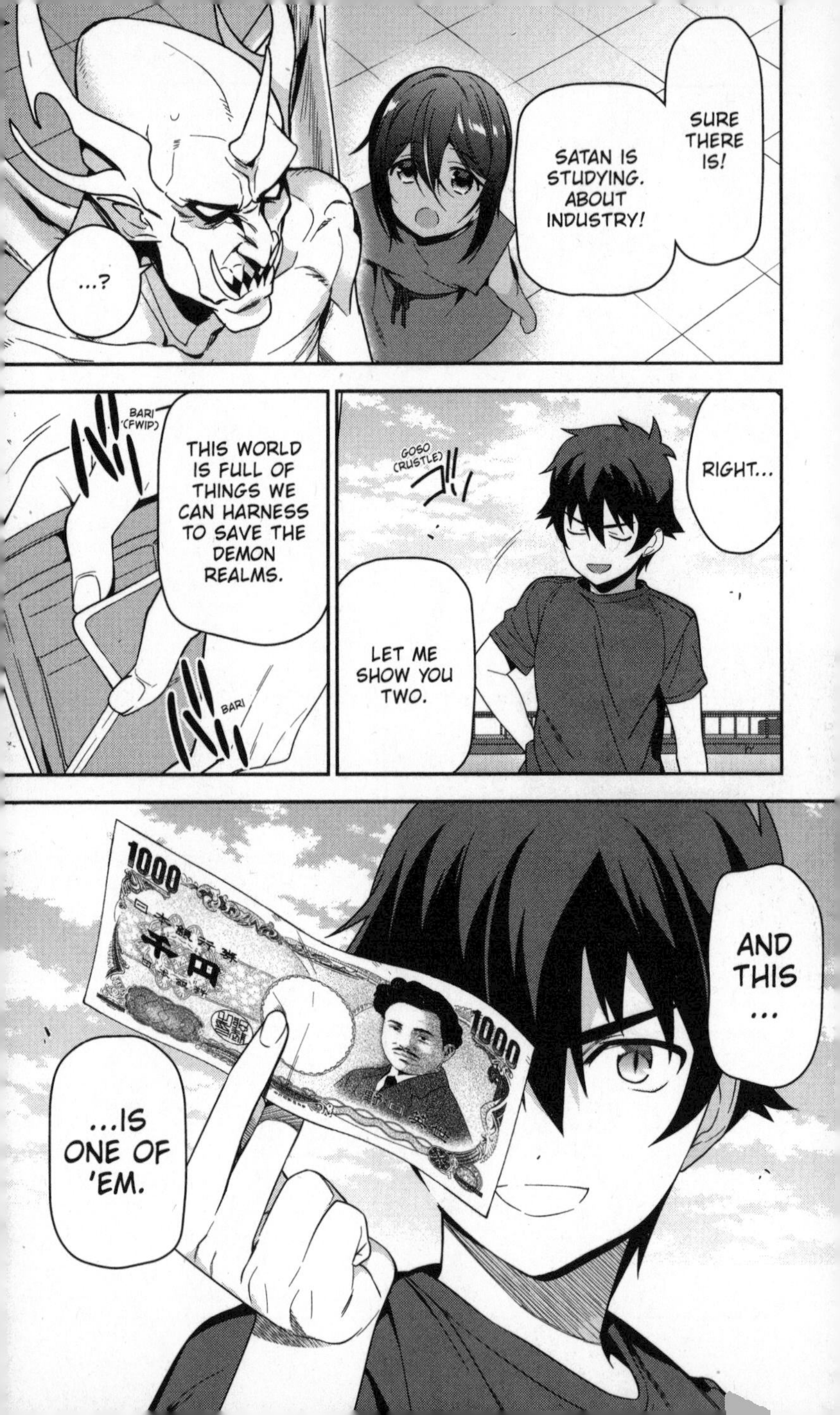
SURE THERE IS!
SATAN IS STUDYING. ABOUT INDUSTRY!
...?
RIGHT...
GOSO (RUSTLE)
LET ME SHOW YOU TWO.
BARI (FWIP)
THIS WORLD IS FULL OF THINGS WE CAN HARNESS TO SAVE THE DEMON REALMS.
BARI
AND THIS...
...IS ONE OF 'EM.

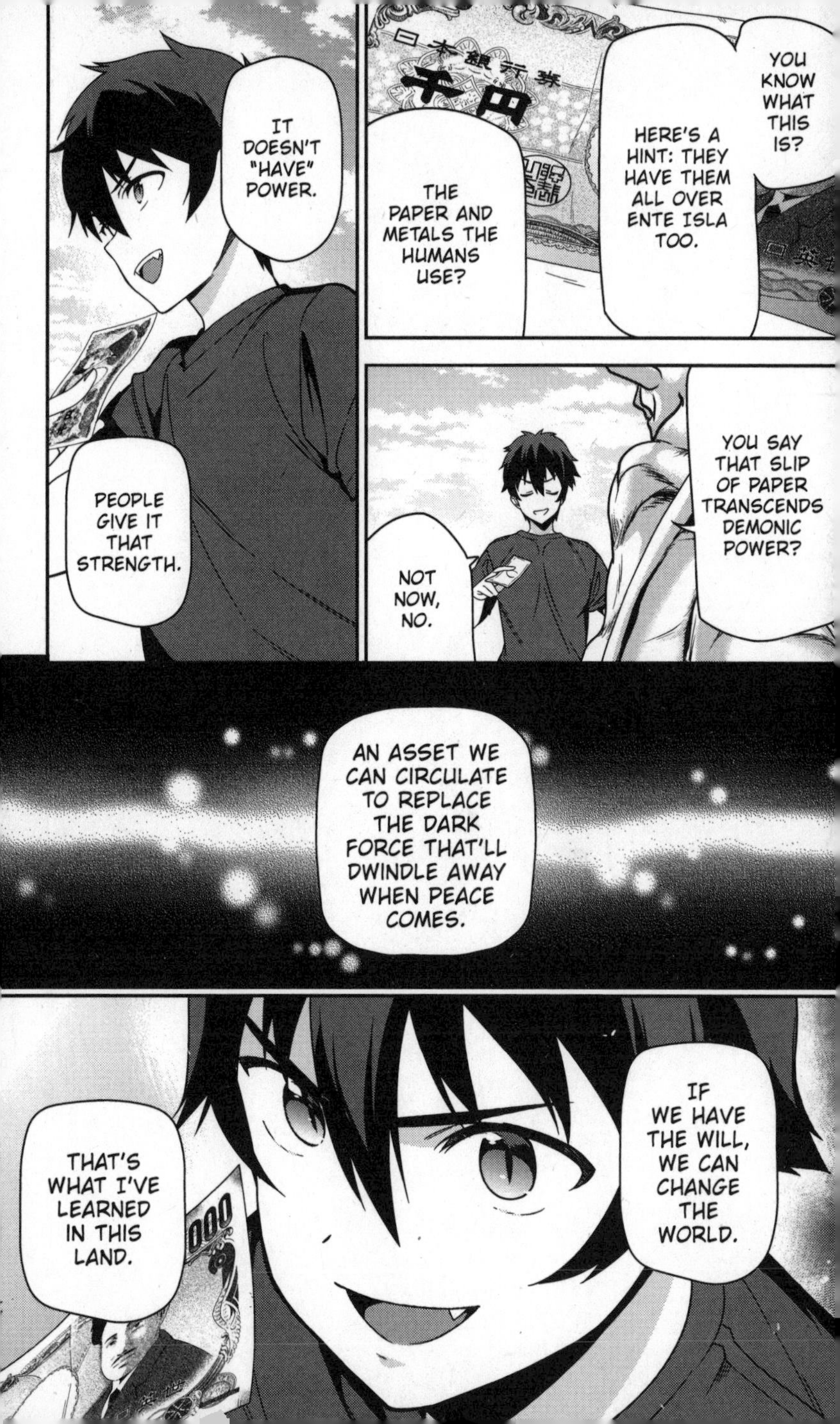
YOU KNOW WHAT THIS IS?
HERE'S A HINT: THEY HAVE THEM ALL OVER ENTE ISLA TOO.
THE PAPER AND METALS THE HUMANS USE?
YOU SAY THAT SLIP OF PAPER TRANSCENDS DEMONIC POWER?
NOT NOW, NO.
IT DOESN'T "HAVE" POWER.
PEOPLE GIVE IT THAT STRENGTH.
AN ASSET WE CAN CIRCULATE TO REPLACE THE DARK FORCE THAT'LL DWINDLE AWAY WHEN PEACE COMES.
IF WE HAVE THE WILL, WE CAN CHANGE THE WORLD.
THAT'S WHAT I'VE LEARNED IN THIS LAND.

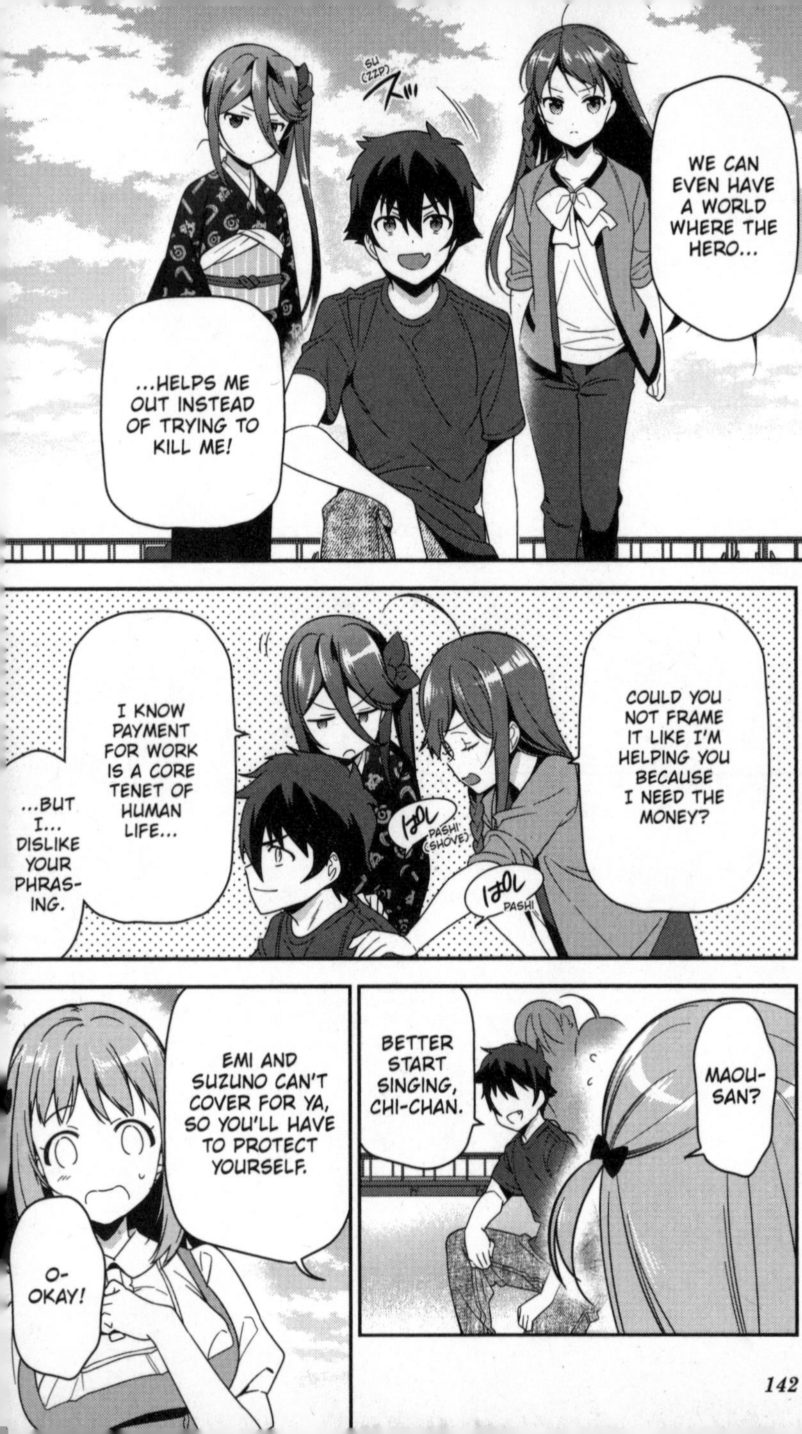
SU (ZZP)
WE CAN EVEN HAVE A WORLD WHERE THE HERO...
...HELPS ME OUT INSTEAD OF TRYING TO KILL ME!
COULD YOU NOT FRAME IT LIKE I'M HELPING YOU BECAUSE I NEED THE MONEY?
PASHI (SHOVE)
PASHI
I KNOW PAYMENT FOR WORK IS A CORE TENET OF HUMAN LIFE...
...BUT I... DISLIKE YOUR PHRAS-ING.
MAOU-SAN?
BETTER START SINGING, CHI-CHAN.
EMI AND SUZUNO CAN'T COVER FOR YA, SO YOU'LL HAVE TO PROTECT YOURSELF.
O-OKAY!

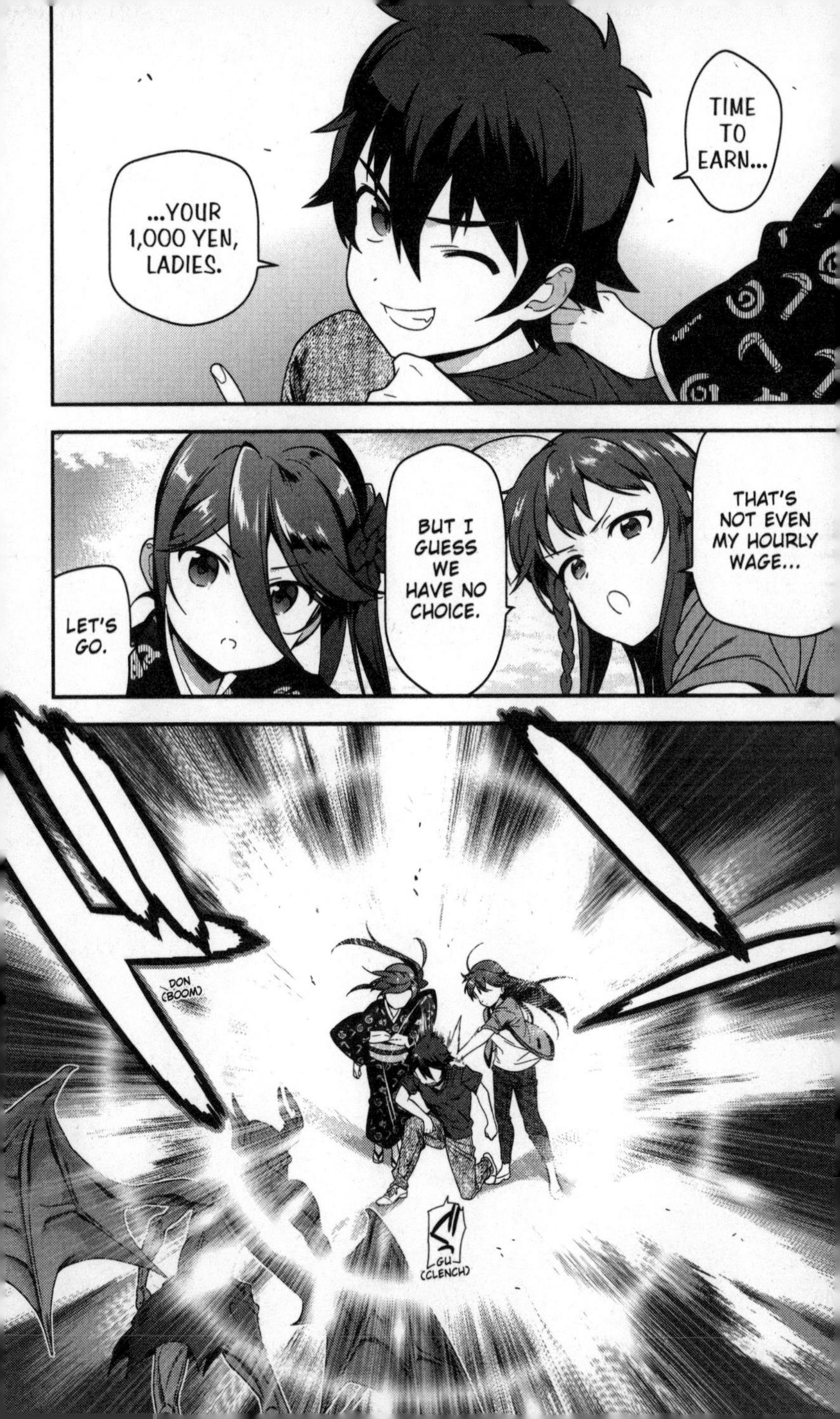
TIME TO EARN...
...YOUR 1,000 YEN, LADIES.
THAT'S NOT EVEN MY HOURLY WAGE...
BUT I GUESS WE HAVE NO CHOICE.
LET'S GO.
DON (BOOM)
GU (CLENCH)

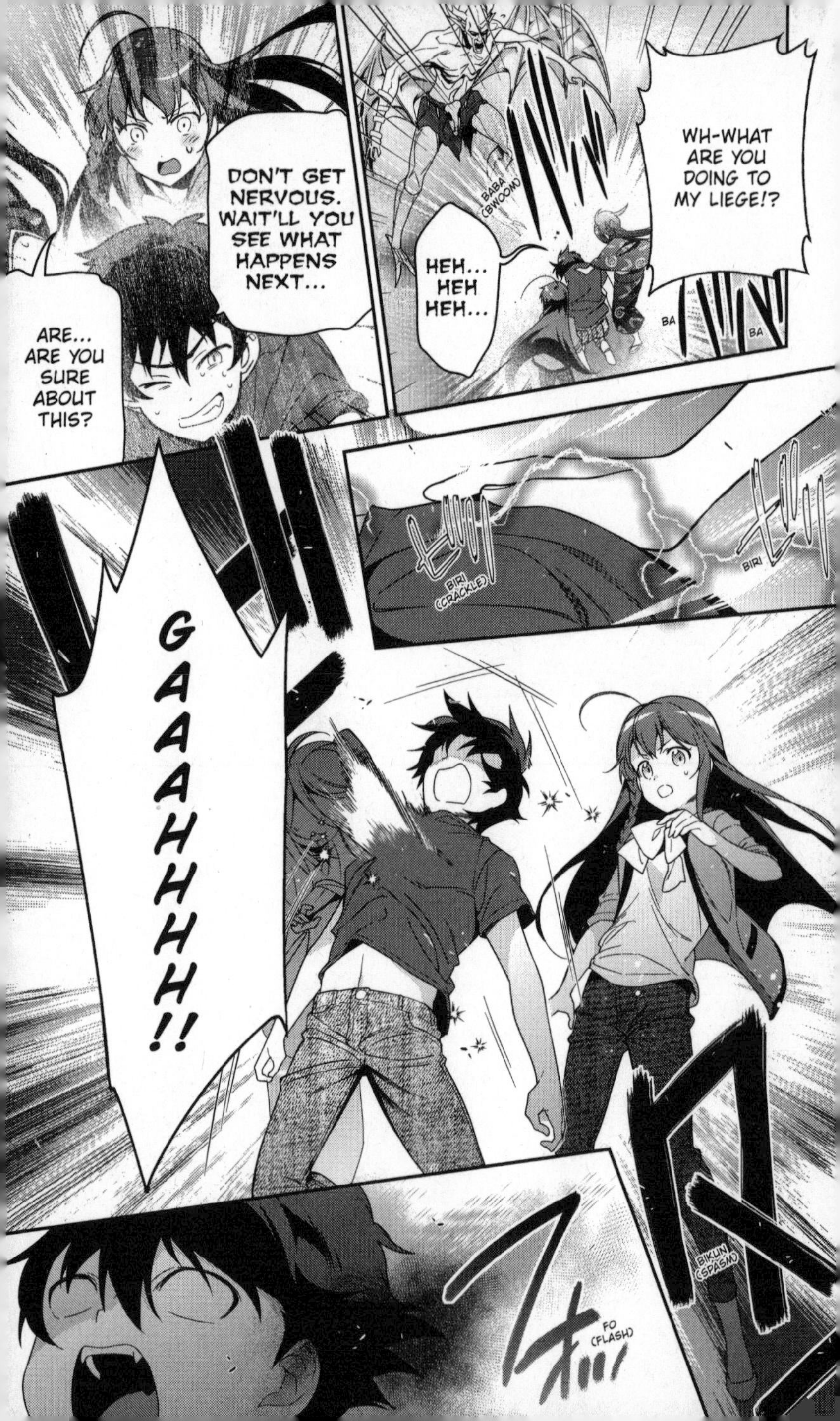
WH-WHAT ARE YOU DOING TO MY LIEGE!?
BABA (BWOOM)
HEH... HEH HEH...
BA
BA
DON'T GET NERVOUS. WAIT'LL YOU SEE WHAT HAPPENS NEXT...
ARE... ARE YOU SURE ABOUT THIS?
BIRI
BIRI (CRACKLE)
GAAAHHHH!!
BIKUN (SPASM)
FO (FLASH)

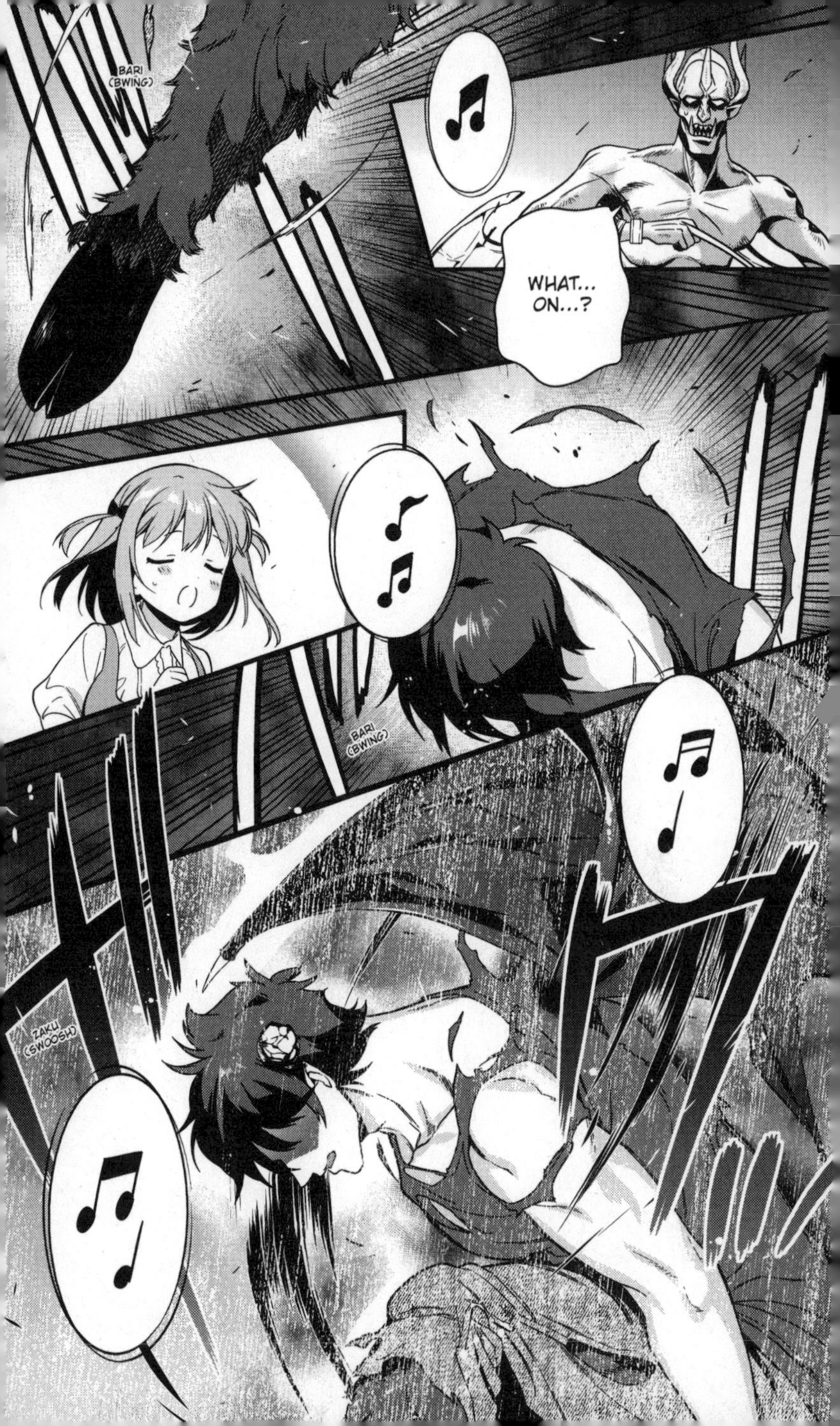
WHAT... ON...?
BARI (BWING)
BARI (BWING)
ZAKU (SWOOSH)

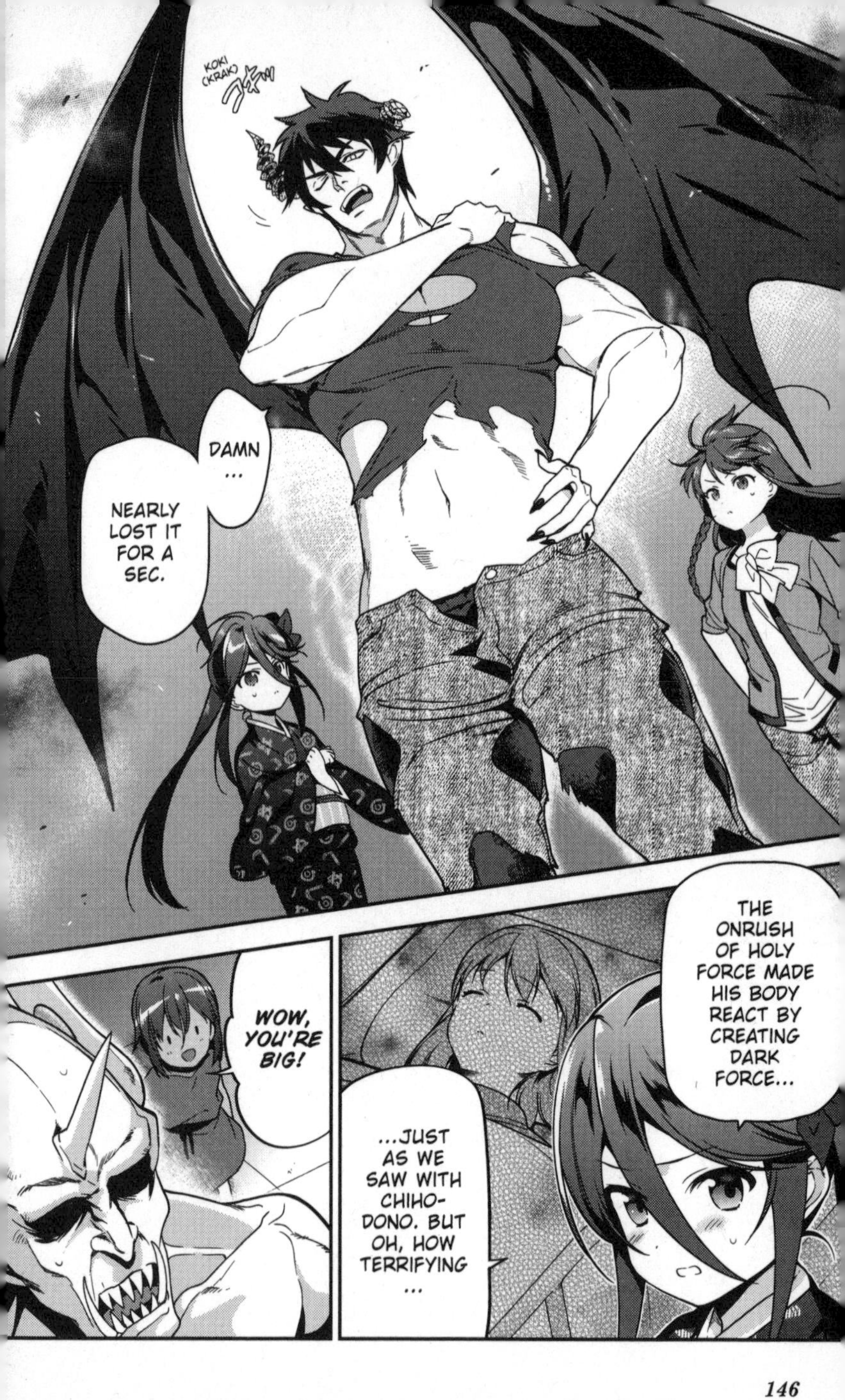
KOKI (KRAK)
DAMN ...
NEARLY LOST IT FOR A SEC.
THE ONRUSH OF HOLY FORCE MADE HIS BODY REACT BY CREATING DARK FORCE...
...JUST AS WE SAW WITH CHIHO-DONO. BUT OH, HOW TERRIFYING ...
WOW, YOU'RE BIG!

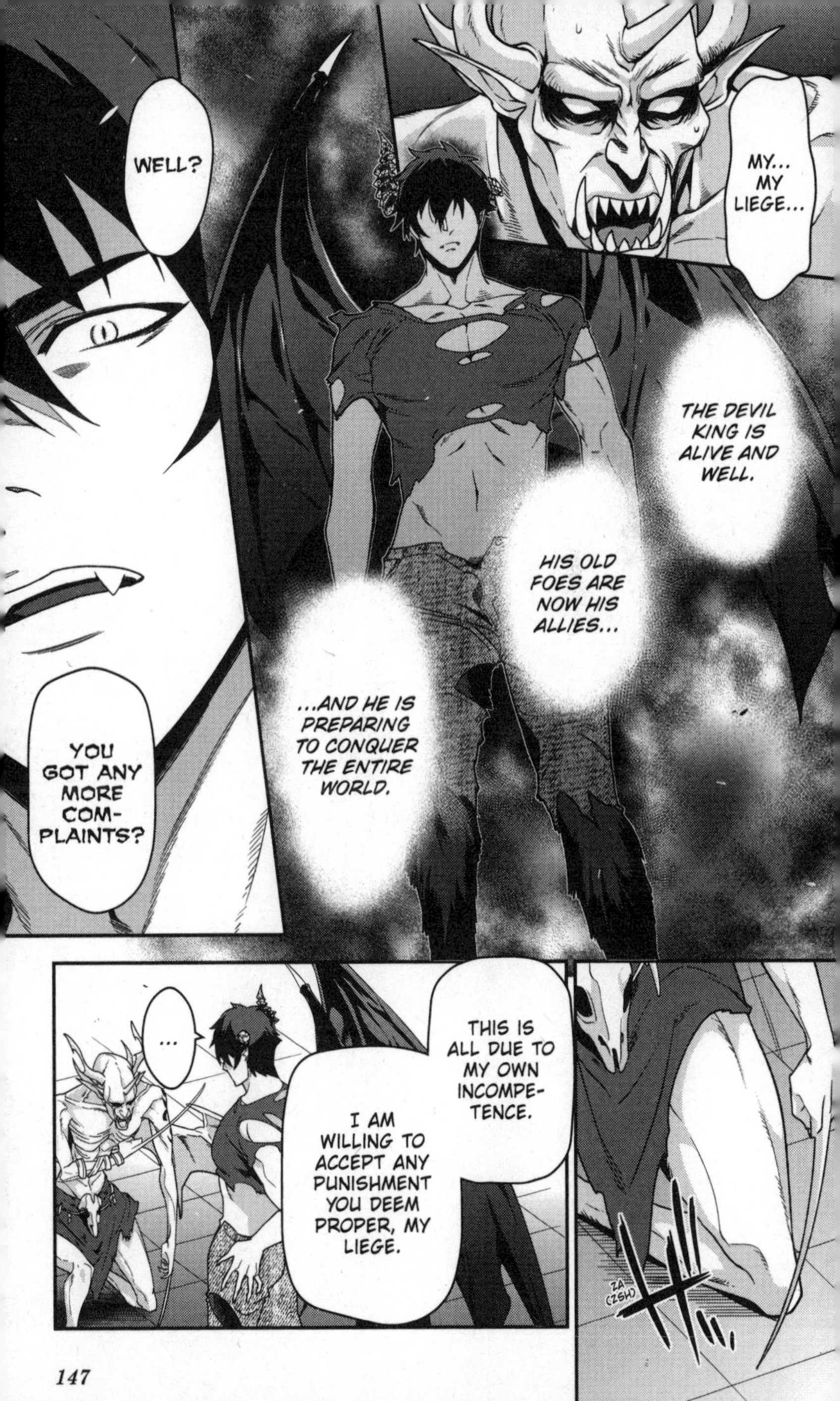
MY... MY LIEGE...
THE DEVIL KING IS ALIVE AND WELL.
HIS OLD FOES ARE NOW HIS ALLIES...
...AND HE IS PREPARING TO CONQUER THE ENTIRE WORLD.
WELL?
YOU GOT ANY MORE COM-PLAINTS?
ZA (ZSH)
THIS IS ALL DUE TO MY OWN INCOMPE-TENCE.
...
I AM WILLING TO ACCEPT ANY PUNISHMENT YOU DEEM PROPER, MY LIEGE.

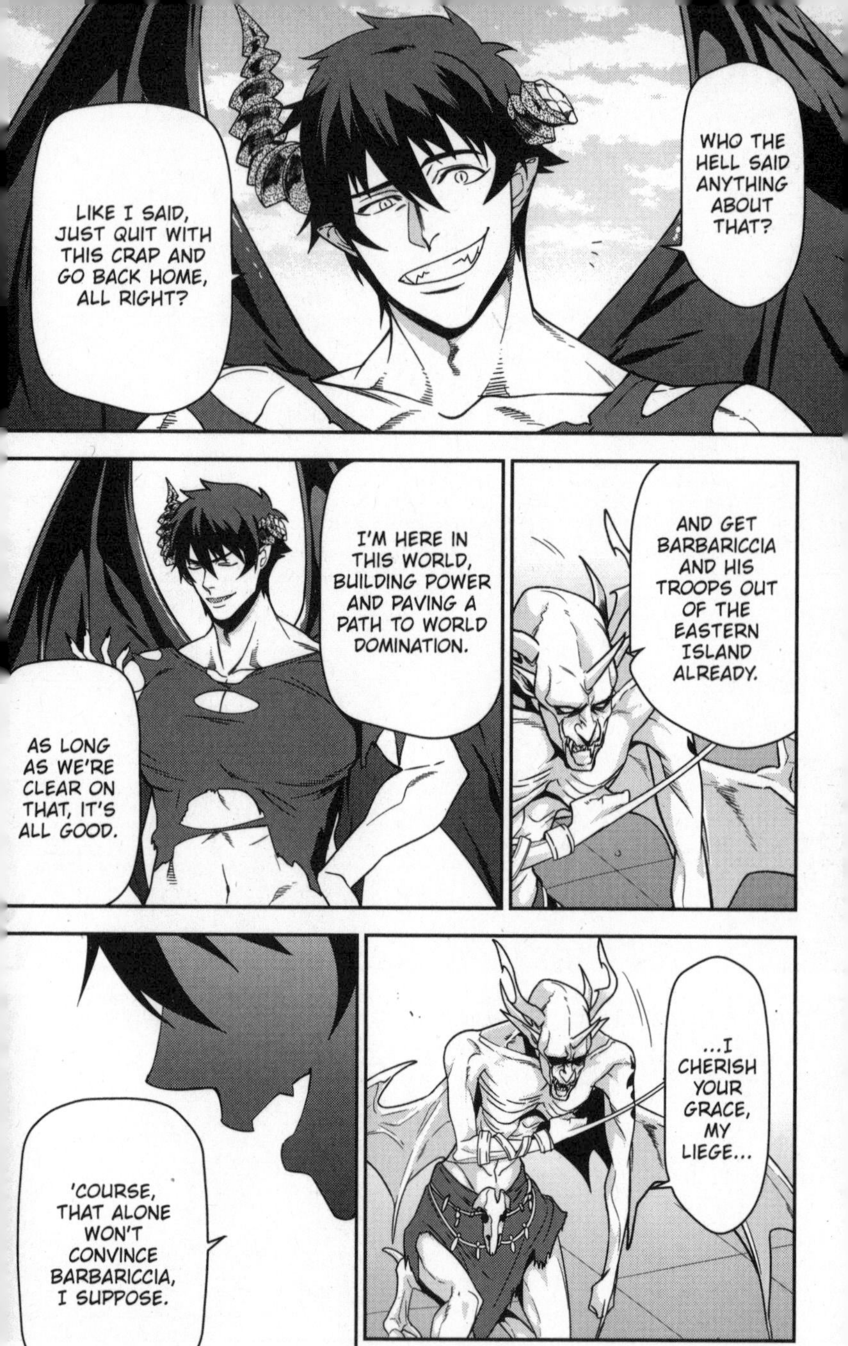
WHO THE HELL SAID ANYTHING ABOUT THAT?
LIKE I SAID, JUST QUIT WITH THIS CRAP AND GO BACK HOME, ALL RIGHT?
AND GET BARBARICCIA AND HIS TROOPS OUT OF THE EASTERN ISLAND ALREADY.
I'M HERE IN THIS WORLD, BUILDING POWER AND PAVING A PATH TO WORLD DOMINATION.
AS LONG AS WE'RE CLEAR ON THAT, IT'S ALL GOOD.
...I CHERISH YOUR GRACE, MY LIEGE...
'COURSE, THAT ALONE WON'T CONVINCE BARBARICCIA, I SUPPOSE.

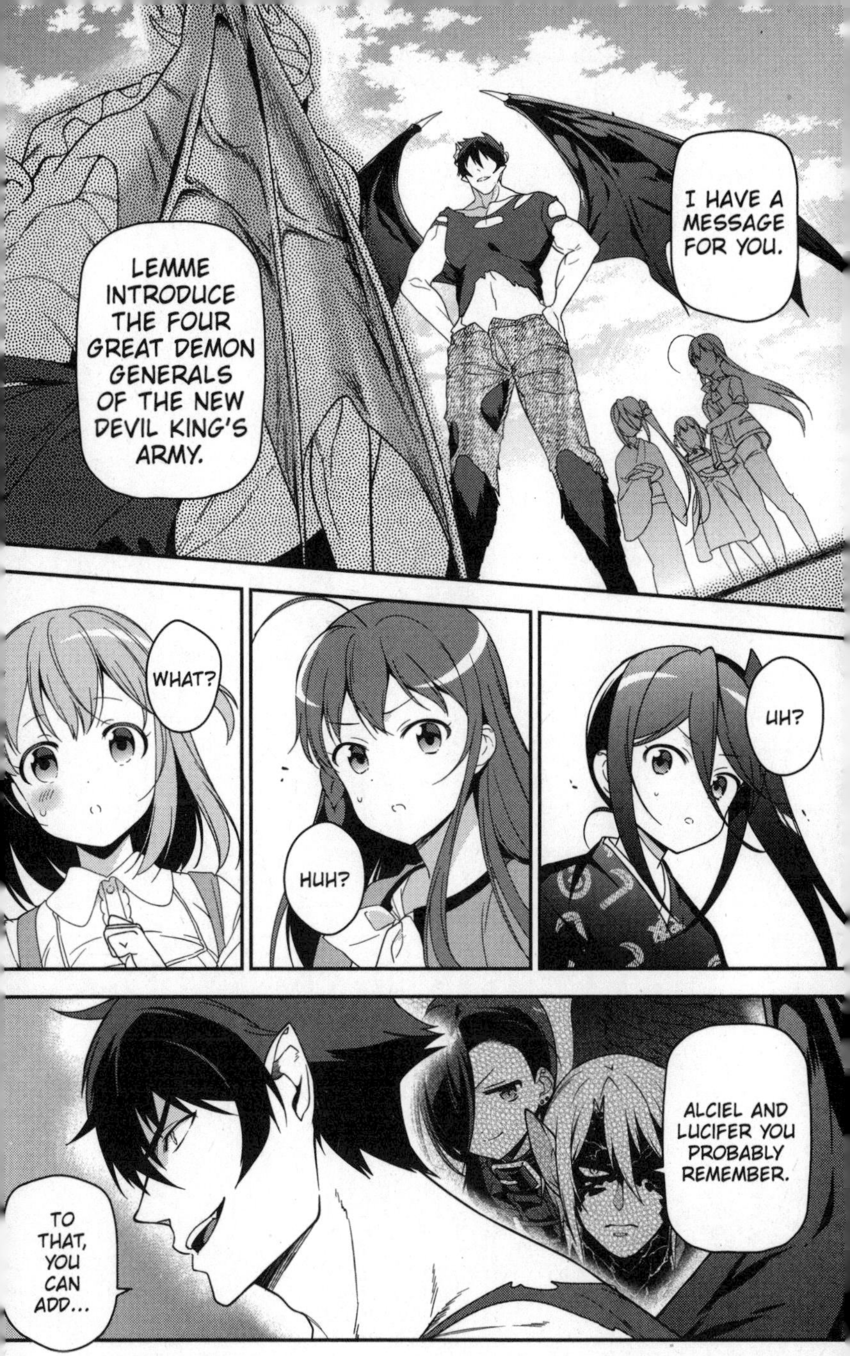
I HAVE A MESSAGE FOR YOU.
LEMME INTRODUCE THE FOUR GREAT DEMON GENERALS OF THE NEW DEVIL KING'S ARMY.
UH?
HUH?
WHAT?
ALCIEL AND LUCIFER YOU PROBABLY REMEMBER.
TO THAT, YOU CAN ADD...

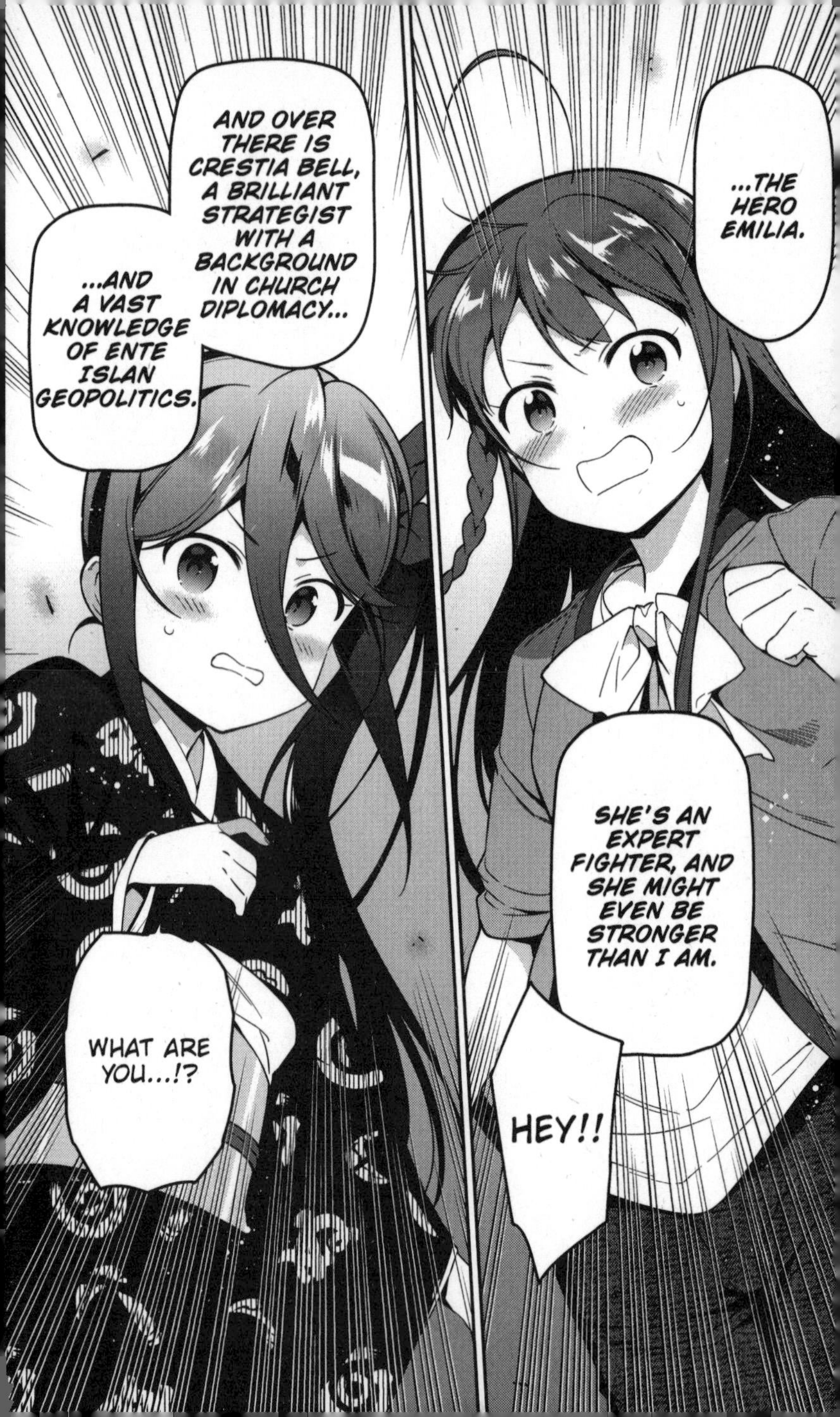
...THE HERO EMILIA.
SHE'S AN EXPERT FIGHTER, AND SHE MIGHT EVEN BE STRONGER THAN I AM.
HEY!!
AND OVER THERE IS CRESTIA BELL, A BRILLIANT STRATEGIST WITH A BACKGROUND IN CHURCH DIPLOMACY...
...AND A VAST KNOWLEDGE OF ENTE ISLAN GEOPOLITICS.
WHAT ARE YOU...!?

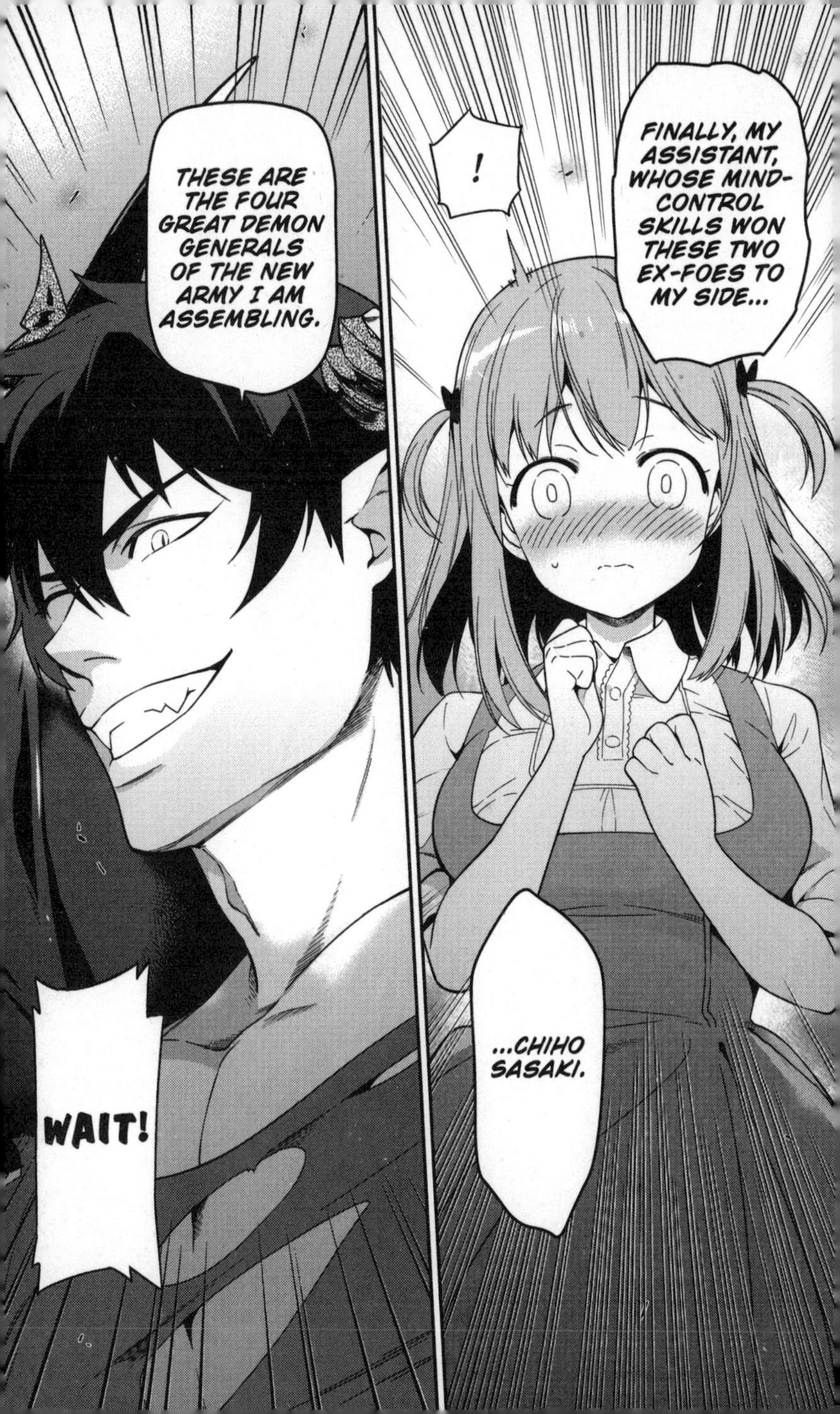
FINALLY, MY ASSISTANT, WHOSE MIND-CONTROL SKILLS WON THESE TWO EX-FOES TO MY SIDE...
!
...CHIHO SASAKI.
THESE ARE THE FOUR GREAT DEMON GENERALS OF THE NEW ARMY I AM ASSEMBLING.
WAIT!

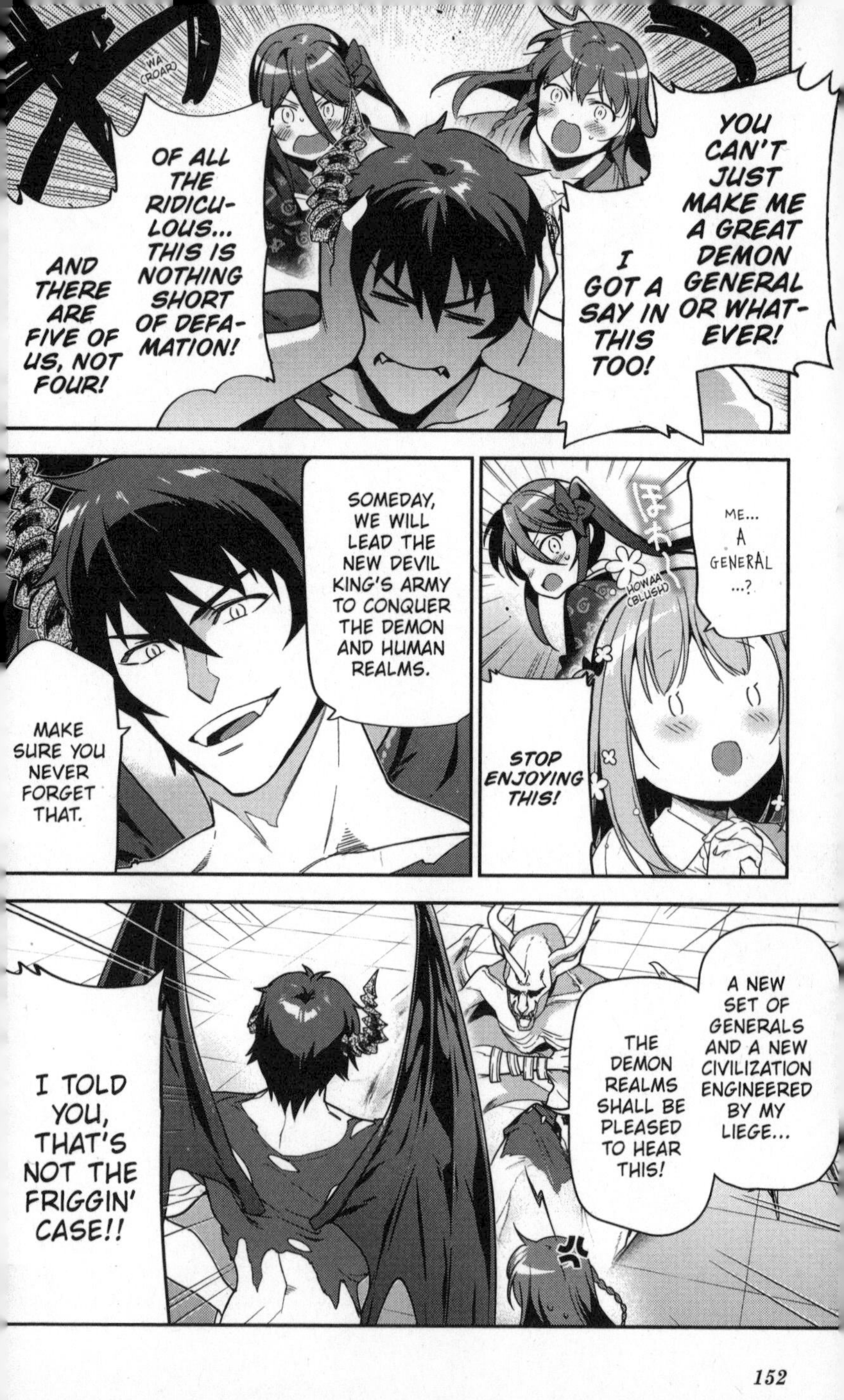
YOU CAN'T JUST MAKE ME A GREAT DEMON GENERAL OR WHATEVER!
I GOT A SAY IN THIS TOO!
WA (ROAR)
OF ALL THE RIDICULOUS... THIS IS NOTHING SHORT OF DEFAMATION!
AND THERE ARE FIVE OF US, NOT FOUR!
ME... A GENERAL ...?
HOWAA (BLUSH)
STOP ENJOYING THIS!
SOMEDAY, WE WILL LEAD THE NEW DEVIL KING'S ARMY TO CONQUER THE DEMON AND HUMAN REALMS.
MAKE SURE YOU NEVER FORGET THAT.
A NEW SET OF GENERALS AND A NEW CIVILIZATION ENGINEERED BY MY LIEGE...
THE DEMON REALMS SHALL BE PLEASED TO HEAR THIS!
I TOLD YOU, THAT'S NOT THE FRIGGIN' CASE!!

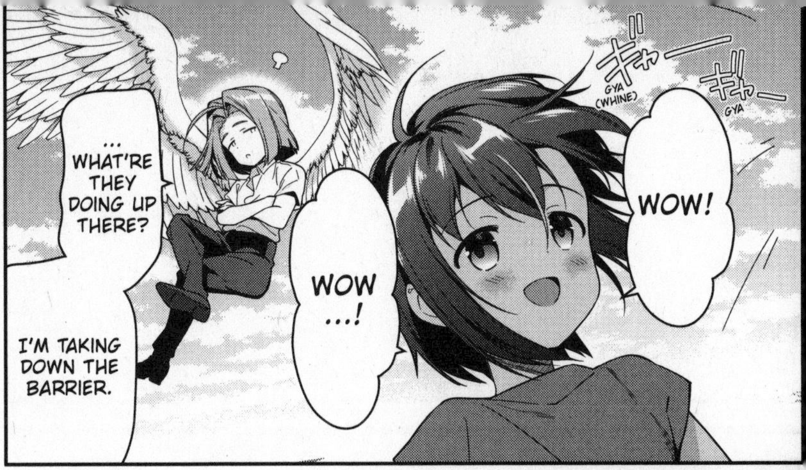
GYA (WHINE)
GYA
WOW!
WOW ...!
... WHAT'RE THEY DOING UP THERE?
I'M TAKING DOWN THE BARRIER.

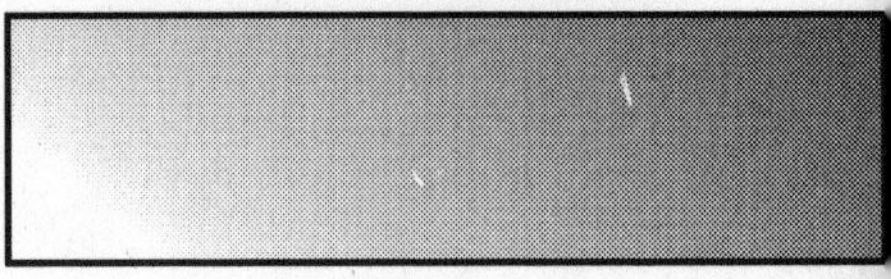

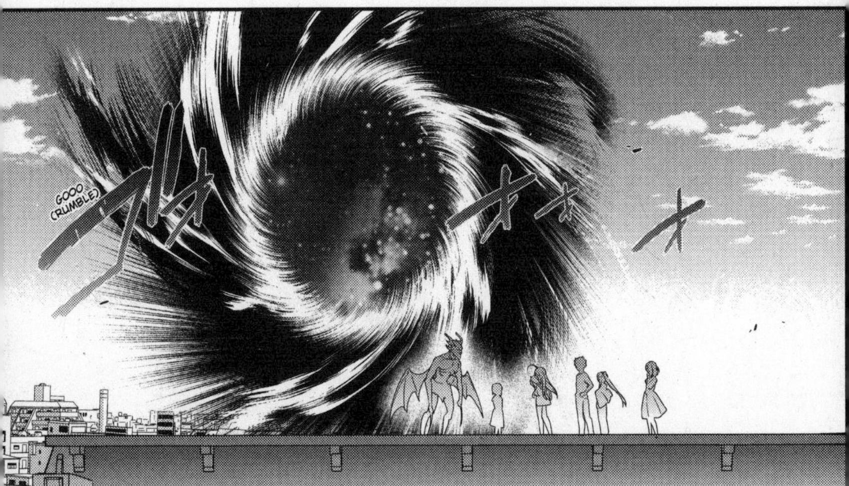
GOOO (RUMBLE)

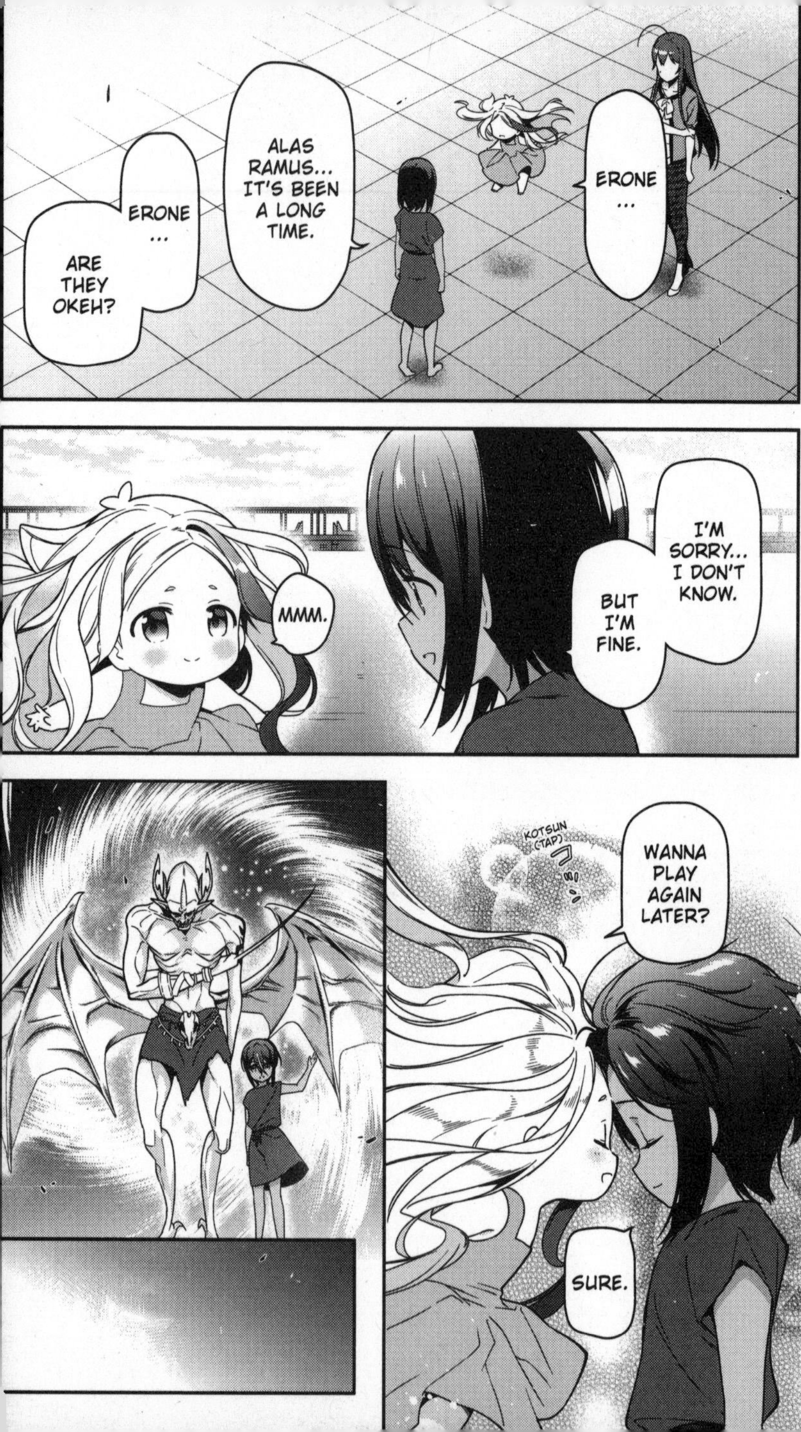
ERONE ...
ALAS RAMUS... IT'S BEEN A LONG TIME.
ERONE ...
ARE THEY OKEH?
I'M SORRY... I DON'T KNOW.
BUT I'M FINE.
MMM.
KOTSUN (TAP)
WANNA PLAY AGAIN LATER?
SURE.

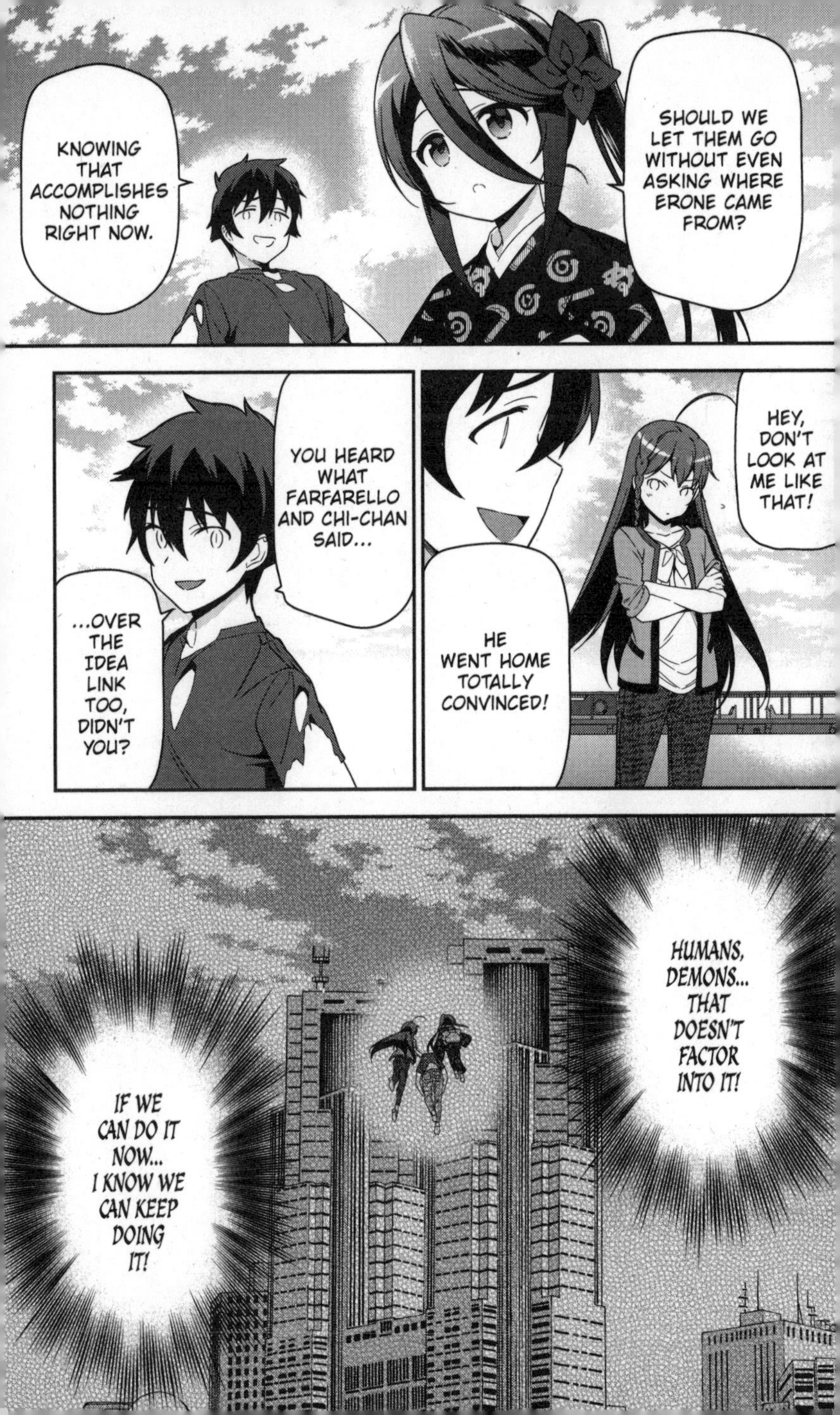
SHOULD WE LET THEM GO WITHOUT EVEN ASKING WHERE ERONE CAME FROM?
KNOWING THAT ACCOMPLISHES NOTHING RIGHT NOW.
HEY, DON'T LOOK AT ME LIKE THAT!
HE WENT HOME TOTALLY CONVINCED!
YOU HEARD WHAT FARFARELLO AND CHI-CHAN SAID...
...OVER THE IDEA LINK TOO, DIDN'T YOU?
HUMANS, DEMONS... THAT DOESN'T FACTOR INTO IT!
IF WE CAN DO IT NOW... I KNOW WE CAN KEEP DOING IT!

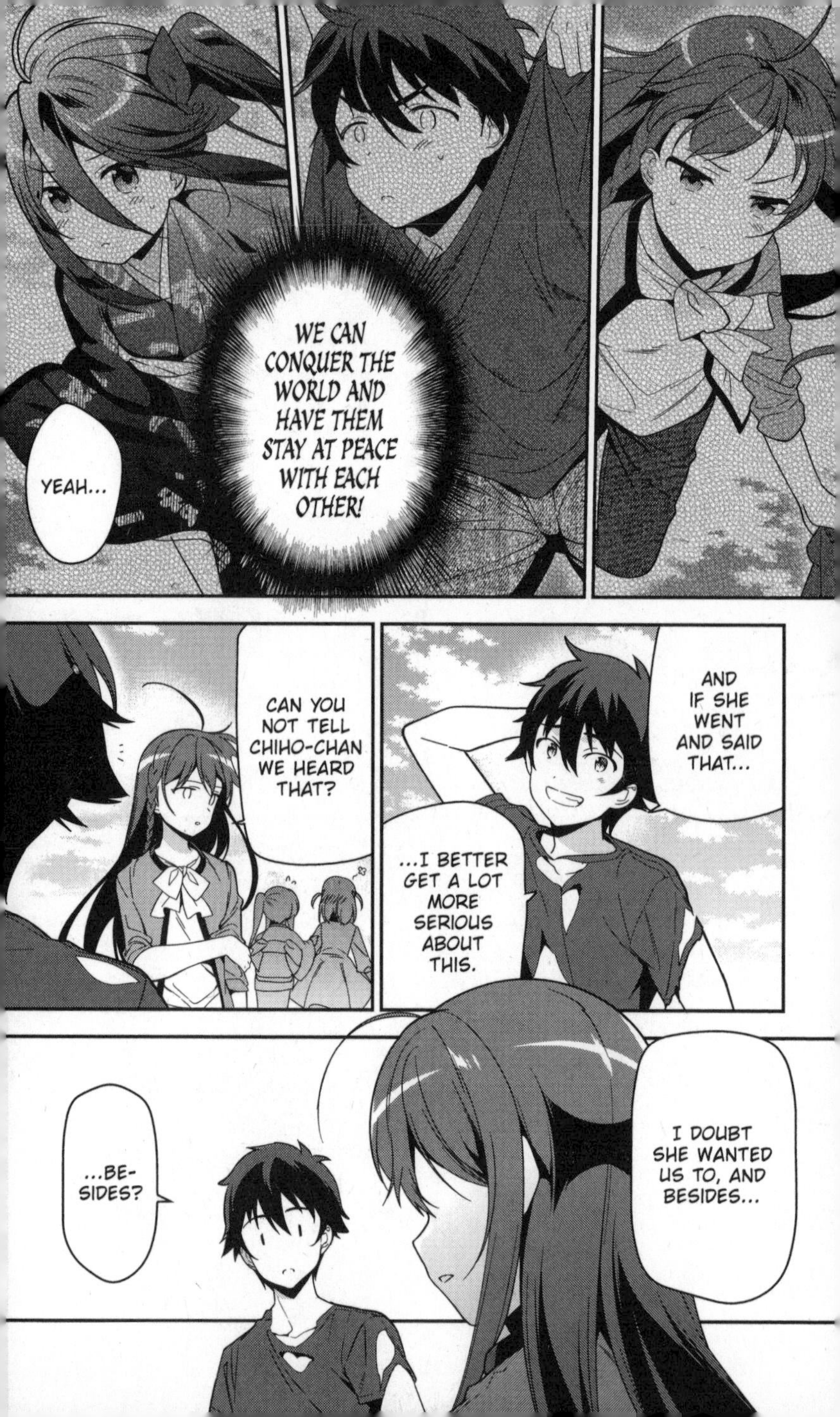
WE CAN CONQUER THE WORLD AND HAVE THEM STAY AT PEACE WITH EACH OTHER!
YEAH...
AND IF SHE WENT AND SAID THAT...
...I BETTER GET A LOT MORE SERIOUS ABOUT THIS.
CAN YOU NOT TELL CHIHO-CHAN WE HEARD THAT?
I DOUBT SHE WANTED US TO, AND BESIDES...
...BE-SIDES?

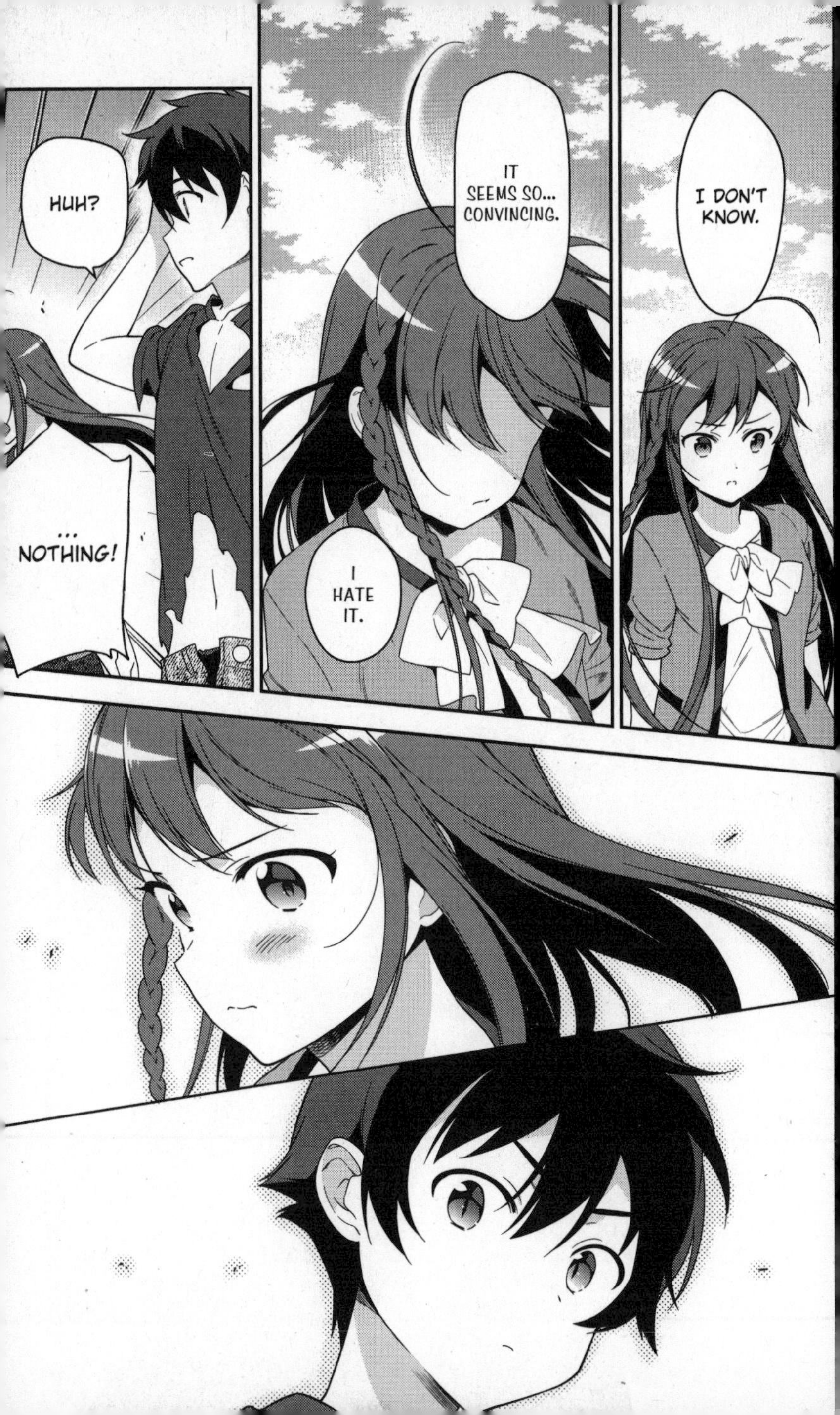
I DON'T KNOW.
IT SEEMS SO... CONVINCING.
I HATE IT.
HUH?
... NOTHING!

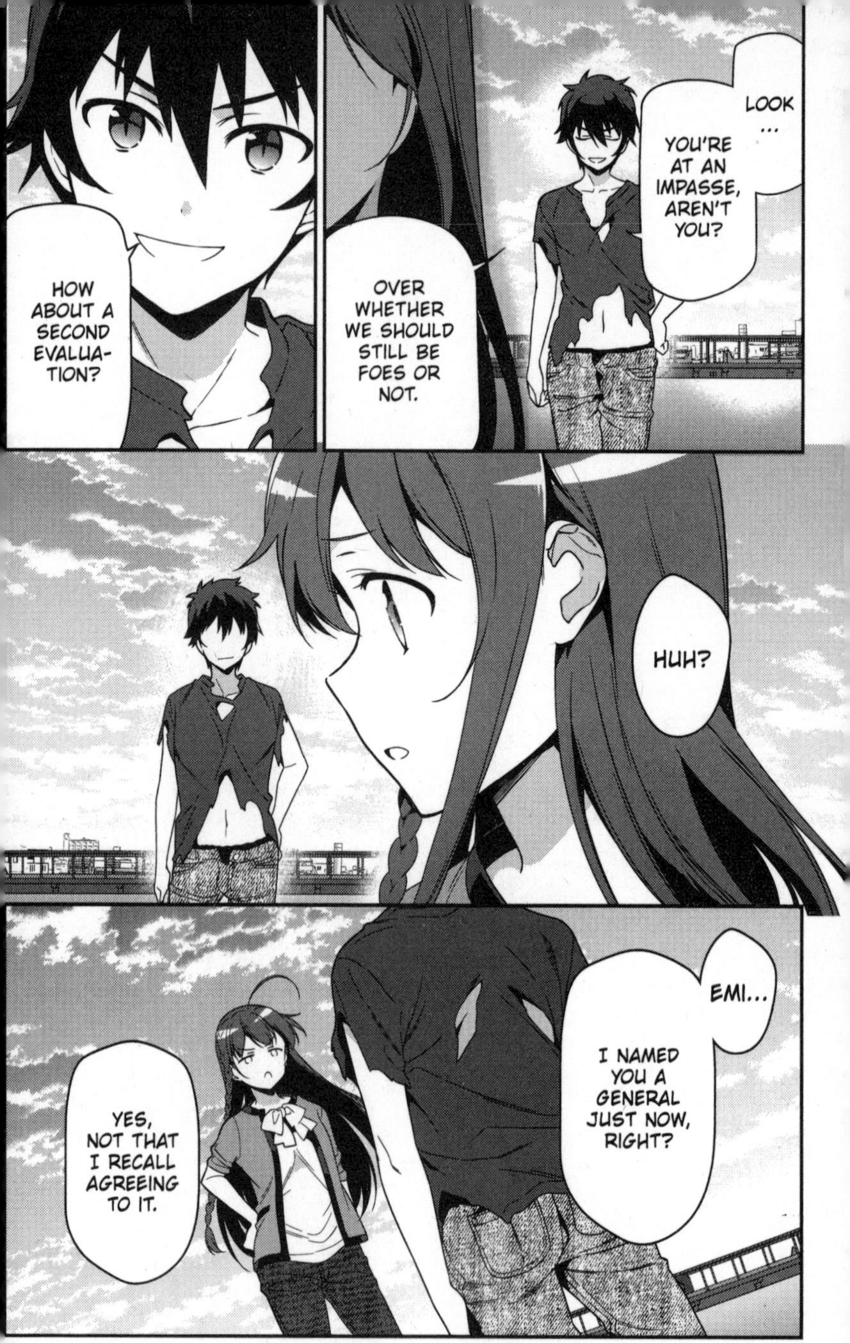

LOOK ...
YOU'RE AT AN IMPASSE, AREN'T YOU?
OVER WHETHER WE SHOULD STILL BE FOES OR NOT.
HOW ABOUT A SECOND EVALUA-TION?
HUH?
EMI...
I NAMED YOU A GENERAL JUST NOW, RIGHT?
YES, NOT THAT I RECALL AGREEING TO IT.

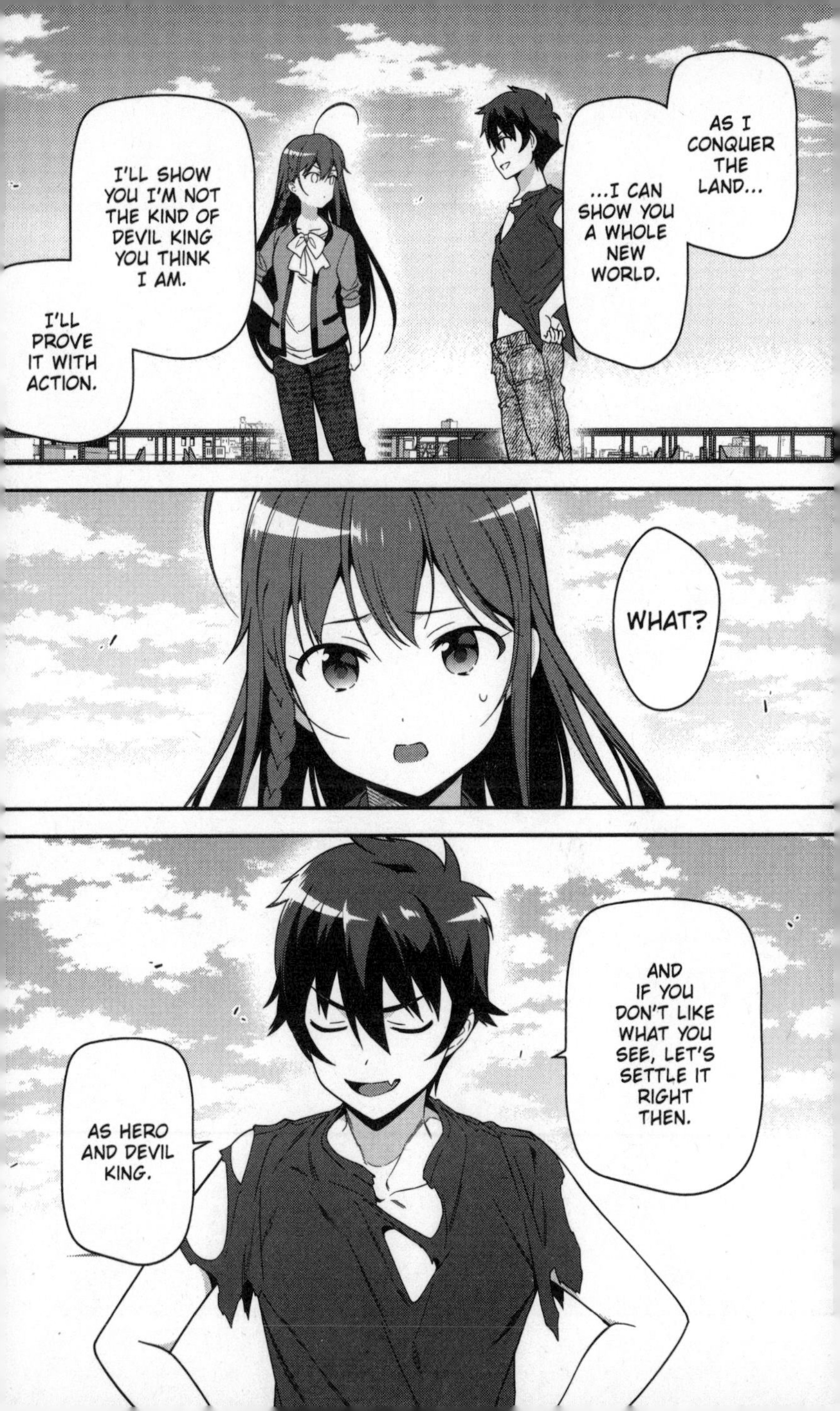
AS I CONQUER THE LAND...
...I CAN SHOW YOU A WHOLE NEW WORLD.
I'LL SHOW YOU I'M NOT THE KIND OF DEVIL KING YOU THINK I AM.
I'LL PROVE IT WITH ACTION.
WHAT?
AND IF YOU DON'T LIKE WHAT YOU SEE, LET'S SETTLE IT RIGHT THEN.
AS HERO AND DEVIL KING.

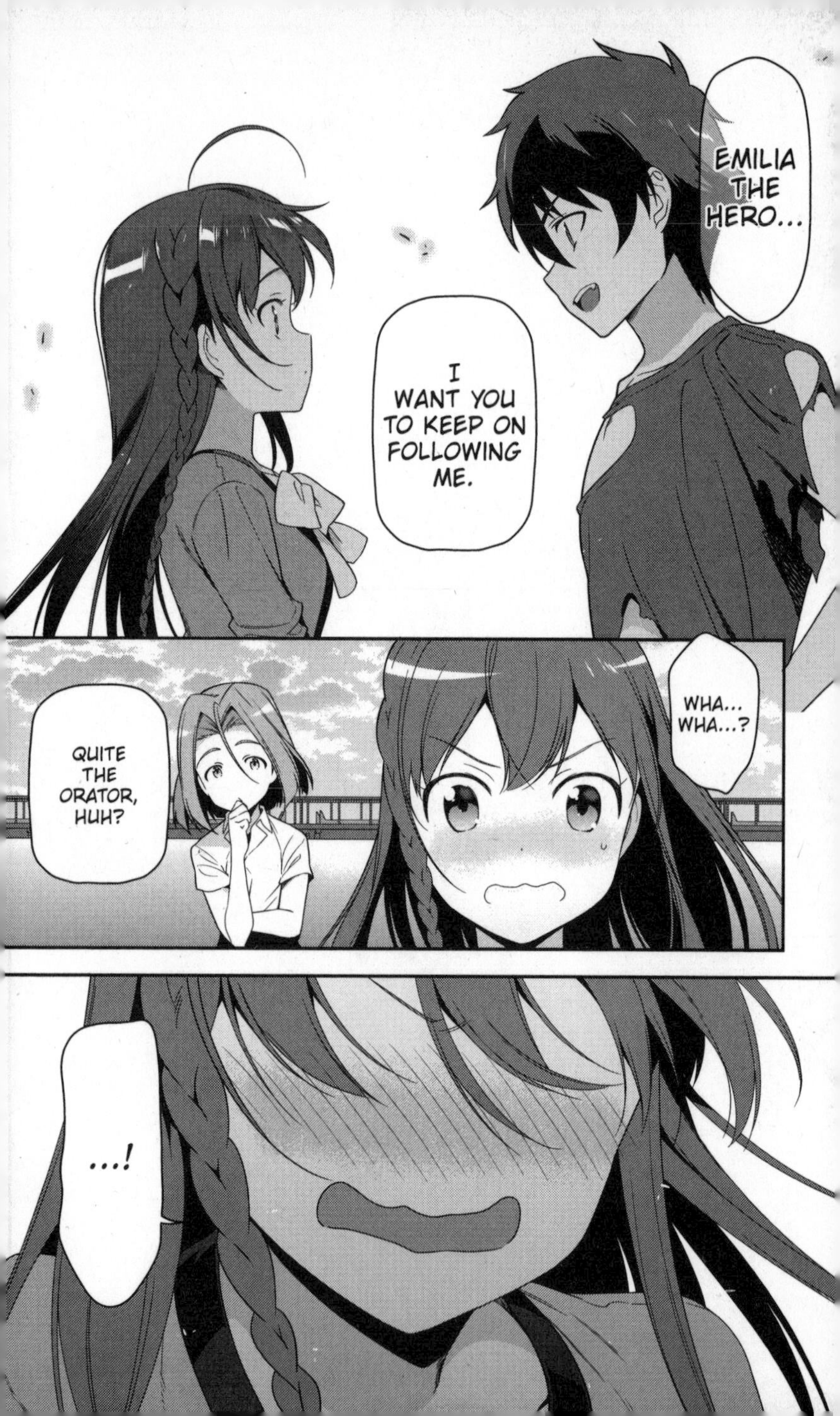
EMILIA THE HERO...
I WANT YOU TO KEEP ON FOLLOWING ME.
WHA... WHA...?
QUITE THE ORATOR, HUH?
...!

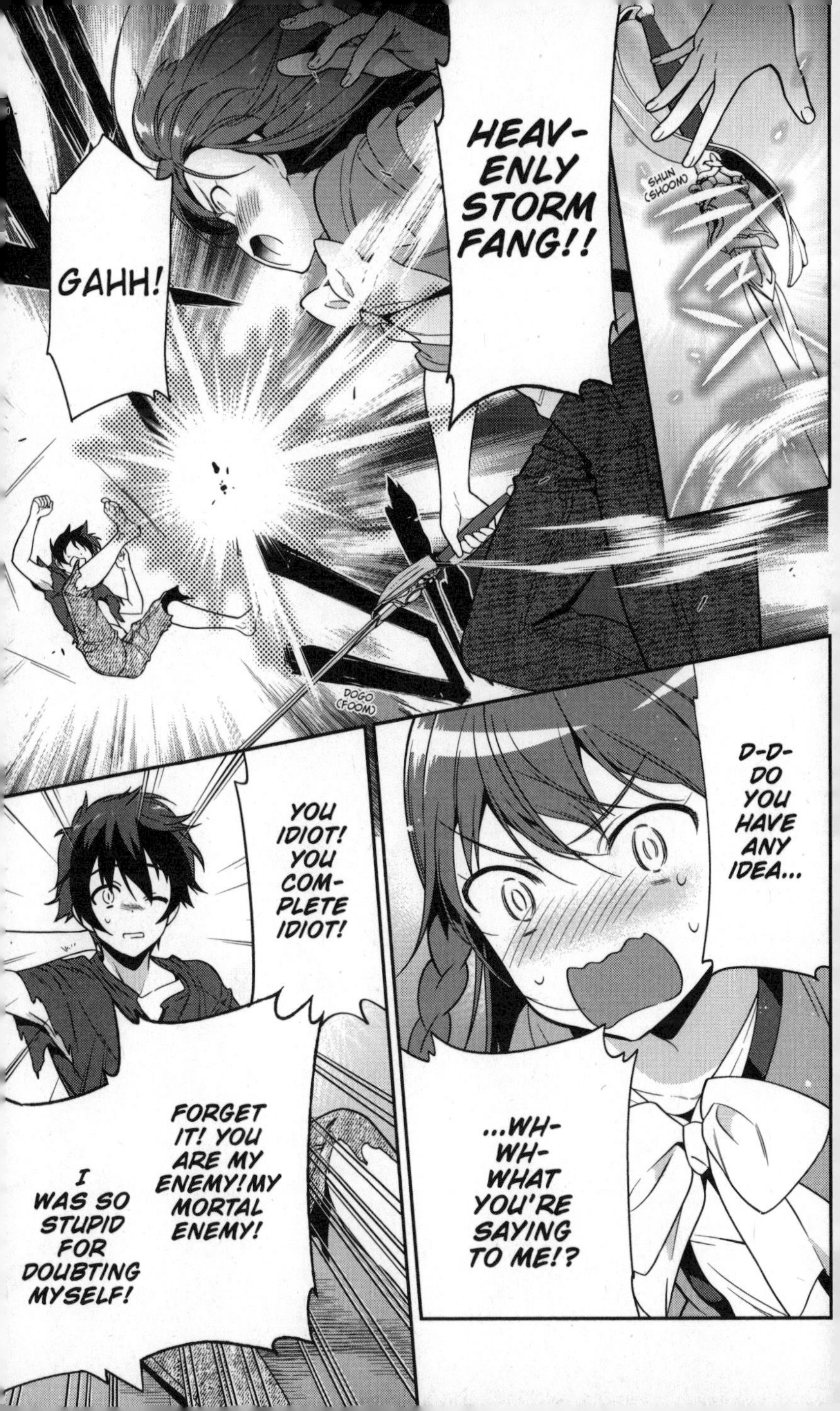
SHUN (SHOOM)
HEAV-ENLY STORM FANG!!
GAHH!
DOGO (FOOM)
D-D-DO YOU HAVE ANY IDEA...
YOU IDIOT! YOU COMPLETE IDIOT!
...WH-WH-WHAT YOU'RE SAYING TO ME!?
FORGET IT! YOU ARE MY ENEMY! MY MORTAL ENEMY!
I WAS SO STUPID FOR DOUBTING MYSELF!

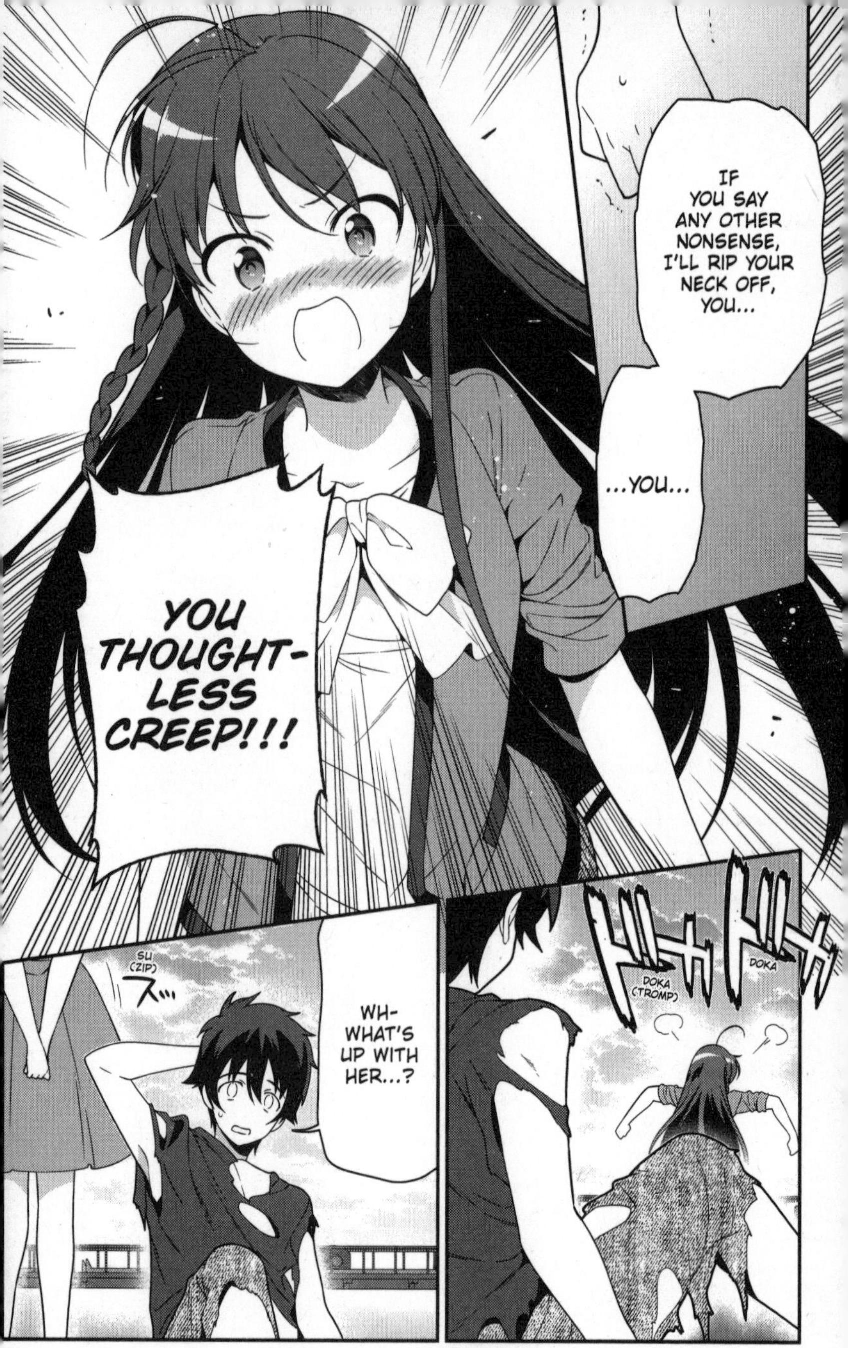
IF YOU SAY ANY OTHER NONSENSE, I'LL RIP YOUR NECK OFF, YOU...
...YOU...
YOU THOUGHT-LESS CREEP!!!
ドカドカ
DOKA (TROMP)
DOKA
SU (ZIP)
ズッ
WH-WHAT'S UP WITH HER...?

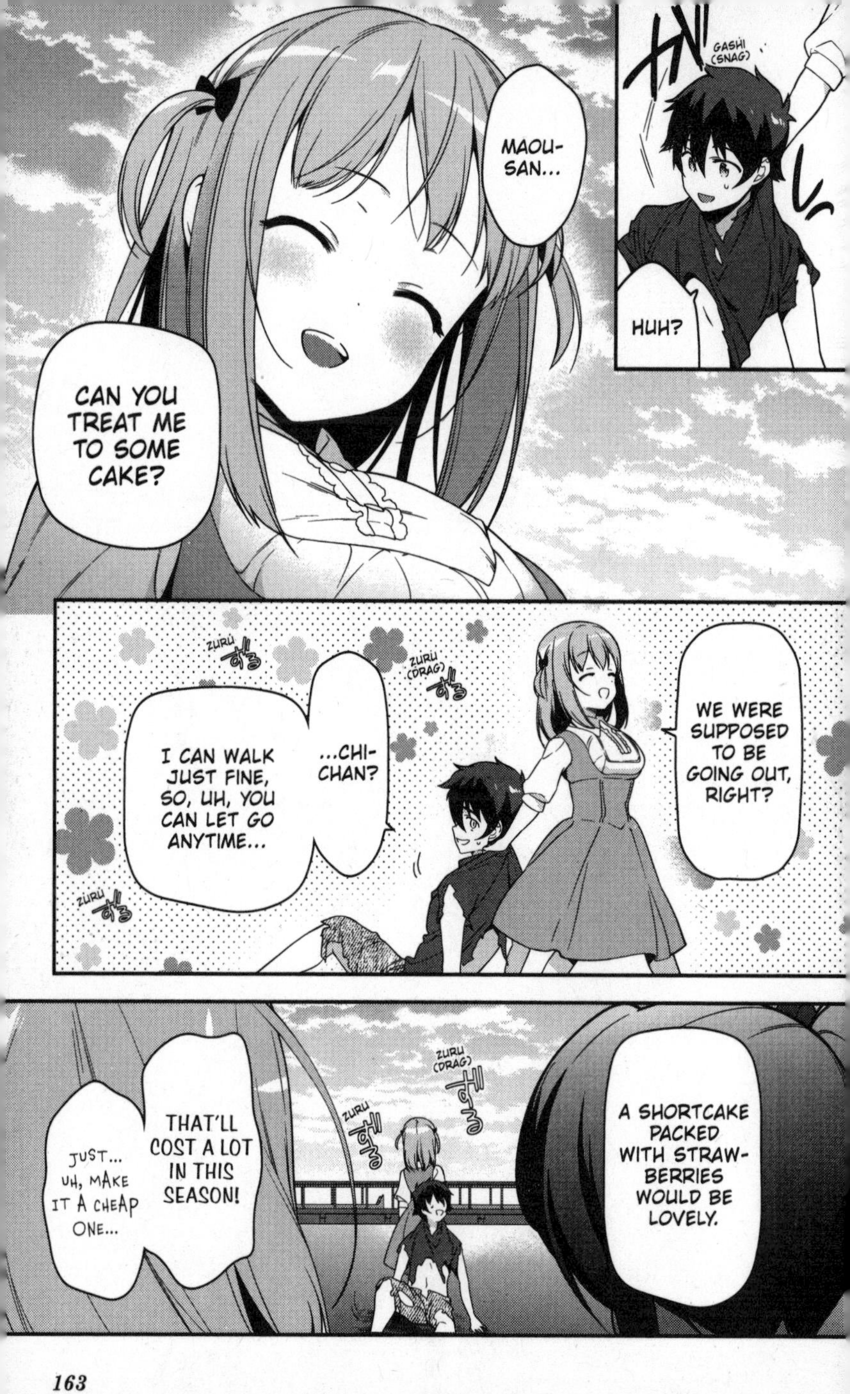
GASHI (SNAG)
HUH?
MAOU-SAN...
CAN YOU TREAT ME TO SOME CAKE?
WE WERE SUPPOSED TO BE GOING OUT, RIGHT?
ZURU (DRAG)
...CHI-CHAN?
I CAN WALK JUST FINE, SO, UH, YOU CAN LET GO ANYTIME...
ZURU
ZURU
A SHORTCAKE PACKED WITH STRAWBERRIES WOULD BE LOVELY.
ZURU (DRAG)
ZURU
THAT'LL COST A LOT IN THIS SEASON!
JUST... UH, MAKE IT A CHEAP ONE...

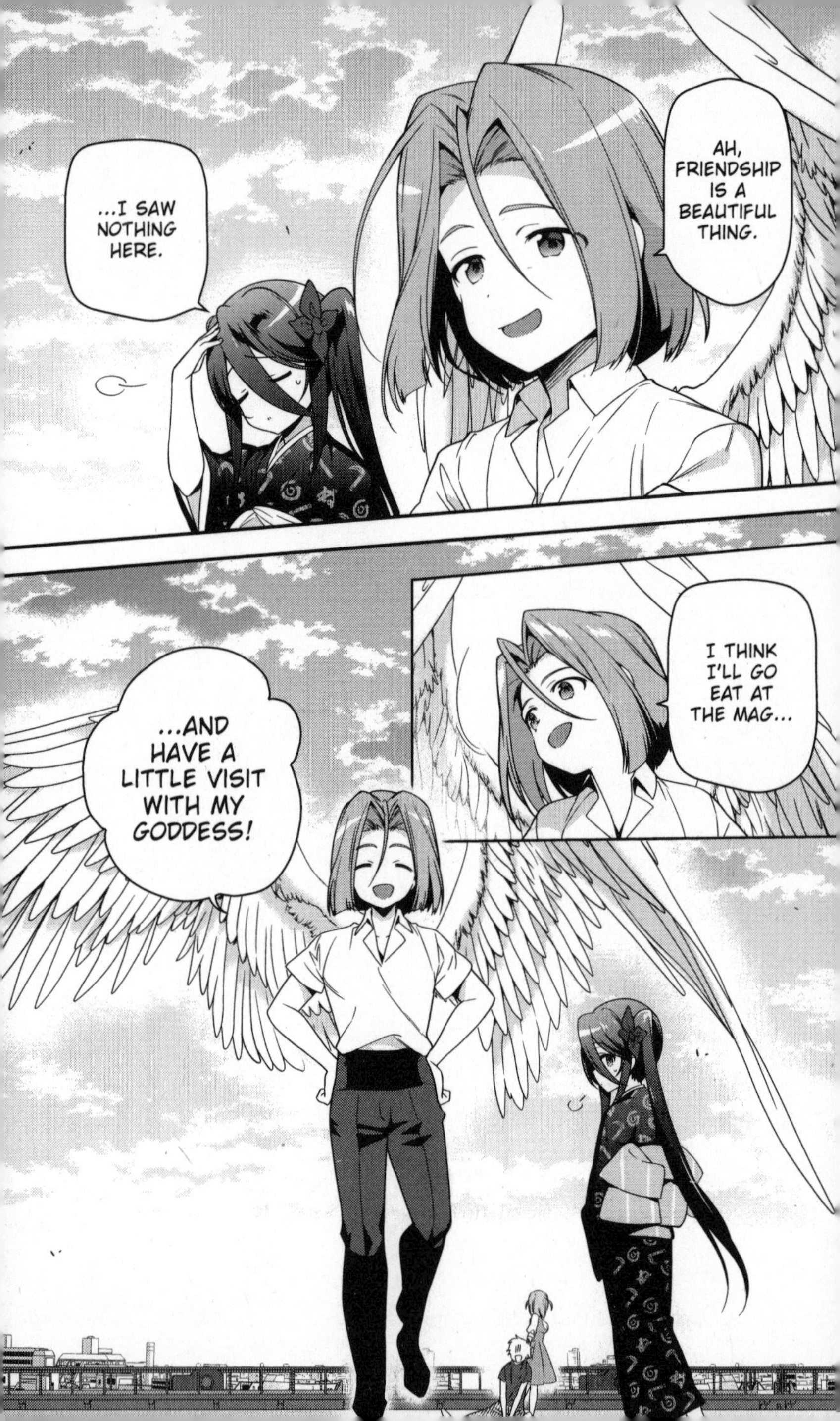
AH, FRIENDSHIP IS A BEAUTIFUL THING.
...I SAW NOTHING HERE.
I THINK I'LL GO EAT AT THE MAG...
...AND HAVE A LITTLE VISIT WITH MY GODDESS!

Chiho
Sasaki

THE DEVIL IS A PART-TIMER!

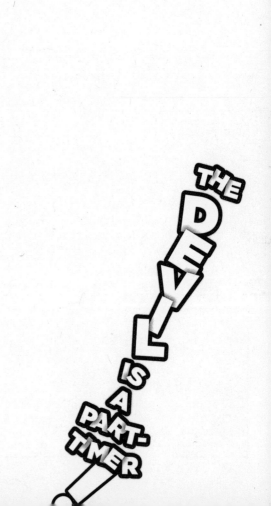

CHAPTER 69: THE HERO COMES HOME

CAN I USE THE MICROWAVE TO HEAT UP MY FRIED CHICKEN, ASHIYA-SAN?

YES. THANK YOU, SASAKI-SAN.

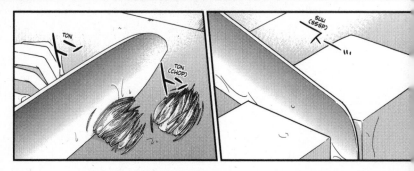

TON

TON (CHOP)

SUU (SSSP)

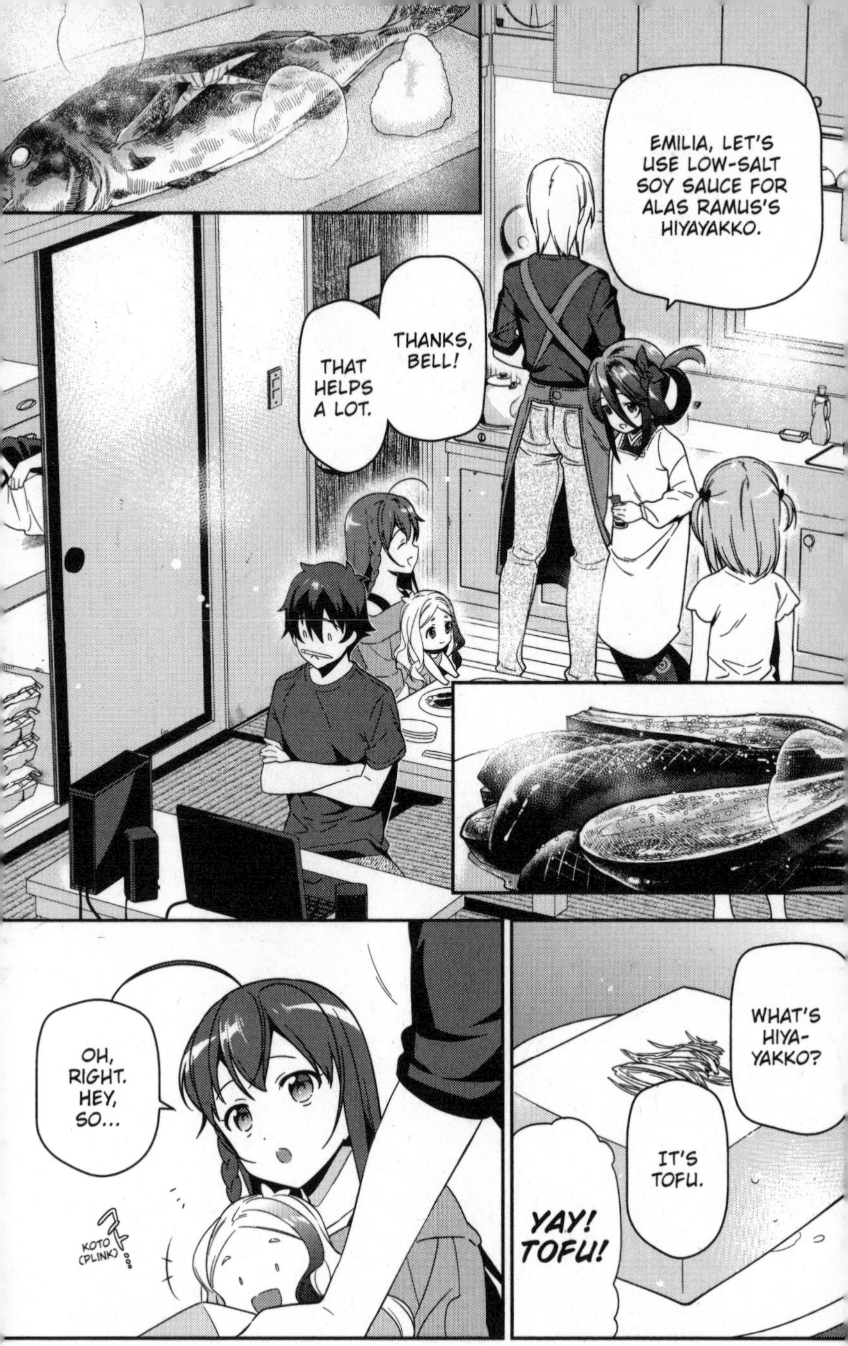
EMILIA, LET'S USE LOW-SALT SOY SAUCE FOR ALAS RAMUS'S HIYAYAKKO.
THANKS, BELL!
THAT HELPS A LOT.
WHAT'S HIYA-YAKKO?
IT'S TOFU.
YAY! TOFU!
OH, RIGHT. HEY, SO...
KOTO (PLINK)

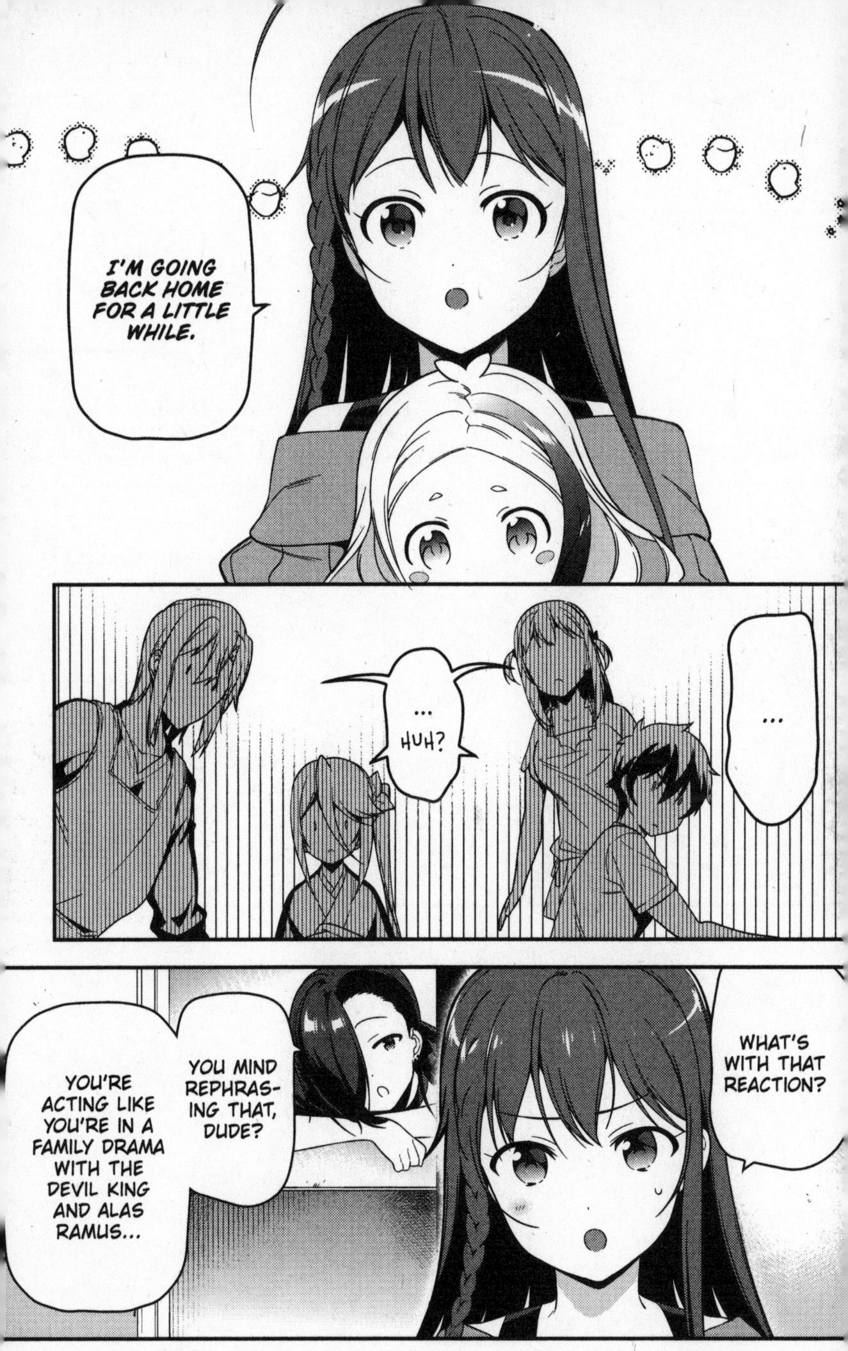
I'M GOING BACK HOME FOR A LITTLE WHILE.
...
... HUH?
WHAT'S WITH THAT REACTION?
YOU MIND REPHRAS-ING THAT, DUDE?
YOU'RE ACTING LIKE YOU'RE IN A FAMILY DRAMA WITH THE DEVIL KING AND ALAS RAMUS...

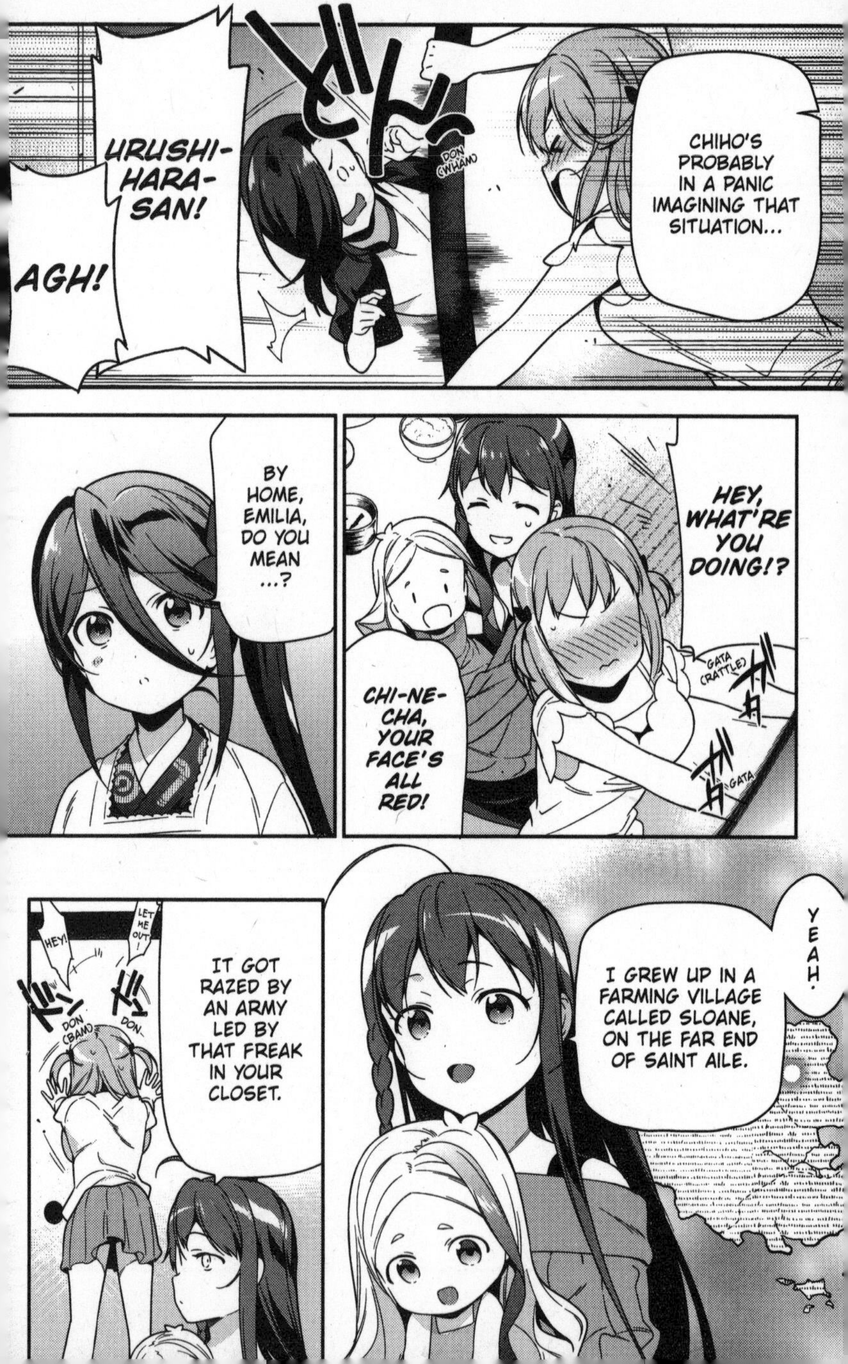
CHIHO'S PROBABLY IN A PANIC IMAGINING THAT SITUATION...
DON (WHAM)
URUSHI-HARA-SAN!
AGH!
HEY, WHAT'RE YOU DOING!?
GATA (RATTLE)
GATA
CHI-NE-CHA, YOUR FACE'S ALL RED!
BY HOME, EMILIA, DO YOU MEAN ...?
YEAH.
I GROW UP IN A FARMING VILLAGE CALLED SLOANE, ON THE FAR END OF SAINT AILE.
IT GOT RAZED BY AN ARMY LED BY THAT FREAK IN YOUR CLOSET.
LET ME OUT!
HEY!
DON (BAM)
DON

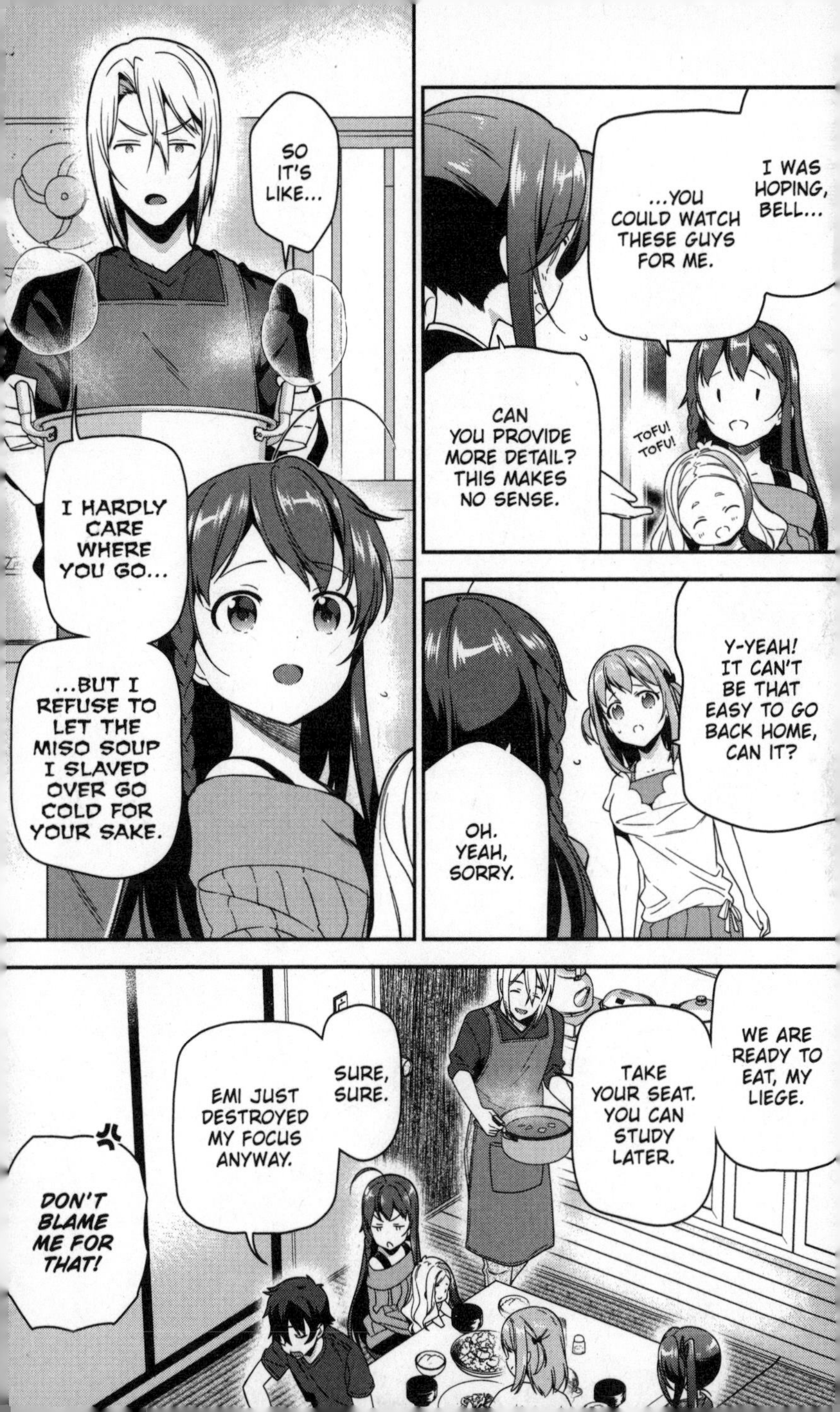

I WAS HOPING, BELL...
...YOU COULD WATCH THESE GUYS FOR ME.
TOFU! TOFU!
CAN YOU PROVIDE MORE DETAIL? THIS MAKES NO SENSE.
Y-YEAH! IT CAN'T BE THAT EASY TO GO BACK HOME, CAN IT?
OH. YEAH, SORRY.
SO IT'S LIKE...
I HARDLY CARE WHERE YOU GO...
...BUT I REFUSE TO LET THE MISO SOUP I SLAVED OVER GO COLD FOR YOUR SAKE.
WE ARE READY TO EAT, MY LIEGE.
TAKE YOUR SEAT. YOU CAN STUDY LATER.
SURE, SURE.
EMI JUST DESTROYED MY FOCUS ANYWAY.
DON'T BLAME ME FOR THAT!

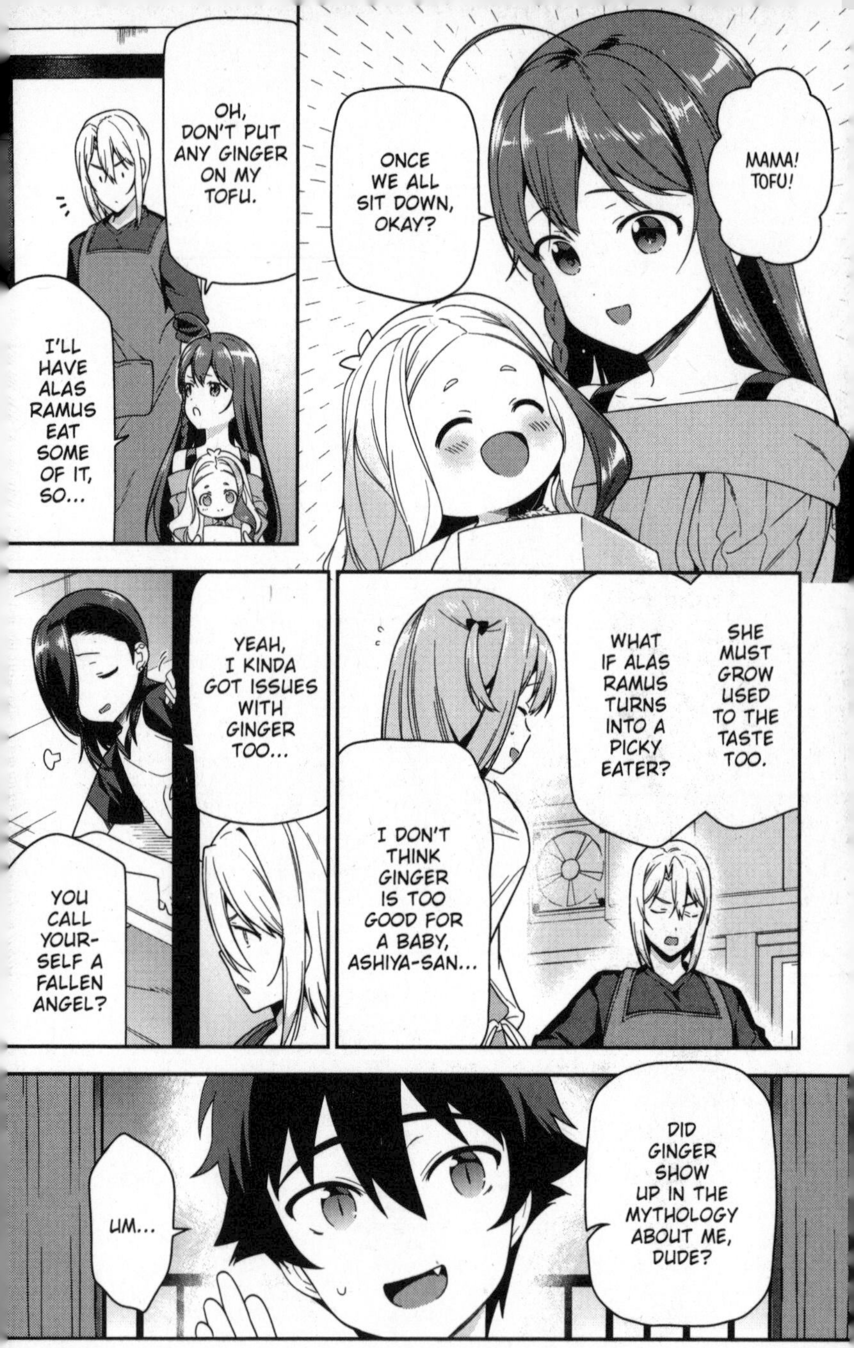
MAMA! TOFU!
ONCE WE ALL SIT DOWN, OKAY?
OH, DON'T PUT ANY GINGER ON MY TOFU.
I'LL HAVE ALAS RAMUS EAT SOME OF IT, SO...
SHE MUST GROW USED TO THE TASTE TOO.
WHAT IF ALAS RAMUS TURNS INTO A PICKY EATER?
I DON'T THINK GINGER IS TOO GOOD FOR A BABY, ASHIYA-SAN...
YEAH, I KINDA GOT ISSUES WITH GINGER TOO...
YOU CALL YOUR-SELF A FALLEN ANGEL?
DID GINGER SHOW UP IN THE MYTHOLOGY ABOUT ME, DUDE?
UM...

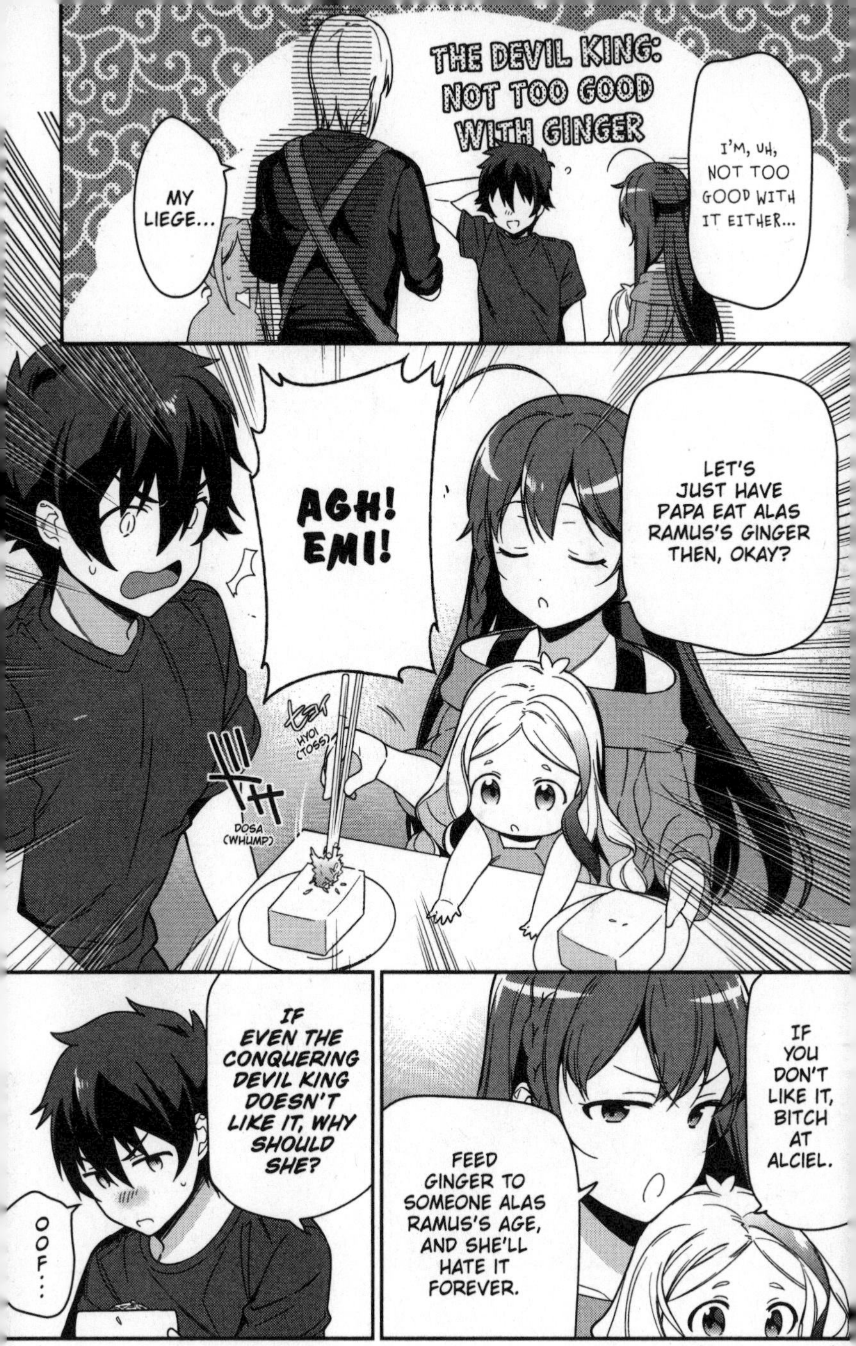
THE DEVIL KING: NOT TOO GOOD WITH GINGER
I'M, UH, NOT TOO GOOD WITH IT EITHER...
MY LIEGE...
LET'S JUST HAVE PAPA EAT ALAS RAMUS'S GINGER THEN, OKAY?
AGH! EMI!
HYOI (TOSS)
DOSA (WHUMP)
IF YOU DON'T LIKE IT, BITCH AT ALCIEL.
FEED GINGER TO SOMEONE ALAS RAMUS'S AGE, AND SHE'LL HATE IT FOREVER.
IF EVEN THE CONQUERING DEVIL KING DOESN'T LIKE IT, WHY SHOULD SHE?
OOF...

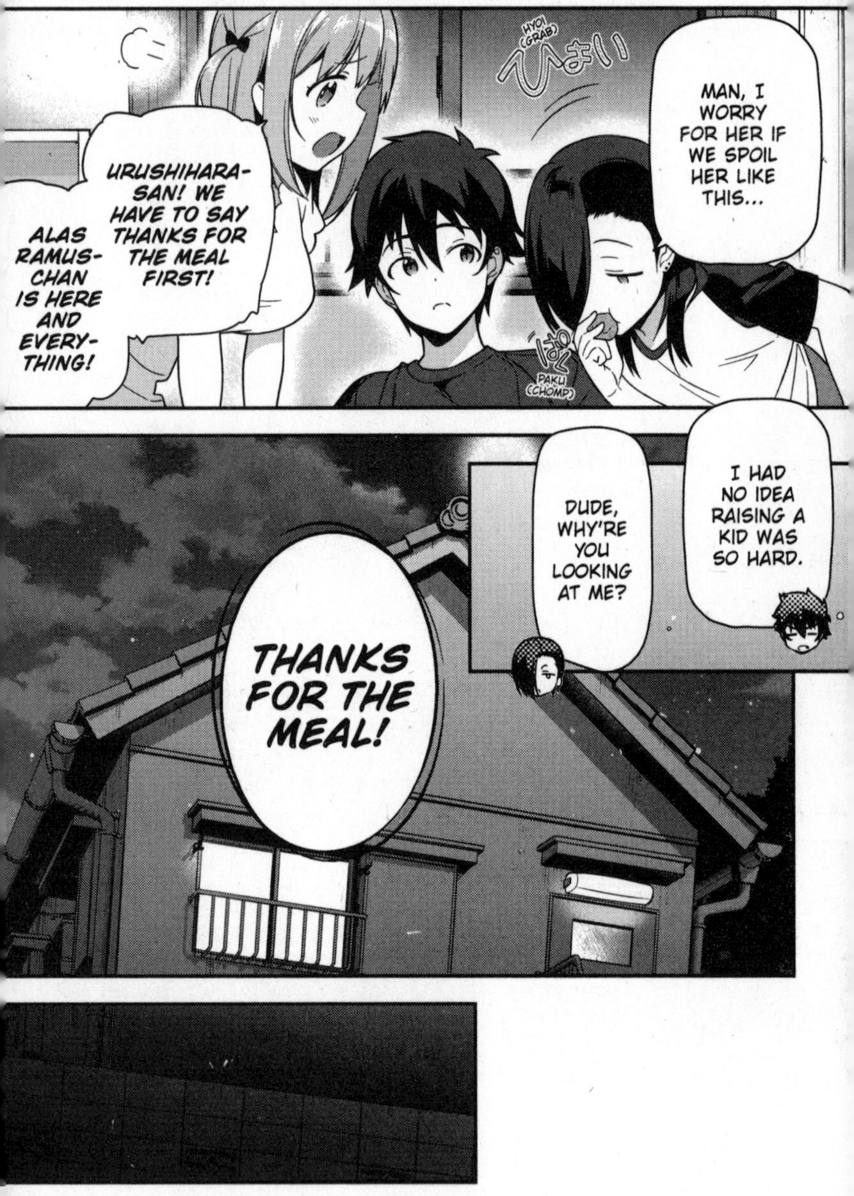
MAN, I WORRY FOR HER IF WE SPOIL HER LIKE THIS...
HYOI (GRAB)
ひょい
URUSHIHARA-SAN! WE HAVE TO SAY THANKS FOR THE MEAL FIRST!
PAKU (CHOMP)
ALAS RAMUS-CHAN IS HERE AND EVERYTHING!
I HAD NO IDEA RAISING A KID WAS SO HARD.
DUDE, WHY'RE YOU LOOKING AT ME?
THANKS FOR THE MEAL!

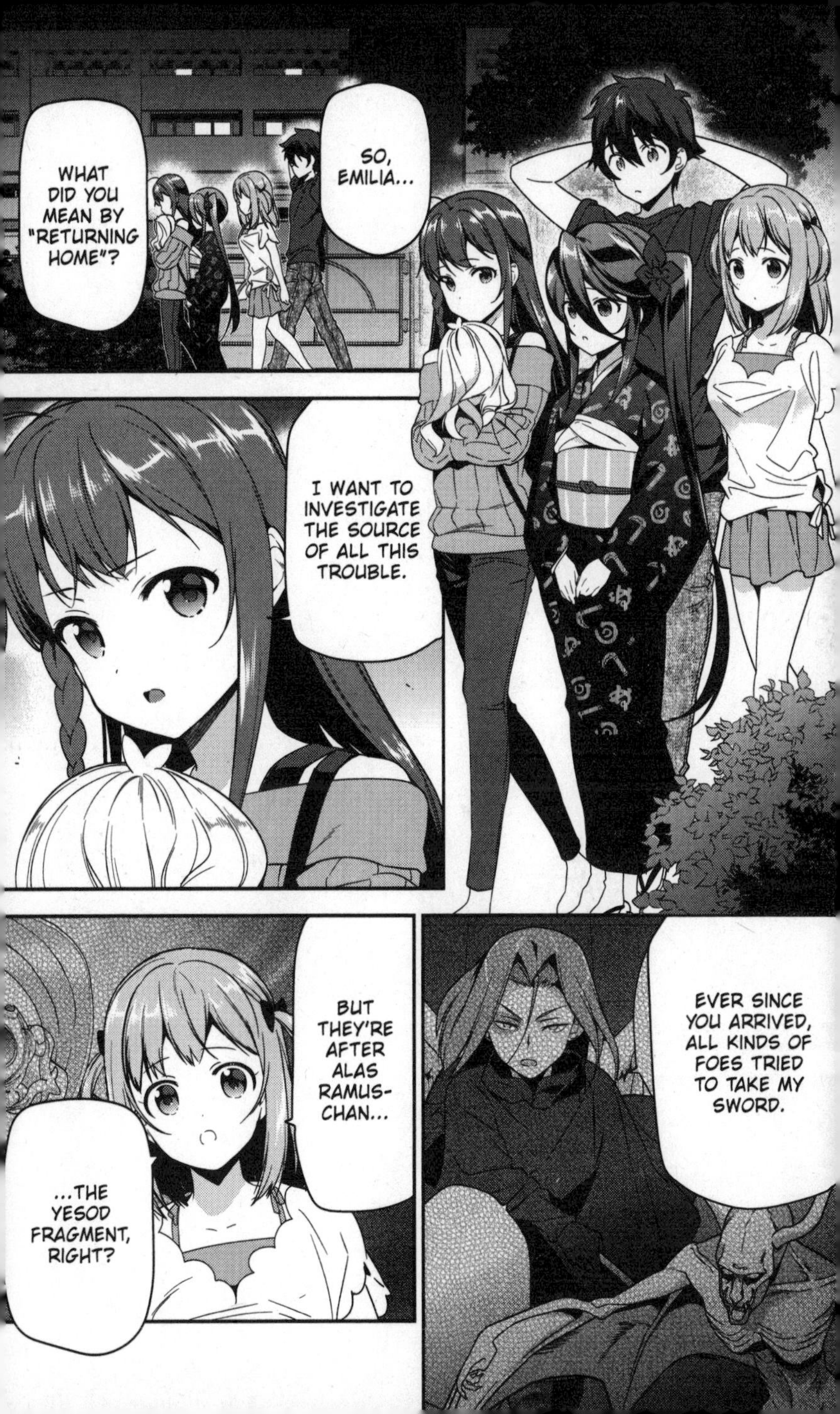
SO, EMILIA...
WHAT DID YOU MEAN BY "RETURNING HOME"?
I WANT TO INVESTIGATE THE SOURCE OF ALL THIS TROUBLE.
EVER SINCE YOU ARRIVED, ALL KINDS OF FOES TRIED TO TAKE MY SWORD.
BUT THEY'RE AFTER ALAS RAMUS-CHAN...
...THE YESOD FRAGMENT, RIGHT?

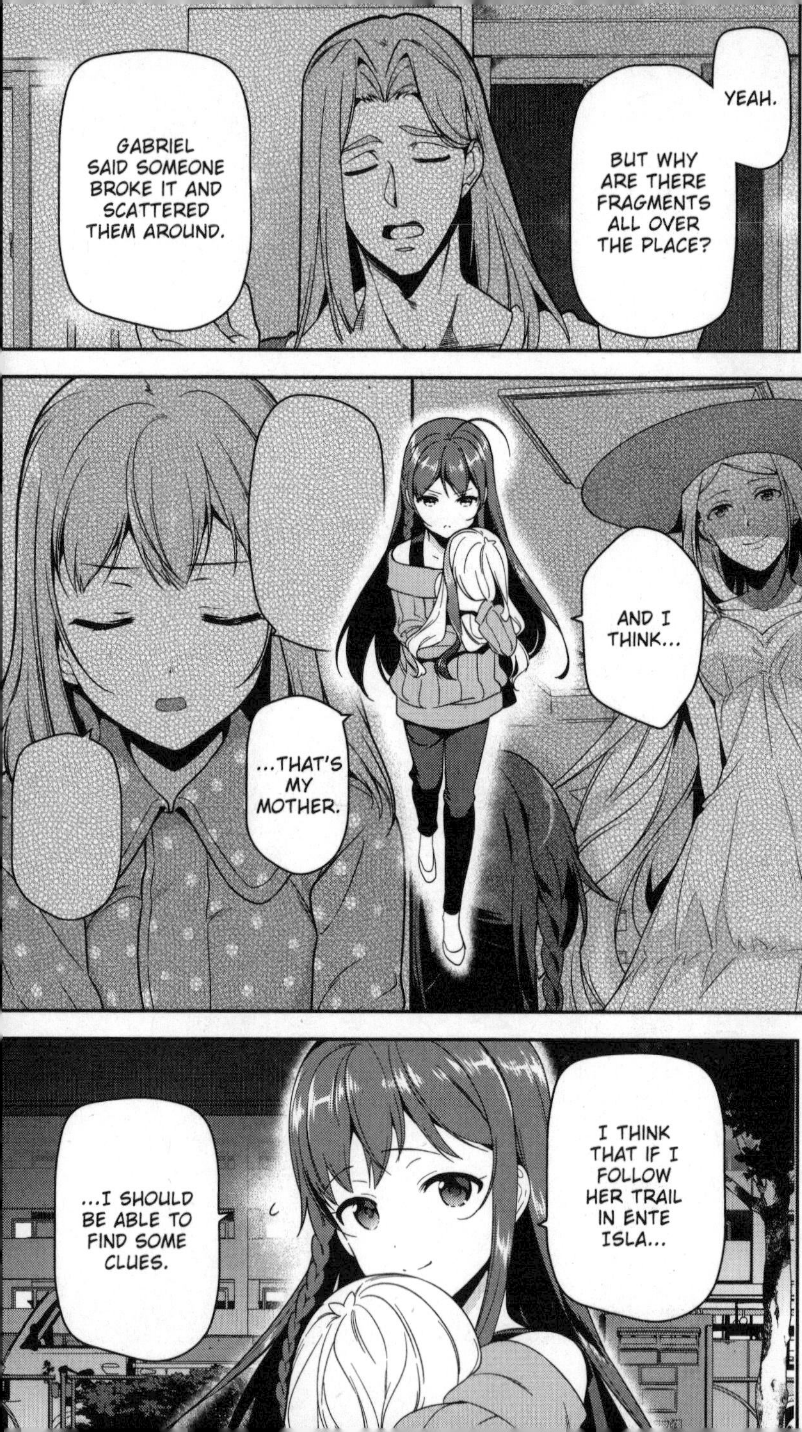
YEAH.
BUT WHY ARE THERE FRAGMENTS ALL OVER THE PLACE?
GABRIEL SAID SOMEONE BROKE IT AND SCATTERED THEM AROUND.
AND I THINK...
...THAT'S MY MOTHER.
I THINK THAT IF I FOLLOW HER TRAIL IN ENTE ISLA...
...I SHOULD BE ABLE TO FIND SOME CLUES.

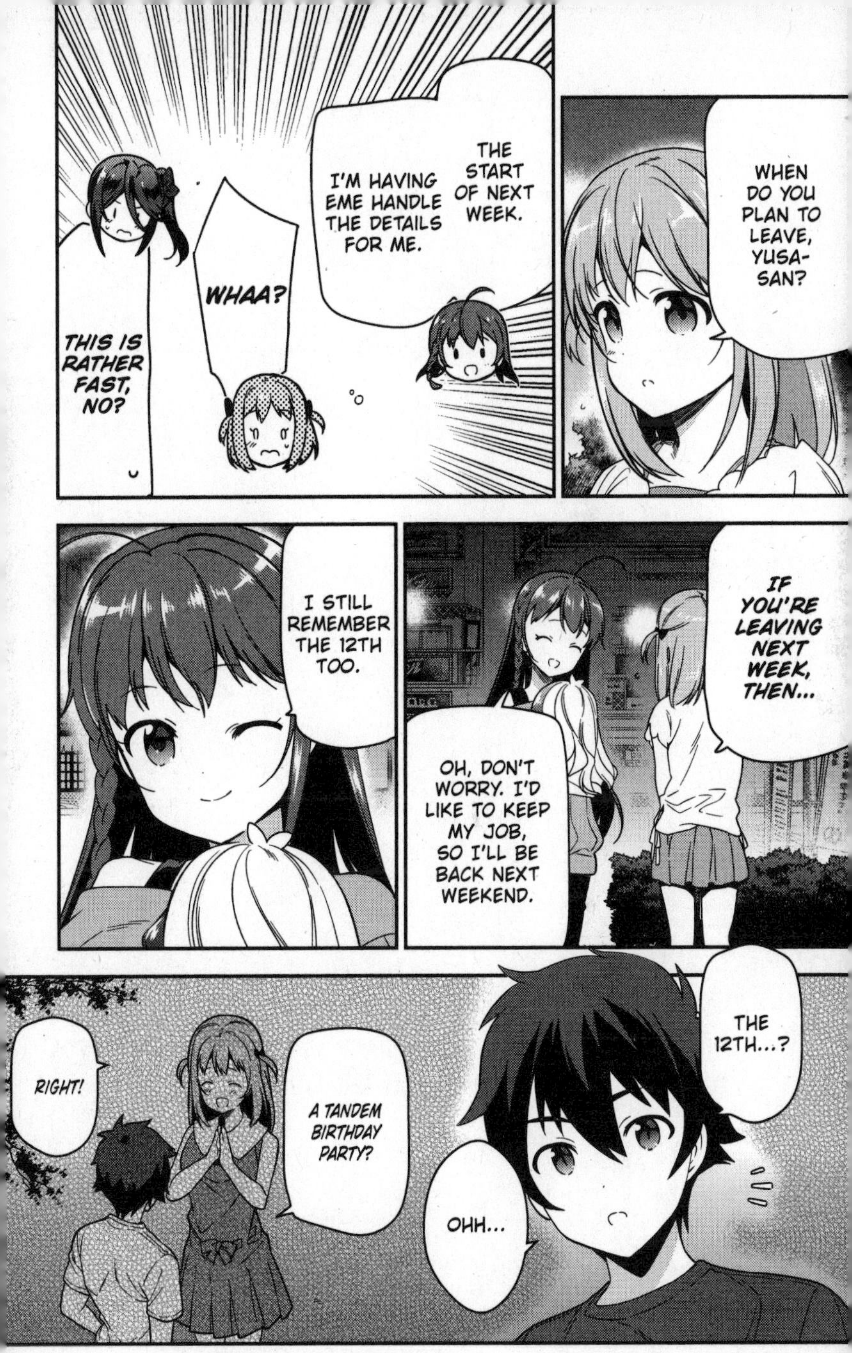
WHEN DO YOU PLAN TO LEAVE, YUSA-SAN?
THE START OF NEXT WEEK.
I'M HAVING EME HANDLE THE DETAILS FOR ME.
WHAA?
THIS IS RATHER FAST, NO?
IF YOU'RE LEAVING NEXT WEEK, THEN...
OH, DON'T WORRY. I'D LIKE TO KEEP MY JOB, SO I'LL BE BACK NEXT WEEKEND.
I STILL REMEMBER THE 12TH TOO.
THE 12TH...?
OHH...
A TANDEM BIRTHDAY PARTY?
RIGHT!

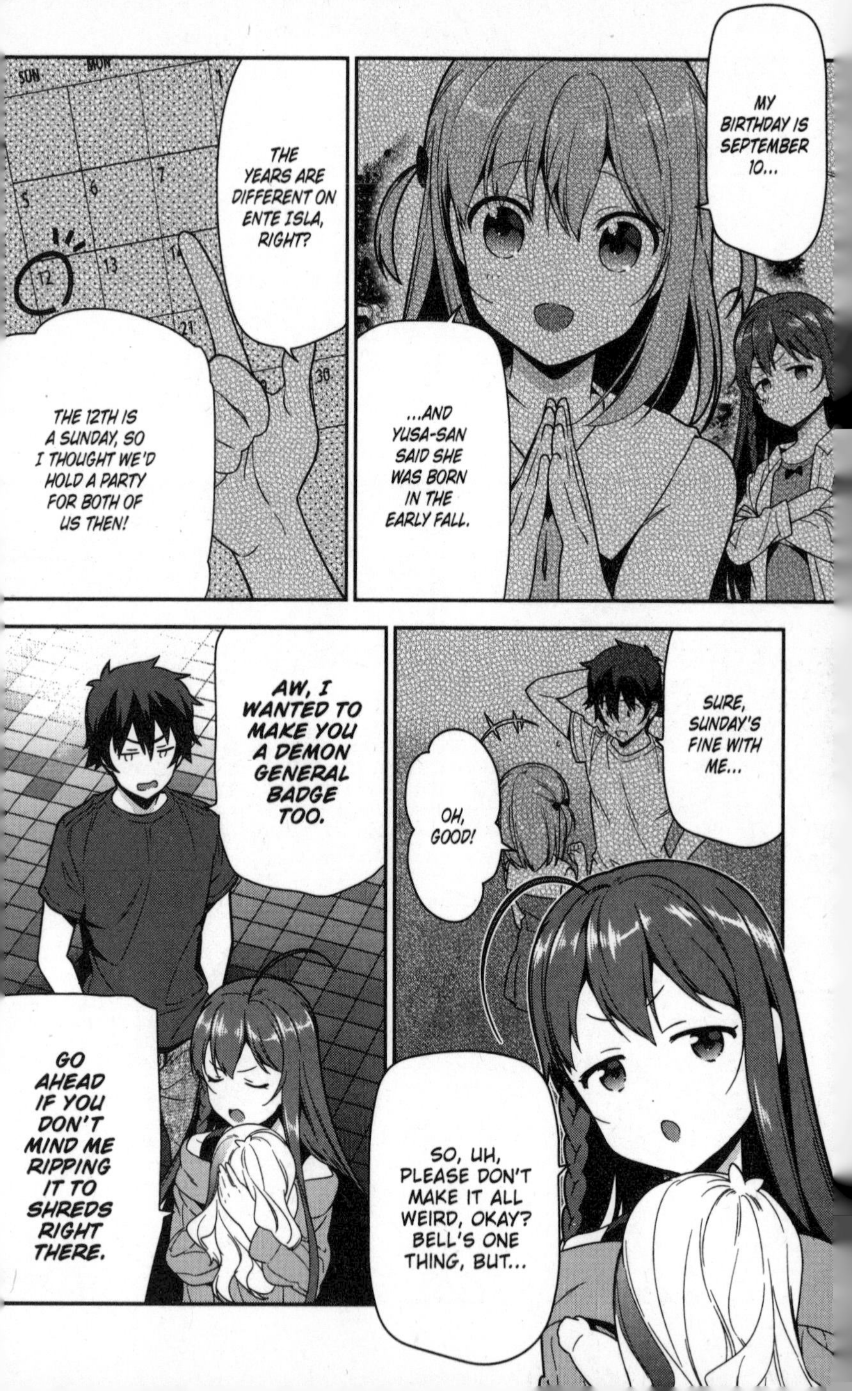
MY BIRTHDAY IS SEPTEMBER 10...
...AND YUSA-SAN SAID SHE WAS BORN IN THE EARLY FALL.
THE YEARS ARE DIFFERENT ON ENTE ISLA, RIGHT?
THE 12TH IS A SUNDAY, SO I THOUGHT WE'D HOLD A PARTY FOR BOTH OF US THEN!
SURE, SUNDAY'S FINE WITH ME...
OH, GOOD!
SO, UH, PLEASE DON'T MAKE IT ALL WEIRD, OKAY? BELL'S ONE THING, BUT...
AW, I WANTED TO MAKE YOU A DEMON GENERAL BADGE TOO.
GO AHEAD IF YOU DON'T MIND ME RIPPING IT TO SHREDS RIGHT THERE.

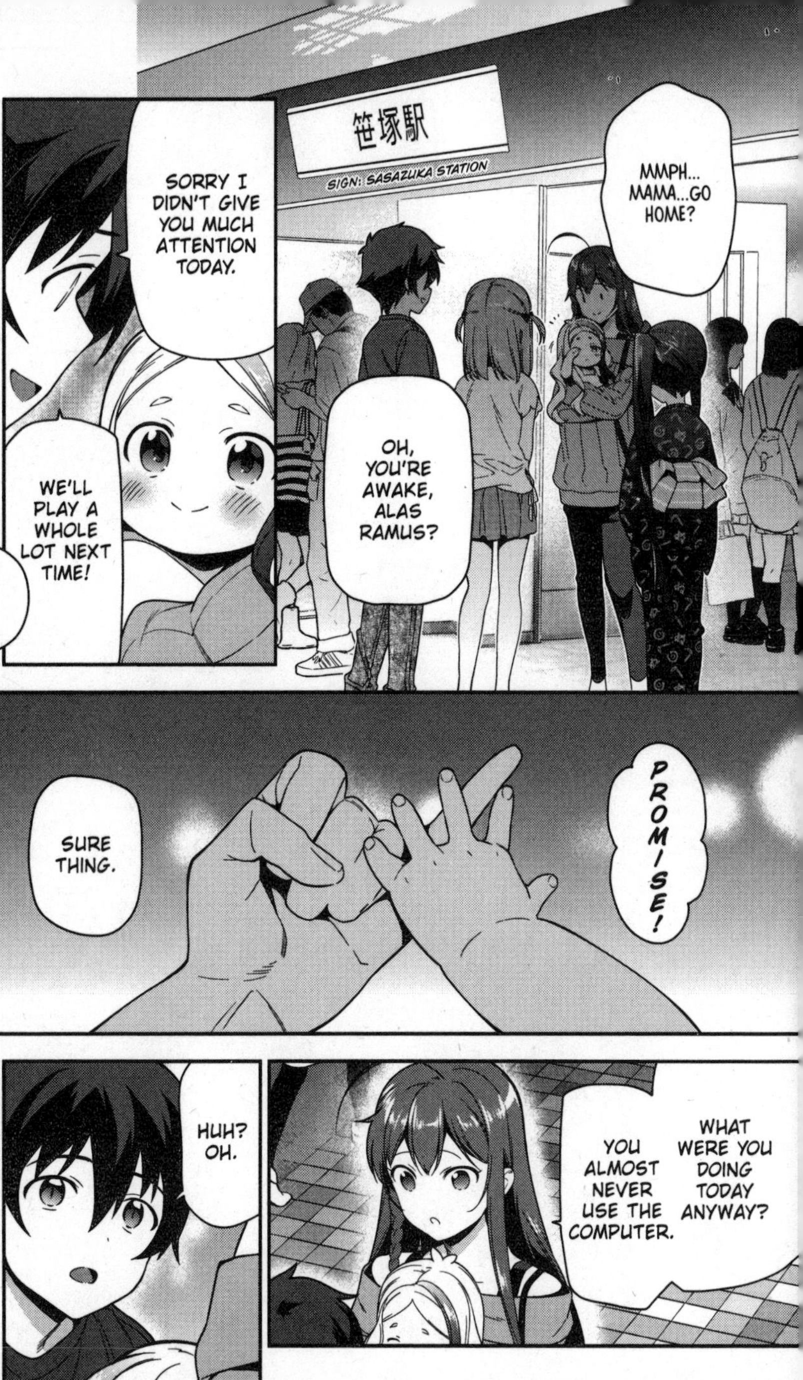
笹塚駅
SIGN: SASAZUKA STATION
MMPH... MAMA...GO HOME?
OH, YOU'RE AWAKE, ALAS RAMUS?
SORRY I DIDN'T GIVE YOU MUCH ATTENTION TODAY.
WE'LL PLAY A WHOLE LOT NEXT TIME!
OKEH!
PROMISE!
SURE THING.
WHAT WERE YOU DOING TODAY ANYWAY?
YOU ALMOST NEVER USE THE COMPUTER.
HUH? OH.

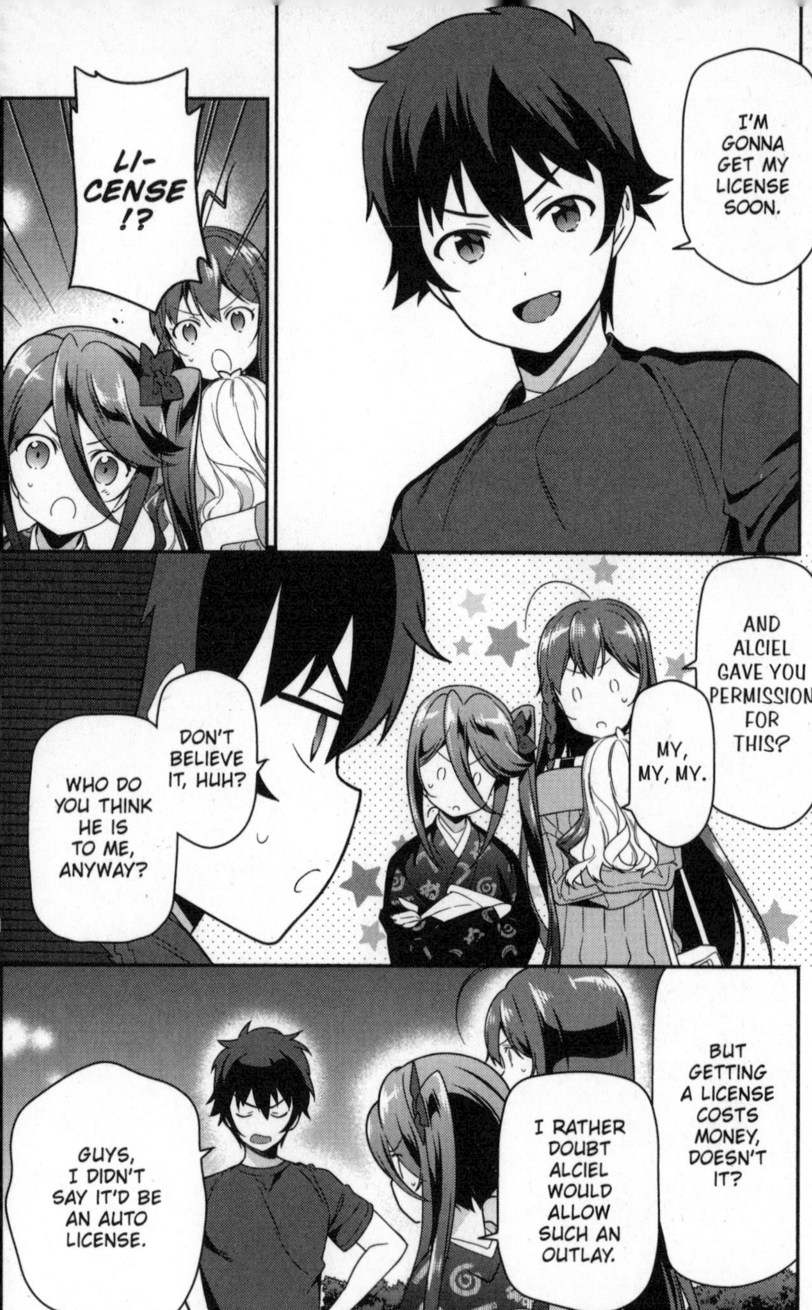

I'M GONNA GET MY LICENSE SOON.
LI-CENSE!?
AND ALCIEL GAVE YOU PERMISSION FOR THIS?
MY, MY, MY.
DON'T BELIEVE IT, HUH?
WHO DO YOU THINK HE IS TO ME, ANYWAY?
BUT GETTING A LICENSE COSTS MONEY, DOESN'T IT?
I RATHER DOUBT ALCIEL WOULD ALLOW SUCH AN OUTLAY.
GUYS, I DIDN'T SAY IT'D BE AN AUTO LICENSE.

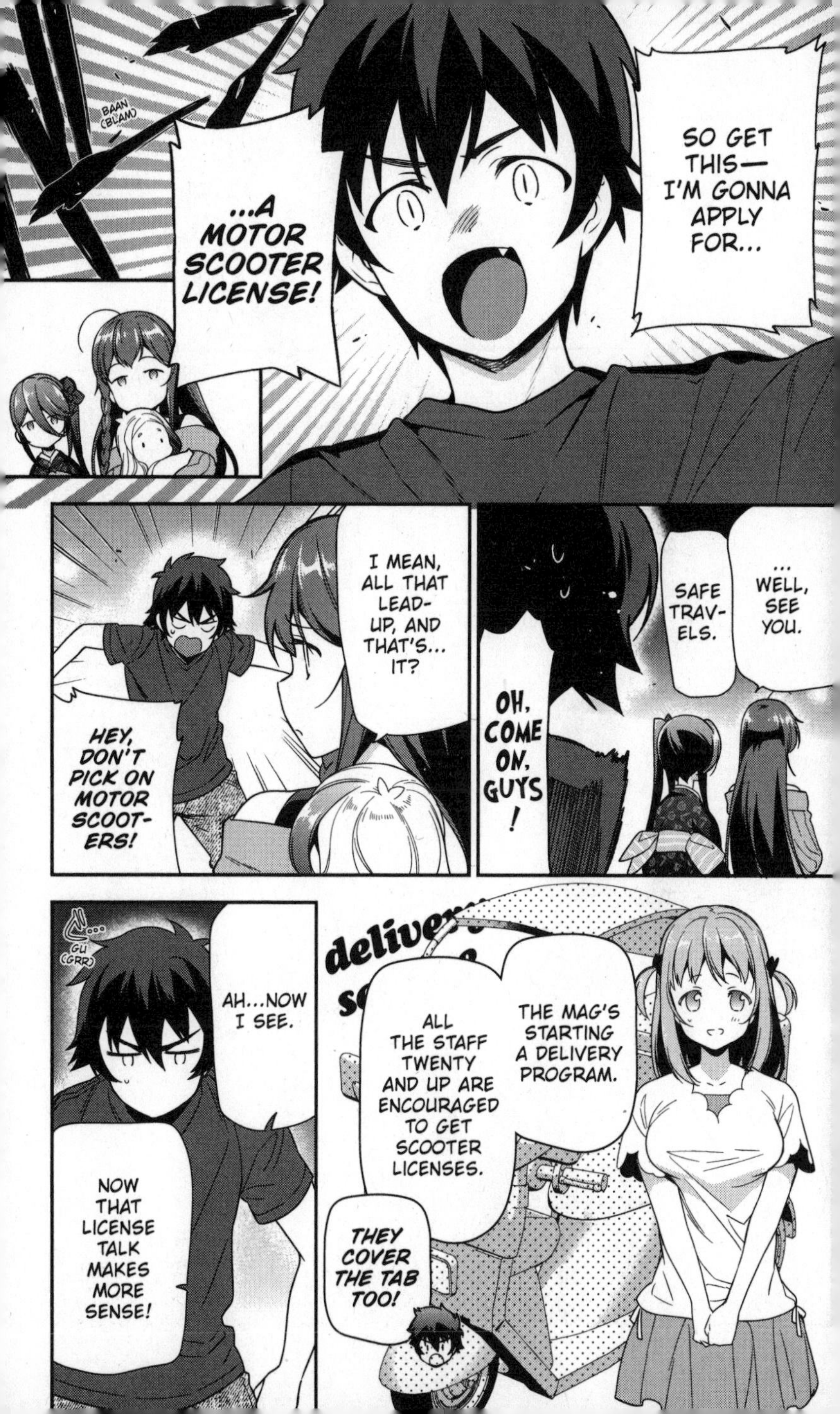
SO GET THIS— I'M GONNA APPLY FOR...
BAAN (BLAM)
...A MOTOR SCOOTER LICENSE!
...WELL, SEE YOU.
SAFE TRAV-ELS.
OH, COME ON, GUYS!
I MEAN, ALL THAT LEAD-UP, AND THAT'S... IT?
HEY, DON'T PICK ON MOTOR SCOOT-ERS!
THE MAG'S STARTING A DELIVERY PROGRAM.
ALL THE STAFF TWENTY AND UP ARE ENCOURAGED TO GET SCOOTER LICENSES.
THEY COVER THE TAB TOO!
AH...NOW I SEE.
GU (GRR)
NOW THAT LICENSE TALK MAKES MORE SENSE!

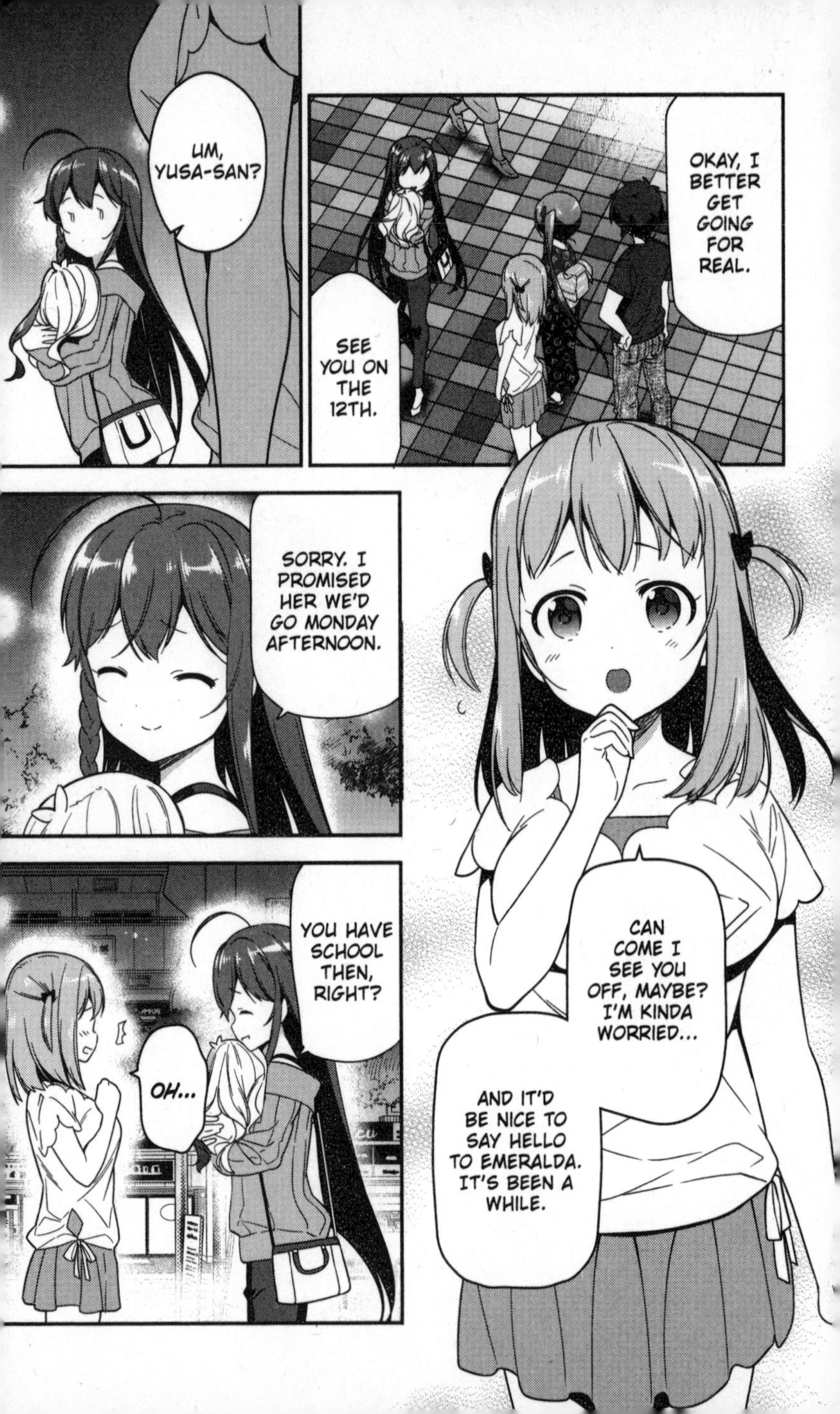
OKAY, I BETTER GET GOING FOR REAL.
SEE YOU ON THE 12TH.
UM, YUSA-SAN?
CAN COME I SEE YOU OFF, MAYBE? I'M KINDA WORRIED...
AND IT'D BE NICE TO SAY HELLO TO EMERALDA. IT'S BEEN A WHILE.
SORRY. I PROMISED HER WE'D GO MONDAY AFTERNOON.
YOU HAVE SCHOOL THEN, RIGHT?
OH...

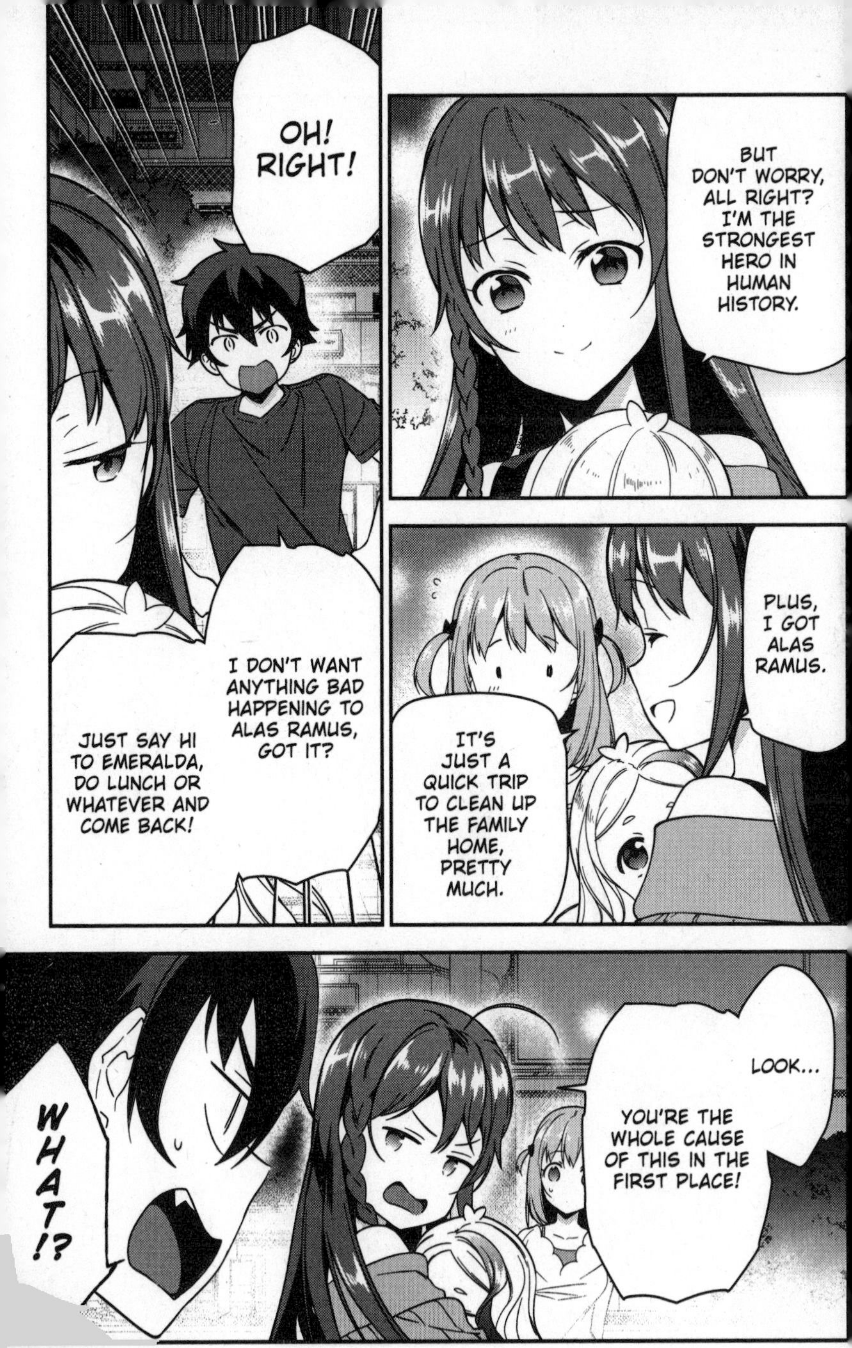
BUT DON'T WORRY, ALL RIGHT? I'M THE STRONGEST HERO IN HUMAN HISTORY.
PLUS, I GOT ALAS RAMUS.
IT'S JUST A QUICK TRIP TO CLEAN UP THE FAMILY HOME, PRETTY MUCH.
OH! RIGHT!
I DON'T WANT ANYTHING BAD HAPPENING TO ALAS RAMUS, GOT IT?
JUST SAY HI TO EMERALDA, DO LUNCH OR WHATEVER AND COME BACK!
LOOK...
YOU'RE THE WHOLE CAUSE OF THIS IN THE FIRST PLACE!
WHAT!?

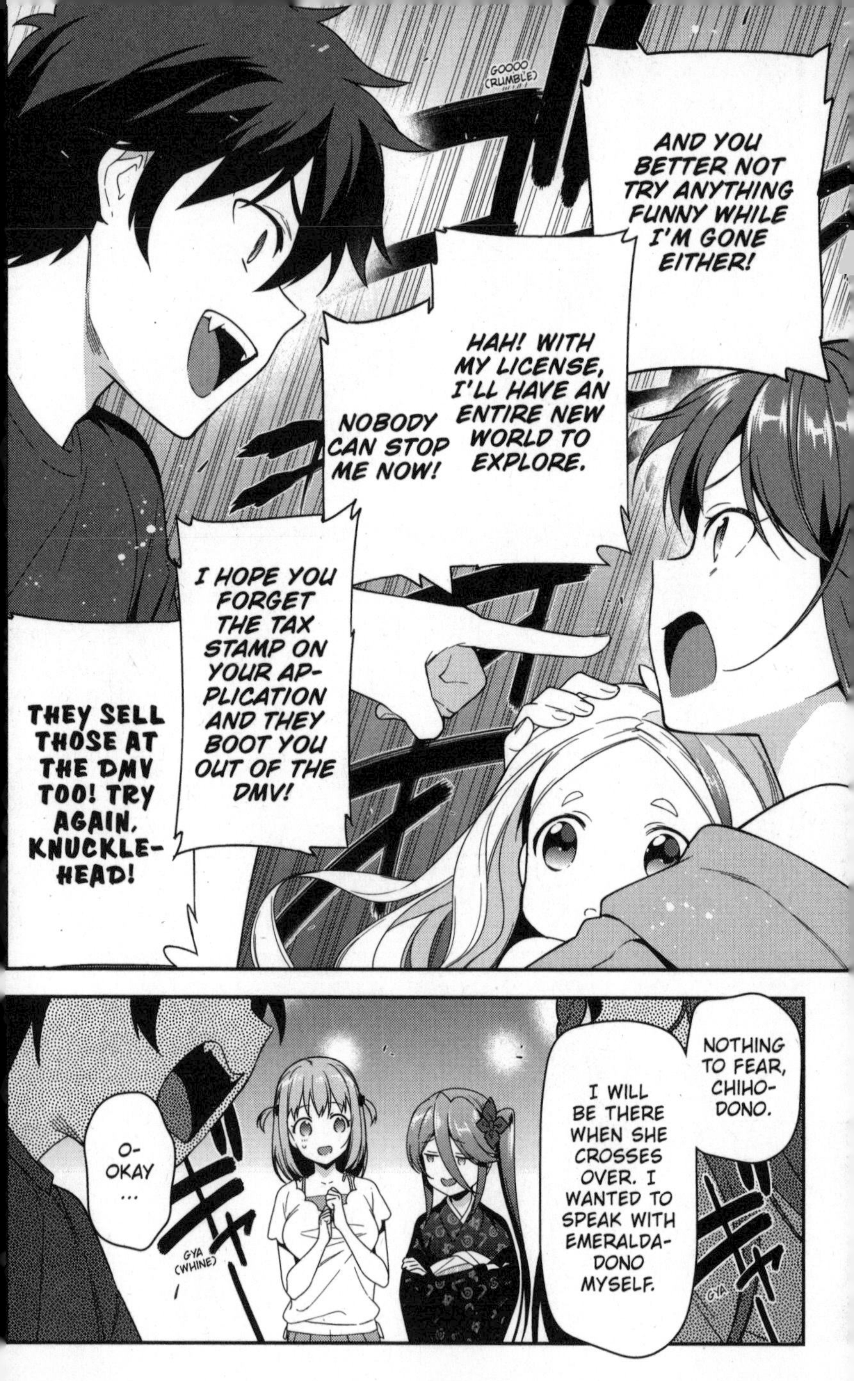
AND YOU BETTER NOT TRY ANYTHING FUNNY WHILE I'M GONE EITHER!
GOOOO (RUMBLE)
HAH! WITH MY LICENSE, I'LL HAVE AN ENTIRE NEW WORLD TO EXPLORE.
NOBODY CAN STOP ME NOW!
I HOPE YOU FORGET THE TAX STAMP ON YOUR AP-PLICATION AND THEY BOOT YOU OUT OF THE DMV!
THEY SELL THOSE AT THE DMV TOO! TRY AGAIN, KNUCKLE-HEAD!
NOTHING TO FEAR, CHIHO-DONO.
I WILL BE THERE WHEN SHE CROSSES OVER. I WANTED TO SPEAK WITH EMERALDA-DONO MYSELF.
GYA
O-OKAY ...
GYA (WHINE)

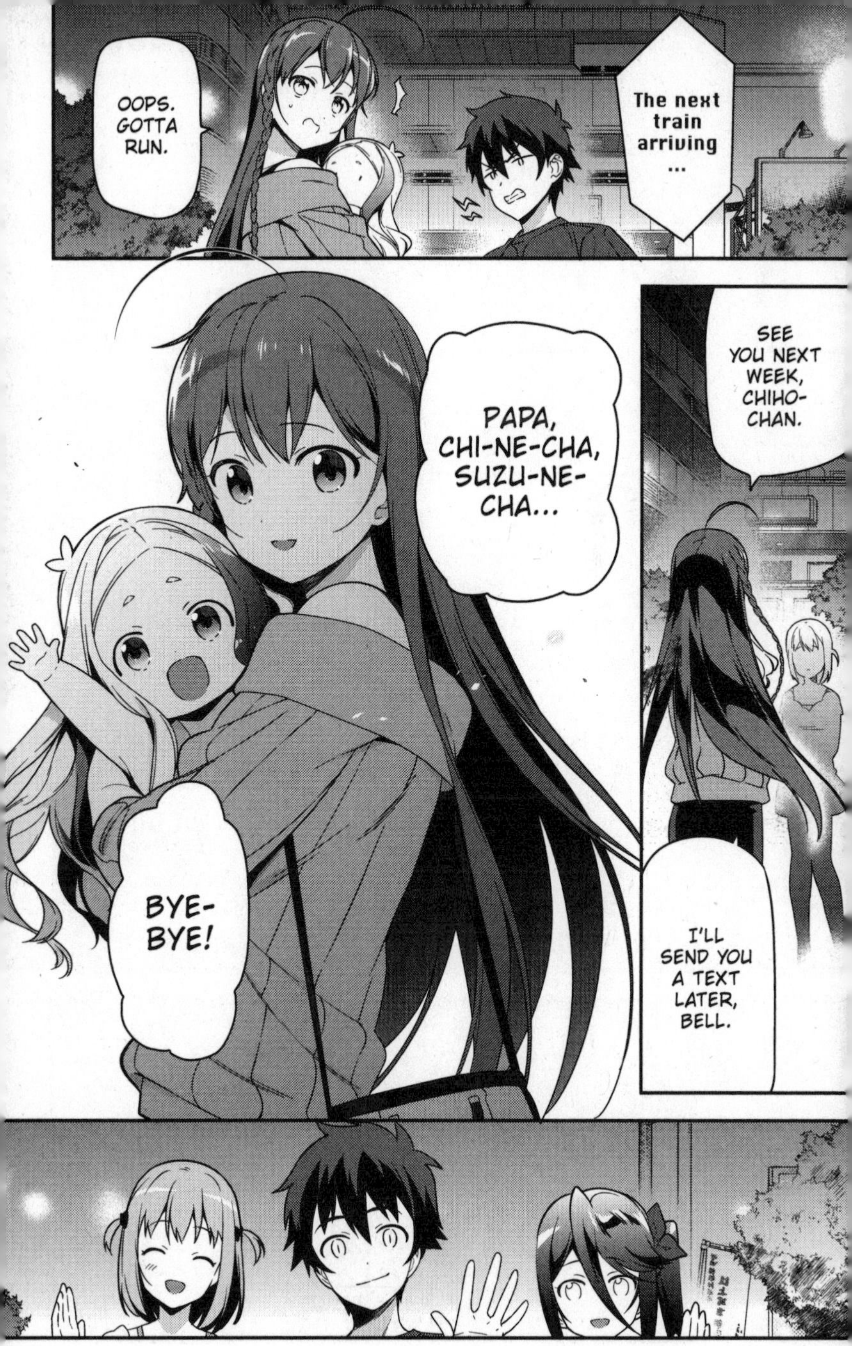
The next train arriving...
OOPS. GOTTA RUN.
SEE YOU NEXT WEEK, CHIHO-CHAN.
I'LL SEND YOU A TEXT LATER, BELL.
PAPA, CHI-NE-CHA, SUZU-NE-CHA...
BYE-BYE!

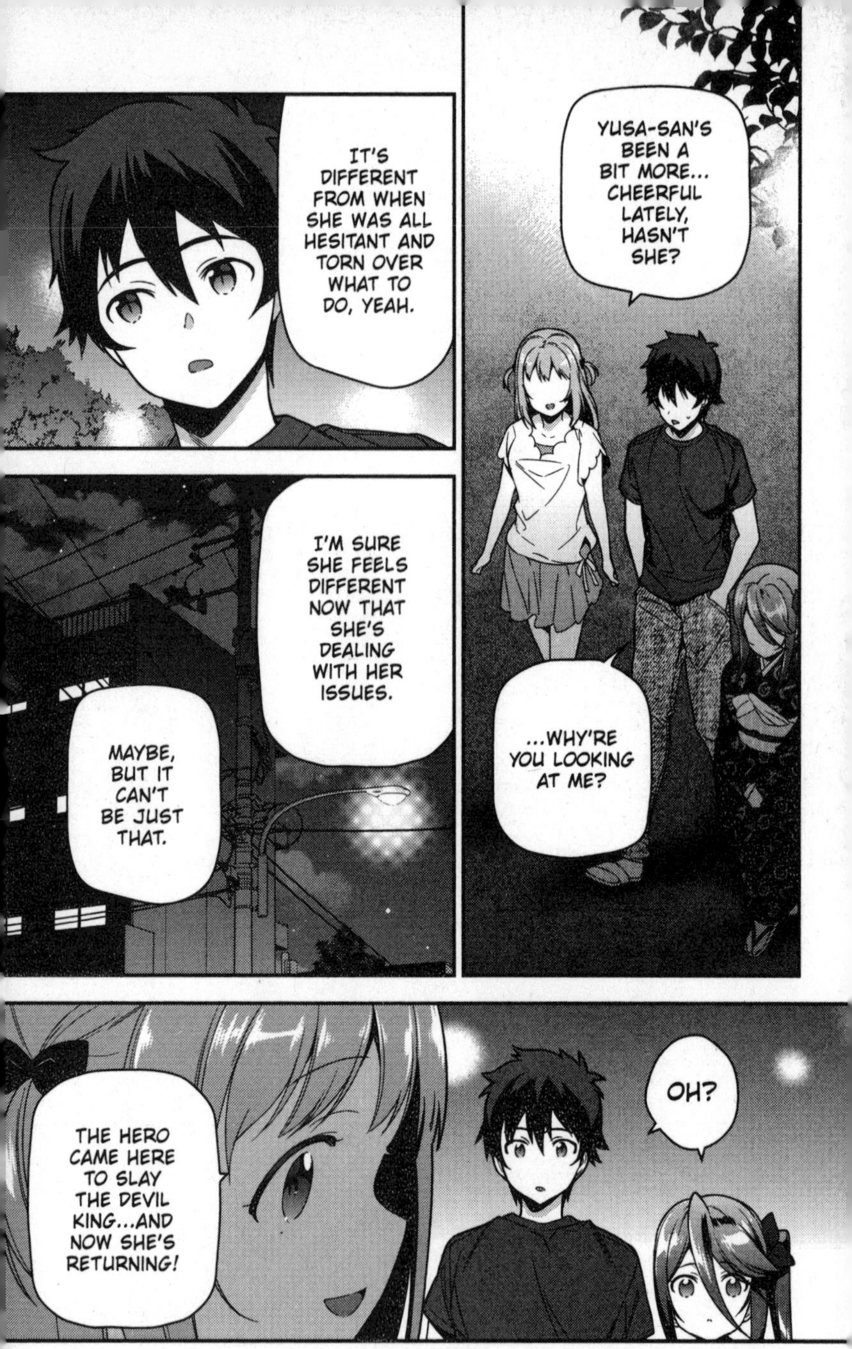
YUSA-SAN'S BEEN A BIT MORE... CHEERFUL LATELY, HASN'T SHE?
...WHY'RE YOU LOOKING AT ME?
IT'S DIFFERENT FROM WHEN SHE WAS ALL HESITANT AND TORN OVER WHAT TO DO, YEAH.
I'M SURE SHE FEELS DIFFERENT NOW THAT SHE'S DEALING WITH HER ISSUES.
MAYBE, BUT IT CAN'T BE JUST THAT.
OH?
THE HERO CAME HERE TO SLAY THE DEVIL KING...AND NOW SHE'S RETURNING!

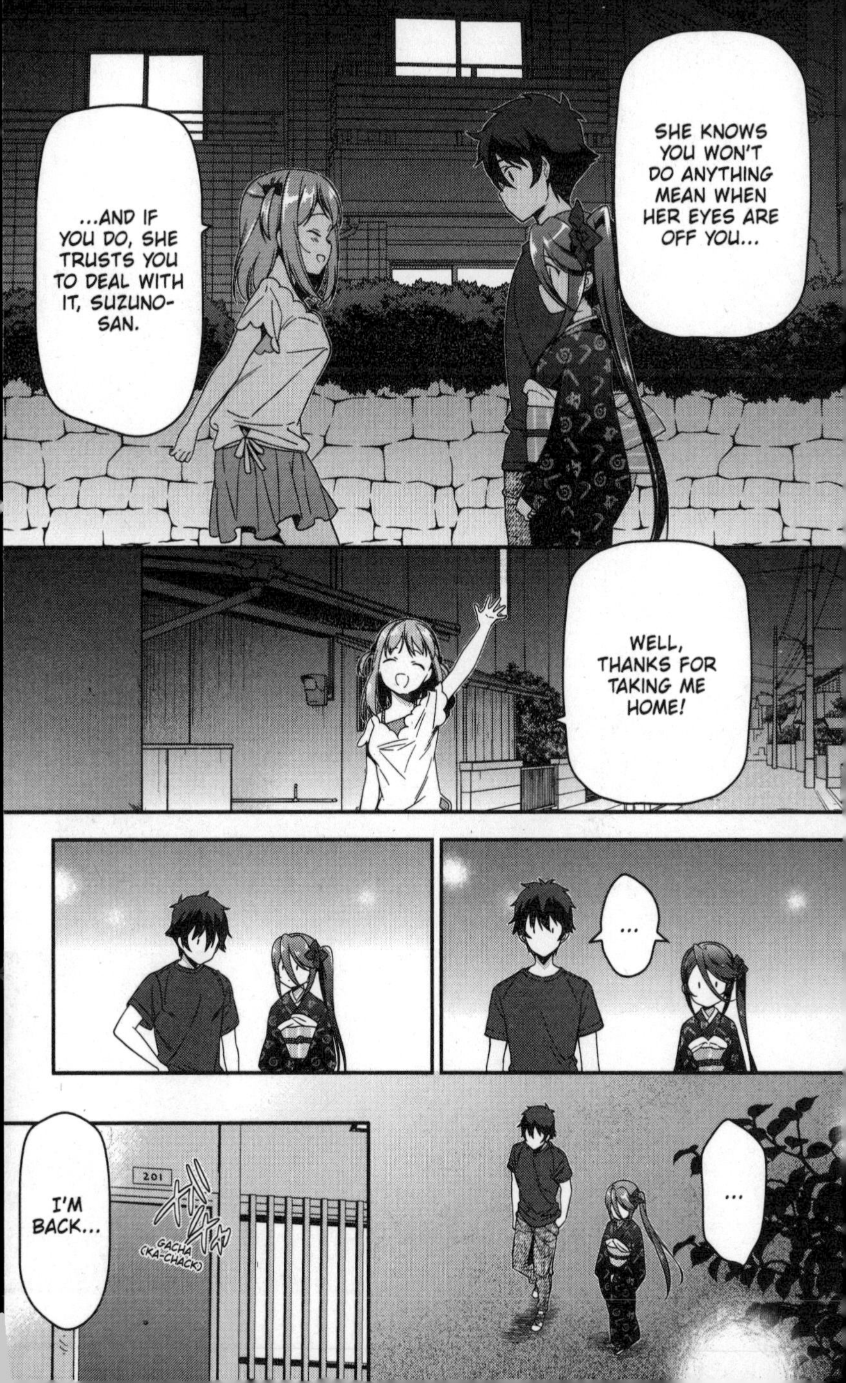
SHE KNOWS YOU WON'T DO ANYTHING MEAN WHEN HER EYES ARE OFF YOU...
...AND IF YOU DO, SHE TRUSTS YOU TO DEAL WITH IT, SUZUNO-SAN.
WELL, THANKS FOR TAKING ME HOME!
...
...
201
GACHA (KA-CHACK)
I'M BACK...

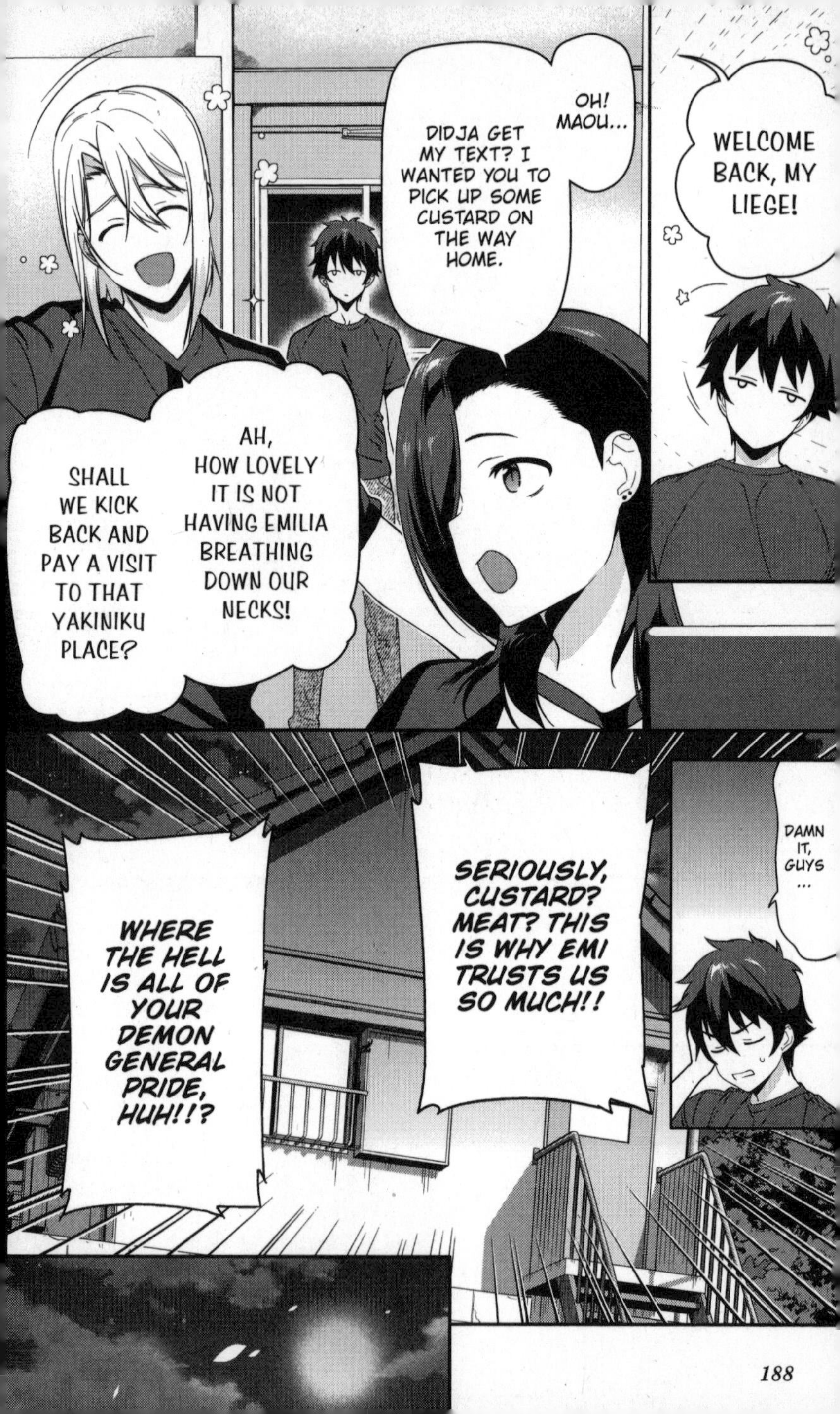
WELCOME BACK, MY LIEGE!
OH! MAOU...
DIDJA GET MY TEXT? I WANTED YOU TO PICK UP SOME CUSTARD ON THE WAY HOME.
AH, HOW LOVELY IT IS NOT HAVING EMILIA BREATHING DOWN OUR NECKS!
SHALL WE KICK BACK AND PAY A VISIT TO THAT YAKINIKU PLACE?
DAMN IT, GUYS...
SERIOUSLY, CUSTARD? MEAT? THIS IS WHY EMI TRUSTS US SO MUCH!!
WHERE THE HELL IS ALL OF YOUR DEMON GENERAL PRIDE, HUH!!?

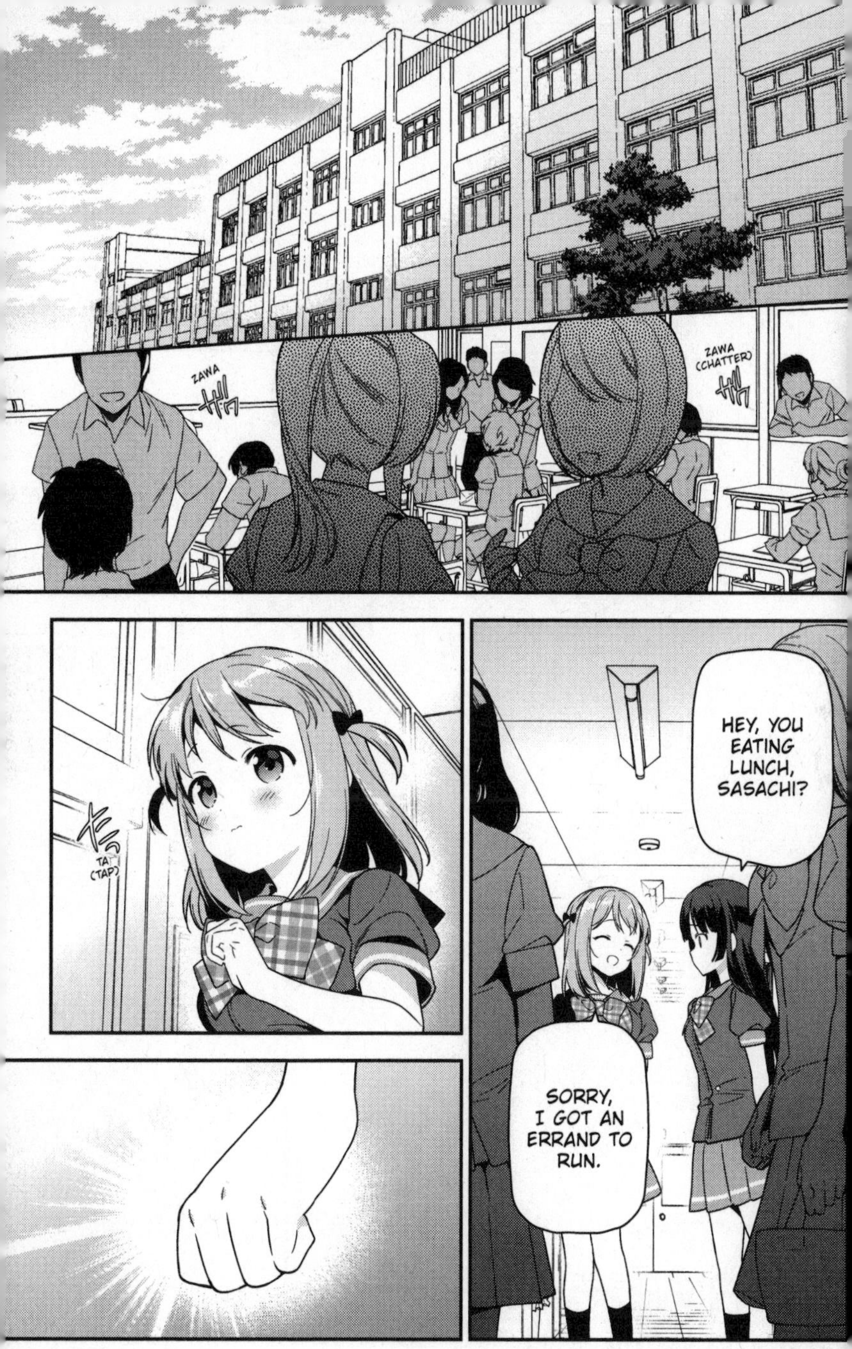
ZAWA (CHATTER)
ZAWA
HEY, YOU EATING LUNCH, SASACHI?
SORRY, I GOT AN ERRAND TO RUN.
TA (TAP)

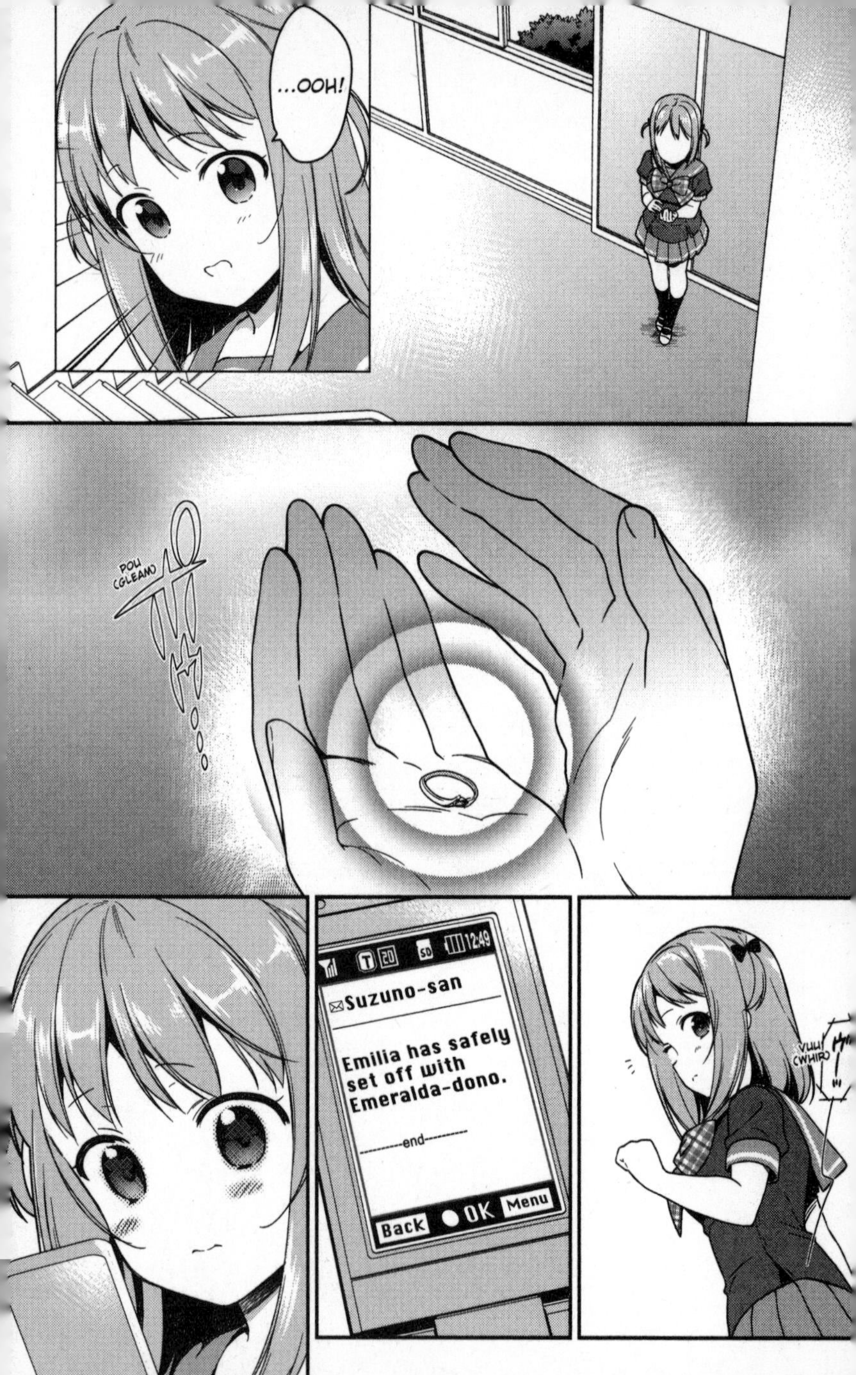
...OOH!
POU (GLEAM)
VUU! (WHIR)
12:49
Suzuno-san
Emilia has safely set off with Emeralda-dono.
----------end----------
Back
OK
Menu

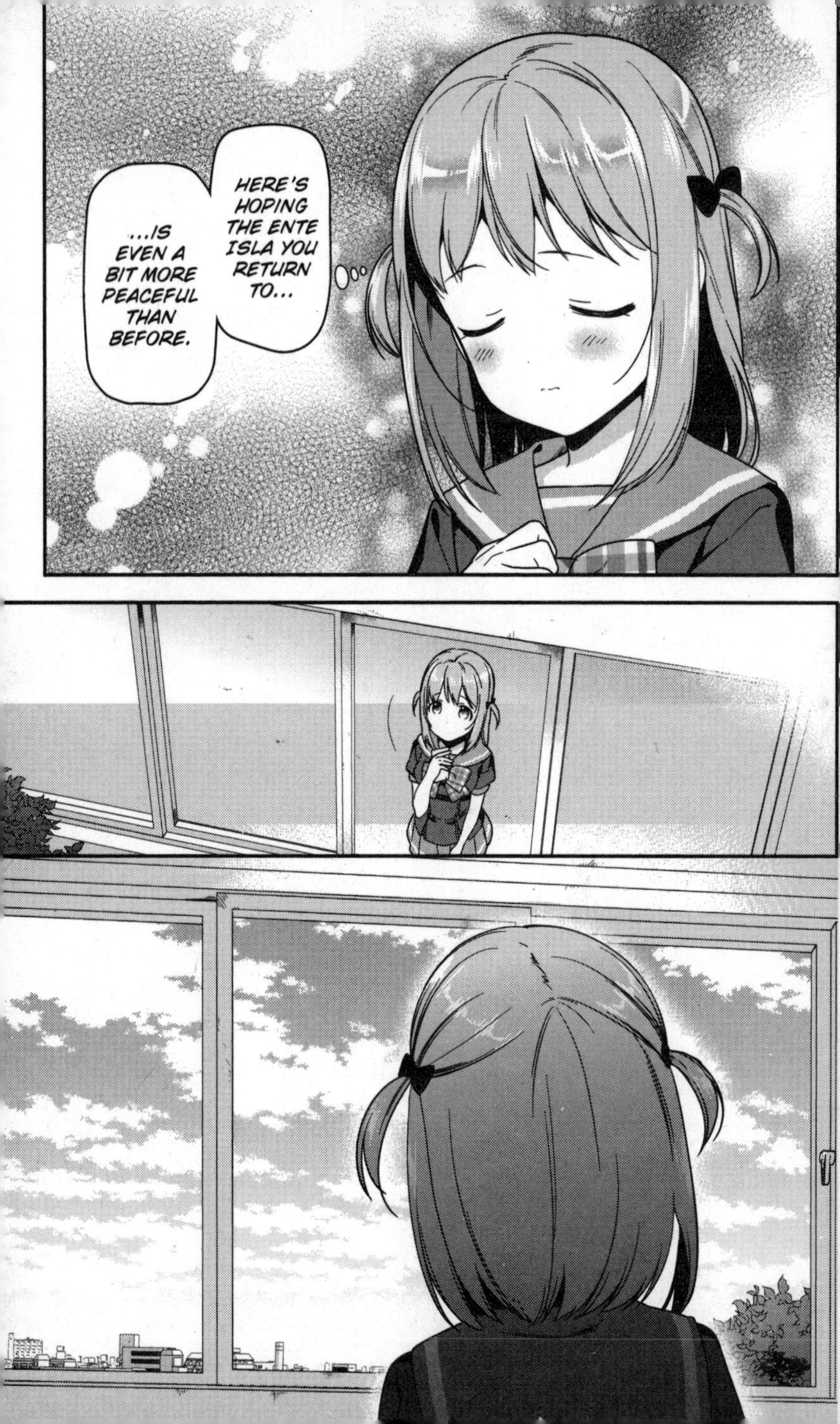
HERE'S HOPING THE ENTE ISLA YOU RETURN TO...
...IS EVEN A BIT MORE PEACEFUL THAN BEFORE.

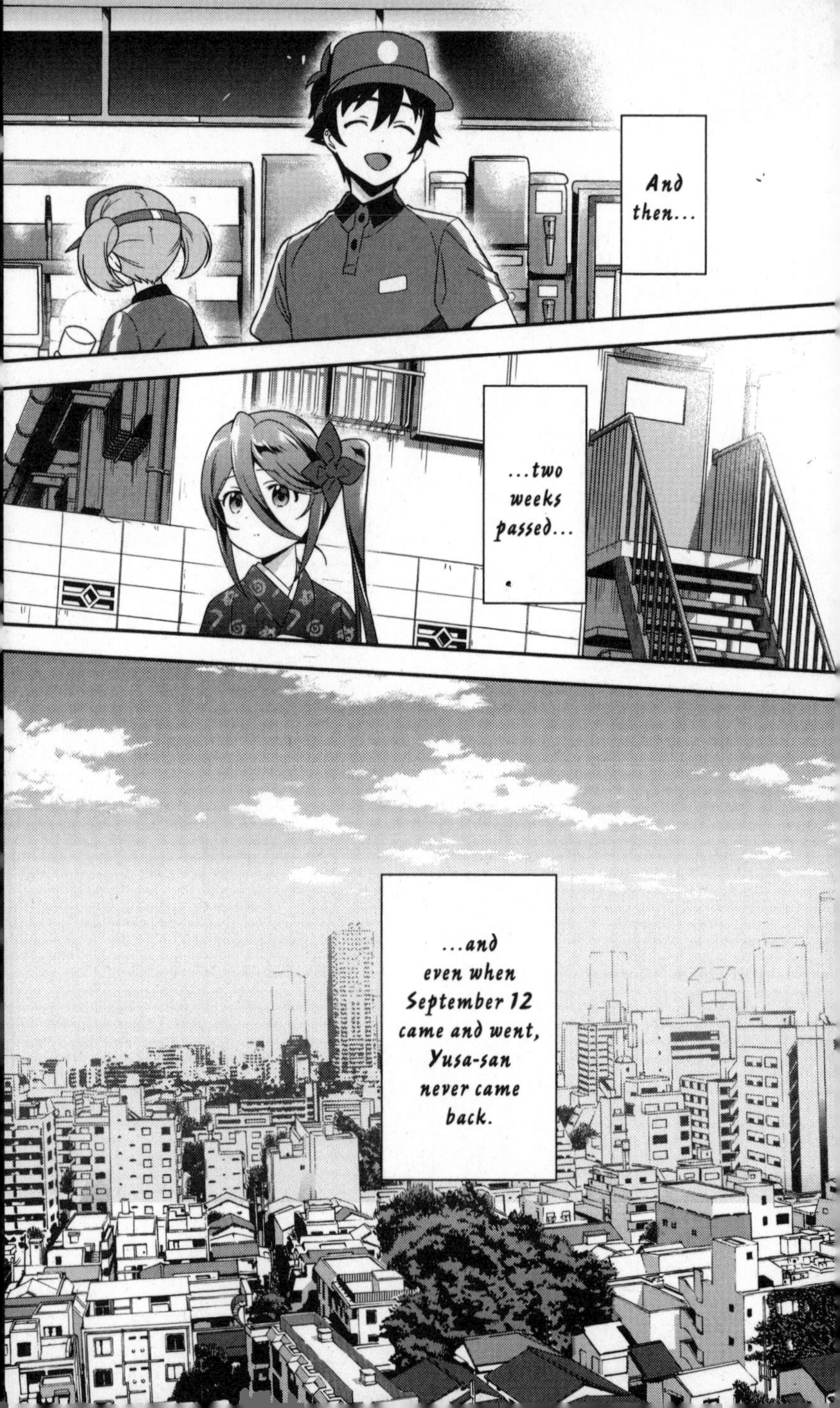
And then...
...two weeks passed...
...and even when September 12 came and went, Yusa-san never came back.

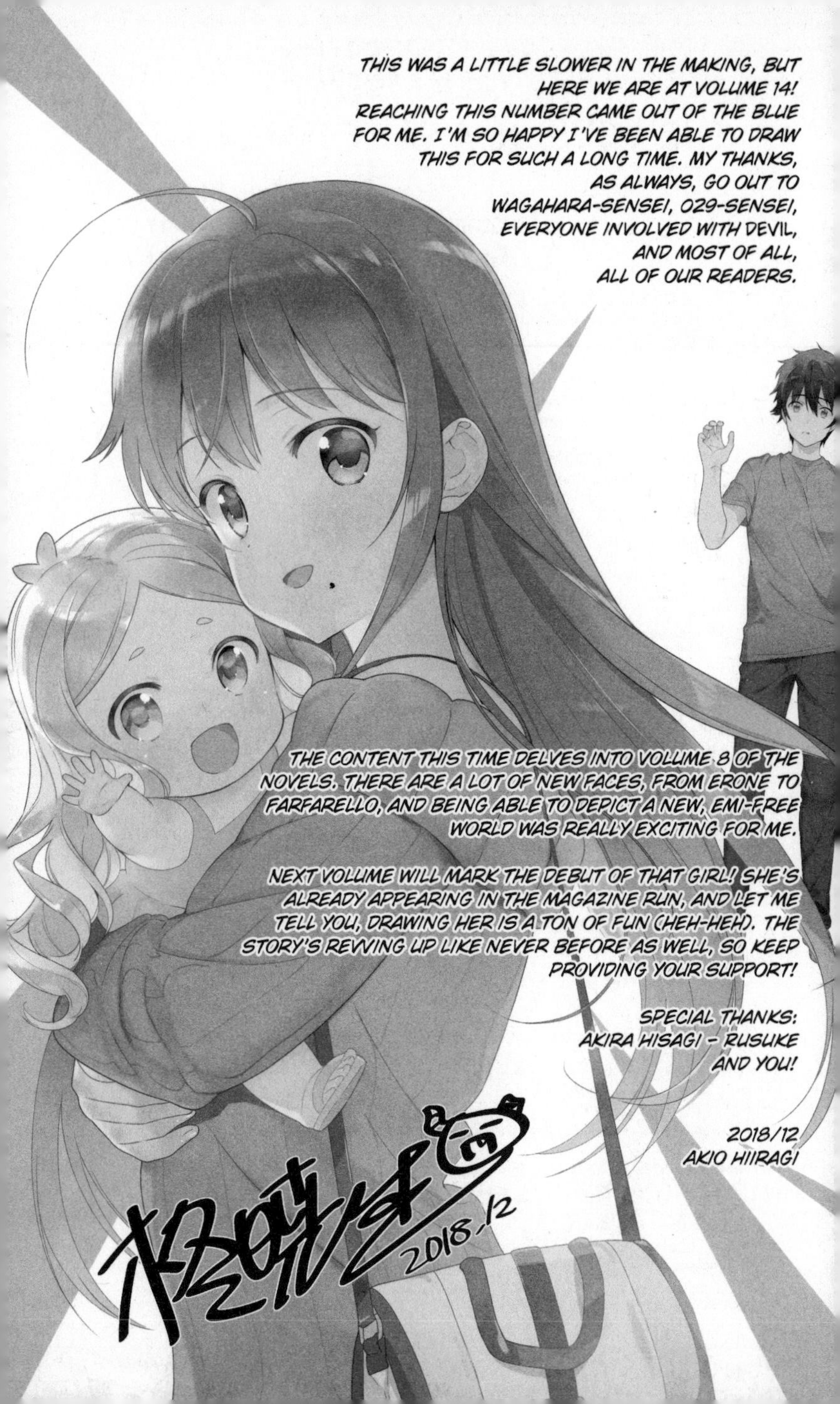

THIS WAS A LITTLE SLOWER IN THE MAKING, BUT HERE WE ARE AT VOLUME 14! REACHING THIS NUMBER CAME OUT OF THE BLUE FOR ME. I'M SO HAPPY I'VE BEEN ABLE TO DRAW THIS FOR SUCH A LONG TIME. MY THANKS, AS ALWAYS, GO OUT TO WAGAHARA-SENSEI, 029-SENSEI, EVERYONE INVOLVED WITH DEVIL, AND MOST OF ALL, ALL OF OUR READERS.

THE CONTENT THIS TIME DELVES INTO VOLUME 8 OF THE NOVELS. THERE ARE A LOT OF NEW FACES, FROM ERONE TO FARFARELLO, AND BEING ABLE TO DEPICT A NEW, EMI-FREE WORLD WAS REALLY EXCITING FOR ME.

NEXT VOLUME WILL MARK THE DEBUT OF THAT GIRL! SHE'S ALREADY APPEARING IN THE MAGAZINE RUN, AND LET ME TELL YOU, DRAWING HER IS A TON OF FUN (HEH-HEH). THE STORY'S REVVING UP LIKE NEVER BEFORE AS WELL, SO KEEP PROVIDING YOUR SUPPORT!

SPECIAL THANKS:
AKIRA HISAGI - RUSUKE
AND YOU!

2018/12
AKIO HIIRAGI

THE DEVIL IS A PART-TIMER! ⑭

ART: AKIO HIIRAGI
ORIGINAL STORY: SATOSHI WAGAHARA
CHARACTER DESIGN: 029 (ONIKU)

Translation: Kevin Gifford

Lettering: Liz Kolkman

HATARAKU MAOUSAMA! Vol. 14
© SATOSHI WAGAHARA / AKIO HIIRAGI 2019
First published in Japan in 2019 by KADOKAWA CORPORATION, Tokyo.
English translation rights arranged with KADOKAWA CORPORATION, Tokyo, through Tuttle-Mori Agency, Inc., Tokyo.

English translation © 2019 by Yen Press, LLC

Yen Press
150 West 30th Street, 19th Floor
New York, NY 10001

Visit us at yenpress.com
facebook.com/yenpress
twitter.com/yenpress
yenpress.tumblr.com
instagram.com/yenpress

First Yen Press Edition: August 2019

Yen Press is an imprint of Yen Press, LLC.
The Yen Press name and logo are trademarks of Yen Press, LLC.

Library of Congress Control Number: 2014504637

ISBNs: 978-1-9753-0555-0 (paperback)
       978-1-9753-5917-1 (ebook)

10 9 8 7 6 5 4 3 2 1

WOR

Printed in the United States of America